MORALITY, POLITICS, AND LAW

MORALITY, POLITICS, AND LAW

A Bicentennial Essay

Michael J. Perry

OXFORD UNIVERSITY PRESS
New York   Oxford
1988

KF
4552
.P47
1988

Oxford University Press

Oxford   New York   Toronto
Delhi   Bombay   Calcutta   Madras   Karachi
Petaling Jaya   Singapore   Hong Kong   Tokyo
Nairobi   Dar es Salaam   Cape Town
Melbourne   Auckland

and associated companies in
Berlin   Ibadan

Published by Oxford University Press, Inc.,
200 Madison Avenue, New York, New York 10016

Library of Congress Cataloging-in-Publication Data

Perry, Michael J.
    Morality, politics, and law : a bicentennial essay / by Michael J.
Perry.
       p.   cm.
    Includes index.
    ISBN 0-19-505296-X
    1. United States.—Constitutional law—Moral and ethical aspects.
2. Law and ethics. 3. Law and politics. 4. Pluralism (Social Sciences). I. Title.
KF4552.P47 1988
340'.11—dc19   87-31289
                                                        CIP

9 8 7 6 5 4 3 2 1

Printed in the United States of America
on acid-free paper.

FEB 2 1 1989

At the still point of the turning world. Neither flesh nor fleshless;
Neither from nor towards; at the still point, there the dance is,
But neither arrest nor movement. And do not call it fixity,
Where past and future are gathered. Neither movement from nor towards,
Neither ascent nor decline. Except for the point, the still point,
There would be no dance, and there is only the dance.
I can only say, *there* we have been: but I cannot say where.
And I cannot say, how long, for that is to place it in time.

T. S. Eliot, "Burnt Norton" (1935), *The Four Quartets*

Acknowledgments

Several colleagues at the Northwestern University School of Law, where I teach, and around the country, too numerous to name, gave generously of their time in commenting on drafts of this book, and I'm grateful to all of them. I'm especially indebted to Milner Ball, Kent Greenawalt, Robin Lovin, John Stick, and Cass Sunstein for particularly extensive comments—and to Yasuji Nosaka of the Faculty of Law of Rikkyo University, Tokyo, for important help with chapter 6. I want to mention, as well, my Northwestern colleagues Ron Allen, Bob Bennett, Bob Burns, Steve Presser, Carol Rose, and David Van Zandt. My greatest debt is to the Northwestern law students who in recent years took my "Law, Philosophy, and Politics" course and my "Constitutional Theory" seminar. That course and seminar were the principal crucible in which the arguments of this book were forged and then tested. I could not have written this book without the help of my students, who have been unfailingly patient, skeptical, and challenging. Two deserve special mention: Tim Bishop (who will be a law clerk to United States Supreme Court Justice William J. Brennan during the 1988 Term of Court) and Richard Manning (who, not content with his law degree, is now pursuing a Ph.D. in philosophy at Northwestern).

Portions of earlier versions of this book were presented to various audiences in the United States and, in one instance, Canada, to whom I'm grateful for helpful comments. I want to mention faculty workshops at the law schools of the University of Chicago (October 1983), Columbia University (October 1983), and Georgetown University (February 1984); the Seminar on Contemporary Social and Political Theory of the University of Chicago (February 1984); the Symposium on "Interpretation" sponsored by the *Southern California Law Review* (February 1984); George Mason University, where I delivered a George Mason Lecture (March 1984); the Conference on "Interpreting the Constitution" sponsored by the Boston College Department of Government (April 1984); the Conference on "The Constitution and Higher Law" sponsored by the San Jose State University Department of Government (May 1984); the annual meeting of the American Society for Political and Legal Philosophy (August 1984); the Conference on "Comparative Perspectives on Constitutional Law" sponsored by the Eason-Weinman Center for Comparative Law of the Tulane University School of Law (November 1984); Illinois Wesleyan University, where I was a visiting scholar (March 1985); Oberlin College, where I was a visiting scholar (April 1985); the Colloquium on "Religion and Politics in a Pluralistic Society" sponsored by the University of Dayton Department of Philosophy (November 1985); the faculty workshop at the University of Iowa College of Law (November 1985); the Symposium on "The Constitution and Human Values: The Unfinished Agenda" sponsored by the University of Georgia School of Law and the Law and Humanities Institute (March 1986); the College of William and Mary, Marshall-Wythe School of Law, where I delivered the 1986 Cutler Lecture in Constitutional Law (March 1986); Case Western Reserve University School of Law, where I was a Halle scholar-in-residence (March 1986); the faculty workshop at the University of Toronto School of Law (April 1986); the Seminar on "Judicial Activism and Judicial Restraint: How Should We Interpret the Constitution?" sponsored by the Intercollegiate Studies Institute and the Henry Salvatori Center of Claremont McKenna College (April 1986); the Seminar on Practical Reasoning of the University of Chicago Divinity School (November 1986); the University of Notre Dame, where I was an Exxon Distinguished Visiting Scholar (November 1986); faculty workshops at the Brooklyn Law School (April 1987) and the University of Maryland School of Law (September 1987); the Conference on "How Does the Constitution Establish Justice?" sponsored by the American Enterprise Institute and the United States Department of Justice (September 1987); Williams College, where I gave a paper on constitutional interpretation (September 1987); the Conference on "The Debate Over Original Intent" sponsored by Northern Kentucky University, Salmon P. Chase College of Law, (September 1987); Cleveland State University, Cleveland-Marshall College of Law, where I was a Bicentennial Visiting Scholar (October 1987); and Brigham Young University, J. Reuben Clark Law School, where I delivered a Bicentennial Lecture on "Interpreting the Constitution" (October 1987).

Finally, I owe a word of thanks to the administration and the secretarial staff of the Northwestern University School of Law, where I've been fortunate to teach since 1982. It's difficult to imagine how an institutional environment could be more supportive. In particular I'm grateful to be, during the 1987–88 academic year, the Stanford Clinton Sr. Research Professor of Law. The holder of the Clinton Professorship is relieved of some of his or her teaching responsibilities; I've therefore been free to devote more time to the preparation of this book for publication. Finally, for their generous help with the tedious but important job of proofreading, I'm grateful to my good friend Joanne Silver and to my mother, Mary Frances Perry.

Contents

MORALITY, POLITICS, AND LAW

Introduction:
The Proper Relation
of Morality to Politics

Several years ago I wrote a book about the proper role of the judiciary—particularly the federal judiciary, and especially the Supreme Court of the United States—in adjudicating constitutional issues.[1] In that book I assumed that there can be right answers—and wrong ones, too—to questions of morality. (I was concerned principally with questions of political morality. I argued that judges should play a relatively large role in the effort to locate the right answers to constitutional questions, understood as an important species of questions of political morality.) That assumption was—and remains—controversial, however, and so I decided to put the assumption in question.

I began this book as an effort to understand and then to address the problem of whether answers to moral questions have truth value—whether moral claims can bear the predicate true/false or any equivalent predicate, such as rationally acceptable/unacceptable. In the course of writing this book my inquiry broadened. Although I do address here the problem of right answers to moral questions, my fundamental subject is the proper relation of moral beliefs—including moral beliefs religious in character—to politics and law, especially constitutional law, in a morally pluralistic society.

The moral culture of the United States is pluralistic: American society comprises many different moral communities, including religious communities.[2] Some observers think that this state of affairs makes the United States a City of Babel[3]—that productive moral discourse among all or even most of the various moral communities is impossible to achieve because the basic moral beliefs of many communities are funda-

mentally different from those of many others.[4] Even if it does not make
the United States a City of Babel, the pluralistic character of American
moral culture gives rise to a number of serious problems concerning the
relation of morality and religion to politics and law, which it is the aim
of this book to address.[5]

My overarching aim is to lend support to the position that a deliberative, transformative politics—as distinct from a politics that is merely
manipulative and self-serving—is possible (though not always actual)
even in a morally pluralistic society like our own. I elaborate and defend
that position mainly in chapter 6, in the course of discussing the nature
and limits of constitutional adjudication, which, at its best, is a species
of deliberative, transformative politics. The opposing position is that
such a politics is not available to us because it is beyond the capacity of
us Americans to engage in productive moral discourse with one another,
which discourse (as I explain in chapter 6) is a prime constituent of a
deliberative, transformative politics; or, more radically but less plausibly, because there is no such thing as productive moral discourse since
there is no such thing as moral knowledge towards which to progress.
That position is sobering, even frightening—it presents a bleak, dispiriting vision of human relations—and ought not to be accepted
uncritically.

The position that a deliberative, transformative politics is beyond the
capacity of us Americans is all the more frightening when we realize
that although the moral culture of the United States is pluralistic, it is
certainly no more pluralistic, almost certainly less so, than the moral
culture of the human species. Human society comprises a multitude of
different moral communities. If we members of American society cannot even engage one another in productive moral conversation, how can
we hope to engage members of other societies very different from our
own in such conversation? In thinking about problems concerning the
relation of morality and religion to politics and law as they arise in a
particular pluralistic country like the United States, perhaps we can
achieve insights that will help us meet the challenge of conducting
productive moral discourse not merely in our own country, but in our
pluralistic world as well.

The questions I address here are, of course, difficult. Indeed, the
questions are so difficult that they are, in one version or another, perennial questions. I don't for a minute suppose that this book puts the
questions to rest. My more realistic aim is simply to contribute to the

ongoing debate about the proper relation of morality/religion to politics/law. My discussion is provisional and reformable—as, of course, any discussion of truly perennial questions must be provisional and reformable. Only a Pollyanna would think that closure could be achieved. Only a fool would think that he had achieved it.

Or, if not a fool, a philosopher. I want to emphasize that I'm not a professional philosopher. I am an academic lawyer—albeit, an academic lawyer with a strong interest in moral and political philosophy as it bears on law. The principal intended audience for this book is not philosophers, although I hope that philosophers and others—such as political theorists and religious ethicists—will be interested in and even engaged by at least some of what I have to say here. The principal intended audience is lawyers and law students, judges and other public officials, and, in general, citizens.

This book was written in the shadow of the Bicentennial of the Constitution of the United States. The Constitution was drafted and signed in 1787 and ratified in 1789. The Bill of Rights to the Constitution was proposed in 1789 and ratified in 1791. Thus, the period from 1987 to 1991 is the Bicentennial of these founding, formative events. I can think of no inquiry more fitting this Bicentennial period than the one I join in this book: the proper relation of moral beliefs, including those religious in character, to politics and law, especially constitutional law, in the morally pluralistic United States of America (and, by implication, in any similarly pluralistic society).

Perhaps the most controversial issue that has been debated this Bicentennial season has been the one I address in the final chapter of this book: what it means, or should mean, to "interpret" the Constitution. In American political-legal culture everyone, or almost everyone, seems to agree that courts should resolve constitutional conflicts on the basis of the Constitution, and that therefore courts should and even must interpret the Constitution. But there is widespread disagreement about what it means to "interpret" the Constitution. There are those—like William Rehnquist, the present Chief Justice of the United States Supreme Court, Edwin Meese, the present Attorney General of the United States, and Robert Bork, formerly a law professor at Yale and presently a judge of the United States Court of Appeals for the District of Columbia Circuit—who argue that the Constitution ought to mean *no more* today than it meant in the past, and that to "interpret" the Constitution, therefore, is simply to uncover its *original* meaning. On the other side of the dispute are those, like William Brennan, the most senior Justice of the United States Supreme Court, who argue that, happily, the Constitution often means *more* today than it meant in the past, and that to "interpret" the Constitution, therefore, is to discern its *present* meaning. Whereas Chief Justice Rehnquist, Attorney General Meese, Judge Bork, and many others want the courts to retreat to the relatively small role of uncovering and enforcing the *narrow* original meaning of the Constitution, many others insist with Justice Brennan that it is important that the courts maintain the larger role of discerning and enforcing the *broad* present meaning of the Constitution. In chapter 6 I elaborate the fundamental differences between, on the one side, the general position associated with Chief Justice Rehnquist, Attorney General Meese, and Judge Bork, and, on the other, the position associated with Justice Brennan. I then defend the latter position.[6]

I want to conclude this introduction with a bibliographical comment. In recent years several books have been published with which this book has some affinity and from which it draws some inspiration. They include: Ronald Beiner, *Political Judgment* (1983); John Finnis, *Natural Law and Natural Rights* (1980); Philippa Foot, *Virtues and Vices* (1978); Stuart Hampshire, *Morality and Conflict* (1983); Stanley Hauerwas, *A Community of Character* (1981); Alasdair MacIntyre, *After Virtue* (1981); Jaroslav Pelikan, *The Vindication of Tradition* (1984); Hilary Putnam, *Reason, Truth and History* (1981); Richard Rorty, *Consequences of Pragmatism* (1982); Michael Sandel, *Liberalism and the Limits of Justice* (1982); David Tracy, *Plurality and Ambiguity* (1987); Michael Walzer, *Interpretation and Social Criticism* (1987); and Bernard Williams, *Ethics and the Limits of Philosophy* (1985). Many more sources, some no less important to me than these, are scattered throughout the notes.

Speaking of the notes, which are extensive: As by now the reader has noticed, the notes are collected at the end of the book rather than at the foot of each page. Although I've deferred to my editor's preference for this format—endnotes rather than footnotes—I want to emphasize that the notes are a central part of the book, often supporting or supplementing the text in important ways.

I

What Is "Morality"?

As I said in the introduction, my fundamental subject in this book is the proper relation of moral beliefs—including moral beliefs religious in character—to politics and law, especially constitutional law, in a morally pluralistic society. If we are to engage in a productive discussion about the proper relation of moral beliefs to politics and law, we must begin by attending to the meaning or meanings of "moral".

What are "moral" beliefs? "Moral" beliefs are beliefs about what? "Moral" has no axiomatic or canonical meaning in either popular or academic-philosophical culture. The neo-Aristotelian understands "moral" differently from the neo-Kantian.[1] In this Part I elaborate and defend a particular understanding—a neo-Aristotelian understanding—of "moral".

That is, I elaborate and defend a particular conception of moral knowledge—a conception of the subject matter of morality (and therefore of moral discourse), of what *moral* knowledge is knowledge of or about. I call it the "naturalist" conception of moral knowledge. (I've just mentioned moral "beliefs" and moral "knowledge". I'll clarify, in due course, the relation between "belief" and "knowledge".) Then I address several issues regarding moral reasoning or justification—issues any proponent of the naturalist conception must face, including the issue of moral relativism, which is an especially important issue for members of a morally pluralistic society like our own.

1

The Naturalist Conception of Moral Knowledge

A vision of future social order is . . . based on a concept of human nature. If in fact man is an indefinitely malleable, completely plastic being, with no innate structures of mind and no intrinsic needs of a cultural or social character, then he is a fit subject for the "shaping behavior" by the state authority, the corporate manager, the technocrat, or the central committee. Those with some confidence in the human species . . . will try to determine the intrinsic human characteristics that provide the framework for intellectual development, the growth of moral consciousness, cultural achievement, and participation in a free community.[1]

I

Can there be moral knowledge? According to moral skepticism (not to be confused with moral relativism, discussed in the next chapter), there cannot be: Moral claims—claims about what is or is not (morally) good or bad, right or wrong, just or unjust—do not have truth value, they cannot bear the predicate true/false or any equivalent predicate, such as rationally acceptable/unacceptable.[2] Therefore, such claims cannot be objects of knowledge (according to moral skepticism). " 'Knowledge', unlike 'belief', is an achievement word; there are true beliefs and false beliefs, but knowledge is of truth."[3] To deny that there can be moral knowledge is to deny that moral claims can be objects of knowledge.[4]

Here are some typical formulations of moral skepticism:

[S]tatements of value, because they cannot be proven true or false, cannot be studied at all. Values can't be analyzed . . .; they can only be chosen, and the choice is irrational, ungovernable, and without criteria.[5]

[A]ll evaluative judgments and more specifically all moral judgments are *nothing but* expressions of preference, expressions of attitude or feeling, insofar as they are moral or evaluative in character. . . . Factual judgments are true or false; and in the realm of fact there are rational criteria by means of which we may secure agreement as to what is true and what is false. But moral judgments, being expressions of attitude or feeling, are neither true nor false; and agreement in moral judgment is not to be secured by any rational methods, for there are none.[6]

While one may have ethical beliefs, ethical knowledge requires that the beliefs be true. Lacking the capacity to be true or false, ethical propositions thus cannot be the subject of knowledge, no matter how much we may pretend that we "know" certain moral "truths."[7]

The choice among competing values [is] . . . arbitrary, . . . a matter of mere taste or preference, . . . a matter of purely personal subjectivity.[8]

It is difficult to find moral skeptics among contemporary philosophers. As Stuart Hampshire has noted, "Few philosophers now subscribe to a theory of belief which excludes the possibility of there being beliefs about good and bad, right and wrong, which have respectable and intelligible grounds no less than beliefs of other familiar kinds."[9] If one wants to find moral skeptics, one would do well to look, among other places, in American law schools, where some provincial lawyer-academics continue to subscribe to the outdated morally skeptical views of an earlier generation of legal philosophers.[10]

We should reject moral skepticism and accept moral cognitivism, which affirms that there can be moral knowledge, that (at least some) moral claims have truth value and therefore can be objects of knowledge.[11] There are different conceptions of what moral knowledge is knowledge of or about. The morally skeptical position is that there can be no moral knowledge, *period.* Put another way, moral skepticism holds that there can be no moral knowledge *no matter how "moral knowledge" is understood or conceived.* The morally cognitivist position is, in a sense, more modest: It holds that if "moral knowledge" is properly conceived, there can be moral knowledge. In this chapter I present what I believe to be the best conception of moral knowlege, which I call the "naturalist" conception. (Moral cognitivism does not exclude moral relativism. Moral relativism affirms that there can be moral knowledge; it insists, however, that such knowledge is "relative". Moral relativism, unlike moral skepticism, is a position worth taking seriously. I examine moral relativism in the next chapter.)

II

According to the naturalist conception, moral knowledge is knowledge of how to live so as to flourish, to achieve well-being. More precisely, it is knowledge about how *particular* human beings—the particular human being(s) I am, or we are, or you are, or she (or he) is, or they are—must live if they are to live the most deeply satisfying lives of which they are capable, or at least lives as deeply satisfying as any of which they are capable.[12] Human beings, like their primate cousins and ancestors, are entities both biological and social in character.[13] Human beings are social in the sense, *inter alia*, that they require society—and the artifacts of society, especially language and concepts—if they are to realize their distinctively human capacities, like speech and thought, and acquire "the information . . . [they] need[] to get . . . [their] bearings, to make up for . . . [their] lack of hereditary instructions";[14] indeed, their very identities, as individual persons, are achieved in and through relationships with one another.[15] Just as we can inquire "How ought I (or you, or she, etc.) to live if as a particular *biological* entity I am to achieve well-being, to flourish?" we can also inquire "How ought I to live if as a particular *social* entity I am to achieve well-being?" Moral knowledge is knowledge of how particular human beings ought to live if as social entities they are to flourish.[16] This conception is "naturalist" in the Aristotelian sense that moral knowledge is conceived as knowledge about human well-being.[17]

Thus, moral knowledge is primarily about what sort of person a particular human being ought to be—what projects she ought to pursue, what commitments she ought to make, what traits of character she ought to cultivate—if she is to live the most deeply satisfying life of which she is capable.

> The study of ethics, according to the classical conception, does not tell one what to do or furnish maxims for conduct; rather, it forms the kind of person that one is—making one, for instance, more reflective, more discriminating, more attentive—and it is only in this indirect way that it has an influence upon practice. . . . "It is sometimes complained that Aristotle does not attempt to outline a decision procedure for questions about how to behave.

But we have good reason to be suspicious of the assumption that there must be something to be found along the route he does not follow."[18]

Moral knowledge is also about, but only secondarily, what choices a particular human being ought to make in particular situations of choice, given the person she is, which means, in part, given the person she is committed to becoming. (If one's basic commitments are partly self-constitutive, then who one is depends in part on who one is committed to becoming.) As Gordon Allport wrote: "I experience 'ought' whenever I pause to relate a choice that lies before me to my ideal self-image."[19]

It bears emphasis that the question how a *particular* human being ought to live so as to flourish does not presuppose that there is but a *single* way for *all* human beings to achieve well-being. The notion that there is only one such way is implausible. Indeed, the question how to flourish doesn't presuppose even that all human beings are alike in any significant respect. The respects in which (all? most?) human beings are alike is an open and contested question.[20]

Even if members of the human species are alike in few significant respects relevant to morality, it is nonetheless the case that, given the naturalist conception of moral knowledge, the morally skeptical claim that there is no moral knowledge no matter how "moral knowledge" is conceived, is manifestly implausible. *Of course* there is moral knowledge in the sense of at least some rationally acceptable beliefs about how particular human beings ought to live if they are to flourish— beliefs about what they should do or refrain from doing if they are to live lives as deeply satisfying as any of which they are capable. Again, moral relativism, discussed in the next chapter, not moral skepticism, is the position worth taking seriously.[21]

III

How can a true *description* of how a particular human being must live so as to flourish support a true *prescription* that she ought or ought not to live a certain way? After all, one cannot deduce an ought-statement from an is-statement.[22] Yet, surely moral knowledge has something to do with ought-statements. The naturalist conception of moral knowledge would be implausible if it failed to account for the ought-statements that are so much a part of ordinary or conventional moral discourse.

The efforts of some contemporary naturalists to deal with the is-ought problem are inadequate. Mortimer Adler, for example, posits a "categorical prescription or injunction"[23] which, according to Adler, is a "self-evident truth".[24] The categorical prescription is this: "We ought to desire (seek and acquire) that which is really good for us."[25] If true, that prescription, coupled with true statements about what is really good for us, supports conclusions about what we ought to desire that are themselves true (and not merely logically valid). The prescription is "categorical" in the sense that the "ought" of the prescription is not contingent on what we do in fact desire. But in what sense is the prescription "true"—and not merely true, but "self-evidently" true? Here is Adler's answer:

> The truth of the categorical prescription that underlies every piece of reasoning that leads to a true prescriptive conclusion is a self-evident truth. Anyone can test this for himself by trying to think the opposite and finding it impossible.
>
> We simply cannot think that we ought to desire that which is really bad for us or that we ought not to desire that which is really good for us. Without knowing in advance which things are in fact really good or bad for us, we do know at once that "ought to desire" is inseparable in its meaning from the meaning of "really good," just as we know at once that the parts of a physical whole are always less than the whole. It is impossible to think the opposite just as it is impossible to think that we ought to desire that which is really bad for us.
>
> We acknowledge a truth as self-evident as soon as we acknowledge the impossibility of thinking the opposite.[26]

If it worked, Adler's argument would explain not how we can get from an "is" to an "ought"—we simply can't do that—but how we get from a categorical "ought" ("we ought to desire that which is really good for us") through an "is" ("X is really good for us") to an "ought" ("we ought to desire X"). However, a fatal problem afflicts Adler's argument.

To respond to the is-ought problem the way Adler does gives rise to the question whether the categorical "ought" is true or justified. If it is not, then the "ought" of the conclusion ("we ought to desire X") is not necessarily true either, since the truth of the "ought" of the conclusion depends on the truth of the categorical "ought". Adler imagines that the categorical prescription is true—indeed, self-evidently true—because it is impossible to think that the prescription is false. However, it is *not* impossible to think that the prescription is beyond justification and, therefore, *neither* true *nor* false. The prescription is beyond justification in the sense that any effort to justify it would be circular.[27] There is nothing strange about an account of "truth" according to which if a proposition cannot in principle be justified (or falsified), it is neither true nor false. To the contrary, there is something mysterious about an account of truth according to which a proposition can be true—"self-evidently" true—even if it cannot be supported by a noncircular argument.[28] Adler's argument in support of the truth of the categorical prescription doesn't work.

John Finnis is another contemporary naturalist. His handling of the is-ought problem bears some resemblance to Adler's. Whereas for Adler the crucial normative proposition is that we ought to desire that which is really good for us, for Finnis it is that flourishing or well-being is good in the sense that it is to be pursued, that we ought to pursue it. If true, that proposition, coupled with true statements about how one must live so as to flourish, supports true conclusions about how one ought to try to live—about what way of living is good.

But is it true that flourishing is good (in Finnis' sense)? For Finnis, the truth of the proposition that flourishing is good or valuable is "obvious ('self-evident') and even unquestionable."[29] At another point Finnis says that the truth of that proposition is "underived". But we must not, cautions Finnis,

> confuse a . . . lack of derivation with a lack of justification or lack of objectivity. Non-derivability in some cases amounts to lack of justification or of objectivity. But in other cases it betokens self-evidence; and these cases are to be found in every field of inquiry. For in every field there is and must be, at some point or points, an end to derivation and inference. At that point or points, we find ourselves in face of the self-evident, which makes possible all subsequent inferences in that field.[30]

What does it mean to say that the truth of the proposition that flourishing is good is "obvious ('self-evident') and even unquestionable"? A move like Adler's—"it means that it is impossible to think that the proposition is false"—is unavailing, because it is possible to think that the proposition is beyond justification and hence *neither* true *nor* false. What else might it mean, then, to say that the proposition is obviously or self-evidently true (or, equivalently, that the good or value of flourishing is obvious or self-evident)? Finnis is right that "in every field there is and must be, at some point or points, an end to derivation and inference." But is he also right that "[a]t that point or points, we find ourselves in face of the self-evident[ly true]"?

Wittgenstein, not Finnis, seems to me to have the better view: "Giving grounds comes to an end;—but the end is not certain propositions striking us immediately as true, i.e., it is not a kind of *seeing* on our part; it is our *acting*, which lies at the bottom of the language game."[31] (Perhaps we should say not "the language game", but "the living game".) The point Wittgenstein seems to me to be making—in any event the point I want to make—is this: "It is not a kind of seeing on our part" but our *existential orientation* "which lies at the bottom of the language game." This point is suggestive of a more satisfying way of dealing with the is-ought problem than the ways Adler and Finnis dealt with it.

Consider the claim "One ought to be rational (rather than irrational)." There is no noncircular way to justify that claim because any putative justification would be rational and thereby presuppose the authority of that which is at issue: rationality.[32] Thus, we cannot justify rationality. Nonetheless, most human beings *are* committed to rationality, they *do* value it. (This is not to deny that there are competing conceptions of rationality.) For virtually every one of us, the commitment to, the value of, rationality is simply not at issue. (Moreover, it is difficult to see how the value of rationality could be put in issue: "[That any attempt to justify] rationality would be circular . . . shows, not that rationality lacks a necessary justification, but that it needs no justification, because it cannot intelligibly be questioned unless it is already presupposed."[33])

Similarly, there is no noncircular way to justify the claim "One ought to try to flourish." Any putative justification would presuppose the authority of that which is at issue: flourishing. (*Q*: "Why ought I to try to flourish?" *A*: "Because flourishing is good for you.") We cannot justify flourishing. Nonetheless, most human beings *are* committed to (their own) flourishing; they *do* value it. (This is not to deny that—just as there are competing conceptions of rationality—there are competing conceptions of flourishing: egoistic, altruistic, materialistic, spiritual, etc.) Just as the commitment to, the value of, rationality is not at issue for most of us, the commitment to, the value of, flourishing is not at issue either.

Rather than saying, with Finnis, that the good or value of flourishing is self-evident, we should say that the value of flourishing is not at issue for most of us. The sense in which the value of flourishing is "underived", as Finnis puts it, is that the value is foundational: Our commitment to flourishing "lies at the bottom of the language game."

Finnis says, in the passage quoted above, that the "non-derivability" of the value of flourishing does not "amount to lack of justification", but merely "betokens self-evidence". It would be better to say that the value of flourishing lacks justification, but that it no more requires justification than does the value of rationality. We might want to *explain* (in evolutionary terms, say) the fact of our commitment to flourishing—just as we might want to explain the fact of our commitment to rationality. But we need not *justify* either commitment. Indeed, as I've explained, we *cannot* justify either commitment.[34]

That the value of flourishing is beyond justification, however, no more undermines the enterprise of moral inquiry than that the value of rationality is beyond justification undermines the enterprise of science. The aim of science is not to "prove" the value of rationality. The aim of morality is not to "prove" the value of flourishing. The impossibility of justifying the value of rationality does not render scientific claims problematic or call into question the notion of scientific "knowledge". The impossibility of justifying the value of flourishing does not render moral claims problematic or call into question the notion of moral "knowledge".[35] Thus, the is-ought "problem"—the fact that an ought-statement cannot be deduced from an is-statement—turns out not to be a problem at all, at least not for naturalism. Naturalism begins with the foundational commitment to flourishing. "In the process of seeking ever more fundamental justifications for our knowledge claims, we must eventually stop at something which is itself in no need of justification."[36]

Moreover, the is-ought problem is not a problem for naturalism even if I am wrong that the value of flourishing is not at issue for most of us. Assume that I *am* wrong. Perhaps someone can be found (or, more easily, dreamt up) who is not committed to flourishing—indeed, who self-consciously, if perversely, pursues a program of "not flourishing". What if most people were like that? No matter. Nothing in my argument depends on the claim, which I nonetheless believe to be true, that the value of flourishing is not at issue for most people. Neither the imagined fact that most people are not committed to flourishing nor, much less, the real fact that at least some people are not, entails that moral knowledge does not exist.

But, one might query, . . . don't David Hume's arguments count for anything? . . . Surely there is a metaphysical gap between facts and values . . .

Such arguments . . . confuse justification with motivation. . . . Whether one is motivated to act [on the basis of moral knowledge] is . . . not a question of reason but of commitment. If I am committed to being ascientific, then scientific justification will be meaningless to me and will not move me. Peter Winch's Azande are a good example of this fact, as are certain modern-day mystics. If I am committed to being amoral, then moral justification will also be meaningless to me and will also fail to move me. Political realists and sociopaths are examples of this fact. However, if I am committed to being moral, then moral facts and moral justification will be as pertinent to my beliefs and my behavior as scientific facts and justification are to those who are committed to being scientific. The fact that something is morally wrong will move us, if we are committed to doing the right and avoiding the wrong, otherwise, such facts will not move us at all.[37]

What can we say to someone not committed to flourishing? "There is perhaps nothing to say to a man who would like to be a centaur. Moral discourse always presupposes the acceptance of humanity and the striving to be and to become ever more fully human."[38]

John Mackie faulted naturalism as an account of the meaning of moral terms. He pointed out that although in ordinary moral discourse moral imperatives—statements about what someone (morally) ought or ought not to do—seem to have a categorical character, in naturalist moral discourse they seem to have a merely hypothetical character:

On a naturalist analysis, moral judgments can be practical, but their practicality is wholly relative to desires or possible satisfactions of the person or persons whose actions are to be guided; but moral judgments seem to say more than this. This view leaves out the categorical quality of moral requirements. . . . Any analysis of the meaning of moral terms which omits this claim to objective, intrinsic, prescriptivity is to that extent incomplete; and this is true of any . . . [naturalist] analysis.[39]

One response to Mackie's point is that naturalist moral theory does not purport to be a theory of what people ordinarily mean when they use moral terms. Rather, a naturalist moral theory is a theory of how to live so as to flourish.[40]

A second and more fundamental response to Mackie is that Philippa Foot has got it just right: Moral discourse can get along quite nicely without categorical imperatives—and indeed *must* get along without them, because there aren't any. There are no moral "ought's" that *necessarily* give a person a reason for choosing or acting one way or another—that is, that give a person a reason for acting regardless of what her interests are or whether or not she is committed to flourishing.[41] Naturalist imperatives or ought-claims, properly understood, are not categorical. Such a claim does not say "You ought (or ought not) to do this no matter what your interests are and even if you are not committed to flourishing". The naturalist imperative is hypothetical. It says, "You ought to do this because of what your interests are and because (or if) you are committed to flourishing".[42] Naturalist ought-talk presupposes that any person to whom an ought-claim is addressed is committed to her own flourishing.[43] That presupposition may be mistaken, of course, in the case of a particular human being. Nonetheless, the naturalist does not—at least, does not on my view of naturalism— pretend to get from an "is" to an "ought" by some sleight of hand. Rather, the naturalist moves from the (perhaps mistakenly) presupposed commitment of a particular human being to her flourishing—which commitment, like the commitment to rationality, is beyond justifica- tion—through an "is" (namely, a statement about what she must do to flourish) to an "ought" (a statement about what she ought to do).

Of course, moral knowledge consists of more than (hypothetical) imperatives. A claim that *A*'s decision to do *X* was wrong, in the sense, for example, that the choice was antithetical to *A*'s flourishing, is not an imperative. Moreover, such a claim or judgment is "categorical" and not "hypothetical" in the sense that it is not necessarily contingent on *A*'s actual preferences or wants or desires.[44] Thus, even on a naturalist analysis moral judgments can have a categorical quality. Categoricality is a feature of moral knowledge, according to naturalism, although moral imperatives are not categorical.[45]

Mackie contended vigorously against what he called the "objec- tivity" of values: "[V]aluing, choosing, preferring, recommending, rejecting, condemning, and so on, are human activities," he argued, "and there . . . [are] no values that are prior to and logicially indepen- dent of all such activities."[46] Mackie was right on that score: Values, including moral values, are not objective (in Mackie's sense of the term).[47] If it presupposed that values *are* objective, the naturalist con- ception of moral knowledge would be unsound.[48] Thus, it bears emphasis that the naturalist conception (as I portray it) does not presup- pose the objectivity of values. Indeed, like Mackie, the naturalist rejects the notion that there are any values prior to and logically independent of the human activities of "valuing, preferring, choosing, recommending, rejecting, condemning, and so on". As my discussion of the naturalist conception illustrates, for the naturalist "the category of values is anthropocentric, in that it corresponds to interests which can only take root in creatures with something approaching our own affective make-up. . . . [V]alues are only ascribable from points of view constituted by human patterns of affective response. A wholly dispassionate eye would be as blind to them as a black-and-white camera to chromatic colors."[49]

IV

As I said at the beginning of this chapter, to flourish (achieve well-being) is to live the most deeply satisfying life of which one is capable (or at least as deeply satisfying a life as any of which one is capable). Flourishing, then, is not an all-or-nothing matter. It is, rather, an ideal and thus a matter of degree. As is the case with many other ideals, most of us rarely, if ever, fully attain it. And even when we do attain it, or come close, there is always the possibility our hold will slip. Any human being who is committed to flourishing is necessarily committed to, *and in that sense has an "interest" in*, whatever is constitutive of her flourishing, even that which she may not presently understand to be constitutive of her flourishing.[50] One is flourishing *to the extent* one's "interests" are satisfied, and not flourishing *to the extent* they are not satisfied.

Naturalist moral theories vary in accordance, *inter alia*, with how they specify human interests—the interests either of human beings generally or of particular human beings. My aim here is not to present a naturalist moral theory, only to sketch a naturalist account of moral knowledge. I do want to suggest, however, some features any naturalist theory must have if it is to be at all plausible.

First. Any naturalist moral theory must acknowledge human variety as well as human commonality. That one human being has an interest in some matter does not mean that other human beings—any or all of them—have an interest in that matter too. Moreover, there is a great variety of ways in which interests—even interests common to all or virtually all members of the human species—can be satisfied. I said near the beginning of this chapter that the notion that there is but a single way for all human beings to achieve well-being is implausible.

Indeed, there is no reason to suppose that there is but a single way for any one human being to achieve well-being, much less for any two or more human beings.[51] (I return to the matter of human commonality and human variety in the next chapter, in discussing moral relativism.)

Second. Any naturalist theory must acknowledge that to have a preference (or want or desire) for something is not necessarily to have an interest in the satisfaction of that preference. A person has an interest (if she is committed to flourishing) in the satisfaction of preferences the satisfaction of which is constitutive of her flourishing. However, a person has an interest in the *nonsatisfaction* of preferences the satisfaction of which is antithetical to her flourishing.[52] (In chapter 4, in criticizing preference-utilitarianism, I comment on the defective character of many preferences.)

Third. Given our commitment to flourishing, we have an interest in the personal capacities and social and political conditions that are prerequisites to flourishing, including capacities and conditions we may not presently understand to be prerequisites. Two such capacities/conditions are worth mentioning here.

Any naturalist theory must acknowledge the importance of the capacity for self-critical rationality and of the conditions for its exercise.[53] Anyone can be mistaken as to one's interests. To the extent, first, a capacity to critically evaluate what we believe about our interests is a condition of correcting such mistakes and, second, correcting such mistakes is, in turn, a condition of flourishing, we have an interest in that capacity, which we might call self-critical rationality.[54] And, correspondingly, we have an interest in social and political conditions that facilitate rather than impede the exercise of self-critical rationality.[55]

More broadly, any naturalist theory must acknowledge the importance of the capacity and conditions for growth. It is often the case that a person desires to change in some regard, to grow. Certainly everyone aware of possibilities for herself that, were she to realize them, would mean a life that, in her own view, would be richer, more deeply satisfying, has such desires. Frequently the best explanation for the fact that a person does not have any such desire is her distorted, diminished vision of her possibilities, her mistaken view of what she would find most deeply satisfying, or both. Our capacity for self-critical rationality is important to our discovery both of our possibilities and of what we would find most deeply satisfying. Similarly, our capacity for growth, for self-transcendence—which consists largely of what we might call strength of will—is essential to our actualization of those possibilities the actualization of which we believe we would find most deeply satisfying. To the extent the realization of such possibilities is constitutive of flourishing, we have an interest in the capacity for growth and in social and political conditions that facilitate its exercise.

V

The commitment to flourishing presupposed by naturalist ought-talk and in need of no justification is a person's commitment to *her own* flourishing. To say that I am committed to *my* flourishing, to satisfying *my* interests, is not to say that I am committed—or that I ought to be committed—to *your* flourishing, to satisfying *your* interests. I might happen to be committed to attending to your interests as well as to (or even instead of) my own. I might happen to have that "preference". But can we somehow get from the fact of my commitment to my flourishing to the proposition that I *ought* to attend to *your* interests? That is, can we get from the fact of a person's commitment to her own flourishing to an altruistic (as distinct from an egoistic) moral theory?

It has been suggested that an egoistic moral theory is irrational or illogical, that it is inconsistent to be committed to the satisfaction of one's own interests but not to the satisfaction of anyone else's.[56] Sometimes the point is put by saying that "the moral point of view" must be "impartial" or "universal", that "universalizability" is a logical requirement of moral judgments.[57] Were such arguments sound, a naturalist moral theory could incorporate some such argument to indicate how a person's commitment to her own flourishing gives her a reason to attend not merely to her interests, but to the interests of others as well. After all, a moral theory hardly constitutes moral knowledge if it is irrational or illogical. Indeed, a theory of any kind, including a scientific theory, hardly constitutes knowledge of any kind, including scientific knowledge, if it violates the consistency constraint, which is a standard, a criterion, of rationality.[58]

However, such arguments are not sound. It would be inconsistent for me to accept that my commitment to my flourishing gives me a reason to attend to my interests, while denying that anyone else's commitment to her flourishing gives her a reason to attend to hers. But there is no inconsistency in claiming that my commitment to my flourishing gives me a reason to attend to my interests but not to anyone else's—or that anyone else's commitment to her flourishing gives her a reason to attend to her interests but not to mine.[59]

My point is not that the consistency constraint—or the universalizability condition—is trivial, only that it does not preclude an egoistic moral theory. The principle "I should look out for myself (or myself and my family/friends/etc.), *period*" is universalizable: "Everyone should look out for herself (herself and her family/friends/etc.), *period*."[60] That principle, however, is not altruistic.[61] And in accepting that *universal* principle, I am accepting that, so far as *I* am concerned, my interests *are* more important, do count more, than the interests of anyone else.[62]

One way of looking out for my interests is to inhabit a society in which people help me and, in return, I help them. Indeed, for most of us that is an indispensable way of looking out for our interests.[63] Does my need for the cooperation (including the noninterference) of some other persons to satisfy some of my interests give me a reason to attend to the interests of other persons? Hardly. At most it gives me a reason to cooperate only with those persons with whom I need to cooperate, and even then only to the extent satisfaction of certain of my interests requires it. Even that claim is problematic, however: Perhaps my need for cooperation gives me a reason to cooperate only when *feigning* cooperation won't do the trick.[64] In any event, such limited self-interested cooperation, if altruism at all, is hardly a robust altruism.

It is an open question, then, whether a sound naturalist moral theory must be altruistic: How, if at all, does a person's commitment to her own flourishing support an imperative to the effect "You shall treat your neighbor lovingly, for he is like yourself"?[65] Perhaps this question brings us to the limits of any truly "secular" moral philosophy. Increasingly I doubt that any such philosophy can support an imperative to the effect that one should "treat one's neighbor lovingly", where "neighbor" is understood in the radical, Gospel sense.[66]

At any rate, for the naturalist it is *that* question—the question of the relation between an altruistic life and flourishing—that requires an answer, *not* the question "Why be moral?" For the naturalist "Why be moral?" means "Why try to flourish?" and, as I explained earlier in the chapter, there is no noncircular way to answer that question, just as there is no noncircular way to answer the question "Why be rational?" If the why-be-moral question is taken to mean something else, namely, "What reason does one have to do what morality requires, other than 'prudential' or 'self-regarding' reasons?", the answer is, "None".

Aristotle was right that no one has any reason to do what morality requires except the "prudential" or "self-regarding" reason that doing what morality requires is somehow constitutive of one's flourishing.[67] What reason does one have, if any, for cultivating in oneself, or at least *trying* to cultivate, the consciousness of a Saint Francis of Assisi, for example, or a Mother Theresa (and then living a life animated by that consciousness) except the belief—perhaps expressed in "religious" terms, perhaps in "secular" terms—that such a consciousness (such a life) is "truly" or "fully" human?[68] (Of course, to the extent one is possessed of such a consciousness, one's motivation for acting or choosing this way or that is scarcely self-regarding.[69])

To say that the value of flourishing is not at issue is not to deny that there are competing conceptions of flourishing, any more than to say that the value of rationality is not at issue is to deny that there are competing conceptions of rationality. There are "deep conflicts over what human flourishing and well-being . . . consist in . . . Aristotle and Nietzsche, Hume and the New Testament are names which represent polar oppositions."[70] Is it possible for a proponent of one conception of flourishing to engage in productive moral discourse with a proponent of a different conception? Is it possible, at least, to *reason* about conceptions of flourishing—to adjudicate among competing conceptions? Or are conceptions of flourishing merely matters of "taste" and therefore (because *de gustibus non est disputandum*) beyond the realm of reason? In the next chapter I present a naturalist perspective on moral reasoning and moral relativism.

2

A Naturalist Perspective on Moral Reasoning and Moral Relativism

> [Y]ou can say of normative argument what has been said of comedy: that it is a narrow escape not from truth but from despair. The emphasis falls on the narrowness of the escape; you cannot even be sure in the end whether you have made it. Perhaps the only view of normative argument that can be made to stick is one that approaches skepticism without being engulfed by it. Better this view than the familiar alternation between boastful moral dogmatism and barely hidden moral agnosticism.[1]

Thomas Scanlon has suggested that there are three basic "questions which a philosophical account of the foundations of morality must answer."[2] They are, first, the question of subject matter: Moral knowledge is knowledge of or about what?; second, the espistemological question: How is moral knowledge achieved?; and, third, the question of motivation: What reason, if any, does one have to take an interest in, to care about, moral knowledge?

In the preceding chapter I addressed the first and third questions. According to the naturalist account of the foundations of morality, moral knowledge is knowledge of or about "how to live"—how particular human beings must live if they are to flourish, to live the most deeply satisfying lives of which they are capable (or at least lives as deeply satisfying as any of which they are capable). If a person is committed to flourishing, then she has reason to take an interest in, to care about, knowledge of how she must live if she is to flourish.

In this chapter I address the epistemological question. I offer an account, from my naturalist perspective, of the nature and limits of moral reasoning and I deal with a matter that bedevils any naturalist account of moral reasoning: moral relativism. The point of departure for my analysis is the observation with which the preceding chapter concluded: There are "deep conflicts over what human flourishing and well-being . . . consist in . . . Aristotle and Nietzsche, Hume and the New Testament are names which represent polar oppositions."[3]

I

My principal aim in this chapter is to portray the nature—*and the limits*—of moral reasoning. This chapter complements and extends the preceding one. As will be apparent, my portrayal is naturalist. The account of moral reasoning—the portrayal of moral discourse—I offer here is opposed, at one extreme, to what is sometimes called moral "foundationalism" and, at the other, to moral skepticism. Moral foundationalism is the position, roughly, that there are first principles, fundamental or "foundational" principles, of morality—of how to live or what to do—that are beyond question and serve as the unquestionable ground of moral justification.[4] (The position that there are basic moral principles somehow implicit in or entailed by one's commitment to "rationality"—principles no one can "rationally" reject—seems to me a species of moral foundationalism.) Moral skepticism, as I indicated in the preceding chapter, holds that there can be no moral knowledge. Moral foundationalism and moral skepticism agree in supposing that a necessary condition of there being moral knowledge is that there be first principles that are beyond question or challenge. Unlike moral foundationalism, moral skepticism denies that there are any such principles. As my discussion in this chapter suggests, it is a mistake to suppose that the existence of moral knowledge—or, indeed, knowledge of any kind, including scientific knowledge—requires unquestionable first principles. My naturalist portrayal of moral reasoning/discourse—that is, of the practices we engage in that constitute what is ordinarily meant by moral reasoning/discourse—illustrates that there are no first principles of morality of the sort moral foundationalists have in mind (in this I'm allied with moral skeptics), but that, nonetheless, there can be, and often is, moral knowledge (in this I'm allied with moral foundationalists).[5]

I shall begin by portraying the nature and limits of reasoning generally. Whatever else it is, moral reasoning is a species of reasoning. "[T]o characterise reasoning as such is to characterise moral reasoning among other species of reasoning."[6]

A particular instance of reasoning constitutes either *inquiry*, in which a hypothesis is tested, or *justification* (or argument or advocacy), in which a claim is defended.[7] Although the elements of reasoning-as-inquiry and the elements of reasoning-as-justification are the same, for convenience I shall talk in terms of reasoning-as-justification and so speak of defending a claim. I mean to portray not a particular mode of reasoning, such as deductive, inductive, or hypothetico-deductive, but reasoning *simpliciter*. For present purposes, distinctions such as deductive/inductive are not important. Later in this chapter I address the question of whether relatively general propositions or, instead, relatively particular ones have justificatory priority in reasoning, including moral reasoning.

The basic elements or constituents of reasoning are *claims*, *warrants*, and *grounds*. A claim is the belief at issue and to be defended (for example, "We should raise taxes"). A warrant is a belief that specifies a belief or set of beliefs—not including the claim-belief or the warrant-belief—the acceptability of which is a sufficient (and sometimes necessary) condition for the acceptability of the claim-belief ("If we must choose between discontinuing essential human services and raising taxes, we should raise taxes"). A ground is the belief, or one of the beliefs, the acceptability of which is, according to the warrant-belief, a sufficient condition for the acceptability of the claim-belief ("If we don't raise taxes, we must discontinue essential human services").

Reasoning is a practice in which two (or more) beliefs—a warrant-belief and a ground-belief(s)—are offered in support of a further claim-belief. Any argument presupposes the "givenness" of two (or more) beliefs: the warrant-belief and the ground-belief(s).[8] The strength of an argument, for a person, depends on the strength with which she adheres to the presupposed beliefs. (The acceptability *vel non* of a belief is a matter of degree.[9]) Of course, one (or more) of the beliefs one wants to use as the warrant or a ground in an argument may, and often will, be at issue. In that case, one must deploy a prior argument in which the contested belief that is to serve as the warrant or a ground in the subsequent argument is defended as a claim.[10]

The constituents of reasoning, then, are beliefs. What are the sources of one's beliefs? A person's beliefs are rooted directly in her own experience. (Although some of a person's "beliefs depend largely upon experience, [and] some largely upon other beliefs of his[,] . . . none depend solely upon experience; for the beliefs he already has affect what beliefs he acquires as a result of experience."[11]) To a very great extent, however, a person's beliefs are rooted indirectly in certain other persons' experience—trusted others, such as family, community, etc., whose reports and interpretations of their experience one often accepts and, to some extent, must accept.[12] A person's experiential, and thus cognitive, condition would be extremely impoverished if she could not rely on others' experience.[13] (This is not to suggest that many of us credit another person's experience as much as we credit our own—though some of us sometimes do, and some of us sometimes should.) Indeed, a person *is* experientially/cognitively impoverished if she forsakes the opportunity for imaginative experience presented by literature and art.[14]

One's beliefs are not fixed for all time. Why does a person revise or at least question her beliefs? What are the occasions of revision?[15] Perhaps she was unaware that she held inconsistent beliefs but is now aware; or perhaps she was aware that she held inconsistent beliefs but now finds herself in a situation in which she can no longer tolerate the inconsistency and must resolve it. Perhaps due to some new experience, whether her own or that of some trusted other on whom she relies, she has acquired a new belief inconsistent with one or more beliefs previously held; or perhaps the new belief is not inconsistent with any previously held belief but nonetheless renders her system or "web" of beliefs less balanced or integrated or coherent and more ad hoc. Perhaps she simply finds herself in a situation in which one or more of her beliefs is subjected to a challenge that, as an existential or at least practical matter, she cannot ignore. Revision of one or more of the beliefs that constitute a person's web of beliefs may require revision of one or more further beliefs, and so on, given the extent to which a person's beliefs are interdependent.[16]

The more important question, for present purposes, is not why a person revises her beliefs, but how. A person's beliefs can arise or change—and in particular be changed—in numerous ways, including "programming" or "conditioning" of various sorts. The principal matrix of someone's most basic beliefs and of the most dramatic changes in her beliefs is surely her lived experience, personal or vicarious. I don't mean to elevate the role of cognition over that of experience in talking about changes in belief. But for present purposes I'm emphasizing the project of belief revision, and a person revises her beliefs only by reference to her beliefs. A person's criteria of belief revision are her beliefs.

Although any (or virtually any) of a person's beliefs can be put in question—intellectually if not existentially—no person can doubt all of her beliefs at once. Everyone must stand somewhere.[17] And everyone does stand somewhere—a place where she says, "I have reached bedrock and this is where my spade is turned."[18] A person revises one or more of her beliefs, which for some reason are in question, by reference to one or more of her other beliefs not in question—that is, not *then* in question. (What is not in question for me today can for a variety of reasons become in question for me tomorrow, just as what was not in question for me yesterday may be in question for me today. Similarly, what is in question for me today may not be in question for me tomorrow.[19]) A person can revise all (or virtually all) her beliefs—but only over time.[20] Those beliefs one finds it difficult to imagine ever abandoning—those beliefs that are, for the present at least, a matter of deep conviction—one tends to think of as "knowledge".[21] Wittgenstein wrote: "One might say: ' "I know" expresses *comfortable* certainty, not the certainty that is still struggling.' "[22]

These observations apply to reasoning *generally* and thus to moral reasoning among other species of reasoning. Moral reasoning and, say, scientific reasoning do not differ *qua* reasoning, although, of course, they differ radically in terms of subject matter. That is, moral *reasoning* does not differ from scientific *reasoning*, although *moral* reasoning differs from *scientific* reasoning.

II

I want to pursue further the questions of the sources of beliefs and of why and, especially, how one revises one's beliefs. And I want to pursue them with reference to moral beliefs, which, according to the naturalist account of the subject matter of morality—the naturalist conception of moral knowledge—are fundamentally about what sort of lives particular human beings should live, what sort of persons they should be, if they are to live the most deeply satisfying lives of which they are capable. It bears emphasis, however, that although my reference in the following discussion is to moral beliefs, the points I make concerning belief revision extend beyond moral beliefs to beliefs generally, including scientific beliefs.[23] Not merely in moral inquiry but "in every sphere of inquiry the learner may come to question what he has been taught, but when he does so he is appealing *to* what he has been taught as well as *against* what he has been taught."[24]

One of the most important sources of one's moral beliefs is certain other persons' experience—trusted others on whom one does and must rely,[25] in particular the moral community and tradition in which one participates.[26] By moral community I mean, in this context, a group of persons who are the present bearers of, and participants in, a moral tradition. By moral tradition I mean a particular history or narrative in which the central motif is an aspiration to a particular form of life, to certain ideals and goals, and the central discourse is an argument—in Alasdair MacIntyre's terms, "an historically extended, socially embodied argument"[27]—about how that form of life is to be cultivated and revised.[28] As Stanley Hauerwas has written, "A community is a group of persons who share a common history [some if only by adopting that history] and whose common set of interpretations about that history provide the basis for common actions. These interpretations may be quite diverse and controversial even within the community, but are sufficient to provide individual members with the sense that they are more alike than unalike."[29] The paradigmatic such community, of course, is religious (and, indeed, Hauerwas' principal reference is to religious communities). (I have put the matter oversimply: Many of us stand at a point of convergence among more than one tradition; we participate in more than one community—for example, we participate in religious, political, and intellectual communities. In that sense, each of us continues more than one narrative.)

The extent to which one's most basic moral beliefs are rooted in the community(ies) and tradition(s) in which one participates bears emphasis. Basic moral beliefs—beliefs about human good, about what sorts of lives are possible and, of those, which are most deeply satisfying—are less the property of individuals than of communities. Thus, in this book I speak of the pluralistic character of American moral culture in terms of a variety of moral *communities* rather than a multiplicity of *individual* moral perspectives. As Bernard Williams has noted, much contemporary moral philosophy obscures the fact that a person's moral beliefs "are part of an ethical life that is to an important degree shared with others. "[30] Such moral thought "actually conceals the dimension in which ethical life lies outside the individual. "[31] (Other sorts of beliefs, too, including scientific beliefs, are less the property of individuals than of communities.[32])

A community—the living embodiment of a tradition—has occasion to participate in the revision of its tradition principally to the extent the lived experience of the community is a source of new beliefs (or new doubts) or of more widespread acceptance of beliefs (or doubts) that had already existed but with only scant support in the community, in particular new beliefs about human possibility and human satisfaction. (Whatever the terms or metaphors in which it is expressed, the moral question-in-chief for any human being or community of human beings is this: Of the sorts of lives that are real possibilities for me or us, which is the most deeply satisfying, or at least as deeply satisfying as any other?) New beliefs must somehow be integrated into the tradition's web of beliefs, and that integration sometimes requires a modification or even adandonment of some traditional beliefs.[33]

It is a feature of many communities and traditions that they acknowledge, implicitly if not explicitly, the provisional and therefore revisable character of their beliefs and thus allow for, even encourage, the exercise of self-critical rationality.[34] Traditions vary, of course, in the extent to which they allow for or encourage self-critical rationality.[35] (As Roberto Unger has written, "The more a structure of thought or relationship provides for the occasions and instruments of its own revision, the less you must choose between maintaining it and abandoning it for the sake of the things it excludes. You can just remake or reimagine it. . . . Society improves by laying its practical and imaginative order ever more open to correction."[36]) Indeed, different subcommunities within the same tradition may vary. No doubt the Polish Pope and many of his bureaucratic staff, most of whom are European, think some things have gotten rather out of hand in parts of the American Catholic Church.

The revision of self and the revision of tradition are analogous. To preview a theme that appears in the next chapter: One's identity—one's "self"—is partly constituted by one's fundamental beliefs.[37] Thus, to revise any of the fundamental aspects of one's web of beliefs is, to that extent, to revise one's self. Similarly, the identity of a tradition is partly, indeed largely, constituted by its fundamental beliefs. To revise any of those beliefs is, to that extent, to revise the tradition. The revision of any aspect of a web of beliefs—whether the web of beliefs of an individual or the web characteristic of a tradition—must be carried out by reference to other aspects of the web of beliefs not then in question. There is no other accessible point of reference for a person or a tradition. A person can revise an aspect of her web of beliefs, and thus an aspect of her self, only by reference to other aspects of her web of beliefs. A tradition—that is, a community that is the living embodiment of a tradition—can revise an aspect of its web of beliefs, and thus an aspect of itself, only by reference to other aspects of its web of beliefs.[38] In that sense, the criterion for the revision of self is self, and the criterion for the revision of tradition is tradition. There is no escaping self or tradition: There is no evaluative perspective outside self or tradition.[39] As Gadamer has written, "Tradition is no proof and validation of something, in any case not where validation is demanded by reflection. But the point is this: Where does reflection demand it? Everywhere? I would object to such an answer on the grounds of the finitude of human existence and the essential particularity of reflection."[40]

My point, however, is not a conservative one. As I indicated in chapter 1, an important condition of the "health"—the flourishing—of persons and therefore of traditions is that they have the capacities for self-critical rationality and for growth, even radical growth, which is conversion. We can use our selves—the beliefs constitutive of our selves—to revise our selves, and, in the same sense, we can use our traditions to revise our traditions.[41] Indeed, at their most vital, traditions are self-transcendent. "It is . . . a mark of an authentic and living tradition that it points us beyond itself."[42] The American Jesuit John Courtney Murray spoke of "the growing edge of tradition". Echoing Murray, Joseph Cardinal Bernardin has said that "[t]he significance of Vatican II is not that it said brand new things, but that it took . . . ideas from the edge of the [Catholic] church's life and located them at the center. . . . Once the growing edge had been taken into the center of Catholic thought, it was time for new growth at the edge."[43] At their most vital, traditions are always growing at the edge and sometimes taking the edge into the center. Persons, too (as well as traditions), at their most vital, are self-transcendent:

> . . . Man is not "finished", finite. Man is open because he is not closed, he is not complete because he is itinerant, not definite, not "finished", in-com-

plete. . . . No person considers himself as finished, as having exhausted the possibilities of becoming. The openness of which we speak is constitutive of the human being, the other side of what we call contingency. . . . Recognizing Man's openness means admitting he is . . . not (yet?) finished, absolute, definitive. It means admitting there is something in him that must evolve; it also affirms the capacity for such evolution.[44]

There are critical moments in the lives of some persons—moments when the situation at hand elicits or provokes a revision of self so thoroughgoing as to constitute a conversion of some sort. Such moments sometimes involve disintegration of personality as well as, hopefully, reintegration. Similarly, there are critical moments in the lives of some traditions. Such a moment has arrived when the dissensus that is a feature of every large community reaches the point of fragmentation, and the revision of the tradition by a faction within the community is so fundamental as to constitute a break with tradition and the beginning of a new tradition—such as when Buddhism emerged from Hinduism or Christianity from Judaism—which then proceeds to develop over time, just as the tradition from which it broke continues to develop. (Sometimes the "parent" and "offspring" traditions develop in similar directions—and sometimes they develop similar internal tensions and divisions—which is not surprising, since sometimes similar pressures push and similar experiences pull the two traditions.) Even such dramatic "breaks", however, develop gradually, over time, and illustrate the fact that *the criterion for the revision of tradition is tradition itself.*[45]

The agent of evaluation in the case of a person questioning an aspect of her web of belief is, of course, the person herself. In the case of a tradition, however, the agent is certainly no one person. As I suggested above, basic moral beliefs are less the property of individuals than of communities. That is, they are less the property of human beings *qua* particular individuals than of human beings *qua* members of particular communities. And, relatedly, the true test or measure of such beliefs is not the experience of just one person. It is, rather, in some large degree, the experience of the community—that is, the experience of the community *not just at a given moment, but over time*. "[T]he justification of our moral principles and assertions", writes Stanley Hauerwas, "cannot be done from the point of view of anyone, but rather requires a tradition of moral wisdom. Such a tradition is not a 'deposit' of unchanging moral 'truth,' but is made up of the lives of men and women who are constantly testing and changing that tradition through their own struggle to live it. The maintenance of such a tradition requires a community across time sufficient to sustain the journey from one generation to the next."[46] Holmes said that the life of the law has been not logic, but experience. Certainly the life of morality is experience.[47]

The general relation between tradition/community and moral reasoning I've sketched here is well understood by, among others, Catholic moral theologians. Consider, for example, these passages in a recent essay by James Burtchaell of Notre Dame's Theology Department:

> The Catholic tradition embraces a long effort to uncover the truth about human behavior and experience. Our judgments of good and evil focus on whether a certain course of action will make a human being grow and mature and flourish, or whether it will make a person withered, estranged and indifferent. In making our evaluations, we have little to draw on except our own and our forebears' experience, and whatever wisdom we can wring from our debate with others. . . .
>
> What we are trying to unpuzzle are things like childbearing and immigration and economic policy and infant mortality and drug use and family fidelity and so much else about which we must frame moral judgments. With our fellow communicants we share commitments and assumptions: that we are happier giving than getting, that there is no greater love than to put down your life for your neighbor, and that your neighbor always turns out to be the most unlikely person.
>
> Nothing is specifically Christian about this method of making judgments about human experience. That is why it is strange to call any of our moral convictions "religious," let alone sectarian, since they arise from a dialogue that ranges through so many communities and draws from so many sources.[48]

III

What is the relation between the particular and the general in moral reasoning? Which, if either, has justificatory priority: relatively general or abstract moral beliefs or, instead, relatively particular or concrete ones? My reference here is principally to beliefs about what to do, given the sort of person one is, rather than beliefs about what sort of person to be. By "relatively general or abstract beliefs", as distinct from "relatively particular or concrete ones", I mean, to quote J. B. Schneewind, beliefs "applicable to a wide variety of cases and circumstances"— "relatively context-free" beliefs. "[U]nlike [the belief that] 'One ought to help old ladies crossing busy streets,' which is relevant only to a fairly limited set of situations, 'One ought to help people in need' is applicable to an indefinitely large number of kinds of cases."[49]

Consider first the position that neither general moral beliefs nor particular ones invariably play the fundamental justificatory role in moral reasoning, but, rather, in some moral arguments general beliefs (or, put another way, general principles) play that role, and in other arguments particular beliefs (principles) do. Schneewind puts it this way:

> Moral philosophers, whatever their theoretical programmes, have in practice always recognised that allegedly basic moral principles depend no less on fairly specific moral propositions than on the other sorts of grounds that have been offered for them; a principle that led to the conclusion that truth-telling was usually wrong, and torturing children normally permissible would be rejected, no matter what kind of proof it might have. But if general principles may sometimes depend on particular moral judgements, and particular judgements sometimes on general principles, then there is no impersonal, necessary order of dependence within the realm of moral knowledge, and we are not compelled to conclude that there must be classical first principles. . . . If particular moral assertions need at times to be justified, so too do moral principles. The facts seem to be that we give reasons for particular judgements in terms of principles, and also that we justify principles in terms of particular judgements. . . . [I]n different types of situations and in response to different problems we use both procedures to justify moral directives . . .[50]

Here the emphasis is on the interdependence of the particular and the general, neither of which invariably has priority.[51]

Consider now the different position that relatively particular moral beliefs are fundamental. Renford Bambrough's statement of the position is exemplary and merits full quotation:

> *All* reasoning . . . is from particulars to particulars. Rules and principles, statements of criteria or conditions for the application of a term or the truth of a proposition or the justification of a valuation, are valuable if at all as *memoranda*, as means whereby we bring particulars to bear upon particulars . . . [A]t the bar of reason the final appeal is always to cases: . . . examples are the final food of thought . . . [W]e need to recognise that the question "are all things of this *sort* good or bad?" cannot be answered by somebody who does not know the answer to any question of the form "is *this* thing good or bad?" We must abandon the idea that to justify a moral or any other conclusion about an instance of an action or person or character or motive is to apply to that instance a principle from which, together with a description

of the instance, the conclusion about the instance logically follows. If the question "is *this x* good?" has not been answered, then the question "are *all x*'s good?" has not been answered. The mistake that philosophers have made in ethics is the mistake that they have made in all other branches of epistemology: they think that the foundations of our knowledge are to be looked for in the sky and not in the soil.

When Wittgenstein urged us to look back at the process of teaching he pointed in the right direction. The ultimate appeal for or against anything that is offered to us as an addition to our knowledge is to something that we have learned before. There can be no justification for any conclusion if there is no appeal to what we have learned before, and, in the end, in ethics as elsewhere, the appeal is to how we learned to think and speak in the first place. If we can build high structures of scientific or logical or moral or any other kind of knowledge, we can build them only on the ground on which we stand. Unless we can understand and know what is primitive and unproblematic we cannot have any confidence in the safety of taller and more complex structures.[52]

Here, in contrast to the preceding passage, the emphasis is on the priority of the particular.[53]

We need not choose between these two positions: the interdependence of the particular and the general, and the priority of the particular. Neither position excludes the other. After all, even if, as Bambrough argues, the particular has priority, sometimes what needs to be justified is a relatively particular moral belief, and an available justification might be one involving a relatively general belief; other times what needs to be justified is a relatively general belief, and an available justification might be one involving a relatively particular belief.

Nonetheless, as Bambrough argues, what is *ultimately* authoritative are not relatively general moral beliefs but relatively particular ones: Relatively general moral beliefs or principles are, as Bambrough explains, simply "memoranda of particulars".[54] Indeed, relatively general beliefs of any kind, whether moral or not, are memoranda of particulars.[55]

In the next chapter I argue that the liberal political-philosophical project—the search for the Holy Grail of official normative impartiality or neutrality—is doomed to failure: No such impartiality or neutrality is possible. Liberal political philosophy of the sort I criticize in the next chapter is fatally flawed for another reason as well: It not merely ignores the priority of the particular; it goes so far as to assert or imply the priority of the general—the general understood not as a memorandum of particulars, but as somehow independent of them.[56] The ambition of such philosophy is to identify a "master" principle the application of which can somehow resolve major political-moral disputes.[57] Bernard Williams' comment on such philosophy—which he calls "ethical theory"—seems correct. "[R]eflective criticism should basically go in a direction opposite to that encouraged by ethical theory", says Williams.

> Theory looks characteristically for considerations that are very general and have as little distinctive content as possible, because it is trying to systematize and because it wants to represent as many reasons as possible as applications of other reasons. But critical reflection should seek for as much shared understanding as it can find on any issue, and use any ethical material that, in the context of the reflective discussion, makes some sense and commands some loyalty. Of course that will take [some] things for granted, but as serious reflection it must know it will do that. . . . Theory typically uses the assumption that we probably have too many ethical ideas, some of which may well turn out to be mere prejudices. Our major problem now is actually that we have not too many ideas but too few, and we need to cherish as many as we can.[58]

The ambition of liberal political philosophy notwithstanding, moral discourse must rely on relatively particular moral beliefs that, for the present at least, have withstood the test of experience, especially the experience of a moral community (or communities) over time.[59] The point of departure for moral discourse must be not some master principle, but whatever "shared understanding"—whatever shared particular beliefs—can be located among the interlocutors. Moral discourse must rely on whatever relatively particular beliefs, "in the context of the reflective discussion, make some sense and command some loyalty." The warrants and grounds in moral argument must be such beliefs.[60]

IV

I'm now in a position to sketch the principal, or at least a principal, role of "rules" and "principles" in moral reasoning. By "rule" I mean a relatively determinate moral norm; by "principle", a relatively indeterminate one. For present purposes I shall ignore the distinction and refer simply to "rules". The particular/general distinction does not track the determinate/indeterminate one. For example, a norm can be both general, in the sense that it is "applicable to a wide variety of cases and circumstances" and thus "relatively context-free",[61] and, at the same time, highly determinate: "Never intentionally kill an innocent human being."

As an action-guiding norm, a moral rule presupposes a belief about how one ought or ought not to act in situations of a certain sort. In that sense, rules represent beliefs. (A rule/belief is relatively particular to the extent the sort of situations it concerns is relatively particular, and relatively general to the extent the sort of situations it concerns is relatively general.) Although rules serve to guide action in the present, the beliefs they represent are, of course, rooted in past experience—namely, experience with situations of the sort in question. The principal function of the rule is to bring that experience, in the form of the belief the experience has given rise to, to bear on a present situation of choice. A moral rule serves to bring the past to bear on the present. "[M]axims of conduct are 'abridgements of tradition' rather than metaphysical abstractions."[62]

To consult a rule in dealing with a situation of choice is, at bottom, to consult those in the past—whether immediate or more distant past—who have dealt with relevantly similar situations and thus have the benefit of experience. Jaroslav Pelikan, following G. K. Chesterton, has characterized appeal to tradition as " 'an extension of the franchise' by 'giving votes to the most obscure of all classes, our ancestors,' . . . [I] affirm and celebrate tradition as 'the democracy of the dead,' a 'democracy extended through time' and through space."[63] Of course, the beliefs that arose in the past may ultimately come to be seen, from the reflective, critical perspective of the present, as inadequate (or no longer adequate). And even if they are not inadequate, there is always the problem that while a present situation of choice can be similar to a past situation of choice, it is never identical to it. *Inter alia*, the past is not the present, and we are not they. ("By including the dead in the circle of discourse, we enrich the quality of the conversation. Of course we do not listen only to the dead, nor are we a tape recording of the tradition. That really would be the dead faith of the living, not the living faith of the dead."[64]) Nonetheless, there is no point in trying to do what we neither can nor, even if we could, should do, namely, begin the world anew in every generation or, more extremely, in every life.[65] It makes sense to mine the experience of the past for whatever insight, if any, might be found there.[66]

Discussing the matter of rules—in particular legal rules—H. L. A.

Hart has emphasized that "a feature of the human predicament . . . that we labour under . . . whenever we seek to regulate, unambiguously and in advance, some sphere of conduct by means of general standards to be used without further official directions on particular occasions . . . is our relative ignorance of fact . . . [and] our relative indeterminacy of aim."[67] Given this "feature of the human predicament", it is sensible that many moral rules (like many legal ones) be relatively indeterminate.

> If the world in which we live were characterized only by a finite number of features, and these together with all the modes in which they could combine were known to us, then provision could be made in advance for every possibility. We could make rules, the application of which to particular cases never called for a further choice. Everything could be known, and for everything, since it could be known, something could be done and specified in advance by rule. Plainly this world is not our world . . . This inability to anticipate brings with it a relative indeterminacy of aim.[68]

Certainly the point is not that relatively determinate rules cannot be achieved. They can. One way of achieving relative determinacy, writes Hart, "is to freeze the meaning of the rule so that its general terms must have the same meaning in every case where its application is in question. To secure this we may fasten on certain features present in the plain case and insist that these are both necessary and sufficient to bring anything which has them within the scope of the rule, whatever other features it may have or lack, and whatever may be the social consequences of applying the rule in this way."[69] The point, rather, is that *given the priority of the particular*, relative determinacy often[70] ought not to be a goal. Relative determinacy is not a principal virtue either of moral rules or of the beliefs they represent. To achieve relative determinacy—in the way, for example, Hart indicates *can* be done—"is to secure a measure of certainty or predictability at the cost of blindly prejudging what is to be done in a range of future cases, about whose composition we are ignorant. We shall thus succeed in settling in advance, but also in the dark, issues which can only reasonably be settled when they arise and are identified."[71]

V

Now we come to the heart of the matter.

There are many different moral communities—many different moral traditions—each with its own set of basic beliefs about human good, about human possibilities and human satisfaction, beliefs constitutive of different conceptions of human flourishing. It is one thing to suggest that the members of a single moral community can engage in moral reasoning—moral discourse—with one another, given their shared basic beliefs about human good. But can members of different moral communities engage in productive moral discourse with one another? If the answer is "no"—or at least "not always"—is it nonetheless possible to adjudicate among competing conceptions of human flourishing? These questions bring us to the subject of moral relativism. "Relativistic attitudes are very widespread and extremely influential in contemporary culture, both in intellectual circles and in popular thought and action about moral and social problems. This is why relativism is one of the chief intellectual and social issues of our time . . ."[72]

What is the morally relativist position? Recall, from the preceding chapter, the morally skeptical position, with which the morally relativist position should not be confused: There can be no moral knowledge no matter how "moral knowledge" is understood or conceived. My argument that we should reject moral skepticism and accept instead the cognitivist position has consisted of an elaboration of a conception of moral knowledge—the "naturalist" conception—such that the claim that there can be moral knowledge is true. If moral knowledge is knowledge of the conditions of well-being or flourishing for particular human beings, then obviously there can be—and, indeed, to some extent there is—moral knowledge. Claims about what particular human beings must have or do in order to achieve well-being have truth value and thus are objects of knowledge. So much for the morally skeptical position.[73]

Again, what is the morally relativist position? A number of positions go by the name "moral relativism". Some are silly.[74] Others are not "relativist" in any sense of the term relevant to the present inquiry.[75] There are two relativist positions we must consider. Call them R1 and R2.

R1 is a position implicit in my discussion of moral reasoning—indeed, of reasoning generally. It is a position about reasoning generally, not just moral reasoning. According to R1, the "truth" (or "falsity") of a belief, in the sense of the "rational acceptability" (or "unacceptability") of a belief[76]—*any* belief—is always dependent on, or "relative to", the acceptance of some further beliefs. (This is not to say that every belief has truth value. A belief that is beyond justification lacks truth value.[77]) The acceptance of some particular further beliefs, as warrant and grounds, is a sufficient condition, and sometimes a necessary condition, for the acceptance of the claim-belief (as "true").

Thus, the truth (or falsity) of any belief is always relative to a web of beliefs. A belief can be true relative to one or more webs, and not true, even false, relative to one or more others. If one or more beliefs necessary to support a claim-belief are not a part of the web of beliefs of a community, then the claim-belief is not true insofar as that community is concerned. The claim is not true relative to that community, even though it may be true relative to a different community. In that sense, "truth" and "falsity" are relative to webs of beliefs.[78]

Furthermore, there is no privileged standpoint from which to adjudicate among different webs of beliefs, in the sense of a perspective that transcends all webs of beliefs. Any such adjudication presupposes beliefs that are constituents of some web of beliefs (though not necessarily of only one web). As Richard Rorty has insisted, there are no " 'natural starting-points' of thought, starting-points which are prior to and independent of the way some culture speaks or spoke. (Candidates for such starting-points include clear and distinct ideas, sense-data, categories of the pure understanding, structures of prelinguistic consciousness, and the like.)"[79]

Because R1 is about not just moral reasoning, but reasoning generally, we should think of the position not as *morally* relativist but as *epistemologically* relativist. Call the position, then, ER.[80]

The principal alternative to ER is the "copy" or "correspondence" theory of truth/knowledge. Mortimer Adler presents this position, which is very likely the man-in-the-street's position and which, were it sound, would constitute a serious alternative to ER. According to Adler, the criterion of the truth of a belief (or statement or claim) is not further beliefs, but (correspondence with) reality-as-it-is-in-itself— "Reality"—independently of whatever anyone may believe about it. Adler writes: "[Truth is—consists in—] a relationship of agreement or correspondence . . . between what a person thinks, believes, opines, or says to himself and what actually exists or does not exist inreality. . . . [T]he truth of thought consists in the agreement or correspondence between what one thinks, believes, or opines and what actually exists or does not exist in the reality that is independent of our minds and of our thinking one thing or another."[81]

The correspondence theory, however, is deeply flawed, as these passages by Richard Rorty and Hilary Putnam, respectively, indicate:

When the correspondence theorist offers that the truth about the world consists in a relation of "correspondence" between certain sentences (many of which, no doubt, have yet to be formulated) and the world itself[,] the pragmatist can only fall back on saying, once again, that many centuries of attempts to explain what "correspondence" is have failed, especially when it comes to explaining how the final vocabulary of future physics will somehow be Nature's Own—the one which, at long last, lets us formulate sentences which lock on to Nature's own way of thinking of herself. . . . *It is the impossible attempt to step outside our skins—the traditions, linguistic and other, within which we do our thinking and self-criticism—and compare ourselves with something absolute.*[82]

[T]he "copy" theory of truth . . . [is] the conception according to which a statement is true just in case it "corresponds to the (mind-independent) facts". . . . On this perspective, the world consists of some fixed totality of mind-independent objects. There is exactly one true and complete description of "the way the world is". Truth involves some sort of correspondence relation between words or thought-signs and external things and sets of things. I shall call this perspective the *externalist* perspective, because its favorite point of view is a God's Eye point of view. . . . The idea that truth is a passive copy of what is "really" (mind-independently, discourse-independently) "there" has collapsed under the critiques of Kant, Wittgenstein, and other philosophers even if it continues to have a deep hold on our thinking. . . . *[T]he notion of comparing our system of beliefs with unconceptualized reality to see if they match makes no sense. . . . [T]he notion of a transcendental match between our representation and the world in itself is nonsense.*[83]

The fatal problem with the copy theory of truth, in short, is that we lack access to Reality. Reality is unmediated reality—prelinguistic, preconceptual reality. As Putnam indicates, the notion of our words and thoughts corresponding to prelinguistic, preconceptual reality is incoherent. The only reality to which we have access, and to which particular words and thoughts of ours could possibly correspond, is mediated reality—the word- and thought-systems we construct and deploy (and revise and even discard) in trying to deal with, in trying to understand, predict, and control, our perceptions, systems that are determined by and also determine our perceptions in ways we don't (yet) fully understand.[84] In any event, as a criterion of truth, Reality is useless: We would never be able to know whether a belief or theory was true because Reality is, through and through, an inaccessible criterion.[85] Thus, Adler (and the man-in-the-street) is wrong in supposing that Reality is the criterion of the truth of beliefs.[86] As Wallace Stevens wrote, "[W]e live in the description of a place and not in the place itself."[87]

Rorty and Putnam agree in rejecting the correspondence theory of truth. They also seem to agree in the alternative they offer, which is essentially the epistemologically relativist position. First, Rorty. Rorty does not deny something "that we have never had any reason to doubt", namely, that "[m]ost of the world is as it is whatever we think about".[88] That is, Rorty does not deny the existence of Reality.[89] For Rorty, however, Reality is not the criterion of truth. Rather, " 'truth' is just the name of a property which all true statements share. It is what is common to 'Bacon did not write Shakespeare,' 'It rained yesterday,' 'E equals mc²,' 'Love is better than hate,' '*The Allegory of Painting* was Vermeer's best work,' '2 plus 2 is 4,' and 'There are nondenumerable infinities.' "[90] But how, according to Rorty, do we determine whether a particular statement has the property truth? (Certainly not by reference to Reality.) What makes a particular statement true? What, for Rorty, is the criterion of truth?

Here is Rorty's answer:

> [The pragmatist thinks that] "the true" is [nothing] more than what Williams James defined it as: "the name of whatever proves itself to be good in the way of belief, and good, too, for definite, assignable reasons." On James' view, "true" resembles "good" or "rational" in being a normative notion, a compliment paid to sentences that seem to be paying their way and that fit in with other sentences which are doing so. . . . [The pragmatist argues] that there is no pragmatic difference, no difference that makes a difference, between "it works because it's true" and "it's true because it works"—any more than between "it's pious because the gods love it" and "the gods love it because it's pious." Alternatively, he argues that there is no pragmatic difference between the nature of truth and the test of truth, and that the test of truth, of what statements to assert, is (except maybe for a few perceptual statements) not "comparison with reality." . . . [For the pragmatist,] knowledge is power, a tool for coping with reality. . . . He drops the notion of truth as correspondence with reality altogether, and says that modern science does not enable us to cope because it corresponds, it just plain enables us to cope.[91]

Rorty's conception of truth/knowledge/rationality is implicitly holistic: We choose among beliefs or sets of beliefs we don't yet accept— presumably including beliefs about our interests and what will satisfy them—accepting some, rejecting others, on the basis of beliefs we already accept, including beliefs about our interests and what will satisfy them.

Now, Putnam. Like Rorty, Putnam rejects the copy theory of truth, or what he calls "the externalist perspective". He proposes, in its stead, "the internalist perspective":

> The perspective I shall defend . . . I shall refer to . . . as the *internalist* perspective, because it is characteristic of this view to hold that *what objects does the world consist of?* is a question that it only makes sense to ask *within* a theory or description . . . "Truth", in an internalist view, is some sort of (idealized) rational acceptability—some sort of ideal coherence of our beliefs with each other and with our experiences *as those experiences are themselves represented in our belief system*—and not correspondence with mind-independent or discourse-independent "states of affairs". There is no God's Eye point of view that we can know or usefully imagine; there are only the various points of view of actual persons reflecting various interests and purposes that their descriptions and theories subserve . . . In an internalist view . . . signs do not intrinsically correspond to objects, independently of how those signs are employed and by whom. But a sign that is actually employed in a particular way by a particular community of users can correspond to particular objects *within the conceptual scheme of those users.* "Objects" do not exist independently of conceptual schemes. We cut up the world into objects when we introduce one or another scheme of description. Since the objects *and* the signs are alike *internal* to the scheme of a description, it is possible to say what matches what.[92]

For Putnam, then, truth is idealized rational acceptability. The actual, as opposed to ideal, property of cognitive statements or claims is not "truth", but "rational acceptability". On this view, a statement is an object of human knowledge if it is rationally acceptable. And Putnam's "internalist" conception of rational acceptability, as the foregoing passage makes plain, is a holistic one: We choose among beliefs or sets of beliefs we don't yet accept on the basis of beliefs we already accept.

Rorty and Putnam agree, then, not only in rejecting the correspondence or copy theory—the externalist perspective—but also in the alternative they offer, which, as I said, is essentially the holistic or epistemologically relativist position (ER).[93] Before considering the implications of ER for moral reasoning, I shall sketch the second morally relativist position we must consider: R2.

As we've just seen, ER is a position on the issue of the nature and limits of reasoning/justification/argument. R2, by contrast, is a position on the distinct issue of the existence *vel non* of human interests. Actually, R2 comprises two positions, one extreme, the other moderate. According to the extreme position, there are no human interests—no interests common to all or virtually all members of the human species, interests the satisfaction of which, in normal circumstances, enhances virtually anyone's level of well-being. Thus, there are no human interests the satisfaction of which can serve as a standard for adjudicating among different ways of life (ideals of the person, moral systems, etc.). According to the moderate position, there may be human interests, but even if there are, as an adjudicatory standard the satisfaction of those interests underdetermines the selection of a single best way of life; a range of ways of life is consistent with the standard. As David Wong has put it, "[T]here is no [determinate] feature or set of features [of human nature] that eliminates all but one ideal [of the good for man] as valid. . . . [I]nsofar as there is such a thing as a fixed human nature, remaining invariant from social environment to social environment, it is not sufficiently determinate to justify the claim that there is a determinate good for man, a complex of activities arranged in an ideal balance, which any rational and informed person would find the most rewarding."[94]

Because they address the issue of the existence *vel non* of human interests, the two positions set forth in the preceding paragraph are *anthropologically* relativist. Call the positions, respectively, AR1 (the extreme position) and AR2 (the moderate one). Anthropological relativism (whether extreme or moderate) does not entail ER, nor does ER entail AR. To be an anthropological relativist is not necessarily to be an epistemological relativist; nor is to be an epistemological relativist necessarily to be an anthropological relativist. One can consistently accept AR and reject ER, or accept ER and reject AR.

Although, as we've seen, Rorty and Putnam agree both in rejecting the correspondence theory of truth and in accepting ER, they disagree with respect to AR1. Rorty is an extreme anthropological relativist; Putnam is not. Rorty is insistent that there is nothing of consequence to say about human beings *qua* members of the same species—human beings *simpliciter*—as distinct from human beings *qua* members of a particular culture, for example, "twentieth-century Europeans".[95] Rorty's position in that regard calls to mind the statement of a French intellectual two centuries ago, commenting on then-recent developments in revolutionary France: "I have seen in my time Frenchmen, Italians, and Russians. I even know, thanks to Montesquieu, that one may be a Persian, but as for Man, I declare that I have never met him in my life; if he exists it is without my knowledge."[96]

Putnam's discussion, in stark contrast to Rorty's, is replete with passages in which he talks about human beings *simpliciter*. This excerpt is illustrative:

> Imagine a society of farmers who, for some reason, have a total disinterest in the arts, in science (except in such products as assist them in farming), in religion, in short, in everything spiritual or cultural. (I don't mean to suggest that actual peasant societies are or ever have been like this.) These people need not be imagined as being bad people; imagine them as cooperative, pacific, reasonably kind to one another, if you like. What I wish the reader to imagine is that their interests are limited to such minimal goals as getting enough to eat, warm shelter, and such simple pleasures as getting drunk together in the evenings. In short, imagine them as living a relatively "animal" existence, and as not wishing to live any other kind of existence.
>
> Such people are not immoral. There is nothing impermissible about their way of life. But our natural tendency (unless we are entranced with Ethical Relativism) is to say that their way of life is in some way contemptible. It is totally lacking in what Aristotle called "nobility". They are living the lives of swine—amiable swine, perhaps, but still swine, and a pig's life is no life for a man. . . .
>
> Let us assume the pig-men are born with normal human potential (if they aren't, then their lives aren't "worse than they might be", and we are not justified in feeling contempt, but only, at most, pity). Then they might be led to appreciate artistic, scientific, and spiritual aspects of life; to live more truly human lives, so to speak. And if any of them did this, they would doubtless prefer those lives (even though they might be less fun) to the lives they are now living. People who live swinish lives feel shame when they come to live more human lives; people who live more human lives do not feel ashamed that they did when they sink into swinishness. These facts give one . . . ground for thinking that they have overlooked alternative goals, and certainly grounds for thinking that they have never made vivid do themselves what realization of those alternative goals would be like.[97]

Notice in particular Putnam's talk about "normal human potential" and "truly human lives".

Is AR1 a plausible position? In one of his more disturbing passages, Rorty writes that "when the secret police come, when the torturers violate the innocent, there is nothing to be said to them of the form

'There is something within you which you are betraying. Though you embody the practices of a totalitarian society which will endure forever, there is something beyond those practices which condemns you.' "[98] Why can't we say to them—to the secret police and the torturers—that there are better ways for human beings, *including them*, to live ("cope")? "Physics is a way of trying to cope with various bits of the universe," writes Rorty, attacking the positivist distinction between science and ethics, fact and value; "ethics is a matter of trying to cope with other bits."[99] But don't we think that there are better and worse ways to do physics—that is, to answer the questions, the "how does reality hang together" questions, that constitute the inquiry which is physics—and that the Third Reich's Aryan physics (or the Stalin-era Soviet Union's Lysenkoist biology) was not a better way? Why, then, shouldn't we also think that there are better and worse ways for human beings to do ethics—to answer the "how to live" questions that constitute the inquiry which is ethics—and that the ethics—the answers— of Rorty's secret police and torturers is not a better way? If we think that there are common human interests better or worse served by different ways of doing physics[100]—interests in understanding, predicting, and controlling the world we inhabit[101]—why shouldn't we also think that there are common human interests better or worse served by different ways of doing ethics, that is, by different ways of living, different forms of life? (Of course, whether Rorty's secret police and torturers will choose to listen to us—or, if they listen, whether they will believe us— is a different matter, which I take up below in discussing the implications for moral discourse of epistemological relativism. In the passage quoted above, Rorty is asserting the extreme anthropologically relativist position. It is that position—AR1—I mean to question, not ER.)

There is a significant passage in his essay "Solidarity or Objectivity?" in which Rorty—*even* Rorty—moves back from the extremity of AR1: "The pragmatists' justification of toleration, free inquiry, and the quest for undistorted communication can only take the form of a comparison between societies which exemplify these habits and those which do not, leading up to the suggestion that *nobody who has experienced both would prefer the latter*."[102] If Rorty is right that no one—no human being, no member of the species—who has experienced both would prefer the latter, what might explain that universal preference? More to the point: Why would Rorty think that "nobody who has experienced both would prefer the latter" *except on the basis of the supposition that there are common human interests—interests the frustration of which is antithetical to the flourishing (or "coping") of anybody*? Rorty's statement that "nobody who has experienced both would prefer the latter" is certainly in tension, if not inconsistent, with his insistence that we cannot meaningfully talk about human beings *simpliciter*, but only about, for example, "twentieth-century Europeans".

AR1 is not a plausible position. Some senses and appetites seem to be shared across the human species. Of course, those senses and appetites are shaped in different ways by different communities/traditions (cultures, societies) *and* by different individual histories within a single community/tradition. Not all differences in senses and appetites are due merely to differences in how common senses and appetites have been shaped: Some senses and appetites are not shared across the human species. Nonetheless, some are shared. Some interests are human and not merely local in character, some interests are shared across the human species. The conclusion is therefore inescapable that AR1 is implausible. Listen to Philippa Foot:

> Granted that it is wrong to assume an identity of aim between peoples of different cultures; nevertheless there is a great deal that all men have in common. All need affection, the cooperation of others, a place in a community, and help in trouble. It isn't true to suppose that human beings can flourish without these things—being isolated, despised or embattled, or without courage or hope. We are not, therefore, simply expressing values that we happen to have if we think of some moral systems as good moral systems and others as bad. Communities as well as individuals can live wisely or unwisely, and this is largely the result of their values and the codes of behavior that they teach. Looking at these societies, and critically also at our own, we surely have some idea of how things work out and why they work out as they do. We do not have to suppose it is just as good to promote pride of place and the desire to get an advantage over other men as it is to have an ideal of affection and respect. These things have different harvests, and unmistakably different connections with human good.[103]

At the same time, there is no reason to suppose that the position at the other extreme from AR1—namely, that there are human interests the satisfaction of which determines a single best way of life—is any more tenable than AR1 itself. To acknowledge that "[t]here are obvious limits set by common human needs to the conditions under which human beings flourish and human societies flourish" is not to deny that "human nature, conceived in terms of common human needs and capacities, always underdetermines a way of life, and underdetermines an order of priority among virtues, and therefore underdetermines the moral prohibitions and injunctions that support a way of life."[104]

The most plausible position, then, is the moderate one: AR2. It is rarely, if ever, the case that the members of a moral community suppose that there is but a single way each and every one of them should live. The more common and much more reasonable assumption is that within the context of the community there is a range of acceptable ways to live, and which way is best for a particular member depends on her particularity. Why, then, should we doubt that within the context not of one moral community, but of the whole human species, there is a plurality of acceptable ways of life, both for human beings individually and for communities of human beings, and which way is best for a particular human being or a particular human community depends on her or its particularity?

> If today we differ with Aristotle it is in being much more pluralistic than Aristotle was. Aristotle recognized that different ideas of Eudaemonia, different conceptions of human flourishing, might be appropriate for different individuals on account of the difference in their constitution. But he seemed to think that ideally there was some sort of constitution that every one ought to have; that in an ideal world (overlooking the mundane question of who would grow the crops and who would bake the bread) everyone would be a philosopher. We agree with Aristotle that different ideas of human flourishing are appropriate for individuals with different constitutions, but we go further and believe that even in the ideal world there would be different constitutions, that diversity is part of the ideal. And we see some degree of tragic tension between ideals, that the fulfillment of some ideals always excludes the fulfillment of some others.[105]

As Putnam goes on to emphasize, however: "[B]elief in a pluralistic ideal is not the same thing as belief that every ideal of human flourishing is as good as every other. We reject ideals of human flourishing as wrong, as infantile, as sick, as one-sided."[106]

If, as it seems, both ER and AR2 are sound positions—sounder, at any rate, than their obvious competitors—what are the implications for moral reasoning? First, AR2. The proper aim of adjudicating among different ways of life (including different conceptions of rationality and different "vocabularies"[107]) is not to locate a single best way of life for human beings *simpliciter*. There is no such thing. The aim, rather, is to identify a range of equally acceptable (unacceptable?) ways of life and, beyond that, to achieve an ever more sensitive understanding of the advantages and disadvantages of different ways of life. "There are many cases in which rationality can do no more than exclude certain alternatives, while not providing any guide to the choice between the remaining."[108]

There is the all too familiar danger, of course, that any effort to evaluate ways of life other than one's own is or will become, unwittingly or not, self-serving and imperialistic. Therefore, it bears emphasis that if there are common human interests the satisfaction of which is the measure for evaluating forms of life, then no way of life, including one's own, is immune to such evaluation. Indeed, least of all one's own: A person should be most concerned to discover, not whether, but how she (and her community/tradition) can do better—how she can live in a more deeply satisfying way.[109] Virtually any person—and her tradition/community—can always do better. The question is not whether, but how.[110]

Perhaps, however, AR2 is, for all practical purposes, the functional equivalent of AR1. Perhaps, that is, that as an adjudicatory standard, the satisfaction of the common human interests we can confidently identify is so underdeterminative that every actual way of life in the world today, or virtually every actual way of life, must be adjudged as acceptable as (virtually) every other actual way of life. (This is not to deny that there are advantages and disadvantages of different ways of life; it *is* to suggest, however, that no way of life is superior insofar as the satisfaction of common human interests is concerned.) Even if true, that possibility is largely beside the real point: Whether there are *shared human interests*—and, if so, whether the satisfaction of those interests is a useful adjudicatory standard—is much less important *for purposes of assessing the possibility, in a given situation, of productive moral discourse*, than whether there are *shared beliefs*—beliefs shared with those with whom we happen to be, at a given point, in conflict and with whom, therefore, we must (or at any rate want to) try to reason.

If there are shared beliefs, some may be to the effect, say, that there are common human interests implicated in the conflict, interests that would be better or worse served by resolving the conflict this way or that. (It seems doubtful that many persons, whatever their moral communities, would reject Foot's belief that "there is a great deal that all men have in common"—that "[a]ll need affection, the cooperation of others, a place in a community, and help in trouble."[111]) Or they may

be to the effect merely that there are interests shared between or among
the disputants that would be better or worse served by resolving the
conflict one way or another, whether or not those shared interests are
also common human interests, indeed, even if clearly they are not.
Whatever the content of the shared beliefs, the important point is that,
as the epistemologically relativist position indicates, even if there are no
common human interests—or no shared beliefs that there are—there
can be productive moral discourse if there are relevant shared beliefs,
for example, beliefs that shared interests would be better or worse
served by pursuing one course rather than another. However, even if
there are common human interests—or beliefs, even shared beliefs, that
there are—there *cannot be* productive moral discourse in the absence of
relevant shared beliefs. Thus, AR1 and AR2 turn out to be much less
important, for purposes of assessing the possibility of moral discourse,
than ER.

We've considered the (limited) implications of AR1 and AR2 for
moral reasoning. As I just said, however, ER, not AR1 or AR2, turns
out to be a more important issue. What, then, are the implications of ER
for moral reasoning? That there is no moral knowledge? No. That moral
knowledge is "relative"? Yes. But according to ER *all* knowledge is
relative, not just moral knowledge.

Certainly ER does not entail that one cannot adjudicate among different ways of life or conceptions of human flourishing. It is true that
according to ER, no such adjudication is from a privileged standpoint—
a transcendent perspective. All such adjudication presupposes the
"givenness" or authority of certain beliefs or criteria. According to ER,
however, *any* sort of adjudication or evaluation or justification whatsoever presupposes the givenness of certain beliefs/criteria. Our questioning and revision of beliefs—whether beliefs a part of our community's
web of beliefs or beliefs a part of some other community's web—is
always carried out by reference to one or more of our beliefs not then in
question. Thus, ER does not entail that one conception of human flourishing is as good as another. (AR2, as I've indicated, doesn't exclude
the possibility that among actual conceptions of flourishing in the world
today, virtually any one is as good, or as bad, as virtually any other
insofar as the satisfaction of human interests is concerned.) ER entails
merely that no adjudication among competing conceptions is transcendent. (Relatedly, ER does not entail that all conceptions of flourishing
or ways of life should be tolerated—as I explain in the next chapter.)

Of course, we don't often set out to adjudicate among different ways of life or conceptions of flourishing. On the other hand, we *do* often try to engage in moral reasoning—moral discourse—with others committed to a way of life, and so to basic moral beliefs, at least somewhat different from our own. ER does not entail that such reasoning is impossible. It's easy to see that the members of a single moral community, because of the many basic moral beliefs they share, can engage in productive moral discourse with one another. But it is also true that even the members of a large, morally pluralistic society like our own, which comprises many different moral communities, might share enough basic moral beliefs that moral reasoning is often a realistic possibility for them. First, "one can maintain that truth is framework-relative, while conceding for a large range of propositions nearly all frameworks coincide."[112] Indeed, as Rorty has sensibly observed, "everything which we can identify as a human being or as a culture will be something which shares an enormous number of beliefs with us. (If it did not, we would simply not be able to recognize that it was speaking a language, and thus that it had any beliefs at all.)"[113]

Although ER does not exclude the possibility that there might be an unlimited number of radically discontinuous webs of beliefs, AR2 indicates why that possibility is not a reality: The facts that human beings are members of a single species, that they have at least some basic interests in common as members of the same species, and that they inhabit the same planetary environment explain why there *are* beliefs common to all human beings.[114] One might want to portray certain of these beliefs—"deep" beliefs about, for example, space, time, causality—as "transcendental" constraints on reasoning or discourse. They are beliefs presupposed by whatever else we believe; in that sense, they can be seen as transcendental constraints on our believing anything at all.[115] But one would be hard pressed to give an other-than-naturalist account of the constraints.

Second, "[a] fully individuable culture [or moral community] is at best a rare thing. Cultures, subcultures, fragments of cultures, constantly meet one another and exchange or modify practices and attitudes."[116] Indeed, moral discourse among members of different moral communities, if conducted in good faith and with a gentle, ecumenical openness to the beliefs, experience, and person of the interlocutor who is not a member of one's own community, can be a principal medium through which different moral communities "meet one another and exchange or modify practices and attitudes."

Any moral community for which love of neighbor (*agape*) is a constitutive ideal—and surely that includes many moral/religious communities in the United States—should understand that ecumenical openness to the Other in discourse facilitates (as well as expresses) such love: I can hardly love the Other—the *real, particular* Other—unless I listen to her and, in listening, gain in knowledge of her.

> In genuine human relations, Gadamer notes, the important point is "to experience the 'Thou' truly as a 'Thou,'" that means, not to ignore his claim and to listen to what he has to say"—an attitude which requires complete existential "openness" and availability. Since openness implies readiness to interrogate and listen to one another, genuine encounter can be said to have the character of a conversation . . .—a conversation which, far from being a series of monologues, is governed by the "dialectic of question and answer" and whose distant ancestor is the Platonic dialogue.[117]

Of course, the more pluralistic the society, the greater the likelihood that those wishing to engage in productive moral discourse with one another will encounter difficulty both in locating relevant shared beliefs that can serve as points of departure and, if such beliefs are located, in concluding the discourse in agreement. But that is true of reasoning generally, and not just moral reasoning.[118]

As to the response that moral discourse can only go a little way, at best, toward resolving disagreement, the best rejoinder is Philippa Foot's: We don't know how far discourse can go in resolving *particular* disagreements between *particular* individuals or groups until it is tried. "One wonders . . . why people who say this kind of thing are so sure that they know where discussions will lead and therefore where they will end. It is, I think, a fault on the part of relativists, and subjectivists generally, that they are ready to make pronouncements about the later part of moral arguments . . . without being able to trace the intermediate steps."[119]

Moreover, the point is *not* that moral discourse is invariably a solvent of moral conflict. Of course it is not. The point, rather, is that—especially given the alternatives—moral discourse ought to be tried. We do not have a priori knowledge, after all, that moral discourse cannot resolve particular disagreements between particular individuals or groups; there is always the possibility that it can, at least to *some* extent.

> The question here is not whether there is some ascertainable moral-political framework that will guarantee a resolution in all cases; but rather,

whether there is, in principle, any limit to the possibility of overcoming incommensurability. . . . [T]here is no such limit: at no point are we justified in terminating an unresolved argument, for it always remains open to us to persevere with it still further. The next stage of argument may yet bring an enlargement of moral vision to one of the contending parties, allowing this contender to integrate the perspective of the other into his own in a relation of part to whole. . . . Therefore at any point there remains the possibility, though not the guarantee, of resolving deep conflict. . . . Confronted with apparent stalemate, there is no need to give in to moral or intellectual "pluralism", for it always remains open to us to say "Press on with the argument".[120]

There is surely nothing to be gained in underestimating the possibility of productive moral discourse. Even if moral discourse probably can't go very far in resolving a particular conflict, such discourse is almost surely worth attempting, given the alternatives. To say that moral discourse might not be able to go very far in resolving a particular conflict is a far cry from saying that moral discourse is a sham, that it's all a matter of "taste", and that *de gustibus non est disputandum*. John Dewey buried that silly there's-no-disputing-taste shibboleth some time ago.[121] May it rest in peace.

As I indicated at the beginning of this chapter, my naturalist account of moral reasoning/discourse is opposed, at one extreme, to moral foundationalism and, at the other, to moral skepticism. The epistemological differences between foundationalists and naturalists like myself are not consequential at the level of moral discourse about particular issues (like abortion), which, ultimately, is the level that really matters. Both foundationalists and naturalists take seriously the possibility of productive moral discourse, and both can engage in moral discourse—even moral discourse *with one another*, giving reasons for and against particular choices and, at their discursive best, maintaining a genuine openness to the possibility that the other is correct. (To be a foundationalist is not to claim infallibility, after all.)

By contrast, the epistemological differences between moral skeptics and naturalists *are* consequential at the level of moral discourse about particular issues. The person who takes seriously the morally skeptical position does not, *qua* skeptic, take seriously the possibility of productive moral discourse and cannot, *qua* skeptic, engage in moral discourse. Thus, I'm principally interested in reaching, not the committed foundationalists, but the reluctant skeptics—persons who mistakenly believe that because there are no unquestionable moral foundations, there can be, alas, no moral knowledge/reasoning/discourse. (My strong sense is that in the professional setting in which I work—the American law school—there are many more skeptics than foundationalists.) If such persons can be helped to see that the choice between moral foundationalism and moral skepticism is a false choice—that the premise that there are no unquestionable foundations does not entail the conclusion that there can be no moral knowledge—then they can, with naturalists and foundationalists, take seriously the possibility of productive moral discourse. And, taking that possibility seriously, they can even begin to participate in such discourse.

Even when it is available, however, moral discourse often runs out—for the time being, at least—before agreement is reached. What are the implications of that fact for politics and law? How ought politics and law to respond—that is, how ought we to respond, in our politics and law—to the reality of deep, pervasive, persistent moral dissensus?

II

The Liberal Vision of
Morality and Politics

The fundamental subject of this book is the proper relation of moral beliefs—including moral beliefs religious in character—to politics and law in a morally pluralistic society. In this Part I argue that the liberal vision of the proper relation is a failure. In Part III I present an alternative vision.

The point of departure for the liberal vision is the observation with which I concluded the preceding chapter: In American society (and similar societies) moral dissensus is deep, pervasive, and persistent. Different moral communities within the society adhere to different—sometimes very different—conceptions of human good, of how it is good for (some or all) human beings to live their lives, of how they must live their lives if they are to flourish, to achieve well-being. Moral discourse can sometimes diminish dissensus, but it is unrealistic to expect such discourse, even at its patient best, always or even often to overcome dissensus. (I think here of the debate, in the United States and elsewhere, as to what public policy regarding abortion should be.)

According to the liberal vision, our politics and law must aim to be "neutral" or "impartial" among the basic differences that constitute the moral dissensus. The ambition to achieve a politics that transcends the deep, pervasive, persistent differences among us—a politics less divided, less fragmented, than we, a politics that unites us—is easy to understand. Indeed, the ambition to avoid a divisive politics in our morally pluralistic society and to achieve, instead, a unitive politics is noble.

The nobility of the ambition, however, ought not to obscure its futility. As I argue in the next chapter, our politics and law simply cannot be neutral or impartial among the differences that constitute the dissensus. The relation between morality/religion and politics/law envisioned by liberal political philosophy is impossible to achieve. We must forge an alternative vision, an alternative understanding, of the proper relation of moral beliefs to politics and law.

3

A Critique of the Liberal Political-Philosophical Project

In this chapter I conclude that the relation between morality and politics envisioned by liberal political philosophy is impossible to achieve. I base this conclusion on a critical examination of the political philosophies of three liberal thinkers—John Rawls, Bruce Ackerman, and Ronald Dworkin—whose work has been prominent, among other places, in the academic setting in which I teach: the American law school. (Both Ackerman and Dworkin are academic lawyers. Rawls, of course, is a philosopher.) None of these three philosophical liberals has succeeded in portraying a politics that is neutral or impartial among the basic differences—in particular among the competing conceptions of human good—that constitute the moral dissensus of our pluralistic society. Of course, it is *possible* that eventually someone will succeed where Rawls, Ackerman, and Dworkin have failed. However, Rawls, Ackerman, and Dworkin are exemplary philosophical liberals, and their failures are exemplary. It is difficult to imagine anyone succeeding where they have failed. The liberal political-philosophical project is spent. It is past time to take a different path.

I

John Rawls is our most prominent contractualist political philosopher.[1] Rawls' theory of justice is contractualist in the sense that for Rawls "the principles of justice . . . are the principles that free and rational persons concerned to further their own interests would accept in an initial position of equality as defining the fundamental terms of their association."[2] (I discuss contractualism generally—as distinct from any particular contractualist theory—in the next chapter.)

According to Rawls, we should try to base our politics and law on principles of justice the justification of which satisfies certain conditions, the principal one being impartiality "among citizens with opposing religions, philosophical and moral convictions, as well as diverse conceptions of the good".[3] Rawls' effort is to identify the requisite liberal principles—principles whose justification is "impartial" or "neutral" among certain opposing religious, philosophical, and moral views. (Hereafter I'll say "moral" rather than "religious, philosophical, and moral".)

Liberal epistemology holds that one cannot resolve such differences rationally.[4] At least, such differences have not been rationally resolved in the past and, according to liberalism, will not be in the foreseeable future. The liberal political-philosophical project, therefore, is to transcend the differences by being impartial among them. "Our social order is not only an arena for competing interests; it is also one for competing views, religious and nonreligious, as to the best way for human beings to live", Alasdair MacIntyre has written. "On the dominant [liberal] view", continues MacIntyre, "it is held that either because rational agreement on the nature of the good life for human beings cannot be reached or just because as a matter of fact it has not been reached . . . the rules that constitute morality must be neutral between alternative and conflicting views of the good for human beings. Pluralism about the good is to coexist with rational agreement on the rules of morality."[5]

Rawls is "not trying to find a conception of justice suitable for all societies regardless of their particular social or historical circumstances."[6] His aim, rather, is "to settle a fundamental disagreement over the just form of basic institutions within a democratic society under modern conditions."[7] To understand why Rawls thinks that settling that disagreement requires impartial principles of the sort he aims to provide, we must understand how Rawls envisions "a democratic society under modern conditions".

The relevant modern conditions for Rawls are what he calls the "circumstances of justice", and they are of two kinds:

> first, the objective circumstances of moderate scarcity; and, second, the subjective circumstances, namely, that persons and associations have contrary conceptions of the good as well as of how to realize them, and these differences set them at odds, and lead them to make conflicting claims on their institutions. They hold opposing religious and philosophical beliefs, and affirm not only diverse moral and political doctrines, but also conflicting

ways of evaluating arguments and evidence when they try to reconcile these oppositions.[8]

The second of the circumstances of justice—the "subjective" circumstances—is crucial for Rawls: "[A]lthough moderate scarcity may be overcome or largely mitigated, justice as fairness assumes that deep and pervasive differences of religious, philosophical, and ethical doctrine remain. . . . Justice as fairness tries to construct a conception of justice that takes deep and unresolvable difference on matters of fundamental significance as a permanent condition of human life."[9] Rawls' view of the subjective circumstances explains his view that if principles of justice are to fulfill what Rawls calls "the practical task of political philosophy"[10]—namely, "to settle a fundamental disagreement over the just form of basic institutions within a democratic society under modern conditions"—they must be ones all members of the society can accept, notwithstanding their "deep and unresolvable" moral differences. Specifically, they must be principles whose justification is impartial among the differences that constitute the subjective circumstances of the society. The justification of the principles must not presuppose a position on any of the basic moral issues as to which there are "deep and pervasive differences" in the society. In that sense, the justification must transcend the subjective circumstances.[11]

But there is no such transcendent justification. At least, Rawls fails in his effort to provide one. The category or set of principles whose justification is impartial among the differences that constitute the subjective circumstances seems empty.

Consider the primary justification Rawls offers for his principles of justice.[12] They are, he argues, the principles all ("free and rational") persons, *understood or conceived a certain way*, would accept ("in an initial position of equality").[13] Thus, Rawls' justification presupposes—*explicitly* presupposes, as these passages from Rawls' Dewey Lectures illustrate—a particular conception of the person:

> [T]he task of justifying a conception of justice becomes: how can people settle on a conception of justice . . . that is (most) reasonable for them *in virtue of how they conceive of their persons*? . . . The task is to articulate a public conception of justice that all can live with *who regard their person and their relation to society in a certain way* . . . [R]ather than think of the principles of justice as true, it is better to say that they are the principles most reasonable for us, *given our conception of persons as free and equal* . . . [In

contractualism, first principles are those that] are most reasonable for those *who conceive of their person as it is represented in the procedure of construction* [which, for Rawls, is the "original position"].[14]

What conception of the person does Rawls' justification presuppose? As Michael Sandel and others have argued, Rawls understands the person as an entity whose identity or "self" is prior to, rather than constituted by (even in part), her moral convictions and commitments.[15]

That conception of the person, however, is not impartial among the differences that constitute the subjective circumstances of a modern democratic society, of which American society is, for Rawls, the paradigmatic example. Rawls suggests that the conception of the person he proffers is *the* conception "implicit" in our culture "or at least congenial to its deepest tendencies."[16] But, contrary to Rawls, there is not just one conception of the person implicit in American culture. There is, in addition to Rawls' conception, one according to which the person is partly constituted by her moral convictions and commitments. "[T]hink of the moral self, the embodiment of rationality," writes the American philosopher Richard Rorty, "not as one of Rawls' original choosers, somebody who can distinguish her *self* from her talents and interests and views about the good, but as a network of beliefs, desires, and emotions with nothing behind it—no substrate behind the attributes. For purposes of moral and political deliberation and conversation, a person just *is* that network, as for purposes of ballistics she is a point-mass, or for purposes of chemistry a linkage of molecules."[17]

Rawls has recently acknowledged the sort of criticism I'm making: "The description of the parties may seem to presuppose some metaphysical conception of the person, for example, that the essential nature of persons is independent of and prior to their contingent attributes, including their final ends and attachments, and indeed, their character as a whole."[18] Rawls then tries "to explain why . . . [his conception of justice] does not . . . depend[] on philosophical claims . . . about the essential nature and identity of persons."[19] According to Rawls, our "reasoning for principles of justice in accordance with the" restrictions represented by the original position,[20] which require, *inter alia*, that we not rely on our particular moral convictions, "no more commits us to a metaphysical doctrine about the nature of the self than our playing a game like Monopoly commits us to thinking that we are landlords engaged in a desperate rivalry, winner take all."[21]

The problem with this response, as Rawls' reference to role playing in *Monopoly* makes clear, is that for a person to forgo reliance on—to "bracket"—her particular moral convictions in reasoning towards principles of justice is not for *her*—the *particular* person *she* is—to reason towards principles of justice, since those convictions are partly self-constitutive; it is, rather, for her to play the role of *someone else* reasoning towards principles of justice—someone without the bracketed convictions. That is, it is for her to play the role of someone else *unless* she brackets one or more of her particular moral convictions at some step in her reasoning towards principles of justice *because* certain other of her convictions require her to do so—or, put another way, *unless* she brackets one or more aspects of her particular conception of the good at some step in her reasoning towards principles of justice *because* certain other aspects of her conception of the good require her to do so. In that case, however, she has not, at the beginning, bracketed her conception of the good. To the contrary, it is precisely because, at the beginning, she *has* relied on her conception of the good that at a later step in her reasoning towards principles of justice she forgoes *further* reliance on her conception. For her, then, the principles of justice at which she finally arrives are not prior to her conception of the good, but derivative of it.

Rawls' theory of justice, however, has been thought by many commentators to be one in which the Right is prior to the Good in the sense that no conception of the good plays a role in the derivation (justification) of the principles of justice.[22] If Rawls' theory is indeed of that (Right-prior-to-Good) sort, then, in Rawls' theory, for a person to bracket her conception of the good in reasoning towards principles of justice is necessarily for her to play the role of someone else reasoning towards principles of justice—someone without her conception of the good, indeed, someone without any conception of the good. What sort of entity is that? Rawls calls such an entity a "person", but it is difficult to see why principles of justice derived in that way have any claim on real persons, each of whom not merely has, but is partly constituted by, a conception of the good.[23]

Perhaps, however, this critique misconceives the character of Rawls' theory of justice. (Richard Rorty has written that "Rawls' writings subsequent to *A Theory of Justice* have helped us realize that we were misinterpreting his book—that we had overemphasized the Kantian and underemphasized the Hegelian and Deweyan elements."[24]) Perhaps Rawls' theory is one in which the Good is prior to the Right in the sense that a person's conception of the good plays a determinative role in her acceptance of the principles of justice. If so, then Rawls' contractualist theory is not, as has commonly been thought, of the Right-prior-to-Good sort, but of the Good-prior-to-Right sort. I discuss the latter sort of contractualism (including Rawls' theory understood as such a theory), and contrast it to the former sort, in the next chapter. For present purposes, suffice it to say that *if* Rawls' theory is of the Right-prior-to-Good sort, then it presupposes a problematic conception of the person: someone—or, better, some "thing"—whose identity or self is prior to, rather than constituted by (even in part), her conception of the good, her moral convictions and commitments.

I reject that conception of the person and accept a conception according to which a person's convictions are partly self-constitutive.[25] My present point, however, is *not* the one made by, for example, Sandel, namely, that Rawls' justification of his principles of justice is ineffective to one who rejects Rawls' conception of the person (though that point is true and important).[26] (It is possible, of course, that there may be one or more justifications—albeit nontranscendent justifications—for Rawls' principles of justice, or for something like them, that *would be* effective to someone who rejects Rawls' conception of the person. I address that possibility in the next chapter, in discussing contractualism of the Good-prior-to-Right sort.) My point is more fundamental: Rawls' liberal project must be adjudged a failure even by one who *accepts* Rawls' conception of the person. The project, recall, was to locate principles of justice whose justification is impartial among the differences that constitute the subjective circumstances of a modern democratic society. But Rawls' justification of his principles, in presupposing a particular conception of the person, presupposes a position on a basic issue—"What is a 'person'? What are the constituents of personal 'identity'?"—as to which there are deep differences in American society, differences partly constitutive of our subjective circumstances.

And, indeed, it is difficult to imagine any such project succeeding—difficult, that is, to imagine any justification of principles of justice that does not presuppose a position on one or more of the basic issues as to which there are differences constitutive of the subjective circumstances of our society. As MacIntyre has written, "the morality spoken of by contemporary liberal moral philosophers . . . is constituted by a set of principles or rules to which any rational agent would assent. . . . [N]o such set of rules has as yet been identified."[27]

Thus, the Rawlsian vision of the proper relation between morality/religion and politics/law is a failed vision: The requisite principles of justice—principles whose justification transcends the subjective circumstances—simply don't exist. At least, Rawls has not succeeded in identifying any such principles.

It is possible, of course, to redefine the Rawlsian project. One might argue along these lines, for example:

> [O]nce one agrees that the original position, in virtue of possessing features that some rational people reject, embodies an ideal of the person that some rational people appear not to share, then the conclusion seems inescapable that the more defensible way of presenting Rawls' two principles is as part of a system of hypothetical imperatives . . . Since the original position models a particular ideal of the person, Rawls can simply be construed as making a claim of the following hypothetical form: If one prizes this ideal of the person, *then* it is rational to abide by these principles of justice.[28]

One might even try to defend the Rawlsian ideal of the person. But thus redefined, the project is no longer liberal. The search is no longer for a transcendent conception of justice. The Rawlsian conception of justice is within the subjective circumstances of fundamental disagreement and must compete there. It does not, as Rawls hoped, transcend those circumstances. Thus, "Rawls must defend [his] theory . . . against the sorts of objections he elsewhere raises against the notions of rationally justified final aims. That is, he must enter into precisely that arena of conflicting perfectionist claims that the formal structure of justice as fairness was designed to sidestep."[29]

II

Bruce Ackerman's political philosophy is based on a master principle—the principle of "neutrality"—the function of which is to test distributive principles on which the state might want to rely in allocating resources, like food, or other things, like the right to vote. No distributive principle is legitimate, according to Ackerman, the justification of which violates the neutrality principle. A justification violates the neutrality principle if (and only if) it relies on either a claim to the effect that one conception of human good—of what way or ways of life, or what political arrangements, are good for human beings, whether human beings generally or particular human beings—is better than another or a claim to the effect that one human being is intrinsically superior to another.[30]

I don't know what it means to say that one human being is intrinsically superior to another.[31] Moreover, any argument in support of a particular distribution of a resource that relies on such a claim seems to rely as well on a claim that it is good to distribute the resource on the basis of intrinsic worth. However, that further claim seems to be ruled out by that part of the neutrality principle banning claims that one conception of the good is better than another.[32]

Let's put aside the question of what it might mean to say that one human being is intrinsically superior to another and ask instead whether there is any distributive principle whose justification does not presuppose that one conception of human good is better than another. If there is none, then the former question is unimportant for present purposes. Ackerman assumes that the principle of equal distribution[33] is consistent with the neutrality principle—that it can be justified without relying on a claim that one conception of human good is better than another. But can it? Assume that an equal distribution of some resource is challenged. Can it be defended consistently with the neutrality principle? Consider these strategies.

1. *The distribution must be equal, because the justification of any unequal distribution fails the neutrality principle.*

This defense fails the neutrality principle. It presupposes that there is a presumption in favor of equal distribution (and, so, against unequal distribution) such that if no unequal distribution can be justified in terms that pass the neutrality principle, the distribution must be equal. But that presumption fails the neutrality principle. It is an open question whether any distributive principle can survive the neutrality principle. (We're presently inquiring whether the principle of equal distribution can survive it.) It is possible, of course, that none can. If no distributive principle can survive the neutrality principle, then whatever distributive principle gets the benefit of the presumption—the benefit, that is, of being tested last and getting to say "all the others failed, therefore I win (by default)"—will prevail. The question thus becomes whether the decision to award the benefit of the presumption to the principle of equal distribution rather than to some other distributive principle can be justified in terms that pass the neutrality principle. And the answer, of course, is no.[34]

2. *The distribution must be equal (as between A and B), because A is*

at least as good as B and A's conception of human good is at least as good as B's.[35]

This defense presupposes that if *A* is at least as good as *B* and *A*'s conception of human good is at least as good as *B*'s, then *A* is entitled to at least as much as *B*—an equal share. Why should we accept that presupposition?

a. One possible answer is: To say "*A* is at least as good as *B* and *A*'s conception of human good is at least as good as *B*'s" is to say—that is, it simply *means*—"*A* is entitled to at least as much as *B*". However, that response renders Ackerman's neutrality principle anything but neutral. Thus understood, the neutrality principle rules out any principle other than that each person is entitled to the same share of resources as every other person. To begin there is to begin with an *ipse dixit* on the question-in-chief—namely, the question of what distribution(s) is (are) legitimate.[36]

b. A second possible answer is: It is just obvious—self-evident—that if *A* is at least as good as *B* and *A*'s conception of human good is at least as good as *B*'s, then *A* is entitled to at least as much as *B*. The problem with that response, as Gilbert Harman has observed, is that "[o]n its face, that assertion [of obviousness or self-evidence] would seem to violate neutrality. The egalitarian would be claiming to have a privileged insight into the moral universe."[37] That is, she would be claiming to have a privileged insight—an intuition—as to what distribution is legitimate assuming the equality both of human beings and of conceptions of human good.

c. A third possible answer is: Resources should be distributed proportionately to the worth of one's person and of one's conception of human good. But *why* should resources be distributed proportionately to worth? Because it is *good* to do so? Why prefer that conception of what it is good to do to some other conception, say, the utilitarian conception? The claim that resources should be distributed proportionately to worth "violates neutrality for it stands, boldly, for a conception of the good. It asserts that it is good to distribute [resources] in shares proportional to . . . merit."[38]

Thus, Ackerman's equal-distribution principle cannot be justified in terms that pass the neutrality principle.

Rawls sought impartiality in the justification of his theory of justice, but he did not find it there, because no justification of principles of justice can be impartial among the philosophical-religious-moral differences that constitute the subjective circumstances. Ackerman sought neutrality in his master principle itself (rather than in the justification of the principle). As our examination of Ackerman's position suggests, however, a truly neutral master principle is of no help in resolving conflicting distributive claims: Either the neutrality principle is weak, in which case it rules out *no* distributive principle, or, like Ackerman's, it is strong, in which case it rules out *every* distributive principle, even the principle of equal distribution.

The relation between morality and politics, as envisioned by Ackerman, like that envisioned by Rawls, is unattainable: Ackerman's neutrality principle is not one with which politics can comply. Ackerman's neutral politics is an impossibility.

III

Ronald Dworkin argues that a "certain conception of equality," which he calls "the liberal conception of equality," is "the nerve center of liberalism."[39] According to Dworkin, "liberalism takes, as its constitutive political morality, [this] conception of equality:"[40] "[G]overnment [must] treat all those in its charge *as equals*, that is, as entitled to equal concern and respect."[41] Or, as Dworkin puts it elsewhere, "government must treat people as equals in the following sense. It must impose no sacrifice or constraint on any citizen in virtue of an argument that the citizen could not accept without abandoning his sense of his equal worth."[42]

Dworkin's master principle—the equality principle—is vague. It is not clear precisely what the principle requires or forbids government to do. Happily, however, Dworkin offers us another, less vague principle—call it the "neutrality" principle—according to which "government must be neutral on what might be called the question of the good life. . . . [P]olitical decisions must be . . . independent of any conception of the good life, or of what gives value to life."[43] Politics, says Dworkin, "must be neutral in one particular way: among conceptions of the good life. Whatever we may think privately, it cannot count, as a justification for some rule of law or some political institution, that a life that includes reading pornography or homosexual relationships is either better or worse than the life of someone with more orthodox tastes in reading or sex. Or that a life suffused with religion is better or worse than a wholly secular life."[44]

It is difficult to tell whether, in Dworkin's view, the neutrality principle is a distinct principle somehow derived from, or is instead simply a (partial) specification of the meaning or content of, the equality principle.[45] If the latter, it bears mention that Dworkin doesn't defend the equality/neutrality principle, but merely treats it as "axiomatic" for authentic liberals.[46] If the former, it bears mention that not only doesn't Dworkin defend the equality principle, he doesn't even show how the neutrality principle is derived from the equality principle. Dworkin's political theory is, then, to say the least, underdeveloped.[47]

Recall that whereas Rawls sought impartiality in the justification of his principles of justice, Ackerman sought neutrality in his master principle itself. Dworkin is like Ackerman on that score, or at least closer to Ackerman than to Rawls: If the neutrality principle is simply a specification of Dworkin's master principle (the equality principle), then Dworkin seeks neutrality in his master principle; if the neutrality principle is somehow derived from Dworkin's master principle, then he seeks neutrality in the derived principle.[48]

In any event, this is the crucial question: Are there any—indeed, can there be any—political institutions or policies that are consistent with Dworkin's neutrality principle, institutions or policies that do not presuppose that one conception or range of conceptions of human good is better or worse than another?[49]

It is simply not possible for government, in making the sorts of choices any government must make, to comply with Dworkin's neutrality principle. Indeed, in enacting the very sort of nonmoralistic and nonpaternalistic program Dworkin obviously has in mind as appropriate for a truly "liberal" state, a government would *thereby* act inconsistently with the neutrality principle. Consider this example: *A* has a conception of human good according to which, all things considered, it is better for her (and for persons generally) to have lawful access to pornographic materials if and when she wants to read or view them— better, that is, to live in a society in which her access to such materials is not impeded by law. *B* has a rather different conception of human good—one according to which, all things considered, it is better for him (and for persons generally) *not* to have lawful access to pornographic materials if and when he wants to read or view them. A public policy concerning access to pornographic materials cannot be neutral. The policy must either affirm *A*'s conception of human good (and deny *B*'s) and permit access or, instead, affirm *B*'s conception (and deny *A*'s) and forbid access. There is no neutral standpoint.

Thus, no government can satisfy Dworkin's neutrality principle, not even one steadfastly pursuing Dworkin's vision of "liberal" justice.[50] Dworkin's theory of justice presupposes that a certain conception or range of conceptions of human good is sound and that other conceptions are infirm. In particular his theory presupposes that certain political and legal arrangements are good for human beings and others are bad, or at least that certain arrangements are better than others, given the nature of real human interests. In Dworkin's view, moralistic and paternalistic arrangements are inferior to nonmoralistic and nonpaternalistic ones, because the former frustrate what Dworkin implicitly sees as the fundamental human interest in autonomous decisionmaking with respect to the shape of one's life. In Dworkin's moral universe "freedom is considered an essential and indispensable constituent of a good life; only a life in which I pursue goals that I have freely chosen can be a genuinely good life for me, and only in leading such a life can I be truly happy."[51] What Isaiah Berlin said of "[t]he ideas of every philosopher concerned with human affairs" applies to the political-philosophical ideas of Dworkin: "[I]n the end [his ideas] rest on his conception of what man is and can be."[52]

Dworkin has tried to answer the sort of objection I'm raising, but he fails. His liberalism does not presuppose a conception or range of conceptions of human good, Dworkin asserts, because "the liberal conception of equality is a principle of political organization that is required by justice, not a way of life for individuals, and liberals, as such, are indifferent as to whether people choose to speak out on political matters, or to lead eccentric lives, or otherwise to behave as liberals are supposed to prefer."[53] In short, liberalism is a theory of justice or of the Right, not a theory of the Good (according to Dworkin). That response is little more than an attempt to win the point by terminological fiat. Dworkin can call his theory a theory of justice if he wants, but that doesn't alter the fact that at bottom Dworkin is arguing that certain political and legal arrangements are better than others for human beings, given a particular understanding "of what man is and can be."

(If Dworkin wants to insist that he has been misunderstood and that his theory of justice is indeed of the Right-prior-to-Good sort—a sort that, significantly, even Rawls has now apparently abandoned[54]—then we may, *arguendo*, give Dworkin the point, for thus understood his theory is vulnerable to precisely the same critique leveled at Rawls' theory, interpreted as a Right-prior-to-Good theory, earlier in this chapter: Any Right-prior-to-Good theory presupposes a conception of the person controversial within the subjective circumstances of justice and therefore fails to transcend those circumstances. Perhaps, however, Dworkin does not aspire or, at least, claim to provide a transcendent theory of justice. Even if so, there remains this insurmountable difficulty: As I explained earlier, any Right-prior-to-Good theory of justice—including, therefore, Dworkin's theory, if it is indeed of the Right-prior-to-Good sort—presupposes a deeply problematic conception of the person.)

Ackerman's neutrality principle, as I've argued, is so severe that no principle of distributive justice can satisfy it. Although Dworkin has criticized Ackerman's principle on that ground,[55] it is difficult to see how Dworkin's own neutrality principle is any less severe. It is difficult to see, that is, what political choices Dworkin's principle would allow, once it is understood that even "liberal" choices presuppose a conception or range of conceptions of human good. (Alternatively, they presuppose a Right-prior-to-Good theory of justice vulnerable to the critique made earlier in this chapter.) There are no political institutions or policies—not even institutions and policies of the "liberal" kind Dworkin has in mind—that do not involve the very sort of presupposition Dworkin's neutrality principle disallows.

I hope I'm not misunderstood. To say that government and politics cannot possibly comply with Dworkin's neutrality principle is not to say that government and politics cannot be neutral with respect to particular disagreements. *Of course* government can be neutral with respect to particular disagreements—for example, some theological disagreements among religious sects. However, for government to maintain a neutral stance towards particular disagreements is not for it to comply with Dworkin's neutrality principle. The decision to maintain a neutral stance towards, say, some theological disagreement concerning the nature of God is necessarily for it to proceed on the basis of a particular conception or range of conceptions of human good, according to which a certain constitutional arrangement regarding "church and state" is better for human beings—whether all human beings or simply some—than certain other arrangements, all things considered.

So much for Dworkin's neutrality principle. But what about his equality principle, the principle of equal concern and respect? As I argued in the preceding chapter, it misconceives the nature of moral rationality, including political-moral rationality, to think that moral discourse should or even can proceed on the basis of a master principle.[56] If, however, equality were to be the master political principle, it could not reasonably be conceived as Dworkin conceives it, because thus conceived government cannot avoid denying persons the equal concern and respect due them: As we've seen, government cannot avoid taking sides with respect to conceptions of human good, affirming some and denying others. John Finnis' lucid discussion of the matter merits full quotation:

> It is sometimes said that to prefer, and seek to embody in legislation, some conception or range of conceptions of human flourishing is unjust because it is necessarily to treat with unequal concern and respect those members of the community whose conceptions of human good fall outside the preferred range and whose activities are or may therefore be restricted by legislation. As an argument warranting opposition to such legislation this argument cannot be justified: it is self-stultifying. Those who put forward the argument prefer a conception of human good, according to which a person is entitled to equal concern and respect and a community is in bad shape in which that entitlement is denied; moreover, they act on this preference by seeking to repeal the restrictive legislation which those against whom they are arguing may have enacted. Do those who so argue and so act thereby necessarily treat with unequal concern and respect those whose preferences and legislation they oppose? If they do, then their own argument and action is itself equally unjustified, and provides no basis for political preferences or action. If they do not (and this must be the better view), then neither do those whom they oppose. Nor can the argument be rescued by proposing that it escapes self-stultification by operating at a different "level of discourse": for example, by being an argument about entitlements [justice] rather than about good. For there is no difficulty in translating any "paternalist" political preference into the language of entitlement, by postulating an entitlement of every member of a community to a milieu that will support rather than hinder his own pursuit of good and the well-being of his children, or an entitlement of each to be rescued from his own folly. Whether or not such entitlements can be made out, they certainly pertain to the same "level of discourse". Nor, finally, can the argument we are considering be saved by a stipulation that arguments and political programmes motivated, as it is, by concern for "equal respect and concern for other people" must be regarded as showing equal concern and respect for everyone, even those people whose (paternalist) arguments and legislation they reject and override. For . . . such a stipulation is merely an *ad hoc* device for escaping self-stultification; if overriding someone's political preferences and compelling him to live in a society whose ways he detests were *ipso facto* to show unequal concern and respect for him in one context, so it would be in any other.[57]

Thus, if it were to be the master principle, equality would have to be conceived so that government *could* avoid acting in contravention of it. Thus conceived, the equality principle would rule out some evaluations of human good, *but not all.*[58]

IV

As I've indicated, one need not take issue with Rawls' effort to justify his principles of justice to see that his project has failed: It is enough to realize that in presupposing a controversial conception of the person—a conception controversial in the subjective circumstances of the United States and other modern democratic societies—Rawls' justification does not transcend the subjective circumstances but is immanent to them. Similarly, one need not take issue with Ackerman's effort to justify his neutrality principle; indeed, I haven't found it necessary even to discuss that effort:[59] Ackerman's principle is not one with which government and politics could possibly comply. Finally, one need not take issue with Dworkin's failure even to try to justify his equality principle: "Liberal" political choices of the sort Dworkin has in mind presuppose a conception or range of conceptions of human good (or, alternatively, they presuppose a Right-prior-to-Good theory of justice subject to the critique presented earlier).

The appeal of the liberal project is obvious. The moral and other differences that constitute what Rawls calls the subjective circumstances of justice are deep, pervasive, and persistent. If there were some way government and politics could transcend those differences by achieving the impartiality Rawls sought, or the neutrality Ackerman and Dworkin sought, perhaps it would make sense to do so. But, as I've explained in this chapter, there is no way for government and politics to transcend the subjective circumstances. The liberal project—the search for the Holy Grail of official normative impartiality or neutrality—is doomed to failure. For all their differences, the arguments of Rawls, Ackerman, and Dworkin are united in their failure to show otherwise.

Although only Rawls, Ackerman, and Dworkin have been discussed here, it bears emphasis that other, kindred theorists—Alan Gewirth, for example[60]—have not succeeded where Rawls, Ackerman, and Dworkin have failed. For the reasons elaborated in this chapter, any "deontological" or Right-prior-to-Good liberal theory—any liberal theory in which no particular conception or range of conceptions of human good plays a role in the derivation of a principle or principles of justice—is doomed to failure, as is any theory, like Ackerman's or Dworkin's, rooted in a neutrality principle.[61] The liberal political-philosophical approach to the problem of the relation of morality/religion to politics/law, therefore, is a dead end. An alternative approach (or approaches) must be tried. (To say that liberalism-as-neutrality is an impossible goal, however, is *not* to deny the possibility and worth of a different goal, liberalism-as-tolerance, which I discuss in the next chapter.)

Ackerman has written:

> In one way or another we must learn to deal with our competitors in the struggle for power. A first response is to persuade them to abandon their errors and adopt our truths; a second, to convince them that toleration is in their self-interest; third, to induce them to sympathize with us, despite the error of our ways. But is there a fourth way—a way we may travel together when, to our dismay, the others lead nowhere?
>
> Yes: we *can* speak Neutrally to one another when we find we have nothing better to say. The dialogic effort does not lead to self-contradictory gibberish but to a form of community that, for all its difficulties, permits us to sustain communication without lying about our ultimate disagreements.
>
> And if we disdain the art of constrained conversation, how *will* we come to terms with one another?
>
> Is there a fifth way beyond excommunication and brute suppression?[62]

Given the inadequacy of Ackerman's fourth way—neutral dialogue— his final question becomes all the more urgent.

How can we, the members of a morally pluralistic society, hope to resolve our conflicting political claims through a discursive process given, first, our deep moral differences and, second, the absence of a transcendent conception of justice? From the perspective of the person as inevitably a partisan in the subjective circumstances—as inevitably a member of some particular moral (perhaps religious) community within the larger pluralistic society—the question is: How can I, a member of one moral community among many, hope to engage in productive moral discourse with persons outside my moral community, given our moral differences and the absence of transcendent principles of justice?

If it is the case (as I believe it is) that a person—a "self"—is partly constituted by her moral convictions,[63] then, in choosing principles of justice, the partisan cannot bracket her membership in her moral community, her particular moral convictions, for that membership, those convictions, are constitutive of her very self. To bracket them would be

to bracket—indeed, to annihilate—herself. And doing that would preclude *her*—the *particular* person *she* is—from engaging in moral discourse with other members of society. Because the partisan's membership in a particular moral community—her participation in a particular
moral tradition—is self-constitutive, she must find a way to engage
persons outside her moral community in moral discourse that does not
require her to do what in any event she cannot do—bracket that
membership.

But is there such a way?[64]

III

An Alternative Vision: Towards a Deliberative, Transformative Politics

The relation between morality/religion and politics/law envisioned by liberal political philosophy is impossible to achieve. In this Part I present an alternative vision.

I concluded the preceding chapter with a question about the possibility of productive moral discourse among persons who are members of different moral communities. Chapter 2 of this book is, in part, an effort to respond to that question. In discussing there the nature and limits of moral discourse, I indicated that—and why—the possibility of productive moral discourse is often quite real, even in a morally pluralistic society like our own. Moreover, as I said near the end of chapter 2, even if moral discourse probably can't go very far in resolving a particular dispute, such discourse is almost surely worth attempting, given the alternatives. Even if moral discourse can do no more, in a particular situation, than diminish the area of disagreement—indeed, even if it can do no more than promote a better understanding of the nature of the disagreement—it is worthwhile. (Achieving a better understanding of the nature of a disagreement is a first step.) So, chapter 2 began the project of presenting an alternative vision of morality and politics.

Even when it is available, however, moral discourse often runs out—for the time being, at least—before agreement is reached. How should we respond, in our politics and law, to the fact of moral dissensus? In this Part (chapters 4–6) I continue the project of presenting an alternative vision.

In chapters 4 and 5 I pursue the question of what to do, what alternatives remain, when moral discourse runs out. Or, resisting the conclusion that moral discourse should often be conceded to have run out, perhaps I should say: I pursue the question of what *else* to do, what complementary or supplementary strategies exist, when moral discourse has become exceedingly difficult (as it has, for example, with respect to the bitterly divisive issue of abortion). Two strategies in particular are important to consider: coercive legislation (chapter 4) and conscientious disobedience (chapter 5).

Then, in chapter 6, in discussing constitutional adjudication, I return to the question of the possibility, in a morally pluralistic society, of productive moral discourse and of the sort of politics of which moral discourse is a prime constituent: a deliberative, transformative politics, as distinct from a politics that is merely manipulative and self-serving. At its best, constitutional adjudication is both a species of moral discourse and a model of a deliberative, transformative politics (as I explain in chapter 6).

The vision of the proper relation between morality and politics I offer here—a vision that is sometimes explicit and sometimes implicit in the next three chapters—is, unlike the liberal vision, capable of realization. Indeed, it is a vision already realized, already embodied, to some extent, in the practices of the American political-constitutional community. Thus, although my discussion is prescriptive, it is, to some extent, descriptive as well.

4

Making Law: The Problem of Coercive Legislation

As I noted in the introduction to this book, the moral culture of the United States is pluralistic. The existence of many different moral communities (including religious communities) in American society entails the existence of competing beliefs about human good, about what it is possible and most deeply satisfying for human beings—whether some human beings or all human beings—to be and to do. Those differences give rise to fundamental disagreements about many issues that engage legislators and other policymakers, like the issue of abortion. In politics, and therefore in law, moral discourse often runs out before agreement—consensus—is reached, especially in a morally pluralistic society like our own.

Consider, then, the predicament of a policymaker who, like everyone, is inevitably a member of some moral community—"inevitably", because everyone shares with some other persons some conception of human good—but who, like every policymaker in the United States, especially those with large constituencies, represents a morally pluralistic political community:[1] On what moral beliefs ought she to rely, in her capacity as policymaker, in reasoning about and ultimately determining public policy? As Governor Mario Cuomo, a member of the Catholic community, has asked: "Must politics and religion in America divide our loyalties? Does the 'separation between church and state' imply separation between religion and politics? Between morality and government? . . . [W]hat is the relationship of my Catholicism to my politics? Where does the one end and the other begin? Are the two divided at all? If they are not, should they be?"[2] In particular, on what moral beliefs ought the policymaker to rely in deciding whether to use the law to coerce a person to make a choice the person believes to be, for her, the wrong choice? The predicament of the policymaker is also the predicament of a citizen intent on evaluating proposed or existing public policy. Like the policymaker, the citizen is a member of one moral community among many. But she is also a member of a morally pluralistic political community. (Indeed, she is a member of more than one such political community: state and local as well as national.) On what moral beliefs ought the citizen to rely, in her capacity as judge of public policy?

Two responses to the predicament of the policymaker (and of the citizen-judge) have been prominent in contemporary American political thought: the utilitarian and the contractarian. Beginning with utilitarianism and then turning to its "major current rival (at least in Anglo-American precincts)",[3] contractarianism, I explain why both responses are inadequate. I then offer an alternative response.

I

A utilitarian theory might be accepted as a general moral theory, a theory for all choice, personal as well as public. Or it might be accepted, more narrowly, merely as a theory for public choice, a decision procedure for public policymaking.[4] In this chapter I criticize utilitarian theories taken as general moral theories. However, because utilitarian theories can be taken merely as theories for public choice, my critique needs to be supplemented by a critique of utilitarian theories taken simply as decision procedures for public policymaking.[5]

"There never has been any canonical formulation of utilitarianism."[6] Indeed, "[t]here is nothing which is 'utilitarianism' *per se*: the term refers not to a single theory but to a cluster of theories . . ."[7] For present purposes many of the differences among the various sorts of utilitarianism—for example, act-utilitarianism,[8] rule-utilitarianism,[9] utilitarian-generalization,[10] and cooperative utilitarianism[11]—are unimportant. It is important, however, to understand what the various utilitarian theories have in common. According to R. G. Frey, the "cluster of theories" to which "utilitarianism" refers

> are variations on a theme, the components of which can be distinguished. This theme, taken here to revolve around acts . . ., involves (at least) four components: (i) the consequence component, to the effect that the rightness or wrongness of acts is tied in some way to (the production of) good and bad consequences; (ii) the value component, to the effect that the goodness or

badness of consequences is to be evaluated by means of some standard of intrinsic goodness; (iii) the range component, to the effect that it is the acts' consequences affecting everyone and not just the agent himself that are to be considered in determining rightness; and (iv) a principle of utility, to the effect that one should seek to maximize that which the adopted standard of goodness identifies as intrinsically good.[12]

One might want to criticize utilitarian theories generally. That is, one might want to criticize some element common to all utilitarian theories, such as "the consequence component". (John Finnis has criticized utilitarian theories by attacking their consequentialist character.[13] I've argued elsewhere that Finnis' criticism is not persuasive.[14]) My aim, however, is to criticize, not utilitarian theories generally, but the two principal contemporary utilitarian theories: experience-utilitarianism and preference-utilitarianism. I criticize "the value component" of each theory.[15] The distinction between experience-utilitarianism and preference-utilitarianism cuts across the distinctions among act-utilitarianism, rule-utilitarianism, utilitarian generalization, and cooperative utilitarianism: For example, an experience-utilitarian theory may be either of the act-utilitarian or of the rule-utilitarian sort. Again, the distinctions among act-utilitarianism, etc., are unimportant for present purposes.

According to experience-utilitarianism, the fundamental good for human beings[16] is a mental state, or experience, sometimes called "happiness".

[F]or persons to be happy is for them to be undergoing a conscious experience that they like or enjoy for its own sake. One important feature of the happiness conception of value is that while persons can be mistaken about whether some activity will make them happy, it is generally thought that one cannot be mistaken about whether one is enjoying an experience or activity at the time one undergoes it. On the happiness conception then, it is conscious experience enjoyed for its own sake that has intrinsic value, and each person is in a privileged position for determining what they enjoy or what makes them happy.[17]

This conception of human good or well-being is utterly implausible. To achieve the mental state in question is not necessarily to have achieved well-being or even to have come close. It is not necessarily to be flourishing. For example, a person may have masochistic or even sadistic sensibilities and thus be "happy" when she is engaged in masochistic or sadistic activities. (If that example doesn't appeal to you, pick another. Our sometimes painful experiences with some family members, friends, colleagues, acquaintances, figures in literature and film, people on the street, etc., surely suggests a multitude of examples.) However, such "happiness" does not entail that she is necessarily living anything close to a life as deeply satisfying as any of which she is capable. She *might* be living a life as deeply satisfying as any of which *she*, poor woman, is capable. We don't know a priori—and so we shouldn't say a priori—that she's not living such a life. But her "happiness" does not entail that she is *necessarily* living such a life.[18] The fundamental problem with the experience-utilitarian standard of value is that it takes as a given—it presupposes the authority of—existing sensibilities. What makes a person "happy" depends on her sensibilities, yet a person's sensibilities might be antithetical to, subversive of, her flourishing.[19]

According to preference-utilitarianism, the fundamental good is the satisfaction of preferences (or desires or wants). This conception of human good or well-being is no more plausible than the experience-utilitarian conception. Putting aside the problem of conflicting preferences, which can be overcome to some extent by reference to preference intensity, it remains the case that to achieve preference satisfaction is not necessarily to be flourishing. As I indicated in chapter 1, a person is flourishing to the extent her interests are satisfied, and not flourishing to the extent they are not satisfied. It is the satisfaction of a person's interests, and not necessarily of her preferences, that constitutes her flourishing. To have a preference for something is not necessarily to have an interest in the satisfaction of that preference. A person has an interest (if she is committed to flourishing) in the satisfaction of preferences the satisfaction of which is constitutive of her flourishing. However, she has an interest in the *nonsatisfaction* of preferences the satisfaction of which is antithetical to her flourishing.

The distance between a person's preferences and her interests can be great. What a person prefers partly depends, of course, on what she believes about her possibilities[20] and about what she would find most deeply satisfying. Yet, a person's beliefs can be mistaken.[21] In that sense a person's preferences, too, can be mistaken. It simply makes no sense to give priority to satisfaction of a person's mistaken preferences rather than to strategies for correcting her mistaken vision of her possibilities and of what she would find most deeply satisfying.[22] And, in any event, some people sometimes prefer all sorts of crazy things—like heroin or someone else's misery. Such preferences have no claim to satisfaction.[23] The fundamental problem with the preference-utilitarian standard of value is that it takes as a given—it presupposes the authority of—existing preferences, many of which are problematic.

Both experience-utilitarianism and preference-utilitarianism are species of naturalist moral theory: Each posits a conception of human good or well-being. However, both the experience-utilitarian and the preference-utilitarian conceptions of human good are impoverished—a condition that stems from the fact that experience-utilitarianism takes an uncritical attitude towards existing sensibilities, and preference-utilitarianism, towards existing preferences.

> A person's desires and preferences are the product of biological needs and the socialization process by which he or she is inducted into a society, state and various social groups. They are importantly determined by and will tend to reflect and reinforce the existing social arrangements, power and authority relations, and expectations in one's environment. Consequently, utilitarianism formulated so as to require maximal satisfaction of preferences as they exist, in turn serves to reinforce the existing social structure: it will have a significant conservative bias. For example, a racist or sexist society may foster racist or sexist preferences in its members, and preference utilitarianism seems committed then to seeking the satisfaction of these preferences.[24]

Although this passage proceeds by reference to preference-utilitarianism, the point applies with equal force to experience-utilitarianism: What makes a person "happy" depends on her sensibilities, which are the product of many factors, including "the socialization process . . .", etc.

Among utilitarian theories preference-utilitarianism seems to be dominant. According to the dispiriting view of politics that sometimes attends adherence to preference-utilitarianism, the policymaking process is merely an instrument for "the *aggregation* of given preferences" rather than "the *transformation* of preferences through public and rational discussion."[25] That view of politics sometimes attends adherence to preference-utilitarianism because adherence to preference-utilitarianism as a decision procedure for public policymaking[26] is sometimes rooted in the belief that preferences are simply a matter of "taste" and there's no disputing—no *reasoning* about—taste/preferences.[27] Given that belief, it follows that preferences cannot be transformed "through public and rational discussion". It would be disturbing, to say the least, were it true that we could not reason about our preferences, for "unrelieved by practical judgment, desire is not so much a spontaneous personal as a socially generated and fashioned impulse . . ."[28]—a fact preference-utilitarians (and libertarians) are wont to blink.[29]

The experience-utilitarian and preference-utilitarian responses to the predicament of the policymaker (and of the citizen-judge) are radically inadequate. Let's now turn to contractarianism and see if it fares any better than its "major current rival",[30] utilitarianism, as a response to the predicament of the policymaker.

II

Just as one can discuss naturalist moral theory generally as distinct from any particular naturalist theory, one can discuss contractarian theory generally as distinct from any particular contractarian theory. In the preceding chapter I considered the work of our most prominent contractarian political philosopher, John Rawls, and found it wanting. In this chapter I broaden the focus to consider contractarian theory generally.

In his important essay "Contractualism and Utilitarianism," Thomas Scanlon aims "to [provide] a clear account of the foundations of . . . [contractualist] moral reasoning."[31] (Scanlon prefers the term "contractualism" to "contractarianism". In commenting on Scanlon's essay, I'll follow his usage.) Scanlon identifies three basic "questions which a philosophical account of the foundations of morality must answer."[32] The first one Scanlon calls the "question of subject matter": "[I]t is not at all obvious what, if anything, . . . [moral] judgments can be about, in virtue of which some can be said to be correct or defensible and others not."[33] This is the question: What is *moral* knowledge; moral knowledge is knowledge of or about what; what is its object? The second question is epistemological: How is moral knowledge achieved; what sort of reasoning or testing does the acquisition of moral knowledge involve? Scanlon writes that "given any positive answer to the first question—any specification of the subject matter or ground of truth in . . . morality—we need some compatible epistemology explaining how it is possible to discover the facts about this subject matter through something like the means we seem to use."[34] The third and final question concerns motivation: What reason, if any, does one have to take an interest in, to care about, moral knowledge? "Given any candidate for the role of subject matter of morality we must explain why anyone should care about it . . . A satisfactory moral philosophy will not leave concern with morality as a simple special preference, like a fetish or a special taste, which some people just happen to have. It must make it understandable why moral reasons are ones that people can take seriously, and why they strike those who are moved by them as reasons of a special stringency and inescapability."[35]

How, in Scanlon's view, does contractualism answer these three "foundational" questions? And how *well* does it answer them? In particular, does it answer them as well as naturalism?

Scanlon notes both the naturalist response to the subject matter question and the appeal of the response. According to naturalism,[36] "the only fundamental moral facts are facts about individual well-being . . . [T]his thesis has a great deal of plausibility for many people . . . Claims about individual well-being are one class of valid starting points for moral argument. But many people find it much harder to see how there could be any other, independent starting points."[37] What, then, is the contractualist response to the question of subject matter—the contractualist account of the subject matter of morality?

According to contractualism (as portrayed by Scanlon), moral judgments are about the property "moral wrongness"; in particular, the object of moral knowledge is "any system of rules for the general regulation of behaviour which no one could reasonably reject as a basis for informed, unforced general agreement."[38] As Scanlon puts it, "An act is wrong if its performance under the circumstances would be disallowed by" any such system of rules.[39] "The intended force of the qualification 'reasonably' . . . is to exclude rejections that would be unreasonable *given* the aim of finding principles which could be the basis of informed, unforced general agreement. Given this aim, it would be unreasonable, for example, to reject a principle because it imposed a burden on you when every alternative principle would impose much greater burdens on others."[40]

As I now explain, there are two ways of interpreting the contractualist account of the subject matter of morality. On the first interpretation, the contractualist account is a genuine alternative to the naturalist account, but the contractualist account is deeply problematic. On the second interpretation, the contractualist account is not an alternative to the naturalist account, but merely an aspect of it.

Is there "any system of rules for the general regulation of behaviour which no one could reasonably reject as a basis for informed, unforced general agreement"? A person cannot reasonably reject rules that, relative to her web of beliefs, are justified to her. However, she *can* reasonably reject rules that, relative to her web, are not justified. If there are rules *no one* can reasonably reject, they must be rules justified to *everyone*. (If they are rules not justified even to one person, they are rules one person can reasonably reject.) Are there any such rules? Or is moral knowledge thus conceived—knowledge of rules justified to everyone— an empty set?

A person's basic beliefs about human good are fundamental to her web of beliefs. Obviously a rule is not justified to a person if the justification presupposes that her basic beliefs about human good—her conception of human good—are wrong or inferior. Therefore, if there are rules justified to everyone, they must be rules the justification of which does not presuppose that anyone's conception of human good is wrong or inferior. Is there any such justification (of rules for the general regulation of behavior)—a justification in which the Right is prior to the Good, that is, in which the determination of what is right or just does not depend on any conception or range of conceptions of human good? Recall that Rawls (as commonly interpreted and as I, in the preceding chapter, interpreted him) tried to provide such a justification.[41] However, Rawls' justification relied on a deeply problematic conception of the person, of the constituents of personal identity—a conception not unreasonable to reject (even if not unreasonable to accept either). Any such Right-prior-to-Good justification—any justification forsaking reliance on a conception or range of conceptions of human good— would seem to be similarly problematic. Pending development of such a justification not similarly problematic, I conclude that there is no "system of rules . . . which no one could reasonably reject". Moral knowledge thus conceived—knowledge of such a system of rules—is an empty set.

Consider now the second, alternative interpretation of the contractualist account of the subject matter of morality. On this interpretation "no one" means "no one whose conception of human good falls within a certain range of such conceptions". The question, then, is whether there is "any system of rules"—at least one system—"for the general regulation of behavior which no one whose conception of human good falls within a certain range could reasonably reject as a basis for informed, unforced general agreement". The number and character of rules in any such system depends on the breadth or extensiveness of the range of conceptions of human good to be accommodated. The broader the range, the thinner the system of rules. If the range is *very* broad, contractualism may engender nothing more than "a mere nonagression treaty", if that.[42] Nonetheless, for at least some (actual or imaginable) ranges of conceptions of human good, some (actual or imaginable) systems of rules exist such that no one whose conception fell within the relevant range could reasonably reject the system. They are systems of rules—or, if not systems, simply unsystematized rules—the justification of which does not presuppose that any conception of human good within the range in question is wrong or inferior. Putting aside justifications that forgo reliance on *any* conception or range of conceptions of human good, the justification must be one that presupposes the authority of some conceptions of human good, namely, those within the range in question. That is, the justification must be one in which the Good is prior to the Right—in which the determination of what is right or just depends on a range of conceptions of human good.

Whereas contractualism according to the first interpretation is of the Right-prior-to-Good sort, contractualism according to the second interpretation is of the Good-prior-to Right sort. On the second interpretation, a contractualist system of rules is a "*modus vivendi* among people having different ultimate commitments (often at home in different subcommunities), a system of mutual advantage, to which we primarily adhere, not because it expresses our deepest self-understandings, but rather for the more prudential reason that it serves our other values . . . a *modus vivendi* among persons having constitutive views of the good life which are shared with some but different from those of many others."[43] It is important to understand that a contractualist-according-to-the-second-interpretation system of rules or doctrine of justice is quite different from a contractualist-according-to-the-first-interpretation doctrine. The former "will be agreed upon by a process of reasoning quite different from" the latter: "[D]ifferent ideals of the good, far from being excluded from the argument for the doctrine of justice, will form the starting points of this argument. . . . [A]s a result, supporters of different conceptions of the good will follow different routes in arguing for the doctrine of justice. There will be a unanimity in the conclusion but (given the different starting points) no unanimity on the route to it."[44]

Although, as I noted in the preceding chapter, Rawls' contractualist theory of justice is commonly understood to be of the Right-prior-to-Good sort, in a recent essay Rawls makes a number of statements that seem to indicate that his theory is of the Good-prior-to-Right sort. For example: "We hope that this political conception of justice may at least be supported by what we may call an 'overlapping consensus,' that is, by a consensus that includes all the opposing philosophical and religious doctrines likely to persist and to gain adherents in a more or less just constitutional democratic society."[45] For Rawls, then, the relevant range of conceptions of human good seems to consist of conceptions a part of the "overlapping consensus". As Rawls elaborates:

> [I]n such a consensus each of the comprehensive philosophical, religious, and moral doctrines accepts justice as fairness in its own way; that is, each comprehensive doctrine, from within its own point of view, is led to accept the public reasons of justice specified by justice as fairness. We might say that they recognize its concepts, principles, and virtues as theorems, as it were, at which their several views coincide. . . . [I]n general, these concepts, principles, and virtues are accepted by each as belonging to a more comprehensive philosophical, religious, or moral doctrine.[46]

Thus understood, Rawls' theory is a *modus vivendi*. Rejecting "views . . . that regard the acceptance of the principles of justice as a prudent *modus vivendi* given the existing balance of social forces",[47] Rawls insists that his theory is not "simply" or "merely" a *modus vivendi*:

> [J]ustice as fairness is a moral conception: it has conceptions of persons and society, and concepts of right and fairness, as well as principles of justice with their complement of the virtues through which those principles are embodied in human character . . . This conception of justice . . . is no less a moral conception because it is restricted to the basic structure of society . . . Thus, in an overlapping consensus (as understood here), the conception of justice is not regarded merely as a *modus vivendi*.[48]

For the naturalist, the prudential/moral distinction is problematic, as I explained in chapter 1.[49] In any event, the fact that Rawls' theory (thus understood) is "moral" as distinct from "prudential" in character does not make it any the less a *modus vivendi* "among people having different ultimate commitments . . . among persons having constitutive views of the good life which are shared with some but different from those of many others."[50]

Perhaps, then, Rawls' theory of justice is *not* of the Right-prior-to-

Good sort but, instead, of the Good-prior-to-Right sort. After all, Rawls now allows that for anyone who adheres to any of the philosophical, religious, or moral doctrines—in effect, to any of the conceptions of human good—that together constitute what Rawls calls the "overlapping consensus", her acceptance of Rawls' principles of justice depends on (is "supported by") the particular doctrine or conception of human good to which she adheres. In that sense, her conception of human good plays a determinative role in her acceptance of the principles of justice, according to what Rawls now seems to say. It is not surprising, then, that Richard Rorty has revised his earlier characterization of Rawls as a Kantian and now sees him as more Deweyan than Kantian.[51]

However, to conclude that Rawls' theory is of the Good-prior-to-Right sort has implications that Rorty, in his recent discussion of Rawls, seems not to understand. Such a theory implicitly concedes that, contrary to what Rorty maintains, there *is* a need for "a religious or philosophical preface to politics",[52] that "democratic politics" can *not* be given justificatory "priority over religion and philosophy".[53] As I suggest in the second half of this chapter, a tolerant, democratic politics finds its sole and deep support in the "religion and philosophy"—in the basic normative commitments—of many of the moral communities that together constitute the pluralistic American political community. The various philosophical, religious, and moral doctrines—in effect, the various conceptions of human good—that constitute Rawls' "overlapping consensus" have priority over democratic politics. As Rawls now seems to understand, that consensus supplies the only available justificatory basis for principles of justice. Happily, in America the overlapping consensus happens to support and nourish, rather than subvert, democratic politics.

In any event, in the preceding chapter I criticized Rawls' theory understood as a contractualist theory of the Right-prior-to-Good sort. If, instead, Rawls' theory is of the Good-prior-to-Right sort, then what I'm about to say about such theory—contractualism according to the second interpretation—is applicable to Rawls' theory.

On the first interpretation, the contractualist account of the subject matter of morality is deeply problematic in that it relies on a flawed conception of the person. On the second interpretation, the contractualist account is not a genuine alternative to the naturalist account but merely an aspect of it. For the naturalist, moral knowledge is knowledge of how to live so as to flourish. Such knowledge *includes* knowledge of whatever rules for the general regulation of behavior a person ought to obey, in the sense that she cannot reasonably reject them as a basis for informed, unforced general agreement, given, first, the subjective circumstances of justice and, second, her conception of human good (or, more broadly, a range of conceptions that includes her own). After all, an aspect of trying to flourish, for those who inhabit the subjective circumstances, is trying to locate mutually acceptable bases of accommodation with those with whom we find ourselves in fundamental moral disagreement. Thus, the contractualist response to the first foundational question—the question of subject matter—is either (on the first interpretation, in which the Right is prior to the Good) deeply problematic or (on the second, in which the Good is prior to the Right) merely an aspect of the naturalist response.

How does contractualism respond to the second foundational question? Scanlon doesn't have much to say, that I can see, about contractualism's response to the epistemological question. He writes that "contractualism . . . can be understood as an informal description of the subject matter of morality on the basis of which ordinary forms of moral reasoning can be understood and appraised . . ."[54] The force of that comment obviously depends on what Scanlon counts as "ordinary" forms of moral reasoning. Early in his essay, Scanlon analogized moral reasoning to reasoning in mathematics: "[I]n both morality and mathematics it seems to be possible to discover the truth simply by thinking or reasoning about it. Experience and observation may be helpful, but observation in the normal sense is not the standard means of discovery in either subject."[55]

Scanlon's questionable analogy is asserted rather than defended. In the naturalist tradition in moral philosophy, from Aristotle to the present, experience is the root of moral knowledge. I discussed the crucial role of experience—whether one's own experience or the experience of one's community/tradition—in chapter 2. Contemporary philosophers such as Owen Flanagan,[56] Virginia Held,[57] and many others[58] have understood that, as Robin Lovin puts it, "moral reality . . . [is] about an interaction between persons and the world which can only be known from the reports of those who experience that interaction."[59] (Indeed, Held has explicitly taken a position directly contrary to Scanlon's, arguing that ethics should *not* "be thought of as analogous to . . . mathematics."[60])

How does contractualism respond to the third foundational question, the question of motivation? "According to contractualism," writes Scanlon, "the source of motivation that is directly triggered by the belief that an action is wrong is the desire to be able to justify one's actions to others on grounds they could not reasonably reject. I find this an extremely plausible account of moral motivation . . . and it seems to me to constitute a strong point for the contractualist view."[61] By contrast, according to naturalism the fundamental source of moral motivation is a person's commitment to her well-being, to flourishing.

The naturalist account of motivation is much more plausible than the contractualist account. Given a person's commitment to her well-being, to flourishing, her *fundamental* desire is to do what she must do if she is to flourish, not to be able to justify her choices to others. Of course, one of the things a person will want to be able to do in the subjective circumstances of justice, in her effort to flourish, is justify certain of her choices to others in terms that, given a particular range of conceptions of human good, they cannot reasonably reject. Thus, the naturalist account of moral motivation subsumes the contractualist account. Naturalism accounts for moral motivation not only in situations in which the desire to justify one's choices is triggered, but also in situations in which there is no conceivable need for the sort of interpersonal justification (as distinct from intrapersonal: a person's justification to herself) Scanlon obviously has in mind. Even in such situations of choice one faces questions that, in terms of ordinary language, are "moral" in character: for example, whether to become a priest or, instead, to marry; whether to raise a (larger) family; what career path to follow—in sum, *what sort of person to be, what way of life to follow.* Even in such situations—indeed, *especially* in such situations—a person is moved, by her commitment to flourishing, to do the (or a) right thing and to avoid doing the wrong thing. Contractualism does not—not easily, at any rate—account for moral motivation in such situations.[62]

Scanlon concludes his essay with an expression of "hope that I have said enough to indicate [contractualism's] appeal as a philosophical theory of morality and as an account of moral motivation."[63] In my view, it seems quite clear that naturalism is a much more appealing theory of morality and account of moral motivation. Recall the three "questions which", according to Scanlon, "a philosophical account of the foundations of morality must answer."[64] As we've seen: (1) The contractualist response to the subject-matter question is, at best, merely an aspect of the naturalist response. (2) The contractualist response to the epistemological question, in contrast to the naturalist response, implausibly discounts the crucial role of experience in moral reasoning. (3) The contractualist response to the motivational question is implausibly narrow; moreover, the naturalist response to the motivational question subsumes the contractualist response.

We've considered the utilitarian and the contractarian responses to the predicament of the policymaker (and of the citizen-judge). I now want to sketch an alternative and, in my view, much more satisfying response.

III

A fundamental aspect of the predicament of the policymaker concerns coercion. As I acknowledged at the conclusion of chapter 2, moral discourse sometimes runs out—for the time being, at least—before agreement is reached. When that happens, one alternative that remains is coercive legislation. (Another alternative, considered in the next chapter, is conscientious disobedience.) On the basis of what criterion or criteria—of what principle or principles—ought the legislator or other policymaking official to decide whether to use the law to coerce someone to do something she does not want to do or to refrain from doing something she wants to do?

Two misconceptions need dispelling. A naturalist moral theory is a cognitivist moral theory—a theory according to which moral claims have truth value, they bear the predicate true/false or some equivalent predicate, such as rationally acceptable/unacceptable, and thus are objects of knowledge. According to naturalism, then, there can be right answers (and wrong ones too) to moral questions. The first misconception is that *qua* cognitivist, naturalism entails or at least is conducive to intolerance (of moral beliefs thought false) and, attendantly, coercion. This position about naturalism—and, more generally, about any cognitivist moral theory—is both incorrect and misguided, as Hilary Putnam has explained:

> [C]ommitment to ethical objectivity [should not] be confused with what is a very different matter, commitment to ethical or moral authoritarianism. . . . [D]iehard opposition to all forms of political and moral authoritarianism should not commit one to . . . moral scepticism. The reason that it is wrong for the government to dictate a morality to the individual citizen is not that

there is no fact of the matter about what forms of life are fulfilling and what forms of life are not fulfilling, or morally wrong in some other way. (If there were no such thing as moral *wrong*, then it would not be wrong for the government to impose moral choices.) The fact that many people fear that if they concede any sort of moral objectivity out loud then they will find some government shoving *its* notion of objectivity down their throats is without question one of the reasons why so many people subscribe to a moral subjectivism to which they give no real assent.[65]

An aspect of the overall naturalist view I've elaborated in this book is the epistemologically relativist position (ER) presented in chapter 2. The second misconception is that this naturalism therefore entails tolerance of moral systems different from one's own and, attendantly, noncoercion. According to this misconception, an epistemological relativist cannot consistently hold that any moral system—any coherent set of moral beliefs—is false or, therefore, that any choice made in accordance with a moral system different from her own is wrong. This position is confused. ER does not entail that no moral system is false— that with respect to truth/falsity, one moral system is as good as another. Rather, ER holds merely that any belief about the truth/falsity of a moral system is "relative to" a web of beliefs—as indeed any belief about the truth/falsity of *anything* is relative to a web of beliefs. There is no inconsistency in adhering to ER and, at the same time, insisting that a particular moral system—or a particular moral belief, including one coherently nested in a moral system—is false, just as there is no inconsistency in adhering to ER and insisting that the position of the members of the Flat Earth Society is false.[66] As Richard Rorty has written, "[T]here is a difference between saying that every community is as good as every other and saying that we have to work out from the networks we are, from the communities with which we presently identify. . . . The view that every tradition is as rational or as moral as every other could be held only by a god, someone who had no need to use (but only to mention) the terms 'rational' or 'moral,' because she had no need to inquire or deliberate. Such a being would have escaped from history and conversation into contemplation and metanarrative."[67]

The naturalist conception of moral knowledge does not entail intolerance/coercion. Nor, however, does epistemological relativism entail tolerance/noncoercion. Let's return, then, to the problem of coercive legislation. Few, if any, persons seriously contend that it is *never* legitimate to use the law to coerce someone to make a choice she does not want to make (whether to do something she does not want to do or to refrain from doing something she wants to do). Similarly, no one contends that it is *always* legitimate to use the law coercively. Putting aside the silly extremes of radical tolerance and radical intolerance, the serious question is: When—under what conditions—is it legitimate to pursue a strategy of legislative coercion? What criteria or principles determine the legitimacy of such a strategy?

a

Consider John Stuart Mill's "one very simple principle", which, argued Mill, is

> entitled to govern absolutely the dealings of society with the individual in the way of compulsion and control, whether the means used be physical force in the form of legal penalties or the moral coercion of public opinion. That principle is that the sole end for which mankind are warranted, individually or collectively, in interfering with the liberty of action of any of their number is self-protection. That the only purpose for which power can rightfully be exercised over any member of a civilized community, against his will, is to prevent harm to others. His own good, either physical or moral, is not a sufficient warrant. He cannot rightfully be compelled to do or forbear because it will be better for him to do so, because it will make him happier, because, in the opinions of others, to do so would be wise or even right. These are good reasons for remonstrating with him, or reasoning with him, or persuading him, or entreating him, but not for compelling him or visiting him with any evil in case he do otherwise. To justify that, the conduct from which it is desired to deter him must be calculated to produce evil to someone else. The only part of the conduct of anyone for which he is amenable to society is that which concerns others. In the part which merely concerns himself, his independence is, of right, absolute. Over himself, over his own body and mind, the individual is sovereign.[68]

Mill's principle is a partial response to the problem of coercive legislation, although it is more than that. The principle governs use of "the moral coercion of public opinion" as well as use of legislative coercion. The response is partial in this sense: To say that "the only purpose for which power can rightfully be exercised over any member of a civilized community, against his will, is to prevent harm to others" is *not* to say that power exercised for that purpose is necessarily rightfully exercised.

Mill's condition purports to be necessary, not sufficient. Mill's principle does not purport to distinguish the occasions when power exercised for the requisite purpose is rightfully exercised from those when it is wrongly—illegitimately—exercised.

Does Mill's principle presuppose a distinction between self-regarding acts and other-regarding acts? Mill's principal contemporary critic, James Fitzjames Stephen, thought so, and he thought the principle problematic for that reason, among others: "[T]he distinction upon which . . . [the principle] depends . . . assumes that some acts regard the agent only, and that some regard other people. In fact, by far the most important part of our conduct regards both ourselves and others . . ."[69] However, Mill seemed to understand that any act might have other-regarding aspects as well as self-regarding ones (though some acts, Mill insisted, were only "indirectly" or "contingently" other-regarding). These passages are illustrative:

> [T]here is a sphere of action in which society, as distinguished from the individual, has, if any, only an indirect interest: comprehending all that portion of a person's life and conduct which affects only himself or, if it also affects others, only with their free, voluntary, and undeceived consent and participation. When I say only himself, I mean directly, and in the first instance; for whatever affects himself may affect others through himself . . .[70]

> [W]ith regard to the merely contingent, or, as it may be called, constructive injury which a person causes to society by conduct which neither violates any specific duty to the public, nor occasions perceptible hurt to any assignable individual except himself, the inconvenience is one which society can afford to bear, for the sake of the greater good of human freedom.[71]

In any event, whatever Mill might have thought, the Millian principle does not presuppose a distinction between acts that are solely self-regarding and acts that are, in whole or in part, other-regarding. As one commentator has put it:

> It is not essential to Mill's position that there should be an area of conduct which must always remain completely free from intervention. The absoluteness of Mill's barrier against intervention, or the "theoretical limit" he sets to the power of the state and society to exercise coercion, is of a different kind. There are certain reasons for intervention in the conduct of individuals which must always be ruled out as irrelevant. Even when intervention is justified in a particular case it is on the basis of certain reasons rather than others.[72]

It is a good thing for Mill's principle that it does not presuppose a distiction between solely self-regarding acts and other acts, for virtually no nontrivial choice is solely self-regarding. Virtually anything anyone chooses to do or not to do has a positive or negative effect on some interest or interests of some other person or persons. For example, if I choose to go to a movie, then I am, to that extent, unavailable to minister to the needs of the poor.

Given that virtually any choice a person makes has an other-regarding aspect, virtually no choice is immune to coercion under Mill's principle. Mill's critic Stephen wrote that "[t]o force an unwilling person to contribute to the support of the British Museum is as distinct a violation of Mr. Mill's principle as religious persecution."[73] Stephen's argument was that such a tax could not fairly be described as for the purpose of self-protection or prevention of harm to persons other than those coerced. However, whether forcing a person to contribute to the British Museum is a violation of Mill's principle depends on whether the person has a duty to contribute. After all, as Mill emphasized, the violation of an other-regarding duty is not a solely self-regarding act: "There are . . . many positive acts for the benefit of others which he may rightfully be compelled to perform . . . things which whenever it is obviously a man's duty to do he may rightfully be made responsible to society for not doing. A person may cause evil to others not only by his actions but by his inaction, and in either case he is justly accountable to them for the injury."[74] A crucial question, obviously, but one Mill's principle does not help us answer and, indeed, was not designed to answer, is: In what ways, and to what extent, ought one to attend to the interests (which interests?) of others (which others?)?

We're considering the problem of coercive legislation: When—under what conditions—may the legislator use the law to coerce someone to make a choice she does not want to make? Mill's principle does not get us very far in grappling with that problem. Although Mill's principle is, again, a partial response, as a practical, real-world matter, the principle is very weak and thus largely insignificant. It is not a violation of the principle to use the law to coerce someone to make a choice she does not want to make so long as the reason for the coercion is nonpaternalistic—in particular, so long as the aim is to compel her to abide a moral duty she is believed to have. My aim here is not to discuss paternalism or to evaluate the strength *vel non* of Mill's case against it. Even if we assume *arguendo* that Mill's antipaternalistic principle is persuasively grounded, it is nonetheless true that as a limitation on legislative coercion the principle is trivial. Little, if any, such coercion is solely paternalistic. For example, laws forbidding the use of heroin or requiring the use of motorcycle helmets are certainly not solely paternalistic—or even primarily paternalistic. (This is not to say that such laws are primarily nonpaternalistic either, although I can well imagine legislators voting for them for primarily nonpaternalistic reasons.)

Let's put aside Mill's principle, then, and try to locate more significant criteria or principles for determining the legitimacy of particular instances of legislative coercion. Given that virtually any coercive legislation is nonpaternalistic (even if also, in part, paternalistic), we should be wary of putting much weight on criteria, like Mill's principle, aimed solely at paternalism.

b

In addressing the issue of "the enforcement of morals" by means of legislative coercion, Lord Patrick Devlin "framed three interrogatories . . . to answer:"

1. Has society the right to pass judgement at all on matters of morals? Ought there, in other words, to be a public morality, or are morals always a matter for private judgement?
2. If society has the right to pass judgement, has it also the right to use the weapon of the law to enforce it?
3. If so, ought it to use that weapon in all cases or only in some; and if only in some, on what principles should it distinguish?[75]

Devlin's first two questions can be collapsed into one: May legislators, on behalf of the political community they represent, make moral judgments and embody them in law? That's an easy question. How could legislators possibly avoid making moral judgments and embodying them in law? To enact a law—any law—is to make a moral judgment, a judgment about how some matter ought to be dealt with, about how it is good or right or just to deal with some matter, and then to embody that judgment in law. Consider this variation on the question: May legislators ever use the law coercively? That's an easy question too. To enact a homicide statute is to use the law coercively. The serious question is the third one, or the second half of it, which is *pro tanto* the question: What criteria/principles determine the legitimacy of pursuing a coercive legislative strategy?

Devlin was skeptical about the existence of a master principle for separating legitimate from illegitimate exercises of legislative coercion. Given my distaste for master political principles, which I explained in chapter 2 (in discussing "the priority of the particular"), I find Devlin's skepticism congenial. The absence of a master principle, however, as Devlin wrote,

> does not mean that it is impossible to put forward any general statements about how in our society [which in Lord Devlin's case was British society] the balance ought to be struck. Such statements cannot of their nature be rigid or precise; they would not be designed to circumscribe the operation of the lawmaking power but to guide those who have to apply it. . . . [I]t is possible to make general statements of principle which it may be thought the legislature should bear in mind when it is considering the enactment of laws enforcing morals. . . . This then is how I believe my third interrogatory should be answered—not by the formulation of hard and fast rules, but by a judgement in each case taking into account the sort of factors I have been mentioning.[76]

What "sort of factors" did Devlin mention? "[T]he chief of these elastic principles", wrote Devlin, is that "[t]here must be toleration of the maximum individual freedom that is consistent with the integrity of society. . . . Nothing should be punished by the law that does not lie beyond the limits of tolerance. It is not nearly enough to say that a majority dislikes a practice; there must be a real feeling of reprobation."[77] How helpful is this admonition? "Beyond the limits of tolerance" of *which* moral community (or communities) among the many that together constitute the pluralistic society? Homosexuality obviously does not lie beyond the limits of tolerance of the gay community. In the absence of a monistic moral culture, the standards or sensibilities of *which* moral community(ies) should be determinative? Devlin asked, "How are the moral judgements of society to be ascertained?" A prior question is whether and to what extent there is such a thing as "the moral judgements of society" as distinct from the judgments of particular moral communities within the pluralistic society. Ronald Dworkin too has written of "the community's morality", meaning the morality of the political community.[78] But if the political community is, like our own, highly pluralistic, then we must speak not of the political community's morality but of its *moralities*. In our morally pluralistic context, I don't know what rendering to give a notion like "the moral judgements of society" except something like this: "the moral judgments common to the politically dominant moral communities within the society".

The heart of Devlin's advice, then, is that "nothing should be punished by the law that does not lie beyond the limits of tolerance" of the politically dominant coalition. Unfortunately, that advice is not helpful. First: How likely is it that many practices will be punished that do not lie beyond the limits of the politically dominant coalition's tolerance? Second: In any event, we're looking for criteria/principles for determining what *ought* to be tolerated, whatever at the present time happens to be tolerated—criteria/principles that, *inter alia*, can be used to test, measure, challenge the present limits of tolerance.

C

I shall now sketch some general criteria for guidance of the legislative decision whether, in dealing with a perceived problem, to pursue a coercive strategy.[79] Of course, whether to pursue a coercive legislative strategy is a moral question, and any list of criteria for answering that question is rooted in a set of moral beliefs. The criteria I'm about to sketch presuppose—indeed, express—a set of normative commitments, to be sure. But the presupposed commitments are, I think, fairly standard ones—beliefs/commitments common to many moral communities in American society, and certainly to the politically dominant or "mainline" ones.

I begin with the principal consideration supporting (weighing in favor of) a strategy of legislative coercion and then turn to several considerations opposing (weighing against) such a strategy. The principal consideration supporting a coercive legislative strategy is the fact, if it is a fact, that the strategy is an important means of protecting a fundamental interest or interests: interests the satisfaction of which significantly enhances one's level of well-being and the frustration of which significantly diminishes it. This consideration has special force if the coercive strategy is an important means of protecting one or more of the fundamental interests of human beings themselves relatively incapable of protecting those interests, and if those considering the strategy are committed to protecting the weak among them—the "least of my brethren".[80] The protection of fundamental interests is, after all, a

principal aspect of the *raison d'etre* of government. (". . . Thomas
Aquinas, a natural lawyer if ever these was one, . . . argues that the law
should not seek to prohibit all vices, but only the more serious ones, and
'especially those which involve harm to others, without whose prohibi-
tion human society could not be preserved. . . .' "[81])

Relatedly, a coercive strategy is supported by the fact that the strategy is an important means of protecting basic social institutions—the
courts, for example—institutions whose effective functioning is itself
crucial to the satisfaction of fundamental interests.[82]

Inevitably, of course, there are disagreements as to which interests
are fundamental. And there are disagreements, too, as to when an entity
(for example, a slave or an unborn child) is a member—or to what
extent a member—of the human community. (An instance of this disagreement looms very large in the abortion controversy.) In a highly
pluralistic society like our own, however, the views of no single moral
community can be determinative, and thus the chance that truly idiosyncratic views might prevail is diminished.

Several general considerations militate against pursuing a strategy of
legislative coercion. I shall take them up in no particular order. One of
the more obvious such considerations is the fact that human judgment,
including legislative judgment, is fallible. There is always the possibility that the moral judgment in the service of which the coercive
strategy is being proposed is wrong. This consideration has special
force in the case of paternalism. What John Stuart Mill wrote seems
correct as a *general* matter:

> [W]ith respect to his own feelings and circumstances the most ordinary man
> or woman has means of knowledge immeasurably surpassing those that can
> be possessed by anyone else. The interference of society to overrule his
> judgement and purposes in what only regards himself must be grounded on
> general presumptions which may be altogether wrong and, even if right, are
> as likely as not to be misapplied to individual cases, by persons no better
> acquainted with the circumstances of such cases than those are who look at
> them merely from without.[83]

The consideration of human fallibility must not be discounted. History
is replete with examples of erroneous judgments that a lifestyle unlike
the evaluator's own in some or many respects was not merely different
but (morally) wrong. An antidote to the regrettable tendency to issue
such judgments too quickly is the realization that the moderate anthro-

pologically relativist position (AR2) discussed in the preceding chapter is sound.[84] Recall Hilary Putnam's comment that Aristotle "seemed to think that ideally there was some sort of constitution that every one ought to have; that in an ideal world . . . everyone would be a philosopher. We agree with Aristotle that different ideas of human flourishing are appropriate for individuals with different constitutions, but we go further and believe that even in the ideal world there would be different constitutions, that diversity is part of the ideal."[85]

A second consideration militating against pursuing a coercive legislative strategy, related to the fallibility consideration—indeed, perhaps simply a variation on the fallibility consideration and not distinguishable from it—is the importance of not frustrating a basic interest sketched in chapter 1: the interest in the capacity for self-critical rationality and in the conditions, social and political, for its exercise.[86] We must be wary about interfering with new or unusual ways of life. Such ways of life can test our beliefs about what ways of life are good for human beings and, moreover, fuel our efforts to imagine better ways of life. "Certainly . . . 'self-knowledge' . . .—knowledge of one's wants, needs, motives, of what kind of life one would find acceptable and satisfying—is something agents are very unlikely to attain in a society without extensive room for free discussion and the unrestrained play of the imagination with alternative ways of living. . . . [Self-knowledge requires] knowledge of . . . [one's] own human possibilities and . . . [the ability to] see . . . [one's] form of life against a background of envisaged alternatives."[87]

A third consideration is simple self-interest. A strong tradition or spirit of tolerance—that is, a strong presumption against legislative coercion—will protect us in the event the winds change. We may be members of the politically dominant coalition today, but there is no guarantee we will be tomorrow. As Governor Cuomo put it in addressing a group of fellow Catholics at Notre Dame:

> [Catholic public officials don't always] love what others do with their freedom, but . . . they realize that in guaranteeing freedom for all, they guarantee our right to be Catholics . . .
>
> The Catholic public official lives the political truth which most Catholics through most of American history have accepted and insisted on: the truth that to assure our freedom we must allow others the same freedom, even if it occasionally produces conduct by them which we would hold to be sinful.
>
> I protect my right to be a Catholic by preserving your right to believe as a

Jew, a Protestant or non-believer, or as anything else you choose. We know that the price of seeking to force our beliefs on others is that they might some day force theirs on us. This freedom is the fundamental strength of our unique experiment in government. In the complex interplay of forces and considerations that go into the making of our laws and policies, its preservation must be a pervasive and dominant concern.[88]

A fourth consideration is compassion. To coerce someone to make a choice she does not want to make is to cause her to suffer.[89] If we are compassionate, we will be wary about imposing that suffering on another. A fifth consideration is the friendship or fellowship that nourishes community. For the politically dominant coalition to coerce a member of the political community to make a choice she does not want to make is to provoke resentment in her. If we value friendship/fellowship and the sort of community it makes posssible, we will be wary about provoking such resentment, which is corrosive of community.[90]

Consider what we might call extreme coercion: coercing someone to refrain from doing something she not merely wants to do, but believes essential to her well-being, even obligatory, that she do; or coercing someone to do something she not merely does not want to do, but believes destructive of her well-being to do, even forbidden for her to do. Extreme coercion causes extreme suffering. And extreme resentment. It can engender alienation from community, lack of respect for "authority" and the law, political instability, and the reactive repression that often attends political instability. Commenting on Aquinas' view of the relationship between religion and law, Mulford Sibley has written: "Human beings vary widely in their social and moral development. To make impossible demands on many of them might provoke rebellion and civil war—consummations far worse in their consequences for humanity, perhaps, than those which result from not embodying every moral offense in human law. St. Thomas is constantly emphasizing contingencies in human life, and awareness of them tends to modify what might otherwise be inflexible and absolutist principles."[91] John Noonan has said that "[t]he central problem of the legal enterprise is the relation of love to power."[92] If we are compassionate, and if we value community, we will be especially wary about relying on extreme coercion: The costs—extreme suffering and extreme resentment—are great and sometimes terrible.

Extreme coercion entails another cost as well, and a sixth consideration, militating against reliance on extreme coercion, concerns this cost.
To coerce someone to refrain from doing something she believes herself
obligated to do, or to do something she believes herself forbidden to do,
is to ask her to act contrary to her conscience. A moral community that
values individual conscientiousness or personal integrity—that believes
that ultimately, after careful, informed deliberation, a person should
choose on the basis of conscience—will be wary, therefore, about
pursuing a legislative strategy of extreme coercion. In an essay elaborating "A Catholic Perspective on Morality and the Law," Joseph Boyle
has written that the Catholic

> conception of morality . . . is based on the assumption that human beings
> have choices to make, and that it is by making the choices which they believe
> to be the correct ones that they become good persons. Moral norms in this
> conception of morality are acknowledged guidelines for choices. These
> norms are known within the human conscience, and human dignity lies in
> choosing to act in accord with these norms. [In a footnote at this point, Boyle
> writes: "This formulation is based on Vatical Council II, *Pastoral Constitu-
> tion on The Church in the Modern World (Gaudium et Spes)*, paragraph 16."]
> Thus, what is morally central is making the correct choices in the light of
> personally acknowledged moral standards. . . . [The] legal imposition of
> moral prohibitions can have effects contrary to the moral goal of making
> choices that conform to one's conscience. For, it might be the case that what
> one person or group regards as morally prohibited is regarded by others as
> morally required. The legal enforcement of the moral views of some thus
> becomes a significant temptation for others not to act in accord with their
> consciences. Those who regard morality as choosing to conform to con-
> science can hardly regard this to be acceptable.[93]

This concern that coercive legislation not subvert individual conscientiousness partly underlies the statement of John Courtney Murray, the
American Jesuit theologian, that "the moral aspirations of the law are
minimal. Law seeks to establish and maintain only that minimum of
actualized morality that is necessary for the healthy functioning of the
social order. It does not look to what is morally desirable, or attempt to
remove every moral taint from the atmosphere of society. It enforces
only what is minimally acceptable, and in this sense socially
necessary."[94]

These six considerations militating against pursuit of coercive legislative strategies—fallibility, self-critical rationality, self-interest, com-

passion, community, and conscience—are not exhaustive, but they are, I think, the principal ones.[95] (Others that have been mentioned include not enacting "laws which are difficult to enforce and whose enforcement tends, therefore, to be patchy and inequitable", "laws which are likely to . . . produce . . . evils such as blackmail", or laws "punishing people for what they very largely cannot help."[96]) Note that none of the six considerations, nor the single basic consideration supporting a strategy of legislative coercion, is aimed solely at paternalistic proposals or at nonpaternalistic ones. Each consideration provides guidance whether or not the strategy in question is paternalistic, nonpaternalistic, or both. (Again, a coercive legislative strategy is rarely, if ever, solely paternalistic in inspiration.)

Both individually and, especially, cumulatively, the six considerations set forth above call for a strong reluctance to rely on coercive legislative strategies and, so, for a tolerant legislative agenda.[97] They are, in that sense, "liberal" considerations; they inform a sensible, discriminating wariness about—even a presumption against—the use of coercive state power.

However, the approach I've advanced here is certainly *not* "liberal" in a different sense of the term, the sense at issue in chapter 3. My approach does not purport to be "neutral" or "impartial" among competing conceptions of human good. To the contrary, my approach recognizes that any list of considerations governing the use of political power, including coercive power, is rooted in a set of moral beliefs about human good, a system of normative commitments. No such list is "neutral" or "impartial" (or "liberal" in that sense). Any such list presupposes a conception or range of conceptions of human good, a vision or range of visions of human interests. Liberalism-as-tolerance is an admirable ideal.[98] Liberalism-as-neutrality is a phantom, a will o' the wisp.

Governor Cuomo asked about the relation of his Catholicism to his politics: "Where does the one end and the other begin? Are the two divided at all? If they are not, should they be?"[99] As the foregoing discussion suggests, the answer to Cuomo's inquiry—the correct response to the predicament of the policymaker—is that the legislator's (and the citizen's) moral beliefs, including her religious beliefs about human good, are ultimately determinative of her politics. Thus, what John Courtney Murray said about the relation of a Catholic's faith to her politics is true of the relation of any system of moral/religious beliefs to politics. For a Catholic, wrote Murray, the principles of Catholic faith and morality stand superior to, and in control of, the whole order of civil life. The question is sometimes raised [as it was during the presidential campaign of John F. Kennedy], whether Catholicism is compatible with American democracy. The question is invalid as well as impertinent; for the manner of its position inverts the order of values. It must, of course, be turned round to read, whether American democracy is compatible with Catholicism. [100]

(Murray went on to write that "[a]n affirmative answer to [the question], given under something better than the curbstone definition of 'democracy,' is one of the truths I hold."[101]) How could the relationship of a person's religious/moral beliefs to her politics possibly be different, given that a person's very identity—her "self"—is constituted in part by her moral/religious convictions?[102] For the *particular* person that one is to make a political judgment is for her to bring to bear on the question at issue her basic beliefs, including her moral/religious beliefs. As I explained in chapter 3, to bracket those beliefs is to bracket one's self.

Contrary to what Rorty has recently argued (and to what Rorty has imagined Rawls to be arguing),[103] then, it is not "democracy" that has priority over "philosophy", but philosophy—in the sense of a person's conception of human good—that has priority over politics. Those of us who, like Rorty and Rawls and Murray, are committed to a tolerant, democratic politics can hope that our fellow citizens' conceptions of human good support and nourish, rather than subvert, such a politics. [104] (In the United States that hope is, by and large, fulfilled, albeit imperfectly. [105])

Those of us who believe that conceptions of human good—including conceptions tending to subvert a tolerant, democratic politics—can *sometimes* be transformed to *some* extent through discourse, can do more than hope: We can talk. Those of us who believe that such talk— moral discourse—is a real possibility even in a highly pluralistic society like our own can try to create a politics focused, in part, on questions of human good—a deliberative, transformative politics (as distinct from a politics that is merely manipulative and self-serving)—a politics in which questions of human good, of what way or ways of life human good consists in, are not marginalized or privatized but, instead, have a central, public place. Not only does "philosophy" have priority over "democracy": Without philosophy, in the sense of ecumenical public discussion about human good, democratic politics would be quite vacuous.

There is more I want to say about the enterprise of politics in a morally pluralistic society like our own. In particular I want to elaborate on the notion of a "deliberative, transformative politics". However, what more I have to say is better said not here, but in chapter 6, in the context of a discussion of the nature and limits of constitutional adjudication, which, at its best, is a model of deliberative, transformative politics.

First, however, I shall address a different matter. The issues I've discussed in this chapter arise for persons as creators or sovereigns of law. In the next chapter I turn to a complementary inquiry, one that arises for persons as creatures or subjects of law.

5

Breaking Law: The Problem of Conscientious Disobedience

> I want to make a special appeal to soldiers, national guardsmen and policemen: Brothers, each one of you is one of us. We are the same people. The campesinos you kill are your own brothers and sisters. . . . When you hear the words of a man telling you to kill, remember instead the word of God, "Thou shalt not kill." God's law must prevail. No soldier is obliged to obey an order contrary to the law of God. It is time for you to come to your senses and obey your consciences rather than follow out a sinful command.[1]

As I've remarked, in politics, and therefore in law, moral discourse often runs out—for the time being, at least—before agreement is reached, before consensus is achieved, especially in a society as morally pluralistic as our own. Problems then arise both for those charged with making law and for those asked to obey it. In the preceding chapter I considered a problem that arises for persons as creators or sovereigns of law. That is, I considered an alternative that remains for lawmakers when the discourse runs out: coercion. In this chapter I consider a problem that arises for—an alternative that remains for—persons as creatures or subjects of law: disobeying the law, which includes, but is broader than, resisting coercive law. Thus, the inquiry of this chapter complements the inquiry of the preceding one.[2]

I

Is disobeying the law ever morally acceptable? Is there a moral obligation to obey the law? What does it mean to say that there is such an obligation?

In the preceding chapter I addressed the question: On what beliefs ought a policymaker to rely in deciding whether to use the law to coerce a person to make a choice the person believes to be, for her, the wrong choice? This question arises because although a policymaker is inevitably a member of some moral community, in the United States she is also a member of, and indeed represents, a morally pluralistic political community. A citizen, too, is a member both of some moral community and of a morally pluralistic political community. The question arises, therefore: On what moral beliefs ought a citizen (or other person) to rely in deciding whether, as a matter of "conscience", to disobey a law? In particular, on what moral beliefs ought she to rely in evaluating claims regarding her obligation to obey the law?

Any citizen's evaluation of such claims is, because it must be, rooted in her own, partisan moral beliefs. Recall my comments near the end of the preceding chapter—comments that are fully applicable here—about the relationship between a person's moral/religious beliefs and her politics.[3] The evaluation I'm about to offer (of various claims regarding the matter of obligation to obey the law), therefore, is not "neutral" or "impartial" (or "liberal" in that sense). My evaluation presupposes several partisan normative commitments. The presupposed commitments are hardly idiosyncratic, however; to the contrary, they are fairly standard commitments, representing moral beliefs common to many moral and religious communities in American society, including the politically dominant ones.[4]

Here are eight claims—moral claims—regarding the matter of obligation to obey the law:

1. One ought always (i.e., in every realistically imaginable situation) to obey all laws (i.e., every imaginable law). Put another way, one always has a conclusive reason to obey all laws.[5]
2. One ought always to obey some laws (i.e., at least one imaginable law).
3. One always has a (nonconclusive) reason to obey all laws. (To say one has a reason to obey is not to say that one ought to obey; it is to say merely that one ought to obey unless one has a better reason or reasons not to obey.)
4. One always has a reason to obey some laws.
5. One ought sometimes (i.e., in at least one imaginable situation) to obey all laws.

6. One ought sometimes to obey some laws.
7. One sometimes has a reason to obey all laws.
8. One sometimes has a reason to obey some laws.

Now, my evaluation of these various claims.

Claim 1: Given normative commitments standard in American society, the belief that one ought in every imaginable situation to obey every imaginable law is obviously untenable—especially in this post-Holocaust age.

Claim 2: The belief that one ought in every imaginable situation to obey at least one imaginable law is acceptable only for one who believes that there is at least one determinate rule of conduct—for example, "Do not intentionally kill an innocent person"—that one ought always to obey, that one ought never, under any circumstances, no matter what the consequences, to disobey. For such a person, one ought in every imaginable situation to obey a law embodying such a rule. I've argued elsewhere that there is no such "absolute" or unconditional rule of conduct.[6] If I'm right, then there is no law one ought in every imaginable situation to obey.[7]

Claim 3: I return to this claim below.

Claim 4: The belief that in every imaginable situation one has a reason to obey at least one imaginable law is correct. Which law? Any law the violation of which in every imaginable situation contravenes any of one's normative commitments. (Of course, one might have a reason to disobey the law—if obeying the law in a particular situation contravenes any of one's normative commitments.) For example, anyone committed not to intentionally kill an innocent person has a reason in every imaginable situation to obey a law forbidding the intentional killing of an innocent person.

Claim 5: The belief that one ought in at least one imaginable situation to obey every imaginable law is unacceptable. I can't imagine any situation—other than science fiction ones, perhaps—in which (given standard normative commitments) one ought to obey a law requiring, for example, the killing of all Jews.

Claim 6: The belief that one ought in at least one imaginable situation to obey at least one imaginable law is correct. Which law? Any law the violation of which in a particular situation contravenes any of one's normative commitments, and the obedience of which in that situation either does not contravene any of one's normative commitments or contravenes a commitment less strong than the commitment that would be contravened were one to disobey the law.

Claim 7: The belief that in at least one imaginable situation one has a reason to obey every imaginable law is correct—for example, a situation in which any disobedient conduct will or might be detected and punished.[8]

Claim 8: If, as I've suggested, Claim 4 is correct, then a fortiori this claim is correct too. Further, if, as I've suggested, Claim 7 is correct, then a fortiori Claim 8 is correct too.

Claims 1–4 are the important ones for present purposes. If Claim 1 were correct, we could say that there is an absolute obligation to obey all laws. But, again, Claim 1 is untenable. There is no such obligation. In rejecting Claim 2, I've said that there is not even an absolute obligation to obey some laws. Because Claim 4 is correct, we can say that there is a presumptive obligation to obey some laws—that in *every* imaginable situation one has a reason to obey at least one imaginable law. But is there a presumptive obligation to obey every imaginable law? In other words, is Claim 3—that one always has a reason to obey all laws—correct? To say that Claim 3 is correct is to say that in every imaginable situation the violation of every imaginable law contravenes at least one of the standard normative commitments presupposed by this discussion. What are those commitments, and is it the case that in every imaginable situation the violation of every imaginable law contravenes at least one of those commitments?

One of the standard commitments in question is to "fairness" in the sense of not taking advantage of others in mutually beneficial, cooperative enterprises. Is it the case that in every imaginable situation the violation of every imaginable law contravenes our commitment to fairness? There seem to be some situations in which my obedience to some laws would benefit no one and my disobedience harm no one—for example, my making a U-turn on the street in front of my house at two in the morning. It is difficult to see how my U-turn contravenes our commitment to fairness (which is a presumptive commitment, of course, not an absolute one). As Kent Greenawalt has noted, "some violations of law need not involve either harm to or taking advantage of others. A person who breaks a thirty miles per hour speed limit at four in the morning or trespasses far from anyone's sight may believe that everyone's acting in the same way would be perfectly all right. He is indifferent to whether others forbear from such acts, since their forbearance would confer no benefit."[9] Furthermore, imagine a law forbidding black persons to use "whites only" public bathrooms. In what way does a black person's violation of the law contravene the norm of fairness? Thus, some imaginable *situations* and some imaginable *laws* seem to be counterexamples to the claim that in every imaginable situation the violation of every imaginable law contravenes our commitment to fairness.[10]

Another of our standard normative commitments is a variation on our commitment to promise keeping: doing what we have consented to do and not doing what we have consented not to do. Is it the case that in every imaginable situation the violation of every imaginable law contravenes that commitment? An affirmative answer is untenable. As John Mackie wrote: "An alleged contractual duty to obey the law is the basis of one of the main Socratic arguments [in support of an obligation to obey]. But . . . there is nothing in the lives of most ordinary citizens in a modern state that could constitute even a tacit or an implied agreement to obey."[11] David Lyons makes the same point. The argument from contract or consent "is incredible", he writes, "because few of us have ever been parties to such an agreement. . . . This argument does not work, because its conclusion rests on false premises."[12] As M. B. E. Smith has noted, "residence and use of the protection of the law do not constitute any usual kind of consent to a government nor any usual kind of promise to obey its laws."[13] A. John Simmons adds an "extremely important point about voting", which in any event not everyone does: "we should remember that voting is often a way not of consenting to something, but merely of *expressing a preference*."[14] Thus, it is not the case that in every imaginable situation the violation of every imaginable law contravenes our commitment (presumptively, not absolutely) to honor our consent.

Another standard normative commitment (presumptive, not absolute) is, if not to set a good example, at least to refrain from setting a bad example—to refrain from engaging in conduct that precipitates consequences damaging interests that merit protection. It is difficult to see how in every imaginable situation the violation of every imaginable law contravenes that commitment. As John Mackie, following Joseph Raz, argued:

> One attempt to derive an obligation to obey the law rests on the thesis that, in breaking the law, one is setting a bad example. Even if this particular viola-

tion would otherwise be justified, and even if the particular law violated is a
bad one, this example of lawbreaking would encourage others both to break
the law when this was not otherwise justified and to break good laws which,
by hypothesis, constitute the greater part of the particular legal system. Raz
argues that this attempt to derive a general obligation fails because in some
cases the example that is effectively set will, on balance, be that of breaking
laws where such violation is justified rather than where it is not. In any case,
many violations remain unknown or attract no attention and set no example at
all.[15]

The argument from bad consequences does not work, therefore, even in
the context where, as Mackie put it, "the legal system as a whole is
good",[16] much less in the context of a legal system that deserves to be
overthrown, not maintained. Legal systems that, given normative commitments standard in American society, deserve to be overthrown are
not merely imaginable. There have been, are now, and will regrettably
but undoubtedly continue to be such systems. In any event, it is not the
case that in every imaginable situation the violation of every imaginable
law contravenes the commitment to refrain from engaging in conduct
precipitating consequences damaging to interests meriting protection.

Is there a presumptive obligation to obey all laws at least in a truly
democratic society (in which every member has an opportunity to participate on an equal basis with every other member, freedom of expression is honored, etc.)? The arguments from fairness, consent, and bad
consequences, as we've seen, don't work in the context of *any* legal
system, including a truly democratic one. But is there some other argument that *does* work in the context of a democratic legal system? If there
is such an argument, I've not seen it.[17] Moreover, even if there is such
an argument, the fact remains that a truly democratic legal system is not
a feature of every imaginable situation, and thus no argument from
democracy can support the claim that in every imaginable situation one
has a reason to obey all laws—that there is a presumptive obligation to
obey all laws.

Is the mere fact that a law requires or forbids an act a reason for doing
or not doing the act—a reason in and of itself, without regard to further
reasons? That is, is illegality per se a reason for doing what the law
requires or not doing what it forbids? To answer affirmatively is to
claim that obedience to law is intrinsically and not merely instrumentally good. Surely on reflection no one would accept that claim, except
someone who fetishizes obedience to law.

[T]he mere *existence* of a rule does not by itself provide a reason why it should be complied with; it must be possible to point to *some* objection to non-compliance, other than simply that it is non-compliance, if we are not to regard rules themselves with a kind of idolatry. Whatever one may think of obedience as a virtue, it is scarcely to be supposed that obedience towards just anything and anybody, all other considerations apart, could be, even *prima facie*, a good thing.[18]

In addressing the question of a presumptive obligation to obey the law, Philip Soper has written that "the obligation in issue is an obligation to obey law in general—*just because it is the law*—not because of some independent argument for compliance applicable only to particular laws or in a particular context."[19] Soper's statement presents us with a false choice—namely, between the position that (1) there is a presumptive obligation to obey all laws because illegality per se is a reason for obeying the law and the position that (2) there is no presumptive obligation to obey all laws. The *real* choice is between the position that (1*) there is a presumptive obligation to obey all laws because one always has a reason (or reasons) *beyond the mere fact of illegality* for obeying all laws and the position that (2) there is no such reason, no presumptive obligation to obey all laws. No one defends position (1)— in effect the position that obedience to law is intrinsically good—not even Soper. Soper's argument, rather, is at most a variation on position (1*). According to Soper, the reason (beyond the mere fact of illegality) for obeying all laws is that disobedience constitutes a denial of the respect owed to those who are in good faith conducting the legal system. The heart of Soper's argument is that "[c]oercive government is necessary for human beings, so those who try to govern in the interests of their subjects are not committing a moral wrong against them. Subjects should respect the good faith efforts of those with authority and a crucial way to show this respect is by obeying their directions. Subjects have a prima facie [i.e., presumptive] obligation to obey the law because those with authority care about whether the law is obeyed and they deserve respect."[20]

Actually, Soper's argument is only *apparently* a variation on position (1*). On closer inspection Soper's argument turns out to support not the position that one always has a reason to obey *all* laws but the weaker position that one always has a reason to obey some laws—that there is a presumptive obligation to obey *some* laws, namely, laws that satisfy certain conditions: "Two conditions, I have argued, are sufficient to provide a moral reason to obey a coercive directive. First, the directive must be part of a supremely effective coercive system, thus providing the security that makes legal systems preferable to no law at all. Second, the directives must be defended by those who accept and enforce them as 'just': in the interests of all, including the citizen whose obedience is in question."[21] Soper's argument only appears to support the stronger position that there is a presumptive obligation to obey all laws because, in the relevant passages, he defines "law" restrictively:[22] According to Soper, a "coercive directive" is not "law" unless it satisfies the two conditions set forth in the passage just quoted. Soper's inquiry is not whether law obligates but what law must be—what criteria it must satisfy—if it is to obligate. Under the ordinary-language, positivist understanding of "law" that underlies our discussion in this chapter, Soper's claim is merely that there is a presumptive obligation to obey some, not all, laws. Nothing of consequence depends on whether we stipulate to Soper's restrictive definition of "law" or, instead, to an ordinary-language, positivist definition. The important thing, obviously, is that we not lose sight of what is at stake, however "law" is defined: whether there is a presumptive obligation to obey all laws in the positivist sense.[23]

Does Soper's argument—that there is a presumptive obligation to obey some laws (in the positivist sense, or, equivalently, that there is a presumptive obligation to obey all laws in his special, restrictive sense of "law")—work? Kent Greenawalt's negative answer seems correct: Soper "gives the impression that what is at stake in law compliance is not disappointing and rebuffing officials who are doing their best on our behalf. Were the obligation so understood, it would not reach the many circumstances when law violation is unlikely to have that effect. . . . [R]espect for officials . . . seems not to come into play when official ignorance or indifference is predictable."[24] In any event, it remains the case that even if Soper's argument can be salvaged, the argument does not even purport to support the claim at issue here—Claim 3 on the list of eight claims set forth early in this chapter—namely, that one always has a reason, that there is a presumptive obligation, to obey all laws (in the nonrestrictive sense of "law").

Indeed, no argument we've considered supports that claim.[25] The basic problem with respect to each of the arguments is the same: None of them applies "generally enough. They refer to conditions that can, but do not always, exist."[26] Taking for granted standard normative commitments, then, one does *not* always have a reason to obey all laws. Not only is there no absolute obligation to obey all laws (or even, if I'm right, some laws); there is not even a presumptive obligation to obey all laws (though there is, I suggested, a presumptive obligation to obey some laws, in the sense that there are some laws one always has a nonconclusive reason to obey).

The search for a reason or reasons that can ground a presumptive obligation to obey all laws has been unavailing. We must be content with identifying reasons that require obedience to *some* laws in *some* situations.[27] As the discussion in this chapter suggests, such reasons include fairness, consent, avoiding conduct with bad consequences, the maintenance of good (for example, democratic) institutions, and respect for good faith authority. Related or overlapping considerations include a healthy sense of the fallibility of one's judgment that disobeying a particular law is justified;[28] commitment to values the realization of which is constitutive of a flourishing political community (including fairness and respect for good faith authority, especially democratic authority); the morality or justice of what particular laws require or forbid;[29] and, certainly not least, one's aversion to punishment or to other costs, whether to oneself, one's family or friends, or others.

My principal interest in this chapter, however, as its title indicates, is not considerations militating *for* obedience to law—some laws in some situations—but considerations militating *against* it. Disobedience to law, including resistance to coercive law, is an alternative that remains for the subjects of law when moral discourse runs out.

II

In the preceding section I concluded that there is no obligation, absolute or even presumptive, to obey all laws. Whether one accepts that conclusion or rejects it, one can agree that, given standard normative commitments, we have reasons, sometimes quite powerful reasons, to obey some laws in some situations. What reasons do we have (given standard commitments) to *disobey* some laws in some situations?[30] Surely *that* question is more urgent—surely it is more imperative that we address *that* question—than the question whether we have a presumptive obligation to obey all laws.

One might be tempted to disobey the law—a particular law—for many reasons, some not at all admirable. For present purposes, two sorts of objectives are relevant:

first, to resist a coercive law to which one conscientiously objects—a law requiring one to do what one believes one may not do or forbidding one to do what one believes one must do;

second, to achieve a greater good—a good greater than the evil(s) entailed by the disobedient act; for example, to undermine those in power (Gandhi's objective), to change or at least focus serious attention on a law (e.g., a racially discriminatory one) or policy (e.g., the deployment of cruise missiles), or simply to protect someone (e.g., a Salvadoran refugee illegally in the United States).

In the United States and kindred societies, in which the disobedient stance of figures such as Antigone, Socrates,[31] Thoreau, Gandhi, Bonhoeffer, and Martin Luther King, Jr., are seen to exemplify the proper relationship between conscience and law, it is widely accepted that *some* disobedient acts—undertaken to resist a coercive law to which one conscientiously objects or on the basis of a good faith judgment that the disobedient act will achieve a significantly greater good— can *sometimes* be justified. Certainly such acts are widely understood to be well within the bounds of "civilized" conduct. For example, in its Statement on "Human Law and the Conscience of Believers," reprinted as Appendix B to this book, the American Lutheran Church—a "main-line" Protestant church and one of the several politically dominant moral communities in American society—speaks approvingly of "individual Christians who choose in good conscience to break a law—to keep peace with their conscience, to raise an important issue to public view, or to seek a change in that law . . ."[32] The position of the Catholic Church, now one of the most dominant moral communities in the United States, is not merely that some disobedient acts can sometimes be justified, but that some disobedient acts are sometimes obligatory. Recall the statement by John Courtney Murray quoted in the preceding chapter, that for Catholics "the principles of Catholic faith and morality stand superior to, and in control of, the whole order of civil life."[33] As Ronald Dworkin has put it in a statement that typifies the dominant American view, secular as well as religious, "A man must honour his duties to his God and to his conscience, and if these conflict with his duty to the State, then he is entitled, in the end, to do what he judges to be right."[34] "The rejection . . . of legal absolutism or the fetishism of legality—that one is never justified in violating any law in any circumstances—is a matter of common sense", writes Sidney Hook,[35] whose observation is accurate at least with respect to *American* common sense and, beyond that, to the common sense of the *New Testament*, which is a principal source informing the sensibilities of many of the politically dominant moral communities (secular as well as religious). (According to Peter and the Apostles in *Acts* 5:29: "Obedience to God comes before obedience to men".)[36]

In the pluralistic American political community, therefore, the controversy surrounding the issue of disobedience to law (disobedience of the sorts under discussion here[37]) has tended to focus, not on whether some disobedient acts are sometimes justified, but on what considerations should inform the decision whether to disobey a particular law in a particular situation.

A major such consideration is the fallibility of human conscience. One need not be a Christian to acknowledge the wisdom of this caution expressed by the American Lutheran Church: "While it is true that certain laws may be wrong, unjust, or corrupt, it is equally true that the consciences of all persons, including Christians, can be wrong, misguided, affected by our sinful condition. . . . Christians will recognize always that conscience also is tainted by sin, and can be wrong. They therefore will give the utmost consideration to the counsel of fellow believers, and will contemplate disobedience with prayer and study in Christian community."[38] The admonition at the heart of this message can, of course, be expressed in secular as well as in theological or sectarian terms, as Sidney Hook, among others, has done:

> The voice of conscience may sound loud and clear. But it may conflict at times not only with the law but with another man's conscience. Every conscientious objector to a law knows that at least one man's conscience is wrong, *viz.*, the conscience of the man who asserts that *his* conscience tells him that he must not tolerate conscientious objectors. From this if he is reasonable he should conclude that when he hears the voice of conscience, he is hearing not the voice of God, but the voice of a finite, limited man in this time and in this place, and that conscience is neither a special nor an infallible organ of apprehending moral truth, that conscience without conscientiousness, conscience which does not cap the process of critical reflective morality, is likely to be prejudice masquerading as a First Principle or a Mandate from Heaven.[39]

A second basic consideration concerns proportionality: The good that can realistically be expected to flow from the particular disobedient act contemplated, given all the particularities of context, of time and place, must offset the evils that will or might flow from the act. One must be wary about applying too lenient a standard here. Given the first consideration—human fallibility—one should apply a fairly strict standard, for example: "Will the disobedient act I am contemplating *very likely* achieve a *significantly* greater good?"[40]

Does the proportionality consideration preclude disobedient acts that are violent? Joseph Raz's observations are sound:

> [C]ivil disobedience, it is often said, must be non-violent. It is clear that, other things being equal, non-violent disobedience is much to be preferred to violent disobedience. First, the direct harm caused by the violence is avoided. Secondly, the possible encouragement to resort to violence in cases where this would be wrong, which even an otherwise justified use of violence provides, is avoided. Thirdly, the use of violence is a highly emotional and explosive issue in many countries and in turning to to violence one is likely to antagonize potential allies and confirm in their opposition many of one's opponents. All these considerations, and others, suggest great reluctance to turn to the use of violence, most particularly violence against the person. But do they justify the total proscription of violence as a means to achieving a political aim? They do not. The evil the disobedience is designed to rectify may be so great, may indeed itself involve violence against innocent persons (such as the imprisonment of dissidents in labour camps in the Soviet Union), that it may be right to use violence to bring it to an end. It may be relevant here to draw attention to the fact that certain non-violent acts, indeed some lawful acts, may well have much more severe consequences than many an act of violence: consider the possible effects of a strike by ambulance drivers.[41]

Kent Greenawalt, while in full agreement that there must be a strong presumption against violent disobedient acts,[42] nonetheless acknowledges that such acts cannot be ruled out: "Most observers would commend rather than condemn the conspirators who planned to kill Hitler, even though the bomb which was planted was also likely to kill others more innocent than he was. Few Americans consider the Revolutionary War immoral, although extensive loss of life was a certain consequence."[43] If violent acts cannot be ruled out, then a fortiori disobedient acts damaging or even destroying property cannot be ruled out either. Of course, a particular moral community may happen to espouse ideals that preclude violent disobedience. The Statement of the American Lutheran Church indicates that "[i]f undertaken, . . . [civil disobedience] must be done . . . [o]nly by nonviolent means, intent on avoiding harm to persons or property."[44]

While the proportionality consideration does not preclude violent disobedient acts, it does require that one not pursue a more costly strategy where a less costly strategy—whether an obedient strategy or simply a different disobedient one—will achieve the hoped-for good to the same or at least to an acceptable extent. This does not mean, however, that, as some have argued,[45] a disobedient strategy may be be pursued only as a last resort—that lawful strategies must be preferred. First, lawful strategies may not, in the situation at hand, be nearly as effective as the disobedient strategy. Second, a disobedient strategy may be less harmful to the interests of others, on balance, than a lawful one. As Raz has said, "Which is worse, a miners' march in London which perpetrates various offenses such as obstruction to the highway, or a lawful lengthy miners' strike? . . . It may be wrong not to resort to civil disobedience and to turn to such lawful action first . . . True, other things being equal, . . . [civil disobedience] has by-products (setting a bad example even if the act is justified in the instant case) which lawful political action does not have. But other things are rarely equal and sometimes civil disobedience should be preferred to lawful action even when that action will be effective."[46]

I now want to consider, briefly, three conditions that have been proposed as necessary to the legitimacy of disobedience of law: First, one may not disobey a law unless the law is itself the object of protest; second, one may not disobey a law unless one does so openly or publicly; and, third, one may not disobey a law unless one accepts the legal consequences, including punishment. None of these conditions is necessary to the legitimacy of disobedience.

In the context of the antiwar protests of the Vietnam War era, then-Supreme Court Justice Abe Fortas wrote that "civil disobedience—the deliberate violation of law—is never justified in our nation where the law being violated is not itself the focus or target of the protest."[47] Fortas' position is untenable. First, the crucial question is not whether the law the disobedience of which is contemplated is itself the object of protest, but whether the good sought to be achieved is significantly greater than whatever evils might flow from disobedience. Second, the object of protest might be a policy that cannot be disobeyed by those protesting the policy—for example, congressional support of "contra" activities in Nicaragua—but which can be protested indirectly, for example, by "sitting in" at congressional offices (and thus violating tresspass and other laws not themselves objects of protest). (Howard Zinn has offered this example: "If . . . after a child had been killed by a speeding automobile, housewives blocked traffic on a street to pressure the city fathers into installing a traffic light, this would not be justified, according to Fortas' criteria, because they would be violating a reasonable law (against obstructing traffic) in order to protest something else (the absence of a traffic signal)."[48]) As Kent Greenawalt has concluded, "it may be that an act of disobedience will create a more dangerous precedent if not directed against an unjust law. But that hardly leads to the absolute principle laid down by Fortas."[49] In its Statement the American Lutheran Church has noted that "[a]cts of civil disobedience . . .—both direct *and indirect*—have a long, honored history in Western societies."[50]

The position that disobedience must be open or public to be legitimate is also untenable.[51] In the United States during the era of slavery, did those who operated the underground railroad act illegitimately because they acted covertly? In the present era, do those who hide Salvadoran refugees illegally in the United States act illegitimately because they act covertly? "[P]urposes other than the open protest normally associated with civil disobedience may underlie a valid claim that disobedience is morally justified. Sometimes a law is so wicked that the actor rightly acts to circumvent it. The person who contrary to the law assisted Jews to escape Nazi Germany acted morally."[52]

Similarly, the position that the disobedient person must accept the legal consequences, including punishment,[53] is unacceptable.[54] "If someone was illegally engaged in helping Jews escape from Nazi Germany, to have given himself up would have made it impossible for him to continue in that aid. It would have been perfectly moral for him to try to avoid punishment."[55] Moreover, if someone helping Jews escape Nazi Germany had been detected, he would have been no more obligated to refrain from attempting to escape Nazi Germany than were the Jews he had been helping.[56]

Nazi Germany is one context. By any plausible standard, contemporary American society is quite another. Do any of the conditions I've examined and rejected—that disobedience be nonviolent, a last resort, confined to laws themselves the objects of protest, open, undertaken with a willingness to accept the legal consequences—hold at least in a democratic society?[57] One undoubtedly has more reason to be skeptical about the legitimacy of particular disobedient acts in a democratic context than in a totalitarian one, as Kent Greenawalt has thoughtfully explained.[58] For example, "[i]f leaders are popularly elected and citizens can affect policies by open discussion and peaceable petition, it may be somewhat more likely that policies and laws will promote the social good. If this is accurate, a citizen in a democracy has an additional reason to question whether his fallible judgment that a law or policy may be unjust is wrong. This is particularly true when the democratic system fairly represents competing interests, such as labor and management . . ."⁵⁹ But there is no reason to think that even in a democratic society the several conditions surveyed above hold in their absoluteness:

> If Hitler had been freely elected as an absolute ruler for four years in 1941, would that have made unjustified the attempt on his life? Given the enormity of his crimes and the destruction of German life likely to result from his continuing role as ruler, I should think not. Nor does the fact that a policy is approved, or even made, by a majority necessarily lead to the conclusion that a minority should not use violence to overcome it. If a majority of Germans approved genocide, would not a minority nevertheless have been justified in violent resitance, at least if that resistance promised some greater hope of success than alternative courses?⁶⁰

I indicated at the beginning of this chapter that disobeying the law is an alternative that remains when, for the time being, moral discourse has run out, as it often does in a morally pluralistic society. It would be a mistake, however, to see disobedience simply as an act of conscience in situations where productive moral discourse between ruler and ruled with respect to some matter has become, for the time being, impossible or at least extremely difficult. First, as various comments in this chapter have suggested, by focusing serious attention on an issue that might otherwise receive only scant attention from the political processes, disobedience can sometimes stimulate moral discourse that has broken down or, indeed, not really begun. Second, even in the context of a moral discourse already well under way, disobedience can sometimes serve as a powerful communicative act and thus as a dramatic contribution to the discourse. To use a metaphor that has currency in some religious communities, disobedience can serve as a kind of "witness"—an existential commitment demonstrating the depth of the disobedient person's or persons' convictions and presenting onlookers, including policymakers, with an occasion, difficult to ignore, for reflecting on the character and depth of their own convictions.⁶¹

To disobey the law is to disobey the legally embodied morality and, if the disobedience is "indirect", to protest some further law or policy and the morality embodied therein. In a modern democratic society, the legally/politically embodied morality is likely an important part of the morality common to the politically dominant moral communities. In the next chapter I consider, among other issues concerning constitutional adjudication, the question of the proper role of the judiciary in adjudicating conflicts between, on the one hand, the morality common to the politically dominant moral communities and, on the other, persons who reject that morality (even if they do not, or not always, disobey that morality when embodied in law).

More generally I consider what the nature and limits of constitutional adjudication in the modern period of American constitutional law have to teach us about the kind of politics that is possible, though not always actual, in American society: a deliberative, transformative politics.

6

Interpreting Law: The Problem of Constitutional Adjudication[1]

In this chapter I turn to the problem of adjudication and focus on the sort of adjudication most controversial in American society: *constitutional* adjudication.[2] Among other things, I elaborate and defend my claim that constitutional adjudication, at its best, is a species of deliberative, transformative politics. And I address a question like the one addressed in chapter 4, where I asked: On what moral beliefs ought a person to rely, in her capacity as policymaker, in reasoning about and ultimately determining public policy?

The predicament of the policymaker is also, sometimes, the predicament of the judge. Every judge, like every policymaker, indeed like everyone, is inevitably a member of some moral community, in the sense that everyone shares with some other persons some conception of human good. But every judge in the United States is also a member of—and, as a public official, even represents—a morally pluralistic political community. Discussing constitutional adjudication, Justice William J. Brennan, Jr., of the United States Supreme Court (and, like Governor Cuomo, a member of the Catholic community) has said: "When Justices [of the Supreme Court] interpret the [United States] Constitution, they speak for their community, not for themselves alone. The act of interpretation must be undertaken with full consciousness that it is, in a very real sense, the community's interpretation that is sought."[3] With respect to constitutional adjudication, therefore, the question arises: On what moral beliefs ought a person to rely, in her capacity as judge, in deciding whether public policy regarding some matter is constitutionally valid? Relatedly, what does it mean—what *should* it mean—to say that a policy or other governmental action is or is not "constitutionally" valid?

I'm concerned here with the adjudication of cases on the basis of the Constitution of the United States ("the Constitution"), although some and perhaps even most of what I have to say has force with respect to the adjudication of cases on the basis of a state constitution.[4] Moreover, I'm concerned here with the adjudication of issues regarding the proper relation between, on the one hand, government, whether federal or state, and, on the other, citizens and other persons. The extent to which what I have to say has force with respect to the adjudication of issues regarding the proper relation either (1) between the federal government and state government or (2) among the three branches of the federal government—legislative, executive, and judicial—is an open question.[5] Finally, I'm concerned in this chapter principally with adjudication by the Supreme Court of the United States ("the Court"), although much of what I have to say has force with respect to adjudication by other courts, state as well as federal.[6]

I

On what moral beliefs ought a person to rely, in her capacity as judge, in making constitutional decisions? I explained in chapter 4 why a legislator or other policymaker ought not to rely on either experience- or preference-utilitarianism as a basis for determining public policy. The reasons I gave there serve to explain why no one—judges in constitutional cases included—should rely on any such utilitarian theory as a basis for making decisions. In chapter 4 I also explained why contractualism of the Right-prior-to-Good sort is a deeply problematic basis for any decisionmaking, including, therefore, constitutional decisionmaking. Where does that leave us?

I shall consider two basic responses to the question of the beliefs on which a judge should rely in making constitutional decisions. The first response I call "originalism"; the second, "nonoriginalism".[7] Different originalist theorists present different originalist theories, but the differences are less important, for present purposes, than the similarities.[8] In any event, because I intend to criticize, and reject, originalism, I shall present the soundest—most attractive, least vulnerable—version of originalism I can imagine. Criticizing the soundest originalism I can imagine makes more sense than taking on some weak originalist theory.[9] Different nonoriginalist theorists, too, present different nonoriginalist theories, but the differences, which are often quite important, need not concern us. My aim is simply to present a particular non-originalist theory.[10] I shall present, criticize, and reject the soundest originalist constitutional theory I can imagine, and I shall elaborate and defend a nonoriginalist constitutional theory.

What is the originalist response to the question of the beliefs on which a judge should rely? According to originalism (in the soundest version I can imagine), in ratifying each constitutional provision, the ratifiers, on behalf of those they represented, constitutionalized—that is, they established as supremely authoritative for purposes of the legal system—a belief or set of beliefs about how government should be organized or about what government may, may not, or must do. They established a norm or set of norms about the structure or limits of government. Originalism holds that a judge, in deciding whether public policy regarding some matter is constitutionally valid, ought to rely only on (1) "original" beliefs—that is, beliefs (norms) established as authoritative through the ratification process—and (2) "supplemental" beliefs—that is, beliefs reliance on which is necessitated by reliance on original beliefs. Put another way, a judicial decision that a law or other governmental action is unconstitutional is legitimate, according to originalism, only if[11] the original belief(s) signified by the relevant constitutional provision (in conjunction with whatever beliefs are supplemental to the original belief) entails the conclusion that government has done something it may not do or failed to do something it must do.

I need to say a few words about the notion of beliefs supplemental to original beliefs. Assume that in ratifying the fourteenth amendment the ratifiers constitutionalized the belief—the political-moral norm—that government may not discriminate on the basis of race with respect to *what the ratifiers believed to be fundamental human interests*. Reliance on that belief necessitates reliance on further beliefs, in particular, the ratifiers' beliefs about fundamental human interests. Assume instead that the ratifiers constitutionalized the belief that government may not discriminate on the basis of race with respect to *fundamental human interests*. Reliance on that belief necessitates reliance on beliefs about fundamental human interests. (*Whose* beliefs about fundamental human interests? The judge's own? The beliefs of the branch or agency of government whose action is at issue? The beliefs with the greatest support in society at large? The first answer seems to me the most defensible,[12] but I happily leave that problem to proponents of originalism.)

Why do the ratifiers of a constitutional provision play the crucial role in originalism (as I present it), rather than, say, those who proposed the provision for ratification in the first place ("the framers")? James Madison, as interpreted by historian Jack Rakove, supplied the answer:

> Madison consistently rejected the idea that the intentions of the framers . . . ought to enter into any systematic process of constitutional *interpretation*. He based this position in part on his awareness of the imperfect state of the records of the Convention and the highly political character of many of the speeches summarized in his notes. But his objection ultimately rested on a more fundamental principle. It was an "error," he wrote in 1831, to "ascrib[e] to the *intention* of the *Convention* which formed the Constitution, an undue ascendency in expounding it. Apart from the difficulty of verifying that intention it is clear, that if the meaning of the Constitution is to be sought out of itself, it is not in the proceedings of the Body that proposed it, but in those of the state Conventions which gave it all the validity & authority it possesses." Rather than resolve constitutional disputes by appealing to the stated concerns of the *framers*, Madison believed it was the views of the *ratifiers* that had to be consulted. The Constitution, he had declared on the floor of the House of Representatives in 1796, was "nothing more than the draft of a plan, nothing but a dead letter, until life and validity were breathed into it by the voice of the people, speaking through the several state conventions." Interpretation, if necessary, should accordingly strive to recover not "the opinions entertained in forming the Constitution," but its true meaning as understood *by the Nation* at the time of its ratification."[13]

A possible response is that Madison's argument concerns the original Constitution—the constitutional provisions drafted in Philadelphia in the summer of 1787, and that the situation is more complicated with respect to the Bill of Rights and the other constitutional amendments: The 1787 Constitution established an amendment process; according to one part of that process, amendment of the Constitution requires a $2/3$ majority vote in both the House and the Senate, and then a bare majority in $3/4$ of the state legislatures.[14] Why, then, shouldn't the understanding of those in the Congress play as large a role as the understanding of those in the state legislatures? Perhaps with respect to constitutional amendments the former understanding *should* play as large a role. In any event, the question is largely academic. First, there is no reason to suppose that the understanding or range of understandings of those in the Congress—or of those in Philadelphia in 1787—differed significantly from the understanding or range of understandings of those in the state

legislatures. Second, even if we assume *arguendo* that only the understanding of the ratifiers is authoritative, as a practical matter the understanding of the framers must play the crucial role for the originalist
judge. As Henry Monaghan, a prominent originalist theorist, has put it:
"Although the intention of the ratifiers, not the Framers, is in principle
decisive, the difficulties of ascertaining the intent of the ratifiers leaves
little choice but to accept the intent of the Framers as a fair reflection of
it."[15]

Because critics of originalism often misconceive it, they end up
attacking a straw man. The most prominent misconceptions of how
originalism requires a judge to decide a case are these: (1) decide it the
way the ratifiers (or, if you prefer, the framers and ratifiers) wanted
or would have wanted such a case to be decided;[16] (2) decide it the way
the ratifiers expected or would have expected such a case to be
decided;[17] (3) decide it the way the ratifiers resolved or would have
resolved such an issue in their day;[18] and (4) decide it the way the
ratifiers would have resolved such an issue in our day, were they still
living.[19] Originalism requires a judge to do none of these things.

Assume that in ratifying the fourteenth amendment the ratifiers constitutionalized the belief that government may not discriminate on the
basis of race with respect to fundamental human interests. Imagine a
case in which the Court must decide whether an antimiscegenation law
violates the fourteenth amendment. Originalism requires the Court to
decide whether the law discriminates on the basis of race with respect to
a fundamental human interest. *Inter alia*, it requires the Court to decide
whether one's interest in marrying the person one wants to marry is a
fundamental human interest. According to originalism, if the Court
decides that the law discriminates on the basis of race with respect to a
fundamental human interest, the Court ought to strike down the law.[20]

Assume that the antimiscegenation law *does* discriminate on the basis
of race with respect to a fundamental human interest. Perhaps the
ratifiers did not think that antimiscegenation legislation was inconsistent
with the principle that government may not discriminate on the basis of
race with respect to fundamental human interests, and, indeed, perhaps
if the inconsistency had been pointed out to them, they would have
wanted to amend the principle so as to spare antimiscegenation legislation. Perhaps, that is, they wanted or would have wanted antimiscegenation legislation sustained. Nonetheless, originalism requires
the Court to strike down the law, not decide the case the way the

ratifiers wanted or would have wanted such a case decided.[21] Similarly, perhaps the ratifiers did not think that antimiscegenation legislation was inconsistent with the antidiscrimination principle and so expected or would have expected the Court to decide such a case in favor of the law. Nonetheless, originalism requires the Court to strike down the law.[22] Perhaps the ratifiers did not think that antimiscegenation legislation was inconsistent with the antidiscrimination principle and so, in their day, resolved or would have resolved such a question in favor of the law. Nonetheless, originalism requires the Court to strike down the law (assuming that the law does in fact discriminate on the basis of race with respect to a fundamental human interest).[23]

The most prevalent misconception is that originalism requires the Court to answer the question the way the ratifiers would have answered it in our day, were they still living.[24] However, there is no way a judge can know how the ratifiers would have answered a constitutional question—the antimiscegenation question, say—in our day, were they still living. Moreover, the inquiry is irrelevant: The originalist project is not to speculate about what the ratifiers' beliefs would have been in our day, were they still living, and then to decide the case on the basis of those beliefs. Rather, the originalist project is to discover what belief(s) the ratifiers constitutionalized, and then to decide the case on the basis of that belief (in conjunction with whatever beliefs are supplemental to it). As Robert Bork, a prominent originalist judge, has written: "The objection that we can never know what the Framers would have done about specific modern situations is entirely beside the point. The originalist attempts to discern the principles the Framers enacted, the values they sought to protect."[25]

Of course, "discern[ing] the principles the Framers enacted, the values they sought to protect", is not an unproblematic assignment. Why is the originalist's historical project so difficult (beyond the obvious fact that the available historical materials may be scant or inconclusive or both)? Ronald Dworkin's statement of the problem is useful:

> History alone might be able to show that some particular concrete opinion, like the opinion that school segregation was not unconstitutional, was widely shared within the group of legislators and others mainly responsible for a constitutional amendment. But it can never determine precisely which general principle or value it would be right to attribute to them. This is so not because we might fail to gather enough evidence, but for the more fundamen-

tal reason that people's convictions do not divide themselves neatly into general principles and concrete applications. Rather they take the form of a more complex structure of layers of generality, so that people regard most of their convictions as applications of further principles or values more general still. That means that a judge will have a choice among more or less abstract descriptions of the principle that he regards the framers as having entrusted to his safekeeping, and the actual decisions he makes, in the exercise of that responsibility, will critically depend on which description he chooses.[26]

So, how can an originalist judge, like Bork, choose "among more or less abstract descriptions of the principle" in a way that is faithful to the premises of his originalism? The answer, it seems to me, is this: The originalist, on the basis of available historical materials, must engage in a hypothetical conversation with "the framers"—"the group of legislators and others mainly responsible for" the relevant constitutional provision—in an effort to discern which principle *they* most likely would have chosen, in the conversation, confronted by the various possibilities, that is, the various candidate principles, from relatively narrow/concrete to relatively broad/abstract, as being the one that best captured the purpose or point or meaning of what they did. That counterfactual project, though difficult, is hardly impossible. Granted, the project leaves the judge a lot of room for self-serving conclusions, but thoughtful originalists, like Bork, understand as much: "[E]nforcing the Framers' intentions is not a mechanical process and . . . even a judge purporting to be an . . . [originalist] can manipulate the levels of generality at which he states the Framers' principles."[27] Nonoriginalism, says Bork, "is an explicit warrant for constitution-making but even under . . . [originalism] there are no safeguards against that except the intellectual honesty of the judge and the scrutiny of an informed profession that accepts the premises of . . . [originalism]."[28]

So, a sophisticated originalism, sensitive to the insights of hermeneutics, readily acknowledges that the judge can never retrieve the actual "original understanding", anymore than one person can come to see the world through another person's eyes (even if the other person is a contemporary). Accepting Gadamer's observation that "we understand in a different way if we understand at all",[29] the sophisticated originalist is fully aware that the best the judge can do is construct an imagined "original understanding" by means of a counterfactual speculative act—the hypothetical conversation—that is sensitive to available historical materials. But, for the originalist, the best the judge can do is quite good enough.[30] Trying to arrive at the original understanding, in the sense and way just indicated, is a far cry from, and far more legitimate than—the originalist will want to insist—pursuing an interpretive path that rejects the "in principle" authoritativeness of the original understanding, which is what nonoriginalists do. ("[E]ven if 'original intention' is not the ideal verbal touchstone, surely it is an extreme view of the Constitution that invites a judge to disregard the original meaning of the text as written."[31])

Consider three possible bases for originalism, which give rise to three different sorts of originalism:[32] "democratic" originalism, "structural" originalism, and "constitutional" originalism. Democratic originalism is based on a theory of the proper role of courts in a democratic society. Structural originalism is based on a theory of the proper separation of powers among the legislative, executive, and judicial branches of government. Constitutional originalism is based on the theory that only the originalist judicial role is legitimate because only the judicial role authorized by the ratifiers of the Constitution is legitimate and they authorized the originalist role.

Because constitutional originalism is question begging, it need not be taken seriously. A fundamental question in the debate about proper judicial role is whether the ratifiers' beliefs—including their beliefs about judicial role—should be deemed authoritative. Constitutional originalism begs that question by presupposing, rather than defending, an affirmative answer to it. (Moreover, the claim that the ratifiers of the 1787 Constitution and the Bill of Rights authorized the originalist judicial role is problematic.[33]) A structural originalism could be distinct from democratic originalism in that the underlying theory of the separation of powers could be other than democratic. For example, the underlying theory could monarchical. In American political-legal culture, however, any plausible theory of the separation of powers is democratic. Moreover, any democratic theory will contain a theory of the separation of powers. As a practical matter, therefore, we can collapse the distinction between democratic originalism and structural originalism. By originalism, then, I mean democratic originalism—originalism based on a political theory of the proper role of courts, in particular, electorally unaccountable courts,[34] in a democratic society.

What is the strength of (democratic) originalism, the source of its

appeal? An originalist judicial role accords nicely with a popular—
"civics book"—understanding of American government, in which it is
the function of the electorally accountable legislative branch, sometimes in conjunction with the electorally accountable executive branch,
to make policy choices, it is the function of the electorally accountable
executive branch to administer policy choices, and it is the function of
the electorally *unaccountable* judicial branch merely to enforce policy
choices. According to the view of democracy that underlies originalism,
it is illegitimate for the judiciary to go beyond the enforcement of policy
choices to the making of policy choices—at least, it is illegitimate
unless the judiciary is authorized to do so by the legislative and executive branches.[35] And it is illegitimate *in extremis* for the undemocratic
judiciary to oppose itself, in constitutional cases, to the democratic
branches and agencies of government on the basis of beliefs never
constitutionalized by the ratifiers.

Originalism loses that strength to the extent it turns out that, as an
historical matter, beliefs constitutionalized by the ratifiers constitute, in
effect, delegations of authority to the Court to make fresh judgments of
political morality, and if originalism does not require the Court to
decline such delegations. Assume, counterfactually, that in ratifying the
fourteenth amendment the ratifiers constitutionalized the belief that
government may not act unjustly or otherwise immorally. According to
originalism, should a Supreme Court Justice vote to invalidate, under
the fourteenth amendment, any governmental action she believes to be
unjust or otherwise immoral? Given originalism's basis in democratic
theory, should a judge rely on an original belief if in doing so she must
act undemocratically? What does originalism require a judge to do if
reliance on an original belief is inconsistent with originalism's democratic premises? And when is reliance on an original belief inconsistent
with those premises? For example, when it necessitates that a judge
decide, unaided by original beliefs, what human interests are fundamental? That problem, too, I happily leave to proponents of originalism,
who should reflect on something John Ely has written: "If a principled
approach to judicial enforcement of the Constitution's open-ended
provisions cannot be developed, one that is not hopelessly inconsistent
with our nation's commitment to representative democracy, responsible
commentators must consider seriously the possibility that courts should
simply stay away from them."[36] (Unlike a democratic originalist, a

constitutional originalist doesn't have democratic premises to worry about. However, a constitutional originalist, unlike a democratic originalist, *does* have question begging premises to worry about.[37])

Of course, a proponent of (democratic) originalism can try to establish that the problem is merely academic—that no constitutional provision, properly understood, is *that* open-ended, that the ratifiers did not constitutionalize any belief reliance on which constrains a judge to act undemocratically. And, indeed, it does not seem to me plausible to suppose that the ratifiers of any constitutional provision constitutionalized a belief so indeterminate or "general" that reliance on it necessitates judges acting inconsistently with originalism's democratic premises. As Monaghan has written, with particular reference to the fourteenth amendment, "[E]xcessive generalization" of the ratifiers' beliefs "seems at war with any belief that a constitutional amendment is a *conscious* alteration of the frame of government whose major import should be reasonably apparent to those who gave it life. . . . I am unable to believe that in light of the then prevailing concepts of representative democracy," the ratifiers "of section 1 [of the fourteenth amendment] intended the *courts* . . . to weave the tapestry of federally protected rights against state government."[38]

What are the weaknesses of originalism? One alleged weakness of an originalist approach to constitutional adjudication—one problem such an approach is said to face—is the difficulty, with respect to several key constitutional provisions, of discovering the precise contours of the beliefs (the political-moral norms) the ratifiers acted to constitutionalize.[39] That difficulty is complicated by the likelihood that in voting to ratify the fourteenth amendment—to take but one example—the ratifiers were not all voting to constitutionalize precisely the same belief(s).[40]

Nonetheless—the originalist will want to insist—it is implausible to suppose that there was no core or common belief all or virtually all the ratifiers voted to constitutionalize. The job of an originalist judge is difficult but not impossible: She must simply do the best she can to discover the contours of the core or common beliefs constitutionalized by the ratifiers. I've already indicated how the hermeneutically sophisticated originalist judge would go about that task: the hypothetical conversation sketched above.

Originalism is fundamentally sound that, as American historian Jack Rakove has written, "a historical approach to the problem of the original understanding can produce more rewarding results than . . . [critics of originalism] are ordinarily prepared to concede."[41] Even Mark Tushnet has disputed "[t]he point, which some fanatics of the hermeneutic method" have pressed, "that, because the world of the past is not the world in which we have developed our ways of understanding how others act, we can never understand that past world." That view, says Tushnet, "would go too far."[42] We know enough about the legislative history of section 1 of the fourteenth amendment, for example, to be able confidently to conclude that constitutional doctrine regarding gender-based discrimination, or abortion, cannot easily or perhaps even plausibly be defended on an originalist basis.[43]

Given originalism's democratic premises, presumably an originalist judge should resolve whatever doubt remains, after her historical inquiry is finished, in favor of the governmental action whose constitutionality is at issue. If, given difficulties like those mentioned above, doubt were to remain, that would be a problem, not for originalism, but for those persons trying to persuade the judge *not* to decide in government's favor.[44]

As a general matter, one might make either, or both, of two basic sorts of challenge to originalism. First, one might contend that an originalist approach to constitutional adjudication faces insurmountable difficulties. As my comments in the preceding three paragraphs illustrate, I'm skeptical of such challenges. At any rate, I'm content to leave it to others inclined to make such challenges to do so.[45] Second, one might contend that even if an originalist approach to constitutional adjudication does not face insurmountable difficuties, there is nonetheless a better approach. In this chapter I make such a challenge. I argue that my nonoriginalist approach to constitutional adjudication is better than the originalist approach. Originalism's weaknesses, in my view, are not intrinsic, but comparative: Originalism lacks the strengths of the nonoriginalist theory of judicial role I elaborate and defend in this chapter.

II

Thus far I've said nothing about the text of the Constitution. Yet, in American political-legal culture it is axiomatic that the constitutional text is authoritative—indeed, supremely authoritative—in constitutional adjudication.[46] That is, it is axiomatic that constitutional cases should be decided on the basis of, according to, the Constitution. (Similarly, in American political-legal culture, "the law" is axiomatically authoritative in adjudication: It is axiomatic that judges should decide cases "according to law".[47]) It is *not* axiomatic, however, what it means to say that the constitutional text is authoritative.[48] (Similarly, it is not axiomatic what it means to say that judges should decide cases according to law.) According to originalism, what does it mean to say that the Constitution is authoritative? And what does it mean to "interpret" the Constitution, according to originalism? What does it mean to say that the Constitution is authoritative—and what does it mean to "interpret" the Constitution—according to nonoriginalism (that is, according to the nonoriginalist theory I elaborate and defend in this chapter)?[49]

To say that something (e.g., marks on a page) is a "text" (and not just marks on a page) is to conclude that that something is meaningful— that is, meaning-ful, full of meaning. For a person to say that something is a text when that something is not (yet) meaningful to her—perhaps because it is written in a language or code she doesn't (yet) understand—is for her to conclude, perhaps only tentatively, that that something is a text for someone, that it is, potentially at least, meaningful to someone, perhaps even (potentially) to her.[50]

All agree that the Constitution is a text. What the Constitution means, to the originalist, is what it originally meant. Its meaning to the originalist is its *original meaning*. For the originalist, to enforce the Constitution is to enforce it *as originally understood* (by the ratifiers, or the framers and ratifiers). For originalism, then, to "interpret" the Constitution is to ascertain the original meaning—the beliefs the text was originally understood to signify—and then to answer the question of what significance, if any, those beliefs have for the conflict at hand, what those beliefs mean for the conflict at hand, what those beliefs, if accepted, require the court to do, if anything, with respect to the conflict at hand. Thus, for originalism, the interpretation of a constitutional provision comprises two interpretive moments: a moment in which the original meaning/understanding of the provision is ascertained (to the extent possible) and a second moment in which the significance of that meaning for the conflict at hand is ascertained.[51]

To the nonoriginalist, too, of course, the constitutional text is meaning-ful. But to the nonoriginalist, the meaning of the text is not singular. *One* meaning of the constitutional text, to the nonoriginalist, is the original meaning. To the nonoriginalist, however, that is not the only meaning of the text.

A text can have multiple meanings. (Indeed, one meaning of a text can contradict another meaning of the text.) Meaning is always meaning to someone, and what a text means to one person is not necessarily what it means to another. But is it the case that a text can have more than one meaning to a person?[52] Yes, to the extent the text is more than one thing to her. To very, very many Americans—myself included—the constitutional text (to use the example at hand), in certain of its aspects, is more than one thing: It is a communication to us (the present) from the ratifiers and framers (the past) *and*, in virtue of a role it has come to play in the life of our political community—a role not necessarily foreseen much less authorized by any group of ratifiers and framers—the Constitution is *also* a symbol of fundamental aspirations of the political tradition. That is, what the constitutional text means to us, what it signifies to us (in addition to the original meaning), are certain basic, constitutive aspirations or principles or ideals of the American political community and tradition. Thus, were someone to ask me what the equal protection clause means, I might say: "As a communication to us from the ratifiers and framers of the fourteenth amendment, it means . . . But as a symbol of a fundamental aspiration of our political tradition, it means, it has come to mean, more than that; it means . . ." There is, after all, no rule that a text must be one and only one thing to a person—or, therefore, that it must mean one and only one thing to a person. Things are not so simple. Like some other texts (like every other text?), the constitutional text is polysemic.

To the nonoriginalist, unlike the originalist, what the Constitution means is not merely what it originally meant. Some provisions of the constitutional text have a meaning *in addition to* the original meaning: Some provisions signify fundamental aspirations of the American political tradition.[53] Not every provision of the text signifies such aspirations, but some do. The least controversial examples of such provisions are probably the first amendment, signifying the tradition's aspirations to the freedoms of speech, press, and religion; the fifth amendment, signifying the aspiration to due process of law; and the fourteenth amendment, signifying the aspirations to due process of law and to equal protection of the laws.

It seems invariably (though not necessarily) the case that the aspirational meaning of a constitutional provision, like the free speech clause of the first amendment, has grown out of the original meaning. The aspirational meaning has emerged over time—in the course of constitutional adjudication and, more generally, of political discourse, including political discourse precipitated by constitutional conflict and adjudication—as a progressive generalization of the original meaning. As a progressive generalization of the original meaning, the aspirational meaning of the Constitution is not inconsistent with, but indeed includes, the narrow original meaning.

This point bears emphasis: Constitutional adjudication in particular and political discourse in general are principal matrices of the Constitution's aspirational meaning to us; and constitutional precedent and, more generally, the ways in which political controversies, especially major ones, have been resolved—the story of the New Deal, for example, comes to mind—are principal shaping influences on the contours of that meaning.[54] Which constitutional provisions signify aspirations? How can a judge know? One important place to look, though not the only place, is constitutional case law, constitutional "precedent", not because such materials are necessarily authoritative, but because they are informative, illuminating, as to which provisions are aspirational, and as to the shape, the content, of the aspirations.[55]

Nonoriginalism does not hold that every worthwhile aspiration is necessarily a fundamental aspiration of the tradition, much less signified by some provision of the constitutional text. Nor does it hold that every fundamental aspiration of the tradition is necessarily signified by some provision of the text. It does not even hold that every aspiration of the tradition signified by some textual provision is necessarily worthwhile. Why should a judge bring to bear, in constitutional cases, *only* aspirations signified by the text? Why not all fundamental aspirations, even those not signified by the text? Indeed, why not all worthwhile aspirations, even those not fundamental aspirations of the American political tradition? If someone wants to claim that a judge should bring to bear all fundamental aspirations, or even all worthwhile aspirations, I want to hear the argument. (*Inter alia*, I'm curious to hear what fundamental aspirations are not signified by the text, and also what worthwhile aspirations are not fundamental aspirations of the tradition.) *My* argument is merely that a judge should bring to bear, in constitutional cases, only aspirations signified by the text.

Why should a judge bring those aspirations to bear? By oath a judge has sworn to support the Constitution.[56] It is difficult to see what might be meant by "the Constitution" other than either (1) original beliefs or (2) the aspirations or ideals or principles signified by the Constitution. Given her oath, then, in adjudicating a case arising under a given textual provision, a judge's choice is either to pursue an originalist approach or, instead, to bring to bear the aspiration signified by the provision.[57] My argument is that with respect to some provisions—those signifying fundamental aspirations of the American political tradition—she should forgo the originalist approach in favor of bringing the aspirations to bear.

However, although I'm arguing that a judge should bring to bear only aspirations signified by the Constitution (as distinct from all fundamental aspirations or all worthwhile aspirations), I'm *not* arguing that she should bring to bear *every* aspiration signified by the Constitution. As I remarked a moment ago, nonoriginalism does not presuppose that every aspiration signified by the Constitution is necessarily worthwhile. If a judge believes that an aspiration signified by some provision of the constitutional text is not worthwhile, then she has no reason to bring that aspiration to bear. She may, consistently with her oath, pursue the originalist approach to adjudication under the provision in question. My discussion from this point forward assumes that the judge believes that the relevant aspiration *is* worthwhile and, therefore, that she *does* have reason to bring it to bear.

Originalists and nonoriginalists agree, then, that the constitutional text is authoritative in constitutional adjudication, but they disagree about what it means to say that the text is authoritative. They disagree about that, because they disagree about the meaning of the text. Whereas for the originalist the meaning of the constitutional text is singular—the meaning of the text is the original meaning—for the nonoriginalist the situation is more complicated. For reasons I give later, a nonoriginalist judge *is* interested in the original meaning of the Constitution; for her, too, one meaning of the text is the original meaning. But for a nonoriginalist judge that is not the text's only meaning. In a sense, the originalist's Constitution is *not the same text*—it is *not meaningful in the same way*—as the nonoriginalist's Constitution (as least insofar as judicial review is concerned). For the originalist, the constitutional text is authoritative in the sense that the original meaning is authoritative. For the nonoriginalist, some provisions of the text are authoritative in the sense that their aspirational meaning—the aspirations they signify—is authoritative. For a nonoriginalist judge, the authoritative meaning of some provisions of the constitutional text is not their narrow original meaning, but their broad aspirational meaning.[58]

For nonoriginalism, then, to "interpret" some provisions of the Constitution is, in the main, to ascertain their aspirational meaning and then to bring that meaning to bear—that is, to answer the question of what significance, if any, the aspiration signified by the relevant provision has for the conflict at hand, what that aspiration means for the conflict at hand, what that aspiration, if accepted, requires the court to do, if anything, with respect to the conflict at hand. Thus, for nonoriginalism no less than for originalism, the interpretation of a constitutional provision comprises two interpretive moments: a moment in which the aspirational meaning of the provision is ascertained and a second moment in which the significance of that meaning for the conflict at hand is ascertained.

As I've indicated, for both originalists and nonoriginalists constitutional interpretation comprises two interpretive moments. Whereas the first moment yields a norm to be applied, the second moment—the moment of application—yields the significance of that norm for the conflict at hand. In the second moment the norm yielded in the first moment is specified, it is rendered more determinate. We might say that in the first moment the objective is the "preliminary" meaning of the constitutional provision, and in the second moment the objective is the "final" meaning. Whereas the preliminary meaning is relatively general, abstract, formal, verbal, the final meaning is relatively particular, concrete, substantial, existential. For the originalist, the proper objective, for the first interpretive moment—that is, the proper preliminary meaning—is the original meaning. For the nonoriginalist, by contrast, it is the aspirational meaning.

For the nonoriginalist, then, unlike the originalist, the constitutional text plays an important "prophetic" role: incessantly disturbing the political community, as I shall now elaborate.[59]

III

I want to illuminate the nonoriginalist conception of constitutional text and interpretation I'm presenting here by considering sacred texts and their interpretation.[60] There is an important analogy between, on the one hand, the role of the sacred text and the activity of interpreting the text, in the life of a religious tradition and community, and, on the other, the role of the constitutional text and the activity of interpreting the text, in the life of a political tradition and community.

The notions of community, tradition, and foundational text figure prominently both in my understanding of sacred texts and their interpretation and in my conception of the constitutional text and its interpretation. Consider the connection among (1) a community, whether religious or political, (2) the tradition of which the community is the present embodiment, and (3) the foundational text or texts of the tradition, whether sacred (as in the case of a religious tradition) or constitutional (as in the case of a political tradition). By "community" I mean, in this context, a group of persons united principally by their identification of themselves as the present bearers of, and participants in, a tradition. By "tradition" I mean a history or narrative in which the central motif is an aspiration to a particular form of life, to certain projects, goals, ideals, and the central discourse, in the case of a *living* tradition, is an argument—in Alasdair MacIntyre's terms, "an historically extended, socially embodied argument"[61]—about how that form of life is to be cultivated and revised. By "foundational text" (or "texts") I mean the text that, in the community and tradition in question, is seen to charter, to mandate, the form of life to which the community and tradition aspire, and thus the text that, for the community and tradition, *symbolizes* that mandate.

Consider both the role of the sacred text and the activity of interpreting the text, in the life of a religious community that is the steward of a living tradition. In such a community, the sacred text is not—not simply, at any rate—a book of answers, but rather a principal symbol of, perhaps *the* principal symbol of, and thus a central occasion of recalling and heeding, the fundamental aspirations of the tradition. In that sense, the sacred text constantly *disturbs*—it serves a prophetic function in— the life of the community.[62] Indeed, it is in significant part in virtue of its "writtenness", and thus its "permanence",[63] that a sacred text is (in the life of a community that might prefer, from time to time, to ignore it) irrepressible, disturbing, prophetic. And it is in significant part because of its comprehensiveness and indeterminacy, and thus its "excess of meaning",[64] that a sacred text, as symbol, achieves its power to disturb from one generation to the next and from one place to another, over the lives of communities separated in time and space and with very different experiences and questions.

How shall we understand the activity of interpretation, of a sacred text, in the life of a religious community that is part of a living tradition? The referent of a text understood simply as evidence of past beliefs is, in a sense, "behind" the text. One must look behind the text, to the past beliefs, if one is to understand the text. The referent of a sacred text, however, is not "behind", but "in front of".[65] One must respond to the incessant prophetic call of the text. One must recall and heed the aspirations signified by the text, and thereby create and give always-provisional, always-reformable meaning to the text.

Yet, it is not simply a matter of creating and giving meaning to, rather than taking meaning from, the text. We are creatures as well as creators of tradition. How, and to what extent, is interpretive activity the activity of persons as *creatures* of tradition? How, and to what extent, the activity of persons as *creators* of tradition? That which is taken from the text are the aspirations the text signifies. That which is given to the text are the community's answers as to how those aspirations are to be heeded, realized, in the life of the community, in the light of *its* experience and exigencies. That is the sense in which "interpretation", as David Tracy says, "is a mediation of past and present".[66] Meaning is given to the sacred text in the sense that later communities who enter into dialogic relation to the text will find there the meanings earlier communities have created; they will find them there because, in signifying—symbolizing—the aspirations of the tradition, the sacred text inevitably resonates with the ways the tradition has (provisionally, reformably) responded to those aspirations.[67] Of course, just as meaning is thus given to the sacred text, later communities must sometimes exorcise from the text what they come to conclude are, for them, unacceptable meanings given to the text by earlier communities.

Thus, in the life of a religious community that is the steward of a living tradition, to interpret a sacred text is, in essence, *to interpret the tradition itself, to mediate the past of the tradition with its present*. And because such a community is cognizant of the imperfect and therefore reformable character of its tradition, it will maintain a critical attitude towards the tradition. That attitude is "the route to liberation from the negative realities of a tradition".[68] To exercise stewardship over the tradition, to see that the tradition lives, requires that the community maintain this critical distance. Although the community must mine the tradition for whatever resources the tradition bears that are helpful in fulfilling the fundamental aspirations of the tradition, the community must also, as steward of those aspirations, reject those aspects of the tradition—those "negative realities"—that come to be seen as subversive of the tradition's aspirations. (There is no denying "the brokenness and ambiguity of every tradition and one's own inevitably ambivalent relationship to it".[69]) Consider, for example, the critical efforts of feminist Christian theologians, like Rosemary Ruether,[70] to uncover the patriarchal aspects of their tradition and to establish—in terms of their tradition's central aspirations—the "sinful" (alienated and alienating) character of those aspects. A religious tradition has ceased to live when, *inter alia*, the community that is its present bearer is no longer sensitive to the need to criticize and revise the community's form of life in the light of new experience and exigencies.[71]

In the American experience, the role of the constitutional text and the activity of interpreting the text have been very similar to the role of the sacred text and the activity of interpreting the text in the life of a religious community that is the steward of a living tradition. For the American political community, the constitutional text is not (simply) a book of answers to particular questions (e.g., "What is the minimum age for President of the United States?").[72] It is, rather, a principal symbol, perhaps *the* principal symbol, of fundamental aspirations of the tradition.[73] Recall Alexander Bickel's observation that "[w]ith us the principal symbol of nationhood, of continuity, of unity and common purpose, is, of course, the Constitution, without particular reference to what it means in this or that application."[74] More recently, Justice Brennan has said that "the Constitution embodies the aspiration to social justice, brotherhood, and human dignity that brought this nation into being. . . . [W]e are an aspiring people, a people with faith in progress. Our amended Constitution is the lodestar for our aspirations."[75]

As a principal symbol of fundamental aspirations of the American political tradition, the constitutional text constantly disturbs—it serves a prophetic function in—the life of the political community. The referent of the constitutional text, conceived as originalism conceives it, is "behind": One must look behind the text, to the original beliefs, if one is to comprehend the text. The referent of the constitutional text conceived in nonoriginalist terms as the symbolization of fundamental aspirations of the political tradition, however, is not behind, but "in front of". The political community must respond to the incessant prophetic call of the text—must recall and heed the aspirations signified by the text—and thus create and give (always-provisional, always-reformable) meaning to the text, as well as take meaning from it. In *Poe* v. *Ullman* Justice Harlan spoke of the importance of "approaching the text which is the only commission for our power not in a literalistic way, as if we had a tax statute before us, but as the basic charter of our society, setting out in spare but meaningful terms the principles of government."[76]

I've just spoken of "giving" meaning to the text. (In *Poe* Justice Harlan spoke of "giving meaning to the prohibitions of" the fifth and fourteenth amendments.[77] Justice Brennan has said that "judicial power resides in the authority to give meaning to the Constitution."[78]) Putting the matter that way may be misleading. After all, for the nonoriginalist, as for the originalist, the constitutional text is *already* meaning-ful— full of meaning. Indeed, to conclude that something is a text is to conclude that it is meaningful (to someone, if not necessarily to oneself). For the originalist, the meaning of the constitutional text is the original meaning. For the nonoriginalist, the text is meaningful in that sense *and* in the further sense that certain provisions of the text signify fundamental aspirations of the tradition. For the nonoriginalist, then, the "meaning" of the text includes what those aspirations require in particular cases. Thus, a textual provision can mean different things to different people—including different judges—since different people can understand the aspiration signified by the provision to require different things. And the meaning of a provision can change in two basic ways. First, the meaning can become *fuller*, in the sense that as new cases arise, the meaning—what the aspiration requires—is further disclosed or specified. Second, the meaning can become *different*—that is, different for a particular person if she changes her mind as to what the aspiration requires.

As the American experience bears out—and as with sacred texts—it is in significant measure because of its "writtenness", and thus its "permanence", that the constitutional text has been irrepressible, disturbing, prophetic. The importance of "writtenness" should not be discounted. As Paul Ricouer has emphasized, "[I]t is with writing that the text acquires its semantic autonomy in relation to the speaker, the original audience and the discursive situation common to the interlocutors."[79] The semantic autonomy of the constitutional text helps to explain how the text has come to have, for many of us, a meaning in addition to the original meaning—an aspirational meaning broader, more general, than the original meaning, an aspirational meaning that continues to be irrepressible, disturbing, prophetic.

Moreover, the comprehensiveness and indeterminacy of certain provisions of the constitutional text—in that sense, the text's "excess of meaning"—helps to explain the power of the text to disturb one generation of the political community to the next.[80] The "majestic generalities and ennobling pronouncements [of the Constitution]", Justice Brennan has said, "are both luminous and obscure. The ambiguity of course calls forth interpretation, the interaction of reader and text."[81] The constitutional text, like other foundational symbols for other human communities, serves a crucial role in the life of the political community: With its semantic autonomy and excess of meaning, the text provides a shared basis, in the political community, for confronting and struggling with the not-to-be-forgotten aspirations of the tradition. The text is a principal occasion of mediating past and present.

Under the originalist conception of constitutional text and interpretation, the principal point of amending the text is to control the future by establishing as supremely authoritative for the legal system a certain belief (or beliefs). Under the nonoriginalist conception, however, original beliefs are not necessarily authoritative. What, then, might be the principal point of amending the text?

Not every provision of the Constitution signifies an aspiration of the political tradition, nor need every amendment to the text to do so. To say that key provisions of the constitutional text function as a foundational symbol in and for the political tradition is not to say that every provision does so or that that is the only function of the text. Some parts of the Constitution, after all, cannot plausibly be seen as doing much more than settling housekeeping matters.[82] As I indicated earlier, a nonoriginalist approach to some provisions of the Constitution does not preclude an originalist approach to other provisions.[83] For example, one who urges a nonoriginalist approach to, say, the freedom of speech clause of the first amendment, or the due process clause of the fifth, or the equal protection clause of the fourteenth, may want to accept an originalist approach to the adjudication of federalism issues or of separation-of-powers issues.[84]

Moreover, a political community that wants to curtail the opportunity for constitutional interpreters to give any meaning to an amendment other than the original meaning—that wants to minimize the possibility for the sort of ongoing judicial development of doctrine constitutional amendment often precipitates—can *try* to do so by adding language to the Constitution the conventional or ordinary understanding of which is so determinate and stable that, as a practical matter, the amendment will bear little, if any, new meaning. It is, after all, the indeterminacy or instability (or both) of the understanding of a provision that enables the provision to take on a general aspirational meaning.[85] Imagine how constitutional doctrine regarding equal protection might have looked very different had section 1 of the fourteenth amendment provided, in relevant part, that "no State shall discriminate on the basis of race". There can never be any guarantee, however, that the determinate and stable understanding (meaning) of a provision will not, over time, become indeterminate or unstable.[86]

But, given my conception of constitutional text and interpretation and putting aside both housekeeping amendments and amendments the conventional understanding of which is both determinate and stable, what is the function of constitutional amendment?[87]

Recall the *dialogic* and *critical* character of interpretation understood as mediation of past and present. Constitutional amendment is a principal instrument with which the present can participate in that dialogic and critical encounter with the tradition, in that ongoing interpretation of the tradition, which is mediation of past and present. For example, it is one way the present can decisively reject an aspect of the tradition and establish, in its stead, a new aspiration (or a new understanding of an old aspiration) more consonant with what the present sees as the central, constitutive aspirations of the tradition. Consider, in that regard, the fourteenth amendment or the proposed Equal Rights Amendment. Constitutional amendment is also one way—a principal, dramatic way—the present can speak to the future; today's amendment will be a part of that which the future must mediate with its own present. (We must bear in mind, however, that just as "[w]hat the constitutional fundamentals meant to the wisdom of other times cannot be their measure to the vision of our time", so, too, "what those fundamentals mean for us, our descendants will learn, cannot be the measure to the vision of their time."[88]) In short, constitutional amendment is an important instrument with which the political community can exercise its stewardship over the living tradition. If constitutional adjudication is one occasion for moral discourse and growth, the amendment process is another such occasion. Moreover, whereas, as I suggest later in this chapter, constitutional adjudication should be confined to changes or innovations that are molecular rather than molar in scope, constitutional amendment can introduce changes that are molar rather than molecular. For the nonoriginalist too, then, no less than for the originalist, the amendment process has important roles to play.

Some commentators have recently explored the similarities between interpretation in law and interpretation in literature.[89] The sacred-text analogy, however, is more illuminating than the literary-text one. The relation between a political community (and tradition) and its foundational, or "constitutional", text is much more like the relation between a religious community (and tradition) and its sacred text than the relation between an "interpretive community" (to use Stanley Fish's term[90]) and whatever literary texts happen to engage it. An interpretive community doesn't often approach—read—a literary text with questions as to what the fundamental aspirations of its tradition are or how to fulfill them. (Indeed, it doesn't seem that an interpretive community—a community of readers—has a tradition or aspirations in anything like the sense religious and political communities have them.) But, of course, both religious and political communities approach their foundational texts with questions of just that sort. In that sense, its sacred text is normative for a religious community, and its foundational text for a political community, in a way a literary text is not normative for an interpretive community.[91] (Sacred texts are typically seen less as the work of particular authors than as artifacts of the tradition, whereas literary texts are typically seen more as the work of particular authors— a difference that reflects the fact that sacred texts and foundational texts are normative in a way literary texts are not.) It is more fruitful, then, to explore similarities between interpretation in law and interpretation in religion than similarities between interpretation in law and interpretation in literature—at least, insofar as foundational (constitutional) law is concerned.

I must be careful here. My claim is *not* that all constitutional interpretation is analogous to all interpretation of sacred texts. There are, after all, different sorts of constitutional interpretation *and* different sorts of interpretation of sacred texts. It is a quite common misconception in the secular academic world that interpretation of sacred texts by members of religious communities always and everywhere presupposes that the texts are divinely inspired, if not divinely authored. This great difference between interpretation of sacred texts and constitutional interpretation is thought to overwhelm whatever similarities there might be between the two. However, while *some* interpretation of sacred texts makes theistic presuppositions, not *all* such interpretation does. For example, Buddhism is, in the main, nontheistic, and interpretation of the Buddhist sutras does not presuppose that they are divinely inspired. I'm analogizing nonoriginalist constitutional interpretation to *the sort of interpretation of sacred texts that presupposes no more than that the texts are human artifacts and repositories of human wisdom.*

The Gospels, for example, and the Constitution—more precisely, aspects of the Gospels and aspects of the Constitution—function, in the sort of interpretation I'm portraying, as *symbols* that are both *commemorative* and *prophetic*. They are commemorative in that in each case the text is an occasion of *remembering*. Remembering what? The *founding, constitutive* aspirations of the religious or political tradition of which we, the religious or political community, are the present bearers, in which we, the present community, participate. They are prophetic in that in each case the text is an occasion of *responding*. Responding to what? To the founding, constitutive aspirations of the tradition. "Interpretation" both of the Gospels and of the Constitution consists, then, in remembering those founding, constitutive aspirations and responding to them.

I'm not suggesting that the sorts of constitutional and scriptural interpretation in question are identical, merely analogous. There are, of course, differences as well as similarities. In any event, *this* analogy is considerably more illuminating than that between constitutional and literary interpretation. At least, sacred texts like the Gospels are essentially and paradigmatically commemorative and prophetic. The same cannot be said about literary texts (that are not also sacred texts).

Some commentators—most notably Thomas Grey—have criticized the effort to analogize constitutional interpretation to the interpretation of sacred texts.[92] Grey's critique imputes too much to the analogical effort. I agree with just about everything Grey says, in his essay, about constitutional interpretation and the judges who engage in it.[93] My twofold point is simply this: First, in presenting nonoriginalism I'm not using "interpretation" in an idiosyncratic sense.[94] As interpretation of sacred texts discloses, one common meaning of "interpretation"—the meaning on which I rely in presenting nonoriginalism—is "mediation of past and present".

Second, and more important, if we consider what has been learned about the interpretation of sacred texts, understood as mediation of past and present—of tradition and present, of fundamental aspiration and concrete problem—we may then better understand constitutional interpretation understood as mediation of past and present. Thus, Grey's (largely misdirected) critique to the contrary notwithstanding, I persist in thinking that the analogy between constitutional interpretation and the interpretation of sacred texts is a useful one—although, to be sure, a far from perfect one. In this, I'm allied with Jaroslav Pelikan, the preeminent contemporary historian of the Christian tradition:[95] "[A] mark by which to identify a living tradition [is] its capacity to develop while still maintaining its identity and continuity. There is an analogy, susceptible of oversimplification as all analogies are and yet profound and accurate, between the American-Constitutional tradition and the Judeo-Christian tradition in their manifestation of that capacity."[96]

If, however, for one reason or another, the analogy between constitutional interpretation and the interpretation of sacred texts seems misleading, then ignore it. No argument in this chapter requires the analogy (other than, of course, my arguments *about* the analogy). The essential point remains the same even if the analogy is abandoned, namely, that constitutional adjudication ought to be understood in "hermeneutical" terms. My nonoriginalist conception of constitutional text and interpretation is hermeneutical.

> What would happen . . . if you were to think of legal interpretation not just in terms of the epistemological relationship between the reader of the law and the writer of it, . . . but also in terms of the hermeneutical relationship between tradition and application? On this hermeneutical model it would not be enough to say that the law is a product of an intention or the work of writing . . . On the contrary, on this model the law is simply a superior example of what is meant by tradition. Tradition is the mode of being of the law. The law comes down to us from the past, that is, from a world of situations different from our own, and our hermeneutical task is to determine the applicability of the law to the situation in which we now find ourselves, where we are called upon to address issues and resolve dilemmas that are particular to the moment at hand, or where we are required to provide for what the law, up until now, had never foreseen. Interpretation in this event will be an adjudication of past and present, or between a written text, the history of the understanding of it (that is, the history of its application), and the question currently to be decided. The law will be that by which we understand our present situation, even as our situation will throw its light upon the law or help us to understand the law more fully, or in a way that will enable the law to remain forceful instead of lapsing into a merely documentary existence.[97]

IV

Why is it important that the fundamental aspirations of the American political tradition signified by the Constitution be brought to bear on the life of the political community? Simply because they are fundamental aspirations of the tradition (and signified by the Constitution)? That answer has no appeal to me. It is important that such an aspiration be brought to bear if, *but only if*, the aspiration is a worthy one to which, therefore, the community should try—struggle—to remain faithful. (Recall that a judge in whose view a given provision signifies an aspiration that is not worthwhile has no reason to pursue the nonoriginalist approach to adjudication under the provision.) I would be surprised were many citizens (including judges) to challenge the view that freedom of speech, freedom of the press, freedom of religion, due process of law, and equal protection of the laws are aspirations to which the political community should struggle to remain faithful.

But is it important that the judiciary play the role assigned it by my nonoriginalist theory if the community is to succeed in its struggle to remain faithful to those aspirations—if, at least, those aspirations are to be brought to bear on and in the life of the political community? One might accept my conception of constitutional text and interpretation as proper for members of the political community, in their role as citizens, and for their political representatives, but reject it as illegitimate for the electorally unaccountable judiciary. More precisely, one might insist that insofar as the practice of judicial review is concerned, only part of what the Constitution means to us—namely, what it originally meant, its original meaning—should be deemed authoritative. That is, one might insist that the original meaning should be privileged, and the aspirational meaning bracketed, for purposes of constitutional adjudication. For example, one might think it is one thing, and acceptable, for Congress, or the President, to pursue a nonoriginalist approach to (certain provisions of) the Constitution, as of course both Congress and the President have sometimes done[98]—one might even think it acceptable for the Court to defer to Congress' or the President's nonoriginalist understanding of the Constitution, as of course the Court has sometimes done—but another thing altogether, and illegitimate, for the Court to pursue a nonoriginalist approach to the Constitution in the course of opposing itself to electorally accountable branches and agencies of government. (Thus, to say that a person is an originalist, in the sense that she adheres to an originalist conception of judicial role and of the Constitution *qua* judicially enforceable law, is not to deny that she might accept a nonoriginalist conception of the Constitution—for example, as signifying fundamental aspirations [principles, ideals] of the tradition—for purposes other than judicial enforcement.)

So, why is it important for *the Court*, in constitutional cases involving issues of individual rights, to continue to do what in the main it has done in the modern period of American constitutional law (and earlier), namely, play the judicial role that attends the conception of constitutional text and interpretation I've elaborated here, rather than the much more limited role entailed by the originalist conception? (In the modern period the Court has certainly *not* privileged the original meaning and bracketed the developing aspirational meaning.) I've addressed that question elsewhere,[99] so I can be brief here. By virtue of its political insularity, the federal judiciary has the institutional capacity to engage in the pursuit of political-moral knowledge—a search for answers to the various questions as to how we, the political community, given our basic aspirations, should live our collective life, our life in common—in a relatively disinterested manner that has sometimes seemed to be beyond the reach of the electorally accountable branches of government, for many of whose members the cardinal value is "incumbency".

This is not to suggest that judges are moral "prophets" (in the Biblical sense of "prophecy") or that the President or Congress (or state legislatures) shouldn't also pursue political-moral knowledge. Nor is it to suggest that the persons who occupy the executive and legislative branches of government aren't also capable of moral leadership.[100] My argument is simply that because of its political insularity, the federal judiciary is institutionally advantaged in dealing with controversial political-moral issues.[101] Although it is quixotic to expect truly prophetic individuals to end up on the Supreme Court of the United States, it is not at all quixotic to suppose that the members of the Supreme Court, because of their political insularity, are in an institutionally advantaged position to play a prophetic role: first, by taking seriously the prophetic potential of aspirational meaning of the constitutional text; second, by taking seriously the prophetic voices that emerge, from time to time, in the community (Martin Luther King, Jr.,'s voice, for example, or Abraham Joshua Heschel's, or Dorothy Day's).[102]

The judiciary is institutionally advantaged in other important respects. Listen to Bickel:

> [An] advantage that courts have is that questions of principle never carry the same aspect for them as they did for the legislature or the executive. Statutes, after all, deal typically with abstract or dimly foreseen problems. The courts are concerned with the flesh and blood of an actual case. This tends to modify, perhaps to lengthen, everyone's view. It also provides an extremely

salutary proving ground for all abstractions; it is conducive, in a phrase of Holmes, to thinking things, not words, and thus to the evolution of principle by a process that tests as it creates.[103]

(Recall my comments, in chapter 2, about "the priority of the particular",[104] which are relevant to Bickel's point.) Listen, too, to Hart and Wechsler:

> Does Congress in voting to enact a bill or the President in approving it actually make or purport to make . . . a determination [that the bill is constitutional]? So far at least as concerns questions of the validity of the statute as applied in particular situations, how can they?
>
> Both Congress and the President can obviously contribute to the sound interpretation of the Constitution. But are they, or can they be, so organized and manned as to be able, without aid from the courts, to build up a body of coherent and intelligible constitutional principle, and to carry public conviction that these principles are being observed? In respect of experience and temperament of personnel? Of procedure for decision? Of means of recording grounds of decision? Of opportunity for close examination of particular questions?[105]

Moreover, not every case is seminal. Many "individual rights" cases present disputes insufficiently important to capture the attention or merit the time of the legislative or executive branches of government, which, given scarce time and resources, have enough trouble dealing with the truly major issues of the day.

So, an eminently sensible division of labor as well as the federal courts' political insularity helps justify the judicial role in question.[106]

V

Recall the basic question with which this chapter began: On what moral beliefs ought a person to rely, in her capacity as judge, in deciding whether public policy regarding some matter is constitutionally valid? The originalist answer, as we've seen, is: original beliefs (in conjunction with whatever beliefs are supplemental to them). The nonoriginalist answer is: with respect to certain provisions of the constitutional text, original beliefs, and with respect to certain other provisions, the fundamental beliefs of the American political tradition signified by the provisions—beliefs or aspirations as to how the community's life, the life in common, should be lived. As Justice Brennan has said, "[T]he genius of the Constitution rests not in any static meaning it might have had in a world that is dead and gone, but in the adaptability of its great principles to cope with current problems and current needs."[107]

However, the fundamental aspirations signified by the Constitution—what Justice Brennan calls "its great principles" —are highly indeterminate.[108] And, so, different persons will have different views as to what an aspiration requires—in conjunction with all other relevant considerations[109]—in a given case or conflict. On what beliefs as to what an aspiration requires in the case at hand should a judge rely? Conventional beliefs—beliefs as to which there is a consensus in the political community? Or at least majoritarian beliefs—beliefs that enjoy majoritarian support in the community? (If no beliefs as to what an aspiration requires enjoy ascertainable majoritarian support, then the beliefs implicit in, or presupposed by, the policy choice whose constitutionality is at issue can fill in for majoritarian beliefs.) Or, instead, should the judge rely on her own beliefs as to what the relevant aspiration requires in the case at hand?

Why should a judge rely on conventional or at least majoritarian beliefs as to what the relevant aspiration requires? (1) Because that's the "democratic"—in the sense of majoritarian—thing to do? But why should judicial review be majoritarian? For the nonoriginalist no less than for the originalist, judicial review is a deliberately counifestommajoritarian institution. (2) Because the majoritarian beliefs are correct? By hypothesis, the judge thinks them incorrect. (I'm assuming a difference between what the majority believes and what the judge believes. If there is no difference in a given case, then the judge need not decide whether to rely on what the majority believes or, instead, on what she believes, for in that case it and she believe the same thing.) Because the majoritarian beliefs might be correct, and the judge should humbly accept them? The virtue of humility may call for judicial self-restraint or self-limitation (a matter I address below), but surely it does not invariably require a judge to defer to majoritarian beliefs as to what the aspiration requires.

For the very reasons I gave in the preceding section of this chapter, in support of a significant judicial role, the judge should rely on *her own beliefs* as to what the aspiration requires. Is that a worrisome proposition? The judge is almost certainly not a radical (of either the right or left).[110] The real danger is not that the judge will go too far, against government, but that she will not go far enough. To say, as I have,[111] that at their best judges can play a prophetic role in constitutional adjudication, is not to suppose that many real, live judges have either the capacity or inclination to be "prophets".[112] But even if some judges are radicals, the beliefs of such a judge cannot, in the nature of things, be determinative. No belief can be determinative in constitutional adjudication unless it is widely shared among judges. A federal trial judge is subject to reversal by a federal appeals court. A federal appeals judge needs at least one ally, since federal appeals court panels typically consist of three judges. A federal appeals court panel is subject to reversal by the federal appeals court as a whole. Moreover, any federal appellate decision is subject to reversal by the Supreme Court, where, since there are nine Justices of the Court, a Justice needs at least four allies.[113]

To say that the judge should rely on her own beliefs as to what the relevant aspiration requires in the case at hand is not to say that she should ignore original beliefs. She should not. The ratifiers, too, were participants in the tradition. In their day, they were among the stewards of the tradition. The ways in which they shaped and responded to the aspirations of the tradition may well shed important light on how we should shape and respond to those aspirations. Why assume we have nothing to learn from our past? The judge should consult original beliefs.[114]

Nor am I suggesting that the judge should ignore the beliefs of past judges. She should not ignore those beliefs—including "precedent"— or, indeed, any other source that may shed light on the problem before the court. (She cannot be immune to precedent, even if she wanted to be, if "the interpretation of a work is invariably conditioned by the prior history of the effects of that work. Any prior interpretation will count as part of that history."[115]) A thoughtful judge will rely on her own beliefs as to what the aspiration requires only after *forming* those beliefs, or at least *testing* them, in the crucible of dialogic encounter with the wisdom of the past, of the tradition, including original beliefs, precedent, and anything else relevant and helpful. As Bickel understood, "The function of the Justices . . . is to immerse themselves in the tradition of our society and of kindred societies that have gone before, in history and in the sediment of history which is law, and . . . in the thought and the vision of the philosophers and the poets. The Justices will then be fit to extract 'fundamental presuppositions' from their deepest selves, but in fact from the evolving morality of our tradition."[116] Moreover, the thoughtful judge will rely on her own beliefs only after forming or testing them in the crucible of dialogic encounter with the beliefs of her contemporaries, in particular, other judges struggling with the same or similar problems.[117]

To consult original beliefs (and precedent, etc.) is one thing, and admirable; to accord them determinative status, however, as the originalist does, is something else, and deeply problematic. Bickel observed that "as time passes, fewer and fewer relevantly decisive choices are to be divined out of the tradition of our founding. Our problems have grown radically different from those known to the Framers, and we have had to make value choices that are effectively new, while maintaining continuity with tradition."[118]

VI

Paul Brest has suggested that "the line separating law from politics is not all that distinct and . . . its very location is a question of politics."[119] Certainly the line separating adjudication from politics is not all that distinct, and its very location—that is, its *proper* location—is a question of politics in the sense of political theory. Indeed, as I said at the beginning of this chapter, at its best, constitutional adjudication is a species of deliberative, transformative politics. It is now time to elaborate and defend that claim.

A principal aim of this essay, as I indicated in the introduction, is to lend support to the position that a deliberative, transformative politics—as distinct from a politics that is merely manipulative and self-serving—is available even in a morally pluralistic society like our own. Constitutional adjudication, particularly in the modern period of American constitutional law,[120] illustrates that such a politics is available. Constitutional adjudication, at its best—that is, *nonoriginalist* constitutional adjudication—*is* such a politics.

A politics is merely manipulative and self-serving if citizens and others treat as a given, a fixed point—and thus are unself-critical towards—what they want (their "preferences") and, therefore, who they are. (One's commitments, and thus one's wants, are partly self-constitutive.[121]) On this view, our political life consists largely of manipulating others—including bargaining with them, to the extent we must—to get what we want. "Fellow humans . . . are not entirely disregarded, but are treated as simply instruments of personal satisfaction: 'Another self is known as the consumer of what I produce, the producer of what I consume, one way or another the assistant in my projects, the servant of my pleasure.' "[122] In manipulative politics, there is talk among citizens, but not talk in the sense of moral discourse. Participants in manipulative politics "certainly maintain the close identity of politics and talk, but they do so by reducing talk to the dimensions of their smallish politics and turning it into an instrument of symbolic exchange between avaricious but prudent beasts."[123]

It is difficult to imagine a politics that is not manipulative and self-serving to *some* extent. A deliberative, transformative politics contains an important further dimension, however. Such a politics, in contrast to a politics that is merely manipulative and self-serving, is one in which the questions of what ought we to want and, therefore, who ought we to be are open, not closed. Whereas manipulative politics presupposes the authority of existing preferences and is simply an instrument a citizen or group uses to maximize her or its preference satisfaction, deliberative politics is in part an instrument for calling (some of) our existing preferences into question—for challenging them—and, ultimately, for "the *transformation* of preferences through public and rational discussion."[124] On this view, our political life includes ongoing moral discourse with one another in an effort to achieve ever more insightful answers to the questions of what are our real interests, as opposed to our actual preferences, and thus what sort of persons—with what projects, goals, ideals—ought we to be. "With regard to fellow humans, the 'I-It' contact to desire gives way to an incipient 'I-Thou' relationship: 'The merely desiring self can go no further than a disingenuous recognition of other selves; in the world *sub specie moris* [as opposed to the world *sub specie voluntatis*], on the other hand, there is a genuine and unqualified recognition of other selves. All other selves are acknowledged to be ends and not merely means to our ends.' "[125]

Why should we want to cultivate or participate in deliberative politics rather than manipulative politics? What claim does deliberative politics have on us? As I explained in chapter 2, any moral community for which love of neighbor (*agape*) is a constitutive ideal—and surely that includes many moral/religious communities in the United States—should understand that ecumenical openness to the Other in discourse facilitates (as well as expresses) such love: I can hardly love the Other—the *real*, *particular* other—unless I listen to her and, in listening, gain in knowledge of her.

In genuine human relations, Gadamer notes, the important point is "to experience the 'Thou' truly as a 'Thou,' that means, not to ignore his claim and to listen to what he has to say"—an attitude which requires complete existential "openness" and availability. Since openness implies readiness to interrogate and listen to one another, genuine encounter can be said to have the character of a conversation . . . —a conversation which, far from being a series of monologues, is governed by the "dialectic of question and answer" and whose distant ancestor is the Platonic dialogue.[126]

Thus, we have an other-directed reason for cultivating and participating in deliberative politics.

We also have a self-directed reason: Deliberative politics is an essential instrument of self-knowledge. It is a basic premise of deliberative politics that we come to know who we truly are—we come to know our authentic selves, in the sense of what sort of persons we should be and thus what we should want—not monologically, but dialogically. Ronald Beiner's elegant articulation of the premise merits full quotation:

Human subjects have no privileged access to their own identity and purposes. It is through rational dialogue, and especially through political dialogue, that we clarify, even to ourselves, who we are and what we want. It is mistaken to assume that we necessarily enter into dialogue with an already consolidated view of where we stand and what we are after, conceiving of speech merely as a means to be used for winning over others, rather than as an end to be pursued for its own sake. On the contrary, communication between subjects joined in a community of rational dialogue may entail a process of moral self-discovery that will lead us to a better insight into our own ends and a firmer grasp upon our own subjectivity. Here politics functions as a normative concept, describing what collective agency should be like, rather than abiding by its present devalued meaning. The political expression of this ideal is the republican tradition. Thus inquiry into the intersubjective basis of moral and political rationality may contribute to a fuller understanding of what Arendt and Habermas call a public realm or public space, what Charles Taylor has called a deliberative culture, and what in the traditional vocabulary goes by the name of a republic. Our hope is that such reflection will ultimately conduct us back to Aristotle's insight that it is through speech and deliberation that man finds the location of his proper humanity, between beast and god, in the life of the citizen.[127]

By now it should be quite clear that, as I indicated in chapter 2, moral discourse is a principal constitutent of a deliberative, transformative politics.[128]

Given the dissensus that is a prominent feature of a morally pluralistic society like our own—given, that is, what Rawls has referred to as the "subjective circumstances" of justice[129]—how are the political disagreements and conflicts that occasion moral discourse to be resolved? At least, how is progress towards resolution to be achieved? A deliberative, transformative politics, and the moral discourse that is one of its principal constituents, require political *community* in the following sense:

> Necessarily, . . . [such questions] must be submitted to criteria of judgment to which (ideally) all those judging can assent. That is, there must be underlying grounds of judgment which human beings, *qua* members of a judging community, share, and which serve to unite in communication even those who disagree (*and who may disagree radically*). The very act of communication implies some basis of common judgment. There must be some agreement of judgment on what would count as valid historical evidence, or valid moral considerations, such as would tend to confirm or contradict one political judgment or the other (although it may well be that none of these considerations is conclusive). For judgment to be at all possible, there must be standards of judgment, and this implies a community of judgment, that is, agreements in judgment at a deeper level that grounds those at the level of ordinary political argument. In this sense, discourse rests upon an underlying substratum of agreement in judgments. The very possibility of communication means that disagreement and conflict are grounded in a deeper unity. This is what may be termed, borrowing Kantian language, a "transcendental" requirement of our discourse.[130]

One reason some persons are skeptical that a deliberative, transformative politics is available in American society—one reason they think that perhaps only a manipulative, self-serving politics is available—is that they believe that, given its morally pluralistic character, American society is not a true community, but a City of Babel. In their view, the United States is a nation of communities, but not itself a community in any significant sense of the term.

In what sense and to what extent is American society a true political community, "a judging community", notwithstanding its morally pluralistic character? In the sense and to the extent the various moral communities that together constitute the pluralistic society share certain basic aspirations as to how the collective life, the life in common, should be lived. There *are* such shared aspirations: for example, the freedoms of speech, press, and religion, due process of law, and equal protection of the laws.

Of course, the aspirations are indeterminate (or, more precisely, "underdeterminate"[131]). If they were not indeterminate, they would not be so widely shared: "[O]ur actual shared moral principles . . . have been rendered indeterminate in order to be adequately shared, adequately shared for the purposes of practical life, that is, with persons of quite different and incompatible standpoints."[132] Every large community—including, indeed especially, the American political-constitutional community—comprises dissensus as well as consensus.[133] The sharing of indeterminate norms partly constitutes the consensus. The dissensus necessitates that the articulation of the norms be indeterminate; otherwise they will not be "adequately shared for the purposes of practical life".

But to say that the shared aspirations are indeterminate is not to say that they, or the sharing of them, is inconsequential. The shared aspirations are what makes political judgment possible. They are, for us in the United States, the "underlying grounds of judgment which" we, "*qua* members of a judging community, share, and which serve to unite in communication even those who disagree (*and who may disagree radically*)." Indeed, without such shared (albeit indeterminate) standards of judgment, articulate disagreement would not even be possible. "Even divergent judgments of the most deep-seated and fundamental kind are rooted in some relation of community, otherwise one would lack the concepts with which to disagree."[134] Imagine a disagreement between two persons about a matter concerning, for example, religious liberty. A discursive effort to resolve the disagreement isn't likely to get very far, or even begin, if only one of the parties is committed to the ideal of freedom of religion. A discursive effort stands a better chance of making progress if both parties accept the ideal.

But, since the principle *is* indeterminate, what work can the ideal (or aspiration, or principle) really do in resolving, or at least diminishing, the disagreement? To accept the ideal of freedom of religion—or any other political-moral ideal—is almost certainly to accept that a particular governmental policy (or policies) is illegitimate, for example, a policy requiring persons to profess allegiance to religious doctrines to which they conscientiously object. Recall the discussion, in chapter 2, of the priority of the particular. Like other general principles, the principle of freedom of religion is a memorandum of particulars, and in the community that embraces the principle, there will be, at any given time, some particulars (at least one)—such as the belief that government may not legitimately compel allegiance to religious doctrines—as to which there is a virtual consensus and which therefore constitute the uncontested core of the principle.[135] So, parties who accept the principle but disagree as to whether policy *A* violates the principle can engage in discourse with one another about the respects in which *A* is relevantly like, or relevantly unlike, another policy (or policies) that would consensually violate the principle. They can also engage in discourse about the respects in which *A* is relevantly like or unlike another policy that has been authoritatively held to violate the principle (assuming that the holding is not then in question). Here the role of "precedent" is apparent. In this way, then, the sharing of principles, even relatively indeterminate ones, serves to ground and focus discursive efforts that otherwise would stand little chance of getting started.

In thus grounding and focusing discursive efforts aimed at diminishing conflict, shared indeterminate principles serve an essential social function: They are an occasion of *the mediation of consensus and dissensus*. In that sense, the constitutional text, understood as the symbolization of fundamental aspirations (principles, ideals) of the American political tradition/community, is a principal occasion of mediating consensus and dissensus.

> [T]he inherently ambiguous character of legal rules [and, we might add, constitutional principles] . . . permits the engagement of parties who submit contending interpretations of legal notions to participate, through the open forum of the court, in the continuous reestablishment of a rule of law that stands as their common property and their warrant of real community. . . . [A]mbiguous talk makes modern politics possible . . . by tempering the assertion of particular interests and parochial understandings with symbols whose common use, in the face of diverse interpretations, provides a mooring for social solidarity and a continuing invitation to engage in communal discourse. And that continuing invitation, finally, engages us as well in quests for meanings that transcend whatever univocal determinations we have achieved at any given moment.[136]

By this point the sense in which nonoriginalist constitutional adjudication is a species of deliberative, transformative politics (and thus demonstrates that such a politics is available to us notwithstanding the morally pluralistic character of our political community) should be evident. Constitutional discourse is simply political-moral discourse in which the operative basic standards of judgment are the fundamental aspirations of the American political tradition/community signified by the Constitution. In constitutional deliberation, as in political deliberation generally, "what is at issue . . . is not 'what should I do?' or 'how should I conduct myself?' but: 'how are we to "be" together, and what is to be the institutional setting for that being-together?' . . . It is not self-deliberation about my life, but mutual deliberation conducted between agents implicated in a common life."[137]

Although in constitutional adjudication the principal "agents" are the parties to constitutional cases (and their lawyers) and the judges, other agents include everyone—public official, editorial writer, public interest lawyer, citizen, etc.—who participates in the larger deliberation about the issue or issues in question. At its idealized best, constitutional deliberation among all the "agents implicated in a common life"—and in particular among appellate judges, especially the nine-member Supreme Court—does not proceed monologically, in which judgment is "submitted to one's fellows for confirmation or negation only subsequent to one's having arrived at the judgment independently of them".[138] Rather, constitutional deliberation is dialogical; it proceeds in a way "that does not abstract from one's discourse with one's fellows."[139] And what David Tracy has said recently of conversation holds true of constitutional conversation—that is, of constitutional deliberation as dialogue/discourse:

> Conversation is a game with some hard rules: say only what you mean; say it as accurately as you can; listen to and respect what the other says, however different or other; be willing to correct or defend your opinions if challenged by the conversation partner; be willing to argue if necessary, to confront if demanded, to endure necessary conflict, to change your mind if the evidence suggests it. These are merely some generic rules for questioning. As good rules, they are worth keeping in mind in case the questioning does begin to break down. In a sense they are merely variations of the transcendental imperatives elegantly articulated by Bernard Lonergan: "Be attentive, be intelligent, be responsible, be loving, and, if necessary, change."[140]

Again, moral deliberation requires community. Many persons participate in more than one community (for example, moral, political, intellectual, etc.). In the United States everyone is a member not only of some moral/religious community, but also of the morally pluralistic political community. Thus, a problem arises: When someone engages in moral discourse, "which community is appealed to for the intersubjective criteria or grounds of judgment, since the latter will vary as one varies the community appealed to . . . [W]here allegiances conflict, it is not decided in advance which community will supply the basis of judgment. Does my commitment to a particular people outweigh, or is it outweighed by, my commitment to" some other group? "[I]t [is not] immediately apparent to whom the judgment is addressed: a community of the past or one projected into the future; a particular national community or a community of nations; a tiny circle or associates or universal mankind. . . . Thus, the claim—judgment implies judging community—gives rise to the question: which community?"[141]

With respect to the species of political-moral deliberation that is constitutional adjudication, the right answer to the question "which community?" seems clear. Nonoriginalist constitutional adjudication implies and requires the constitutional community—the community comprising those persons and groups in the morally pluralistic society who share a commitment to the aspirations signified by the constitutional text. Thus, in constitutional-moral discourse the community appealed to for the fundamental "intersubjective criteria or grounds of judgment" is the constitutional community.

Constitutional discourse, then, *at its idealized best*, is the moral discourse of the constitutional community. Accordingly, what I said in chapter 2 about the nature and limits of moral discourse generally—in particular, about its embeddedness in a tradition/community; about the relation of the particular and the general; about the role of rules and principles; and, especially, about the revision by a community of its tradition (including, therefore, the revision by a political community of its political tradition) on the basis of its tradition—applies to constitutional discourse in particular. James Boyd White has argued that "law is most usefully seen not . . . as a system of rules, but as a branch of rhetoric; . . . the kind of rhetoric of which law is a species is most usefully seen not, as law usually is, either as a failed science or the ignoble art of persuasion, but as the central art by which community and culture are established, maintained, and transformed."[142] As I've presented it, constitutional adjudication is precisely such an enterprise. Nonoriginalist constitutional adjudication is a way—not the only way, but certainly a principal one—the constitutional community is established, maintained, and transformed.[143]

Why should we want to establish and maintain the constitutional community? For many—most?—of us, the constitutional community is a splendid achievement, and our membership in it is deeply satisfying, even ennobling. As members of the constitutional community we participate in a form of life that is both a personal and a collective good

(good for "me" and good for "us")—a form of life that enables us, both individually and collectively, to make progress, however halting, in realizing our true selves and in achieving well-being. Were we deprived of or cut off—alienated—from the constitutional (or an equivalent) community, in the way the victims of authoritarian and totalitarian societies are deprived of such a community, we would, we believe, be seriously diminished. (Membership in the constitutional community need not compete with or detract from membership in other communities, some doubtless more important to us than the constitutional community, including some communities more "local" than the constitutional community, such as family, and some more "universal", such as church.) Why should we want to transform the constitutional community? Because like any human community, the constitutional community is inevitably and always imperfect and therefore inevitably and always in need of revision.

I want to return to the question of the relation between constitutional adjudication and deliberative politics. Constitutional adjudication has a discursive character that is external as well as internal. It is internal in that the discourse is among the principal constitutional decisionmakers, the judges themselves, especially the Justices of the Supreme Court. It is external in that the discourse is between the judiciary, especially the Court, and the political community as a whole. Because of its internal discursive character, constitutional adjudication (at its idealized best) is itself a species of deliberative, transformative politics—in which the judges serve as representatives of the political community. As Justice Brennan has said: "When Justices [of the Supreme Court] interpret the Constitution they speak for their community, not for themselves alone. The act of interpretation must be undertaken with full consciousness that it is, in a very real sense, the community's interpretation that is sought."[144]

Because of its external discursive character, constitutional adjudication is an aspect of a larger deliberative, transformative politics—in which the judges serve as interlocutors of the political community and its elected representatives. Indeed, to the extent constitutional adjudication is disturbing and even prophetic, it can serve to precipitate in the political community, or enhance, a careful deliberation of certain issues as "matters of principle". This is a crucial function in a society in which a variety of constraints—for example, the value legislators place on incumbency, the sheer volume and complexity of the issues with which legislators must try to find time to deal, and a skepticism about the possibility of productive moral discourse—inhibit careful deliberation about matters of principle.

Some persons are skeptical about the possibility of a deliberative, transformative politics. Others who are not skeptical think that such a politics is for citizens and their political representatives, but not for the courts. My position, as I hope I've made clear, is that such a politics is not only for citizens and their representatives, but for the courts as well—and that, indeed, the courts have an important role to play in encouraging citizens and their representatives to take seriously the possibility of a deliberative politics. The courts play that role by (1) exemplifying such a politics in their discursive practice and (2) engaging the other branches and agencies of government in the sort of discourse that is a prime constituent of deliberative, transformative politics.[145]

Consider the matter from a somewhat different perspective: the perspective of Part I of this book, with its observations about the subject matter of "morality" and about the nature of moral reasoning. The constitutional aspirations of the American political community constitute a conception of the good for that community—a conception of how the community should live its collective life, its life in common, if it is to flourish as a political community. The nonoriginalist judicial role I've elaborated in this chapter is one way of helping the community to attend to—to remain faithful to—its (constitutional) conception of the (common) good. Put another way, the nonoriginalist judicial role—more generally, deliberative, transformative politics, of which the nonoriginalist role is a species—is in part a way of institutionalizing the ideal of self-critical rationality, which is an ideal, an aspiration, of the community.[146] My nonoriginalist constitutional theory is an elaboration of the view that, as I said, the courts, too, have an important role to play.

Originalism rejects that view. Why?

VII

That question brings us to the two principal arguments against the nonoriginalist judicial role I've presented, in particular the argument from democracy. A third argument is conspicuously question begging and thus need not be taken seriously: that the nonoriginalist judicial role is illegitimate because only the judicial role authorized by the ratifiers of the Constitution is legitimate and they did not authorize the nonoriginalist role. A fundamental issue in the debate about proper judicial role is whether the ratifiers' beliefs, including their beliefs about judicial role, should be deemed authoritative. This argument begs that question, as I indicated earlier, by presupposing an affirmative answer to it.[147]

The first argument I want to consider we can call "Easterbrook's argument".[148] Here it is, to the extent I can make it out. Whereas government (state and federal) is morally obligated to obey originalist decisions—decisions justified on originalist grounds—it is not obligated to obey nonoriginalist ones.[149] Why? What principle(s) supports that claim? Judge Easterbrook has said[150] that government is not obligated to obey a judicial decision if the judge's (or judges') rationale for the decision is: "The law is one I would oppose as a legislator, therefore it is unconstitutional." I'm not inclined to dispute the point, any more than I'm inclined to dispute the point that government is not obligated to obey a decision the rationale for which is: "The law is inconsistent with Hitler's *Mein Kampf* and, therefore, unconstitutional." However, the assumed truth of those points does not entail the truth of the claim that government is not obligated to obey *Roe* v. *Wade*[151] or any other nonoriginalist decision. Again, what principle supports the claim that whereas government is morally obligated to obey originalist decisions, it is not obligated to obey nonoriginalist ones?

Easterbrook's argument, the principal portions of which I quote in the margin,[152] seems to be that government is obligated to obey originalist decisions for a reason that has no force with respect to nonoriginalist ones. Government is morally obligated to act consistently with original beliefs, the argument runs, but not with beliefs that fall outside the category of original beliefs. Original beliefs, but not nonoriginal ones, are morally binding on government; that is, original beliefs, but not nonoriginal ones, have moral authority. Originalist decisions possess the authority of original beliefs, but nonoriginalist ones do not.[153]

How sound is this argument? *Why* is government morally obligated to act consistently with original beliefs? To say that public officials are obligated to act consistently with the Constitution—because, say, they have taken an oath to do so—is not to say that they are obligated to act consistently with original beliefs. "The Constitution" is not axiomatically equivalent to "original beliefs". "The Constitution" can well mean, in part, "the aspirations or ideals signified by the constitutional text". Indeed, it is counterintuitive to suppose that today's public officials are morally obligated to defer to the beliefs either of the long-dead and mostly WASP men who ratified the original Constitution and the Bill of Rights or of the long-dead and mostly WASP men who ratified the second Constitution—the Civil War amendments.[154] (Again, to consult original beliefs is one thing; to deem them authoritative, something else.)

Are public officials obligated to act consistently with original beliefs because, independently of their oaths to act consistently with the Constitution, they have consented, at least implicitly, to do so? Is the myth of consent to rear its silly head again? If anyone has consented to rule by original beliefs, few have: few public officials (maybe an occasional judge seeking nomination to the Supreme Court by the Reagan administration), and few people generally. (I certainly haven't consented. Has Judge Easterbrook? When? How?) If anything is authoritative for public officials in the American political community, it is, of course, the fundamental, constitutive aspirations of the American political tradition (and the principal textual embodiment of those aspirations: the Constitution). What else could possibly ground claims made in and to that community—claims about what public officials should or should not do—but those aspirations or ideals or principles? In any event, Easterbrook's argument has simply not been made out.

Lest Judge Easterbrook (or someone else) counter by announcing that I haven't made out the argument that government is morally obligated to obey nonoriginalist decisions, let me hasten to add that I've made no such claim—nor need I. Just as the argument that the legislature should play a particular role in government does not presuppose that anyone is morally obligated to obey directives issued by the legislature if it is playing the prescribed role, so, too, the argument that the judiciary should play a particular role in government—whether originalist *or nonoriginalist*—does not presuppose that anyone, including any public official, is morally obligated to obey decisions made by the judiciary if it is playing the prescribed role. The argument that a political institution should play such and such a role in no way requires the premise that those legally subject to the institution are morally obligated to obey the institution if it is playing the prescribed role. Indeed, one can insist that there is no moral obligation, absolute or presumptive, to obey all nonoriginalist constitutional decisions and nonetheless consistently believe that, all things considered, it would be better for us Americans were the federal judiciary to play the nonoriginalist role in (all or some) constitutional cases. Similarly, one can insist that there is no moral obligation to obey all originalist constitutional decisions and yet believe that it would be better were the federal judiciary to play the originalist role. (Recall that in chapter 5 I contended against the claim that there is a moral obligation, absolute or even presumptive, to obey "the law".)

I now want to turn to the second argument against the nonoriginalist judicial role elaborated in this chapter: the argument from democracy. According to this argument, which is more difficult and therefore more important than Easterbrook's argument, the nonoriginalist role is illegitimate because undemocratic. What does it mean to say that the nonoriginalist judicial role is "undemocratic"? And is it?

The value or ideal of electorally accountable policymaking—the principle that governmental policymaking (by which I mean simply decisions as to which values among competing values shall prevail, and as to how those values shall be implemented) should be subject to control by persons accountable to the electorate[155]—has an axiomatic or canonical status in American political-legal culture. But so do certain other values or aspirations, including those signified by certain provisions of the constitutional text. There is a deep and ineradicable tension in the American political tradition between the value of electorally accountable policymaking and certain other values or ideals. As Robert McCloskey put it:

> Popular sovereignty suggests *will*; fundamental law suggests *limit*. The one idea conjures up the vision of an active, positive state; the other idea emphasizes the negative, restrictive side of the political problem. It may be possible to harmonize these seeming opposites by logical sleight of hand, by arguing that the doctrines of popular sovereignty and fundamental law were fused in the Constitution, which was a popularly willed limitation. But it seems unlikely that Americans in general achieved such a synthesis and far more probable, considering our later political history, that most of them retained the two ideas side by side. This propensity to hold contradictory ideas simultaneously is one of the most significant qualities of the American political mind at all stages of national history, and it helps substantially in explaining the rise to power of the United States Supreme Court.[156]

Any conception of proper judicial role represents one way of embodying or institutionalizing the tension. No plausible conception—including the originalist—eradicates the tension. Any plausible conception compromises the value of electorally accountable policymaking ("popular sovereignty") to some extent. A question for constitutional theory is: To what extent ought the value to be compromised, and in the service of what other values? (Or: To what extent should the other values be compromised in the service of the value of electorally accountable policymaking?)

In a previous book I assumed not merely that the value of electorally accountable policymaking has an axiomatic status in American political-legal culture. I made the further, mistaken assumption that in American political-legal culture it is axiomatic that the value of electorally accountable policymaking is lexically prior to all other values, such that any judicial role that compromises the value of electorally accountable policymaking is illegitimate—or, at least, such that any judicial role that compromises the value of electorally accountable policymaking to a greater extent than another judicial role is normatively inferior to that other role.[157] Although the value of electorally accountable policymaking *is* axiomatic in American political-legal culture, it is *not* axiomatic that that value is lexically prior to all other values. Justice Brennan has said that "[f]aith in democracy is one thing, blind faith quite another."[158] Americans have traditionally had faith in democracy, of course, but not blind faith. Consider, in that regard, this passage by Jack Rakove:

> [T]the framers now most commonly appear as the perversely enlightened architects of the maddening obstacle course that has to be run every time a deserving piece of legislation is launched through a treacherous maze of congressional committees and executive agencies more worthy of a byzantine satrapy than the world's greatest democracy. In the view of such prominent political scientists as Robert Dahl and James MacGregor Burns, "the framers deliberately created a framework of government that was carefully designed to impede and even prevent the operation of majority rule." . . . Rather than look for ways to break the deadlock . . . [the framers] bequeathed, modern students of "The Founding" would have us learn to appreciate the timeless concerns that led the framers to prevent government from becoming too vigorous for our own good. . . . In the influential formulation of Martin Diamond: "The reason of the Founders constructs the system within which the passions of the men who come after may be relied upon to operate in safely moderated channels."[159]

So, in evaluating the claim that nonoriginalism is "undemocratic", we must not assume that the value of electorally accountable policymaking has an axiomatic priority over all other fundamental values.

We must avoid as well the false assumption that a particular conception of democracy, of how our overall governmental apparatus should be organized, is axiomatic for the American political tradition, such that the only question is whether the judicial role in question—here, the nonoriginalist role—is consistent with that axiomatic conception. That assumption won't do, because the issue is precisely how our overall governmental apparatus should be organized. No particular conception of democracy—that is, no particular conception of what the judicial role in that governmental apparatus should be—is axiomatic for the tradition. The tradition has never settled, even provisionally, on what the judicial role should be. That issue—unlike, say, the issue of whether blacks, or women, or eighteen-years-olds should be permitted to vote—has been and remains widely contested within the tradition.

The debate, properly understood, is about which conception of democracy should prevail. As Larry Alexander has emphasized, the constitutional-theoretical debate is "a dispute over what authority should be given to the political morality of present popular majorities, past and present Supreme Court justices, the various persons, committees, conventions, and legislatures associated with the framing of the Constitution, the words of the Constitution, and so forth."[160] Any particular conception of democracy, of what the judicial role should be within the overall governmental apparatus, must be defended. To presuppose the authoritative status of a particular conception is to beg the question. One must *argue for* a particular conception. (To argue for a particular conception of democracy, of judicial role within the overall governmental apparatus, is to argue for a particular conception of constitutional text and interpretation, namely, the conception entailed by the prescribed judicial role.) How do we conduct that argument—by reference to what considerations? How else but by reference to the ways in which a particular conception of judicial role comports with (or fails to comport with) the constitutive purposes and projects—the central aspirations—of the political tradition? A lot turns, therefore, on how one understands those central, constitutive aspirations.

One such aspiration, of course, is for governance that is both responsive and, because it is not always responsive, accountable to the electorate. Electorally accountable government is plainly not the only constitutive aspiration of the American political tradition, however. The tradition has aspired to "liberty and justice for all" as well as to "popular

sovereignty". ("As we adapt our institutions to the ever-changing conditions of national and international life, . . . [the] ideals of human
dignity—liberty and justice for all individuals—will continue to inspire
and guide us because they are entrenched in our Constitution", said
Justice Brennan.[161])

A central aspiration of the tradition has been to achieve justice, and
justice has generally been seen to lie partly in the direction marked out
by more particular aspirations signified by various constitutional provisions regarding human rights. Put another way, a central aspiration of
the tradition has been to keep faith with the more particular aspirations
regarding the form of life of the polity, the life in common. To say this
is not to deny that at any given point in the course of the tradition there
have been various competing visions of the requirements of justice, or
that various considerations of self-interest have powerfully distorted
the visions and pursuit of justice. Still, a constitutive aspiration of
the American political tradition has been to achieve "liberty and justice
for all".

If justice can be known and achieved—if, at least, we can make some
progress in that direction, as in Part I of this book I argued we could—is
the judicial role that attends my conception of constitutional text and
interpretation one way to achieve it? (I'm not suggesting it's the only
way.) Consider modern constitutional doctrine regarding, for example,
freedom of speech, freedom of religion, and racial and other sorts of
equality. Imagine what public policy regarding these matters might
have been today had the Supreme Court not played the nonoriginalist
role in the modern period. Which body of doctrine—the constitutional
doctrine we have or the public doctrine we might well have had—is
more defensible as a matter of political morality—as a matter, that is, of
the correct interpretation of our tradition, of its aspirations to freedom of
expression, freedom of religion, and racial equality? This is not to
endorse every detail of modern constitutional doctrine regarding, for
example, freedom of speech, but only to suggest that, on balance, the
doctrine we have is sounder than the doctrine we might have had.[162]

"But", you say, "there's no guarantee the Court won't mess up in
the future. It has in the past. Remember *Dred Scott* and *Lochner!*"[163]
(Or, depending on your point of view, "Look at *Roe* v. *Wade!*") Certainly the Court is a fallible institution; it has made mistakes, and surely
will again. In the modern period, however, on balance, the Court's

record in the service of individual rights has been admirable. (Even Henry Steele Commager, who in the 1940s criticized the Court's record as irrelevant, if not hostile, to individual rights,[164] has recently sung the Court's praises.[165]) As Robert Cover once observed:

> The 20th century has too often witnessed disastrous and cruel degenerations of majoritarianism into totalitarianism. These calamities have often centered either about state-sponsored persecution of religious, racial or ethnic minorities or party-sponsored manipulation of the machinery of information and politics. The first is an attempt to force "society" into the mold of the "state," the second is the further transformation of the state into the party. These processes can plausibly be understood to be diseases exacerbated by contemporary mass politics which a simple appeal to majorities or supermajorities (Constitutional amendment) is incapable of curing.
>
> It is not clear why the Supreme Court has been capable of exercising leadership and leverage in counteracting such tendencies in the United States for the past 25 or 30 years. But it has done so.[166]

One is not obliged to conclude that, in the modern period, the Court's nonoriginalist role has been an important way (which is not to say the only way) of keeping faith with the tradition's aspiration to justice. I suspect most of us would rather have the burden of defending *that* proposition, however, than the proposition that the Court's role has been ineffective or unimportant.

Why focus on "the modern period"—the period, roughly, since 1954, when *Brown* v. *Board of Education* was decided? Because the issue for the polity now living is whether any given judicial role is likely to be, "in our own time", as Bickel said,[167] an effective way of keeping faith with the tradition's aspiration to justice. Any answer is, of course, speculative. But what the Court has done in the modern period—in the past generation—seems more indicative of what it is likely to do "in our own time", if it continues to play the nonoriginalist judical role, than what the Court did several generations ago. This is not to deny that what the Court did several generations ago is relevant to our inquiry, or to say that what it has done in the past generation is an infallible guide to what it will do in our own time.

Consider now another constitutive aspiration of the American political tradition: the aspiration to electorally accountable government. Is the nonoriginalist role a good way of keeping faith with that aspiration? Because the Court is an electorally unaccountable institution, a larger—

that is, nonoriginalist—judicial role is indisputably more problematic than a smaller—originalist—one, in terms of the aspiration to electorally accountable government.

My argument, then, is not that the nonoriginalist role the Court has played in the modern period is as good a way as a more constrained role, much less a better way, of keeping faith with the tradition's aspiration to electorally accountable government. The originalist role is a better way of keeping faith with that aspiration. There is, however, that other constitutive aspiration—to justice. My suggestion, which concededly is speculative (but speculation is all we have to go on here), is that what the tradition is likely to gain, in terms of justice—in terms, that is, of the correct mediation of the past of the tradition with its present—from a judicial role of the nonoriginalist sort the Court has (often) played in the modern period, more than offsets what the tradition is likely to lose, in terms of "responsiveness" and "accountability".

What is the tradition likely to lose? Certainly the electorate cannot exercise the comparatively direct and immediate political control (through its elected representatives) over the constitutional decisions of the Court that it can exercise over the Court's nonconstitutional decisions. But American history leaves little doubt that when a serious tension develops between the direction in which the Court is leading and the direction in which the electorate, in the end, after deliberation, is determined to move, the electorate, not the Court, will prevail.[168] The various mechanisms of political control or influence over the Court—in particular, the appointments power and, ultimately, the amendment power—have proven adequate in that regard.[169]

Constitutional decisionmaking by the Court is responsive to the polity—not immediately, but it is responsive. Still, immediacy counts for something, and there is no denying that time can be lost. (Time is not always lost. In the course of the dialectical interplay between Court and polity I've discussed elsewhere,[170] the political community may eventually come to see it as a good thing it did not get its way. When that happens, time is not lost. But, sometimes, time has been lost, as in the case of child labor legislation.[171]) The significance one attaches to that occasional loss depends mainly on the significance one attaches to the actual or potential gain, in terms of justice. A black person is more likely to attach greater significance to, to value more highly, the gain, in the modern period, than a white person. Whose point of view is more likely distorted? (In South Africa, whose point of view is more likely distorted: the Black's or the Afrikaner's?)

Moreover, one who has a strong sense of herself, of her identity, as a participant in a living tradition, whether religious or political, is likely to be more concerned that institutional authority be allocated so that the tradition stands a better chance of getting it right—achieving justice— than that a majority of the community get its way *here and now*.

Does all this seem inconclusive? It *is* inconclusive—*but for originalists no less than for nonoriginalists*. One's decision to accept or reject, one's argument for or against, any conception of judicial role, including the originalist conception, is always *contingent*, *speculative*, and *provisional* and therefore *revisable*. The decision is contingent because it is rooted partly in one's sense or vision of justice—in one's view of the proper interpretation of the tradition, of the correct mediation of the past of the tradition with its present.[172] The decision is speculative because it is grounded partly on our answers to counterfactual questions about the past and present ("Where would we be today had the Court not played a nonoriginalist role in the last thirty years?") and partly on our predictions of future governmental (both judicial and nonjudicial) behavior on the basis of past behavior.[173] And the decision is provisional and therefore revisable because one's sense or vision of justice may change, one's predictions may prove wrong, or both.

Except for the true believers of various stripes—originalist *and* nonoriginalist true believers—constitutional theory is, alas, an inconclusive enterprise. How could it be otherwise?

> Designing institutional authority to decide future questions that are, at present, only dimly perceived is inherently uncertain and always revisable in the light of new information. . . . [B]ecause all . . . [conceptions of judicial role] . . . are strategic designs, none of them is impervious to constant reassessment and controversy. . . . [B]ecause such conceptions are strategic, they are always up for reconsideration. The issue of judicial review can be settled only tentatively, never for all time.[174]

VIII

An important question, as I indicated in the preceding section, is whether nonoriginalism compromises the value of electorally accountable policymaking to an acceptable extent (in the service of other fundamental values). The answer depends in important part on how moderately or immoderately judges—especially Supreme Court Justices—have played and are likely to play the nonoriginalist role. A theory of judicial self-restraint or self-limitation can and should be an important component of nonoriginalism.

Constitutional aspirations (in conjunction with other relevant considerations) rule out some, but not all, choices. Indeed, they fail to rule out indefinitely many choices. The judicial function is to determine which choices are ruled out. The legislative function is to select among the choices not ruled out (which sometimes requires that the legislature make a provisional determination as to which choices are ruled out). It would be a gross abuse of her function for a judge to invalidate a policy choice not because it was, in her view, ruled out by the relevant aspiration, but because it was a choice she would have opposed as a legislator. According to the nonoriginalist theory I'm presenting, a necessary condition of legitimate judicial invalidation of a policy choice is that the choice be ruled out by the relevant aspiration.

A necessary condition, but not a sufficient one. I haven't argued that if a judge believes a choice to be ruled out, she should invalidate it. (I *have* said that if a judge does not believe a choice to be ruled out, but believes merely that the choice is not preferable, she should *not* invalidate it.) There are other conditions that must be satisfied, according to my nonoriginalist theory, before a judge may invalidate a policy choice.

The judge must be confident of her position that the policy choice is ruled out by the relevant aspiration(s). She must humbly acknowledge the limits of her personal, and the court's, institutional competence with respect to the issue or sort of issue in question and face the possibility that she may be wrong. (Indeed, she should face the possibility that the issue is of a sort with which the judiciary cannot helpfully deal.[175]) If the issue is one about which other public officials—including not merely other judges, but also legislative and executive officials—have truly deliberated, and if, after deliberation, they have concluded that the policy choice is not ruled out by the relevant aspiration, the judge must face the possibility that they are right. To the degree that possibility seems to her a realistic one, to that degree she should hesitate to invalidate the policy choice.

That general caution must be heeded especially when the issue is particularly complex and seems to defy confident resolution one way or another. (Isn't abortion such an issue? In the penultimate section of this chapter I discuss the Court's handling of the abortion issue in *Roe* v. *Wade*.[176]) The caution must be heeded especially, too, when the consequences of resolving the issue the way the judge is inclined to resolve it are difficult to foresee and may be quite problematic.[177]

Perhaps resolution of the issue the way the judge is inclined to resolve it is, all things considered, relatively unimportant and so not worth the expenditure of institutional capital, or at least the provocation, that would be involved. Imagine, for example, a case in which the Court is asked to enjoin the federal government from putting "In God We Trust" on coins.

Or, perhaps resolution of the issue the way the judge is inclined to resolve it is *not* "relatively unimportant", all things considered, but perhaps, nonetheless, resolution of the issue that way would be exceptionally controversial, threatening to precipitate a societal crisis and perhaps even impair the Court's capacity to function effectively. Consider, in that regard, this judgment: "[I]n ordering that [school] desegregation proceed with all deliberate speed [rather than immediately], the Court [in *Brown* v. *Board of Education*[178]] acknowledged the considerable disagreement that currently existed. That should not surprise us, nor is it wrong. The Court is not the supreme actor in American politics; it is only one actor among many seeking to persuade the others within the ongoing political process."[179]

Perhaps, however, a judge believes that she must resolve the issue the way she is inclined to resolve it, notwithstanding the possible political and institutional consequences, lest a grave injustice go unremedied.[180] What then? It is probably impossible to articulate sensible criteria of judicial self-restraint, the unconditional adherence to which will not "destroy . . . [the Court's] legitimate and necessary function of inhibiting at least some of the grosser forms of unconstitutional adventurism undertaken by the other two branches of the national government and by the states."[181]

Obviously, then, the "theory" of judicial self-limitation I've (barely) sketched here is not determinative or determinate. It is meant to be neither. I've merely suggested some considerations the thoughtful judge will want to bring to bear in deciding whether to invalidate a policy choice that, in her perhaps tentative view, is ruled out by the relevant aspiration. (These or similar considerations counseling self-restraint are relevant to originalist judicial practice, too, though because a non-originalist judicial role is larger than an originalist one, the value of self-restraint is more consequential in the context of nonoriginalist judicial practice.) Concededly, different judges will be influenced by these considerations in different degrees. Some judges are more confident of their views than other judges. (Doubtless some judges should be more confident—and, therefore, some should be less confident). Similarly, some judges are more risk-averse than others—or at least more sensitive to the potential political and institutional costs, in certain situations, of invalidating particular policy choices. The basic point is that even a judge who pursues a nonoriginalist approach to constitutional adjudication, rather than an originalist approach, can and should appreciate the importance of acting moderately rather than imperially or precipitously in deciding whether a policy choice regarding some matter is to be invalidated.[182]

Perhaps the most important reason for such moderation concerns a matter I discussed in section VI of this chapter: the salutary potential for productive dialectical interplay between constitutional adjudication on the one hand and, on the other, electorally accountable politics.[183]

IX

Did the Supreme Court act in a properly moderate way in *Roe* v. *Wade*?[184]

In 1973, in *Roe* v. *Wade*, the Supreme Court ruled, in relevant part, that under the United States Constitution no state may criminalize previability abortions—abortions that take place prior to the point at which fetuses become "viable".[185] The Court's decision in *Roe* is perhaps the most persistently controversial constitutional ruling since the 1930s. It is certainly the most controversial constitutional decision since 1954, when, in *Brown* v. *Board of Education*,[186] the Court ruled that public schools may not be segregated on the basis of race. Just as *Brown* was the principal occasion for an earlier generation of constitutional theorists to reflect on the Court's proper role in interpreting the Constitution, *Roe* has been the principal occasion for the present generation of constitutional theorists to reflect on that question. This chapter would not be complete were I to fail to comment, against the background of the constitutional theory I've elaborated here, on *Roe*.

The originalist critique of *Roe* is simple and, accepting *arguendo* originalist premises, powerful. The critique is not merely that the Court in *Roe* gave the wrong answer to the question it set for itself—in effect, the question of what public policy regarding abortion states may adopt. The originalist critique is more fundamental: The Court was wrong to set that question for itself. Because legislation like that ruled unconstitutional by the Court in *Roe*—legislation that outlawed all abortions except those for the purpose of saving the life of the mother—does not implicate, much less violate, any constitutional provision *as originally understood*, the Court simply had no business making abortion its business (according to originalism).[187]

John Ely's famous essay on *Roe*[188] is perhaps the best example of a nonoriginalist critique of *Roe*. According to Ely, legislation like that struck down in *Roe* does not implicate any value or principle that may reasonably be inferred from either the words of, or the structure of government ordained by, the Constitution.[189] Thus, although Ely arrived by a different route—a route that does not confine constitutional interpretation to the discovery of the original meaning—he arrived at the same destination as the originalist: the conclusion that the Court simply had no business making abortion its business. According both to originalism and to the nonoriginalist John Ely, no constitutional principle is substantially (as distinct from trivially or peripherally) implicated in the legislative decision whether or to what extent to outlaw abortions (that is, abortions for a purpose other than saving the life of the mother), any more than a constitutional principle is substantially implicated in the legislative decision, for example, whether or to what extent to explore the solar system. Neither matter—abortion or exploration of the solar system—is any part of the Court's constitutional business.

I reject the originalist critique of *Roe*, because I reject the premises on which the critique is based, which confine constitutional interpretation to the discovery of the original meaning. I reject Ely's nonoriginalist critique as well. Ely is simply wrong in thinking that legislation like that at issue in *Roe* does not implicate any constitutional principle.

Section 1 of the fourteenth amendment says, in relevant part: "nor shall any State deprive any person of . . . liberty . . . without due process of law . . . ." The crucial words, for present purposes, are "liberty" and "due process of law". Whatever its original meaning might have been, "liberty" has come to signify to us—it has come to mean—the freedom of the individual to shape the most fundamental aspects of his or her life according to the dictates of his or her informed and conscientious judgment.[190] This liberty is not absolute, of course. A state may deprive a person of some part of such liberty, but not "without due process of law". Whatever the original meaning of "due process of law", the proposition that a state may not deprive a person of liberty without due process of law has come to mean to us, *inter alia*, the principle or ideal that government may not deprive us of our precious liberty to shape our lives unless government must do so in order to secure some overriding good. That this principle has constitutional status—that it is a constitutional aspiration of the American political tradition/community—has been quite clear for a very long time.[191] And that this principle is substantially implicated in the legislative decision whether and to what extent to outlaw abortions could scarcely be more apparent.[192] Given nonoriginalist premises, abortion *is* a proper part of the Court's constitutional business. As Justice Potter Stewart wrote in his concurring opinion in *Roe*, "Several decisions of this Court make clear that freedom of personal choice in matters of marriage and family life is one of the liberties protected by the Due Process Clause of the Fourteenth Amendment. . . . As recently as . . . [1971], in *Eisenstadt* v. *Baird*, 405 U.S. 438, 453, we recognized 'the right of the *individual*, married or single, to be free from unwarranted governmental intrusion into matters so fundamentally affecting a person as the decision whether to bear or beget a child.' That right necessarily includes the right of a woman to decide whether or not to terminate her pregnancy."[193]

However, to conclude that, contrary both to the originalist critique and to Ely's nonoriginalist critique, abortion is indeed a proper part of the Court's business, is not to conclude that the Court gave the right answer to the question it set for itself in *Roe*. It is to conclude merely that the Court was not wrong to set the question for itself. In my view— my *nonoriginalist* view—the Court gave the wrong answer to the question it set for itself.

The Texas statute at issue in *Roe* outlawed all abortions except those for the purpose of saving the life of the mother. To say that such a statute substantially implicates the constitutional principle set forth above is not to say that, on careful analysis of the competing considerations, such a statute violates the principle. After all, the "liberty" protected by the due process clause is not absolute. Moreover, the protection of fetal life is surely more than a trivial good. In *Roe*, should the Court have sustained the Texas statute? (Perhaps the Texas statute, to use the *Eisenstadt* language that appears in the part of Justice Stewart's opinion in *Roe* quoted above, constituted a "*warranted* governmental intrusion".) Or should it have done what it did, namely, rule that no state may criminalize previability abortions of any sort, even "non-therapeutic" or "elective" abortions? Or, instead, should the Court have done something in between these two extremes.

I strongly doubt that sensitive application of the constitutional principle of due process can support the conclusion that a state may not outlaw previability abortions of any sort. Such a conclusion seems to me to require a premise—that the protection of fetal life is not a good of sufficient importance—obviously not entailed by that principle. Moreover, because the issue the premise addresses—the value of fetal life—is so widely contested in American society, and, further, because the issue is one as to which people of good will and high intelligence (among others) seem irresolvably to disagree, it is not at all clear that the premise is an appropriate basis for constitutional judgment. To the contrary, reliance on the premise as a basis for constitutional judgment seems plainly imperial. I don't see how to avoid the conclusion, therefore, that the Court should not have done what it did in *Roe.*

I also conclude, however, that the Court should not have sustained the Texas statute. What, then, should it have done? What "in between" path, what middle way, should the Court have taken?

The Texas statute made it a crime to "procure an abortion" except "by medical advice for the purpose of saving the life of the mother."[194] The Court should have ruled that three further exceptions are constitutionally required: first, abortions for the purpose of protecting the physical health of the mother from a significant threat of serious damage; second, previability abortions for the purpose of terminating a pregnancy caused by rape or incest; and, third, abortions for the purpose of terminating a pregnancy that would result in the birth of a genetically defective child whose life would be short and painful.[195] Because the Texas statute did not provide for such exceptions, it was constitutionally infirm and should have been invalidated.[196]

Why should the Court have ruled that the enumerated exceptions are constitutionally required? Because it is most unlikely that abortion legislation failing to provide even for those relatively narrow exceptions would be enacted or maintained in contemporary American society unless the importance, the value, of the well-being of the women affected (the importance of the various "liberty" interests at stake)—women whose unwanted pregnancies posed a significant threat of serious damage to their physical health, or were due to rape or incest, or would result in the birth of a genetically defective child whose life would be short and painful—was unfairly, that is, discriminatorily, disregarded or at least discounted by those supporting the legislation.[197] At least, that conclusion seems to me more plausible than any other. Significantly, in 1967 the American Medical Association and in 1972 the American Bar Association gave their support to exceptions like the three enumerated above.[198] Moreover, the American Law Institute's Model Penal Code provided for such exceptions.[199] Legislation that would not exist but for the discriminatory discounting of the value of the well-being of the women affected—like, for example, legislation that would not exist but for the discriminatory discounting of the value of the well-being of the nonwhite persons affected—implicates and indeed offends the constitutional principle of the equal protection of the laws as well as the constitutional principle of due process. Government may not, consistently with the principle of equal protection, count the well-being of one person or group as worth less, by virtue of race or gender, than the value of the well-being of another person or group.[200]

There is no reason to think, and ample reason to doubt, that the ruling I've sketched would have been very controversial.[201] Of course, a vigorous political effort would doubtless have been mounted in Texas (and elsewhere), in response to the ruling, to put criminal laws against abortion—now containing the constitutionally required exceptions—back on the books. However, a ruling that the exceptions enumerated above are constitutionally required, and the Texas statute (and similar statutes) therefore constitutionally infirm, would have shifted the burden of legislative inertia from those opposing criminal laws against abortion to those supporting such laws, thus helping insure that the various considerations against criminalizing previability abortions, including the considerations supporting exceptions beyond those enumerated above, were given due consideration in the legislative process.[202] (Few contend against the constitutional legitimacy of criminalizing most postviability abortions.) Moreover, such a ruling would have given the Court the opportunity to help shape the ensuing political debate by saying something like the following:

> Because it fails to provide for the enumerated exceptions the Texas statute (and similar statutes) is constitutionally infirm. Some persons argue that even more exceptions are constitutionally required—and required for essentially the same reason the enumerated exceptions are required. (Indeed, some persons argue that states may not outlaw previability abortions of any sort, even "nontherapeutic" or "elective" abortions.) This case does not require

that we address that argument. This is just as well: The matter of yet further exceptions is better addressed, in the first instance at least, by state legislatures.

It is imperative that the Texas legislature (and the legislatures of other states whose abortion statutes are like Texas') deliberate anew about the difficult matter of public policy regarding abortion. And as it does so, it must not lose sight of the fact that, as we have indicated today, the matter is one implicating fundamental constitutional principles—the principles of due process of law and of the equal protection of the laws.

The constitutional ruling I'm suggesting the Court should have made in *Roe*, and the politics of judicial role implicit in that ruling, are much more consistent with the premises of my nonoriginalist constitutional theory than the ruling the Court actually made there and the politics of judicial role implicit in that ruling. As I began to suggest at the close of the preceding section of this chapter, an important reason why non-originalist constitutional adjudication must be moderate rather than immoderate, molecular rather than molar—an important reason why a nonoriginalist judge must take seriously considerations counseling self-restraint—is that the constitutional dialogue between the judiciary and the political community as a whole will proceed more productively if the judiciary acts cautiously and incrementally rather than radically or imperially. (Surely a decision that follows the lead of the AMA and the ABA, which are hardly radical organizations, cannot fairly be characterized as imperial.) No conversation is likely to be productive if one of the interlocutors assumes an arrogant stance, pontificating rather than listening patiently and patiently searching for common ground.

The question of what public policy regarding abortion should be is surely an unusually difficult one, and the Supreme Court is an obviously fallible institution. The Court should not have tried to preempt discourse about that question. Rather, it should have acted so as to enhance such discourse. (The fact that the Court failed in its attempt to preempt such discourse is beside the point.) And the Court should have acted that way not simply because that would have been the more "democratic" thing to do, but also, and more fundamentally, because the Court, like the rest of us, might have learned something useful from the ensuing discourse—a discourse hopefully informed by the Court's insistence that the constitutional principles of due process and equal protection were at stake.

When such constitutional conversation is productive, we may hope

that, as I've put it elsewhere, "[i]n the constitutional dialogue between
the Court and the other agencies of government—a subtle, dialectical
interplay between Court and polity—what emerges is a far more self-
critical political morality than would otherwise appear, and therefore
likely a more mature political morality as well."[203]

There is rampant misunderstanding—in the legal-academic community
as well as outside it—that to be a nonoriginalist is to support a no-holds-
barred judicial "activism". As my discussion—my nonoriginalist critique—of *Roe* illustrates, the truth is to the contrary. To be a nonoriginalist is not necessarily to support an imperial judicial role—a
point that bears emphasis, given the extent of the misunderstanding. I
am a nonoriginalist. But I reject an imperial judicial role.

X

It has been suggested that in the modern period of American constitutional law, constitutional adjudication hasn't really achieved all that
much.[204] It has also been suggested that the truly important issues
facing the American political community in the foreseeable future are
not of a sort with which the judiciary can helpfully deal. It has been
suggested, finally, that the most important imperative on the constitutional agenda in the years ahead is not the maintenance of a large
judicial role in American government, but the discovery of ways to
empower the politically powerless and to make possible much more
pervasive and meaningful citizen participation in political life.[205]
    The first two suggestions, as generalizations, seem to me indiscrimi-
nate.[206] With respect to the third suggestion, I can't argue the point
here, but I think it is a mistake to suppose that there is any serious
tension between the maintenance of a significant judicial role in constitutional cases and the empowerment/participation goals.[207]
    However, let's assume, *arguendo*, that, given the nature of the issues
facing the American political community in the next generation, we
cannot realistically expect a judicial contribution to their resolution as
significant as the judicial contribution to the resolution of the critical
issues that faced us in the recent past, like racial discrimination. Let's
assume, too, that in the best of all possible political worlds, the need for
a large judicial contribution would be small. The fact remains that, in
the real world of American politics, constitutional adjudication has an

important role to play in constantly reminding us, by example, of something we seem too often in danger of overlooking or forgetting, or even denying: A deliberative, transformative politics—participation in which, as I've explained, is an important personal as well as collective good—*is* available to us, notwithstanding the morally pluralistic character of our society.

Conclusion

My fundamental subject in this book has been the proper relation of moral beliefs, including moral beliefs religious in character, to politics and law in a morally pluralistic society. That is a large subject. I've addressed it only partially and provisionally.

I began, in Part I, by sketching a particular understanding—a naturalist or neo-Aristotelian understanding—of "moral". I then turned to two basic problems any proponent of a naturalist conception of the moral must face: epistemological relativism and anthropological relativism. I argued that the truth in neither sort of relativism negates the possibility of productive moral discourse.

Nonetheless, the truth in both sorts of relativism makes understandable the appeal of the liberal political-philosophical project—the effort to imagine a politics that is "neutral" or "impartial" among competing conceptions of human good. As I explained in Part II, however, that project is a dead-end. The liberal conception of the proper relation of morality/religion to politics/law is impossible to achieve. One's participation in politics and law is and must be based on one's most basic convictions about human good, including one's religious convictions (if one has any religious convictions).

My discussion, in Part III, of three problems—coercive legislation, conscientious disobedience, and constitutional adjudication—was in part an effort to illustrate and elaborate my "post-liberal" claim that one can participate in politics and law, that one can use or resist power, only as a partisan of particular moral/religious convictions.[1] That claim has force with respect to interpreting law (adjudication) no less than to making law (legislation) and breaking law (disobedience).

My concern in chapter 6 was constitutional interpretation. American constitutional aspirations are not neutral or impartial as to human good; to the contrary, as I explained in chapter 6, those aspirations constitute a conception of human good. To say that the conception comprising those aspirations is one that persons with various and even competing moral and religious convictions about human good may find attractive is not to deny that the conception comprising those aspirations is itself a conception of human good—that is, a conception of how it is good or fitting for us, as human beings who often do not share convictions about human well-being, to organize and live important aspects of our life in common, our political-communal life.

Furthermore, as I explained, a judge's own convictions about human well-being properly, and in any event inevitably, play an important role in guiding the judge's specification of a constitutional aspiration in the setting of a particular case. There is no way to exclude judicial "subjectivity" from the process of interpretation/adjudication; nor, I argued, should we want to. This is not to deny that we should want to moderate or constrain the influence of such subjectivity. I've set forth considerations counselling judicial self-restraint.[2]

Does the realization that judicial "subjectivity" is an inevitable part of the process of adjudication—hardly a novel insight—require that we abandon the ideal of the rule of law? It certainly requires that we reject some versions of the ideal. In particular, the fanciful notion of passive judges mechanically applying determinate and perhaps even "self-evident" norms to reach unavoidable results is, of course, no longer tenable, if it ever was. But the other extreme is also untenable: that, notwithstanding the mystifying patina of reason-giving, adjudication cannot be more than the exercise of power. Adjudication can be and sometimes is more than the mere exercise of power,[3] though it is obviously the exercise of power—power backed by the very real threat of state violence.[4] Perhaps the rule of law is best understood as the rule of practical reason—of judgment (*phronesis*)[5]—in an historically extended political community of a certain sort: a political community committed to certain foundational or constitutional aspirations (principles, ideals). (The aspirations—the constitution—need not be written, of course.) What are the relevant aspirations? Prominent among them, surely, are due process of law, in its procedural aspect, and the equal protection of the laws.

The fundamental point, in any event, is this: One's basic moral/-religious convictions are (partly) self-constitutive and are therefore a principal ground—indeed, the principal ground—of political deliberation and choice. To "bracket" such convictions is therefore to bracket—to annihilate—essential aspects of one's very self. To participate in politics and law—in particular, to make law, to break law, or to interpret law—with such convictions bracketed is not to participate as the self one is but as some one—or, rather, some thing—else.

Because they are the principal ground of political deliberation and choice, one cannot—least of all in a morally pluralistic society like our own—insulate such convictions from challenge. Politics, then, in a morally pluralistic society, is in part about the credibility of competing conceptions of human good. Political theory that fails to address questions of human good—questions of how human beings, individually and collectively, should live their lives—is, finally, vacuous and irrelevant.

Contemporary secular political-moral discourse—especially, perhaps, in Anglo-American precincts—has often been conspicuous in its failure to address questions of human good, much less to risk elaborating and defending a substantial and concrete vision of what it means to be human—truly human, fully human.[6] Consider, in particular, liberal political philosophy of the neo-Kantian variety. Such philosophy has not merely neglected to address questions of human good; a central, animating ambition of such philosophy is to avoid such questions as much as possible. But, as I explained in chapter 3, such questions cannot be bracketed, though, of course, they can be ignored or repressed. Questions of human good—and in particular the deep question of what it means to be authentically human—are too fundamental, and the answers one gives to them too determinative of one's politics, to be marginalized or privatized.

Neo-Kantian talk about "autonomy" or "freedom" doesn't begin to compensate for the studied inattention to the question of the authentically human. Discourse about autonomy or freedom often seems impervious to the fact that autonomy/freedom is at most a *political* category, not an *ontological* one. (I'm not using "political" in any narrow sense. A patriarchal family structure, for example, is a system of political constraints from which one can be free. In talking about the political we must be wary of the public/private distinction, which often functions to obscure the political dimension of the so-called private realm.) The relevant ontological category is not autonomy but authenticity. To have achieved some degree of (political) freedom is not necessarily to have achieved any degree of (human) authenticity. Political freedom or liberty is certainly a very great value, but its value derives ultimately from the extent to which it serves the more fundamental value of the authentically human.

Contemporary theorists on the secular left often seem scarcely more interested than neo-Kantian liberals in dealing with the question of "the human". And secular leftists who are interested in dealing with that question often seem ill equipped, because of their reductionist attitudes to religious thought—reductionist attitudes of either a materialist or a psychoanalytic sort—to explore some of the richest resources for thinking about the human: the resources of the great religious traditions.[7] (I think here of liberation theology, which has been such a potent theoretical *and practical* force in some Third World countries.[8]) There is at least one bright spot on the horizon of political-moral theory, however: Feminist thought is an important discursive space where the question of the human is not invariably marginalized—where, indeed, that question is often a central concern. At its best and at its root, feminist theory is perhaps best understood as an effort to struggle with the question of what it means to be authentically human.[9]

If one can participate in politics and law—if one can use or resist power—only as a partisan of particular moral/religious convictions about the human, and if politics is and must be in part about the credibility of such convictions, then we who want to participate, whether as theorists or activists or both, must examine our own convictions self-critically. We must be willing to let our convictions be tested in ecumenical dialogue with others who do not share them. We must let ourselves be tested, in ecumenical dialogue, by convictions we do not share. We must, in short, resist the temptations of infallibilism. (As I emphasized in Part I, adherence to the naturalist conception of moral knowledge requires that we relinquish neither our pluralism nor our fallibilism.[10]) If necessary we must revise our convictions until they are credible to ourselves, if not always or even often to our interlocutors. We must be willing to lend credibility to our convictions by being faithful to them in our lives and not merely in our polemics and our posturing. We must bring our convictions to bear as we use or as we resist power. We must resist and seek to transform a politics that represses, by marginalizing or privatizing, questions of human authenticity.

We are all partisans of particular convictions about the human. Although we must resist infallibilism if we are to be participants in an ecumenical politics in which questions of human good are a central concern, at any given moment our convictions are what they are: "I have reached bedrock, and this is where my spade is turned."[11] At any given moment we must and do stand somewhere, even if it's not where we stood yesterday, even if we're not quite sure where we'll stand tomorrow.

My convictions are ones I share, in general outline at least, with the man to whom I've dedicated this book and with several other men and women who, like Thomas Merton, are mentors I never met (Dorothy Day, Fyodor Dostoevsky, T. S. Eliot, Shusaku Endo, Thich Nhat Hanh, Abraham Joshua Heschel, Etty Hillesum, James Joyce, Juan Luis Segundo, Leo Tolstoy, Simone Weil). My convictions have been shaped in crucial ways by the morality of what Hilary Putnam, in his recent Carus Lectures, has called "[t]he Jerusalem-based religions",[12] though the heart of the morality in question is rooted in certain Indic spiritualities (for example, in Hindu Vedanta and in Mahayana Buddhism) as well as in the semitic religions. As Putnam states it, "The Jerusalem-based religions had a [moral] image which, while it did not yet include the liberal values of free and critical thinking, stressed equality and also fraternity, as in the metaphor of the whole human race as One Family, of all women and men as sisters and brothers."[13]

Like Putnam, I am a partisan of "Jerusalem-based" morality. Given my particular convictions about what it means to be fully human—given the bedrock where I now stand—for me the fundamental political inquiry is the question of the relation of love to power.[14] As a Catholic, one of my principal moral texts is the Last Supper scene in John's Gospel, in which Jesus, on the eve of his execution, says to those gathered with him to share a Passover seder: "I give you a new commandment: love one another; you must love one another as I have loved you."[15]

Love and power. That is a subject—an even larger subject than the one I've addressed here—for another day. The inquiry I've begun in this book, but not begun to complete, is merely prologue to that inquiry.

Appendix A: Not Taking Rights-Talk Too Seriously

> Creon: And am I wrong, if I maintain my rights?
> Haemon: Talk not of rights; thou spurn'st the due of Heaven.[1]

Rights-talk—talk about *moral* rights (as distinct from legal ones)—is a prominent and pervasive feature of contemporary political-moral discourse.[2] However, rights-talk is anything but a prominent or pervasive feature of this book. A few words of explanation are in order. In this brief appendix, I indicate why rights-talk is a derivative and even dispensable feature of political-moral discourse.

Moral theory, including political theory, is, *inter alia*, a theory of choice. Under many moral theories, some choices are required ("ought to"); some are prohibited ("ought not to"); and some are discretionary ("may").

Rights-talk is in part a way of talking about discretionary choices— about what one may do or decline to do as distinct from what one ought or ought not to do.[3] We don't usually say, "A has a (moral) right to choose X", if choice X is required (although we sometimes say, depending on the particular "ought" in question, "A has a duty to choose X", if choice X is required); nor do we say, "A has a right not to choose X", if choice X is required. (If A has "a right to do wrong"—a right not to choose X even if choice X is required, or a right to choose X even if choice X is prohibited—it is only in the sense that someone, B, has a duty not to interfere with A's choice of X—a duty not grounded on any moral right of A to make a morally wrong choice, for there is no such right.[4]) Similarly, we don't say, "A has a right not to choose X", if choice X is prohibited (although we sometimes say, "A has a duty not to

185

choose *X*", if it is prohibited); nor do we say that *A* has a right to choose *X* if choice *X* is prohibited. We do say, however, "*A* has a right to choose (or not to choose) *X*", if choice *X* is discretionary.

A rights-claim that is primarily a way of talking about a discretionary choice can be a ground of duty in the sense that if *B* ought not to interfere with *A*'s choice of *X*, where *A*'s choice is discretionary, one reason might be that *A*'s choice is discretionary.[5] In that sense, rights are sometimes prior to duties.[6]

Rights-talk, however, is more than a way of talking about discretionary choices. If *A* ought not to choose *X* because choosing *X* would damage some interest of *B* (which *A* ought not to do), then *B* can be said to have a right to be free from *A*'s choice of *X*—a claim that *A* not choose *X*, that *A* abide her duty not to choose *X*. Similarly, if *A* ought to choose *X* because not choosing *X* would damage some interest of *B* (which *A* ought not to do), then *B* can be said to have a right to *A*'s choice of *X*—a claim that *A* choose *X*, that *A* abide her duty to choose *X*. Thus, rights-talk is also a way of talking about duties or obligations from the side of the beneficiary of the duty. In political theory in particular, "the modern vocabulary and grammar of rights is [an] instrument for reporting and asserting the requirements or other implications of a relationship of justice *from the point of view of the person(s) who benefit(s) from that relationship*. It provides a way of talking about 'what is just' from a special angle: the viewpoint of the 'other(s)' to whom something (including, *inter alia*, freedom of choice) is owed or due, and who would be wronged if denied that something."[7]

A rights-claim that is primarily a way of talking about obligations (from the viewpoint of the beneficiary) cannot be a ground of duty. It is circular to attempt to justify the claim that *A* ought not to choose *X* on the basis of *B*'s right that *A* not choose *X*, if *B*'s right is itself explained in terms of *A*'s duty not to choose *X*. As Richard Brandt has put it, "If one person's having a right *logically entails* some other person's(s') having an obligation, then it is just confusion to cite the right as a *reason* for the obligation; the fact of the right just is, or includes, the fact of the obligation."[8]

We can talk about discretionary choices and about obligations, including obligations of justice, without mentioning "rights".[9] By contrast, it is difficult to see how we can dispense with ought-talk, may-talk, and duty- (or obligation-) talk. Rights-talk seems reducible to the latter sort of talk without remainder, but the latter sort of talk does not seem reducible to rights-talk without remainder.[10] This is not to say that we should never use rights-talk. Rights-talk can be useful. For example, "[t]he modern language of rights provides . . . a supple and potentially precise instrument for sorting out and expressing the demands of justice."[11] (However, rights-talk "is often, . . . though not inevitably or irremediably, a hindrance to clear thought when the question is: What are the demands of justice?"[12])

We've been instructed that "[t]here are four crucial issues in an adequate philosophical examination of individual rights: the *definition* of various types of rights; the *justification* of them; the *scope* of them (that is, who can have them); and the *place* of rights—their importance relative to other sorts of considerations—in moral argument."[13]

As my comments on rights-talk suggest, defining the various types of rights—specifying their meaning—is simply a matter of defining the various types of discretionary choices, and the various types of obligations, that are talked about in the language, the rhetoric, of "rights". Justifying rights is a matter of justifying claims that certain choices are discretionary and claims that certain choices are obligatory. Who can have rights? As regards rights-claims that are a way of talking about discretionary choices, anyone for whom some choices are discretionary can have them.[14]

As regards rights-claims that are a way of talking about obligations from the point of view of the beneficiaries of the obligations, anyone or anything who is a beneficiary can have them. If an animal is a beneficiary of a particular obligation, then the animal has a right—namely, a right to the performance of the obligation.[15]

The final of the four issues—the importance of rights relative to other considerations—pertains to rights-claims that are a way of talking about obligations,[16] and raises the problem of the "weight" or "strength" of such rights. That is mainly a problem about how close to being absolute (unconditional), or how far from it, are the rules of conduct that entail the rights in question. At least one such rule—the rule against the intentional killing of an innocent person—is, by most accounts, virtually absolute.[17] The issue of the importance, relative to other considerations, of the right of an innocent person not to be killed is largely the issue of what particularities of context, what consequences, could justify an act in contravention of that right—in contravention, that is, of the rule that entails the right.

Thus, rights-talk is a derivative and even dispensable feature of political-moral discourse, although it can be useful if properly understood and employed. One can take rights very seriously, so to speak, without taking rights-talk too seriously, indeed, without even using rights-talk.[18] And, as it happens, in this book I don't use rights-talk.

Appendix B: Human Law and the Conscience of Believers: A Statement of the American Lutheran Church

A statement adopted October 20, 1984, by the Twelfth General Convention of The American Lutheran Church (GC84.20.xxx): Introduction and Parts I, II, and III as a statement of comment and counsel expressing the views of the Convention to the congregations of The ALC and their members for their consideration and such action as they deem appropriate; Part IV as a statement of policy and practice of The ALC. Ballot vote tally for Introduction and Parts I–III: Yes 883 (94.4%), No 50 (5.4%), Abstain 2 (0.2%); for Part IV: Yes 828 (90.9%), No 78 (8.6%), Abstain 5 (0.5%).

Be subject for the Lord's sake to every human institution, whether it be to the emperor as supreme, or to governors as sent by him to punish those who do wrong and to praise those who do right. (I *Peter* 2:13–14)

But Peter and the apostles answered, "We must obey God rather than men." (*Acts* 5:29)

But if . . . the temporal power and authorities . . . would compel a subject to do something contrary to the command of God, or hinder [one] from doing what God commands, obedience ends and the obilgation ceases. In such a case [one] has to say what St. Peter said, "We must obey God rather than men" . . . [It is] as if a prince desired to go to war, and his cause was clearly unrighteous; we should neither follow nor help such a prince, because God had commanded us not to kill our neighbor or do him a wrong. MARTIN LUTHER in TREATISE ON GOOD WORKS (1520).

189

ITRODUCTION

1. *Summary of this Paper.* The paper treats the requirements of human law and the requirements of the faith-informed conscience of Christians living in a constitutional democracy. It sees obedience to law as normal behavior for Christians and change in law as coming through judicial and electoral means. The paper says that disobeying civil law can be done only as a last resort, nonviolently, and with willingness to pay the required penalty. Finally the paper says that individual Christians who choose in good conscience to break a law—to keep peace with their conscience, to raise an important issue to public view, or to seek a change in that law—may expect the full ministry of the faith community to be available to them. This is true even though others in the faith community may disagree strongly with the law violator's stand or action.

2. *Situations Addressed by this Paper.* Conflicts between the requirements of laws and the demands of Christian conscience have been present from the beginning of the church's history. In this country during recent years the issues at conflict have included use of public funds for abortions, state-required certification of religious schools, payment of social security taxes for church employees, denial of tax exemption for certain ministries of the churches. Within The American Lutheran Church, specific calls for a responsible address to law/conscience conflicts have come to the national church body from:

    a. congregations considering an appropriate ministry to undocumented persons who are present in their communities;

    b. persons considering violation of trespass laws as part of a witness at military or defense-industry locations (a formal request for study in this area has also come from National Lutheran Campus Ministry);

    c. persons considering conscientious objection to payment of taxes for certain military purposes (the matter of conscientious objection to military conscription has been addressed frequently by The ALC during the past two decades).

3. *Purposes of the Paper.* The following discussion seeks to respond seriously to such requests by:

    a. reviewing the biblical and theological tradition of Lutheran Christians on the call to gospel discipleship and the role of human law;

    b. exploring the options to be considered when one believes a conflict exists between legal duty and the call of conscience;

c. assisting the thinking of the community of believers in some specific areas which pose problems of conscience for some members of the church today.

4. Human beings yearn for an ordering of society which they can view as fair and secure. Human beings also experience brokenness and disorder in the scoieties they fashion. Since we are not perfect beings, we neither perfect social systems nor obey perfectly those we do fashion.

5. And yet, human laws, particularly when developed through processes which reflect the will of the people, are to be seen as honorable and responsible tools for enabling us all to live together in socially constructive ways. Thus, accepting both the principle of rule by law and the practice of obedience to specific laws is welcomed as the norm by believers who live in modern, democratic societies such as ours. We see human law, including its elements of restraint and punishment, as valid and essential framework for the benefits which we all derive from living together in complex social environments.

6. There are occasions, however, when particular laws, even in the best of societies, present problems of conscience for believers. ("Conscience" may be defined as "that sense of right or wrong within a person which produces a feeling of obligation to do the right thing as one understands it." Believers whose consciences are formed by their faith in God seek to be faithful to the will of God as they understand it.) This paper explores the dilemma of conflict between requirements of human government and the calling of God as some believers may hear that call.

I. The Gospel and Laws of Human Societies

A. *The Bible on God's Authority and Human Authority*

1. As Christians we affirm the gospel—God's gift of gracious acceptance offered to sinful people who create imperfect social orders—as the essential context in which we live as redeemed persons. The gospel empowers us to live in the new reality of God's kingdom, marked by a higher righteousness than that of the normal human order, the new mandate to love our neighbors, including those called "enemy."

2. The struggle of Christian discipleship is to live on the terms of the New Age while the Old Age continues, we in it and it still in us. Here,

governing authorities and law enter and command the allegiance of Christians. Civil law has a provisional—but essential—place as part of God's patient preservation of broken and fallen creation.

3. Biblically, God's law is understood to be given to the covenant people. God demands more of God's people than any human power can properly require: namely, total allegiance. The first commandment reads, "I am the Lord your God, . . . you shall have no other gods before me" (*Exodus* 20:2–3). The people of God's New Covenant are asked in the New Testament for an equally total response of allegiance to Jesus Christ (see *Mark* 8:34–38). That response will always be in some tension with those realities called "principalities and powers," which include such human structures as governments, family, ethnic loyalties, economic systems, national interests, etc. (See *Romans* 8:38–39; *Ephesians* 6:10–20; *Colossians* 1:15–17.) Powers and principalities are, on the one hand, created by God; on the other hand they are part of fallen creation and wish to claim the priority which can only be accorded to God. Thus, we cannot live without them, and we cannot live in total comfort with them.

4. When any human government asks total allegiance of its people, as do certain states throughout the word today—East and West, North and South—Christians are compelled to refuse and resist. But it is not just in totalitarian systems that conflicts exist between Christian discipleship and the laws of human governments. How does the biblical record help us to view such conflicts?

5. The Old Testament frequently provides examples of disobedience to human authority when it is seen as conflicting with the purposes of God. An early example is the Pharoah's order to the Hebrew midwives to kill every newborn Hebrew son. The midwives "feared God" and disobeyed (*Exodus* 1:16–17). Pharoah's daughter also disobeyed her father's order as a way of saving the infant Moses. Even after the Moses-led Israelites succeed in establishing their own nation, decades later, there are problems for those who would follow God rather than their earthly kings. The prophets, speaking for God, at times disagree with the kings of Israel, affirming the divine purpose rather than courses of action sought by human rulers. (See *Isaiah* 30:1–5 and 31:1–3, *Jeremiah* 21:8–10 and 27:12–15.)

6. By the time of New Testament, the covenant people are living under an occupying government, that of the Roman Empire. Jesus on one occasion is asked about the matter of allegiance to the emperor. He

confounds those who seek to trap him by advising them to give to Caesar what is Caesar's and to God what is God's (*Mark* 12:13–17). His response has been traditionally understood as supporting payment of taxes, even to governments not ruling by will of the people, since the coin of the realm bears the image of Caesar. Jesus' point most likely includes that meaning, but also goes beyond it: that is, the ultimate allegiance of people must be to God their Maker, since human beings do not bear the image of a human ruler but of God.

7. Throughout his earthly ministry, our Lord declares it is the Law of God (the Torah) which he comes to fulfill. In doing so, he often challenges the Torah interpreters of his day—the scribes and Pharisees—and gives the Torah an interpretation other than the conventional view of what it requires. He identifies for them the heart of the law, which is love, and elevates that over the letter of the law. See his attitude toward the Sabbath law (*Mark* 2:23–28) and the sentence of capital punishment for adulterers (*John* 8:3–11). Jesus' point is that God's law, properly understood, is on the side of love and justice for the neighbor.

8. In virtually identical words, Paul and Peter counsel believers to "be subject to" human institutions (*Romans* 13:1 and I *Peter* 2:13–14). They are here asking believers to be obedient to the legal requirements of the Roman Empire. Yet, the early Christians did not hear that advice as requiring them to worship Caesar (which *was* expected by the Caesars at certain periods in the early centuries of Christianity). Nor did most Christians in the first three centuries agree to serve as soldiers in the Roman armies.

9. Paul and Peter themselves disobey specific laws of the empire and find themselves in trouble with its local authorities, often going to prison for such violations (see *Acts* 5, 16, 19, 21). Yet, Paul certainly valued the Roman legal *system*, even insisting on his rights of "due process" as a Roman citizen (*Acts* 16:37–39; 22:25–29; 25:11).

B. *Proper Respect for Human Institutions*

1. How shall we carry the biblical witness to God's activity in and through human order into our own quite different situation today? What are the limits to the authority of human institutions and what constitutes proper respect for such institutions? Four principles can be stated:

    a. *God works through human institutions that are part of the ordering of creation.* God is active in *all* structures that bless and sustain ordinary life, including those that seem far from explicit faith content. That is, societal elements such as family and government are God-ordained just as much in cultures which lack the biblical tradition—or deny and reject it— as in those which recognize publicly the God of the Scriptures. There is no biblical support for separating faith from public life (the institutional separation of religious organizations from government is quite a different matter). In their statement to Emperor Charles V at Augsburg on June 25, 1530, German political representatives who followed Martin Luther included these words:

The Gospel does not overthrow civil authority, the state, and marriage but requires that all these be kept as true orders of God . . . Accordingly, Christians are obliged to be subject to civil authority and obey its commands and laws in all that can be done without sin. But when commands of the civil authority cannot be obeyed without sin, we must obey God rather than men (*Acts* 5:29).—from *Augsburg Confession,* Article 16.

b. *God expects government to be the kind of authority which rewards good behavior and punishes evil.* As Paul writes, "Rulers are not a terror to good conduct but to bad" (*Romans* 13:3 RSV). And Peter defines governors as people who are sent by God "to punish those who do wrong and to praise those who do right" (I *Peter* 2:14). Governing authorities and civil laws are God's servants to preserve order and promote justice in this Old Age. This means that no state is God, for all states are established to be servant to God's purposes and so are accountable to God, whether or not they recognize God's authority. There is no separate, autonomous political realm free from divine moral judgment.

c. *Having respect for the institution of government as ordained of God does not imply acceptance of every specific policy of particular governments.* These are times when one's sense of God's will for one's life may lead—as with Peter, or Paul, or Martin Luther, or Martin Luther King Jr., or Rosa Parks (of the Montgomery bus boycott), or Bonhoeffer, or Dorothy Day or Ruth Youngdahl Nelson, or any number of other deeply faith-filled persons—to disobedience of a particular governmental demand. Christians in the early centuries regularly refused to take part in the military service demanded of them by the Roman government, for which they paid a heavy price of persecution. Luther often quoted the conclusion of Peter when facing the council of Israel (*Acts* 5:20), "We must obey God rather than [human authorities]"—if the two conflict.

d. *"Governing authorities" as used in Romans 13 is not limited to local, state, and national governments.* The nation-state as we know it today is a development of the last several centuries and likely will not be the ultimate stage in the evolution of human political structures. Today the world recognizes certain elements of international order: agreements governing warfare and weaponry, the law of the seas, the covenants concerning treatment of refugees, the judgments of international courts. These have been given a measure of authority by national governments. It is clear that nation-states have a monopoly on the legitimate use of coercive force and thus the structures of international order we do have are functional only as *nations* choose to honor or enforce them. Still, they are an emerging element, beyond the nation-state with some characteristics of "governing authority." Further, when international agreements are adopted by a government such as ours they become a part of that nation's own body of law; our government as well as our citizens can be expected to abide by them as such.

II. CHALLENGES TO HUMAN LAW

A. *The Priority of Legal Resorts*

1. In a democratic society such as ours, respect for the law itself is accepted as a high value. Laws are assumed to be created through an exercise of the will of the citizenry and, when that is questioned, they can be challenged in the courts or changed through the electoral power of the people. Thus, in a constitutional democracy, of which the United States is an example, the rule of law properly has high status. Believers, along with all citizens, will normally give properly adopted legislation their obedience—even if they should find specific laws personally inconvenient or annoying or contrary to their political preferences.

2. Believers who see particular laws as wrong or inappropriate or counterproductive are obliged to join with others in testing such laws in the courts or in seeking their repeal through elected representatives.

3. While it is true that certain laws may be wrong, unjust, or corrupt, it is equally true that the consciences of all persons, including Christians, can be wrong, misguided, affected by our sinful condition. It must also be remembered that faithful Christians can and do differ in understandings of what the gospel (or God's will) requires in the response of discipleship. These cautions apply to any discussion of law and conscience.

B. *When Disobedience is Contemplated*

1. Even in a democracy that functions smoothly and fairly most of the time, some persons, in conscientiously held conviction, may feel

obliged to challenge a particular law through disobedience. Indeed, the only way of testing the constitutionality of a specific law may be deliberately to violate it. Lutheran church agencies have recently done precisely that as a way of challenging federal law interpretations (Internal Review Service attempts to define narrowly the church's mission, excluding social services from the functions for which a church agency may claim an exemption from filing annual informational tax returns).

2. There may also be occasions in which preservation of life leaves one no alternative but to break a law which is considered valid even by the law-breaker. An example would be a situation in which, trying to save a life, an automobile driver will deliberately break a speed law. The driver recognizes the law's validity, but will break it under extraordinary circumstances.

3. The more common situations which some Christians have seen as calling for conscientious violation of law—what is called "direct civil disobedience"—fall under situations such as the following:

   a. When the intent or effect of a law leads to a pattern of discrimination against particular groups within a society. (Examples: in U.S. history, laws that have denied justice and freedom to persons because of their race, national origin, or gender.)

   b. When the law's requirements may lead, for some citizens, to severe violation of what they believe God requires them to do. (Examples: demand that church schools meet state certification requirements; taxation for certain military purposes; use of tax dollars to pay for abortions; conscription of the selective objector to a particular military activity; state-enforced provision of medical procedure, such as a blood transfusion, against one's religious convictions.)

   c. When the implementation of a law is understood to cause great human danger. (Examples: required return of escaped slaves in the mid-19th century; deportation which may result today in people being sent to a life-threatening situation in their country of origin.)

4. In the above examples, when a particular law itself stands in the way for persons who believe Christian discipleship justifies or requires their doing a certain deed, violation of that law is called *direct* disobedience. A violator may have either of two attitudes towards such a law: (a) it is a law one cannot personally obey in good conscience, but the violator does not claim the law is one that should be changed or repealed; (b) it is a law that is wrong for everyone and should thus be changed or repealed. An example of the first attitude would be that of a

selective conscientious objector who accepts a draft as legitimate for those who can in good conscience bear arms, but cannot himself enter armed service in a specific circumstance. An example of the second would be that of the person who sees *any* conscription law as illegitimate under any circumstances, believing governments never have a right to compel people to bear arms against their will.

5. In contrast to direct civil disobedience, there are situations in which citizens choose to violate a law, not in itself a problem, in order to make a public statement on another concern. Such violations are called *indirect* disobedience. The violation becomes the vehicle for protesting something else. Breaking antitrespass laws at military bases or defense plants to protest military preparations or policies would be examples. There is an obvious distinction between direct and indirect disobedience. In the former, people believe they have no choice, since to obey the law would require them to go against conscience. The latter does *not* involve such a dilemma; people choose to break a law to make a witness on a matter they consider serious, but if they had chosen to obey that particular law there would have been no conscience violation resulting from that specific obedience.

6. Acts of civil disobedience such as those noted—both direct and indirect—have a long, honored history in Western societies. The rationale for such acts can be traced to Greek philosophers before the time of Christ. In U.S. history, acts which were at one time illegal were part of the process of gaining full religious liberty, ending slavery, securing the vote for women, recognizing labor's right to organize, legalizing conscientious objection to combatant service, securing civil rights of minority groups. The idea of achieving social change and greater justice through civil disobedience has been developed over many centuries. When social change is the goal, the disobedience must appeal to a rationale which is accessible to public discussion and reflection, that is, based on reasonable societal values and not those solely of a particular religious or philosophical viewpoint.

7. Principles such as these are central to the theory of civil disobedience. If undertaken, it must be done:

   a. *Only as a last resort*. Persons will have differing definitions of what, for them, is "last resort," but legal means of changing an unjust law, or of calling attention to a social problem of injustice, shall have been tried first, when at all possible.

b. *Only by nonviolent means,* intent on avoiding harm to persons or property.

c. *Always for the sake of the larger community,* not simply to satisfy a personal or selfish desire.

d. *Always with respect for the consciences of those who disagree* with the planned disobedience. (See Paul's regard for the consciences of others, I *Corinthians* 10.)

e. *Always with willingness to accept the legal consequences* for violation of law—which is a way of affirming the legitimacy of a system of law itself. This is one way that a civil disobedient is distinguished from a criminal. A criminal actively seeks to avoid getting caught and paying any penalty for his or her action. But, by being public and willing to accept the consequences, the civil disobedient demonstrates respect for the system of law while breaking one particular law.

8. Finally, Christians will recognize always that conscience also is tainted by sin, and can be wrong. They will therefore give the utmost consideration to the counsel of fellow believers, and will contemplate disobedience with prayer and study in Christian community.

C. *Individual and Collective Disobedience*

1. Within the family of believers, we may speak of three situations in which disobedience has implications for the faith community. First, the action of an individual believer, who is convinced that faithfulness to divine law requires violation of human law. When considering disobedience, such a person can be expected to seek guidance from Scripture and the church's tradition. Within that search, the counsel of the person's worship community, including its pastoral care, should be central.

2. Second, the response of persons and groups toward those believers who engage in civil disobedience. The believing community, especially the congregation, is called to help individuals to struggle with any decision of conscience, in the light of biblical witness. That community is also called to support such persons through prayer, counsel, pastoral care, and acts of love, even when the community cannot agree with a stance of law violation which they take.

3. Third, an action done by or in the name of a group of believers such as a congregation. It is important to keep some distinction between what is possible for individuals and what is possible for institutional expression of the church. Violation of law in the name of a corporate entity, such as a congregation, will have legal implications for all members; thus all members should be involved in any decision about a

proposed disobedient act. It is wise to make such a decision by consensus.

4. A special word must be spoken about the role of parish pastors. There may be times when a pastor believes his/her Christian faith is leading him/her to an act of disobedience *as a believing individual.* Yet, the congregation may vehemently object, on grounds that *their* consciences do not lead them in the same way and their pastor is to be a public example of the faith we are all called to exhibit, as well as to be a public representative of that congregation in the eyes of the community. There is need for great caution and understanding on both sides of such a disagreement. If a satisfactory resolution cannot be reached, it may be necessary for a pastor to resign rather than violate conscience on a matter of deep conviction.

D. *The American Lutheran Church and Civil Disobedience*

1. The ALC, through general conventions, has addressed issues of civil disobedience on two occasions.

a. The 1966 convention, in the midst of numerous activities protesting U.S. racial injustice, commended a statement on civil disobedience "to the earnest study and discussion of pastors and of congregations. . . ." Included was this paragraph:

He who decides that the Lord requires him to become involved in civil disobedience, fully expecting to take the consequences of his decision, is to be honored as much as the one who decides, before the Lord, against such involvement. To be pitied, however, are those who refuse to face the issue with its stark alternatives or who allow "what will people think?" to decide the case for them.

b. The 1970 convention committed The ALC to stand by those who conscientiously refuse combatant service in the military as selective objectors and find themselves in violation of law thereby. This position was reaffirmed by the 1982 convention. Both the 1970 and 1982 actions are statements of official policy and practice for the church. (The two conventions also affirmed support for those who conscientiously choose to serve as combatants or seek general conscientious objector status—both of which are legal positions. The ALC in 1971 joined others in urging Congress to legalize selective objection to combatant service, but without success.)

2. Two dilemmas face the organized expressions of the church. One is the need for communities of faith not to abandon persons who, in

obeying consciences that are shaped by the church's own teaching on questions of ethics, find themselves in conflict with a law. Even though a majority of the faith community may disagree with one member's choice, it is simply not responsible or just to ignore or shun that person who believes he/she is following a faith-formed conscience. The other dilemma is to try to say anything helpful about the role of the conscience of believers without the statement itself being heard as binding the consciences of believers! The goal is to affirm conscientious Christian civil disobedience, according to the principles summarized above, without excluding those who disagree. Thus, we repeat: in seeking to respond to the conscientious actions of those who feel compelled to acts of civil disobedience, the church must be equally concerned about respecting the conscientiously held convictions of all who hold another view (Section B-7-d above). It is necessary, though difficult, to seek to maintain an over-riding unity within a community of believers in the face of deep disagreements over particular strategies for seeking justice in our world.

III. Three Current Areas of Tension

A. *Governmental Regulatory Requirements*

1. *Tax Regulations.* Some Christians and some congregations believe they cannot conscientiously pay Social Security taxes for their lay employees (clergy are considered self-employed and have none of their Social Security paid by employing institutions). Certain congregations are challenging the law by refusing to make such payments, which are required under a recent revision of the federal tax code. Other Christians are distressed by tax regulations which seem to define narrowly what are proper functions of religious organizations—that is, limiting them to worship and education endeavors but excluding the church's role in social ministries. Some of these narrow interpretations have been challenged by church organizations which refuse to file required information, in hopes of having the interpretations overturned by the courts.

2. *Certification of Church Schools.* Certain states ask all private schools, including those of the churches, to meet certification requirements of those states. Some churches have refused to comply and their leaders have been willing to face jail sentences because of their conscientious belief that government has no right to make such a demand of religious schools.

3. *Points for Consideration of Protest to Regulatory Requirements.*

a. Those who are opposed to tax or other regulations and their impact on churches may consider filing a civil case which will seek a judicial decision on the regulation in question.

b. Opponents may also work to have the law or regulation changed by legislative action.

c. Opponents may consider violating the law as a way of compelling a judicial review as to constitutionality, consistency with the powers granted to the government agency making the interpretation, or fairness of the regulation at issue.

B. U.S. Military Policies

1. *Conscription.* The U.S. military draft law continues to present problems of conscience for some who are touched by it. Our law does not recognize selective participation/objection, which is the obvious consequence of adherence to the official Lutheran ethic on peace and war, the just/unjust war criteria. Even during the present period of no inductions, the registration requirement in itself is a problem for some young men, since the registration procedure defers the time at which the individual may state a conscientious-objection claim.

2. *Taxes for Military Purposes.* Some Christians conscientiously oppose paying taxes for military purposes in general, or for specific weapon systems (e.g., nuclear, chemical) or military activities they consider immoral. Short of voluntary poverty, there are no legal ways of avoiding participation with one's federal tax payments in our government's military enterprise, just as one cannot choose whether to support the cost of the postal service or of food stamps. There are proposals, such as the World Peace Tax Fund Act, which if adopted by Congress would allow taxpayers to specify that their tax money not be used for military purposes. (The military would still receive the full amount appropriated by Congress but peace-oriented efforts specified by Congress would gain.[1]) Without such a provision, those choosing to refuse payment of taxes for military purposes will be in violation of law. ALC members choosing to make a witness as military tax resisters in good conscience, who also accept any penalty the law requires may legitimately look for counsel, prayers, and pastoral care from their fellow believers, even when others in the faith community disagree with the action taken.

3. *Protest of Military Preparations.* This area is not as well defined

as the issues of conscripting people or their money into military service. It is not a matter of opposing a law which demands an action in violation of one's conscience (*direct* civil disobedience). It is rather a matter of acting to protest a process or system one believes will have evil results, such as military preparations or production of weapons of mass destruction. This indirect civil disobedience seeks to awaken public awareness and to have impact on public policy, through nonviolent, public, symbolic, illegal actions, taken only after regretfully concluding that less drastic actions have proved insufficient. Again, the faith community is obliged to help explore the pros and cons of *all* available options with those contemplating such disobedience, and to offer counsel, prayer and acts of love to those who conscientiously choose such actions, even when most of that community may not favor the strategy.

4. *Points for Consideration of Protest to Military Policies.* Individuals and congregations may wish to reflect on these considerations:

a. When faced by conscription or the draft registration law, consider stating a claim as a general conscientious objector and being willing to give legal service (if called) in a non-combatant role. For persons who do not qualify as all-war objectors, pastors and congregations should provide help in thinking through the pros and cons of selective objection, particularly the traditional Lutheran understanding of the criteria for just and unjust warfare.[2]

b. Consider lawful means of protesting payment of taxes for military purposes, including voluntary reduction of income and increase in charitable contibutions, sending letters of protest to the President and to members of Congress, and working for legislative changes such as the World Peace Tax Fund Act.

c. Pursue lawful kinds of witness against military preparations, including political advocacy, dialogue with leaders of companies holding weapons contracts, efforts to change public attitudes, and (if appropriate) organizing legal economic pressures such as giving consumer patronage to companies whose priorities one favors.

C. U.S. Immigration Policies

1. In recent years, groups of American Christians, on occasion entire congregations, have declared their church buildings to be sanctuaries where undocumented persons who lack legal status in this country may find safe haven. The idea of holy space as public sanctuary is an ancient one. In the Old Testament we read that there were holy places where

persons guilty of crimes such as manslaughter were given protection (*Exodus* 21:12–14). There were also entire cities designated as refuges (*Numbers* 35:9–34), wherein acts of vengeance were prohibited. The Israelites, moreover, were told repeatedly that they would be judged by their treatment of the stranger within their gates, and were reminded that they themselves had been sojourners in a foreign land (*Exodus* 22:21; 23:9).

2. Sanctuary was written into medieval church law and English common law, providing safety for the accused while due process was undertaken on letting the accused leave the country safely. The idea has never been part of U.S. law, but the practice was quite common during slavery, when church buildings and church people alike became important links in the "underground railway" for fugitive slaves. During the Vietnam War a few congregations provided sanctuary to military deserters while their cases were being adjudicated.

3. Helping undocumented persons to live is not illegal. Helping them to avoid arrest or deportation may be, however, whether by providing them sanctuary or by aiding their escape from authorities. Those who feel compelled to help undocumented persons, particularly within the U.S. religious community, have typically cited justifications like these:

a. First and most important, they believe those who need protection may well be in danger of imprisonment, torture, even death, if forced to return to their country of origin. Some may have entered exile as political opponents of vengeful governments. Others who need protection may not be opponents of their government but are simply victims of well-documented arbitrary violence. Many who flee such forms of terror are apolitical, but they do have a "well-founded fear of persecution" (the internationally accepted definition of what makes one a refugee, which the U.S. Immigration Act of 1980 has also accepted).

b. Second, they view U.S. immigration law itself as law unjustly administered, when it fails to give protection to those who face lifethreatening situations in their country of origin. That law may be administered in what its critics consider violation of international covenants concerning the rights of refugees, as when persons from countries whose governments we disfavor receive refugee status but those from countries whose governments we favor do not. When immigration and refugee law is turned to serve foreign policy goals in disregard of the basic humanitarian values of our society, there is reason to protest. Currently it is people from Central America and the Caribbean, especially El Salvadorans, Guatemalans, and Haitians, who are in our country in large numbers without legal standing and who fear for their well-being if forced to return to their home countries at this time.

c. Third, they argue that churches are, by definition, places of sanctuary in a religious sense. Anyone in need should be able to find there a safe haven—physically as well as spiritually. In this reasoning, churches cannot vote whether or not to be sanctuaries: they simply are that, if they are churches. Let the governing authorities do what they must, but the churches are called to be faithful to their mission of sanctuary and hospitality, even if that involves some risks.

d. Finally, churches that have considered this issue claim that offering public sanctuary makes two unique contributions. It is, of course, an act of compassion and an act of resistance to what is considered an unjust application of a law (though there are other ways to express compassion and resistance). More distinctly, it is an occasion for education and empowerment. Public sanctuary brings the voice of suffering peoples into the heart of North American churches and communities, in the person of the refugee, turning statistics and reports into a living relationship. Public sanctuary also empowers the refugee. No longer in hiding, the refugee can tell his or her story and take an active role in the future of fellow refugees and their home countries. Public sanctuary is thus not a one-way service, but two-way partnership, educating North Americans while empowering those who seek asylum.

4. The number of congregations which have formally offered sanctuary is small (some 100 across the country through the spring of 1984). But the issue has raised generally in churches an awareness of (1) the historic role of faith communities in protecting politically, socially, and economically vulnerable people; (2) the intricacies of the provisions and implementation of U.S. immigration laws; (3) the relationship between people of Central America and of the U.S.

5. *Points for Consideration of Sanctuary.* In contemplating declaration of sanctuary, local churches may wish to weigh these points:

a. The most important activity to undertake, on the long term and systematic issue of refugees, is to address the *reasons* that sanctuary for aliens must even be contemplated. Most people anywhere in the world would prefer to remain in their land of birth. Further, it is neither possible nor desirable for the United States to receive all of those who may seek refuge here. Therefore, let us ask what our nation could do to help insure that people are not forced into refugee conditions in the first place. Second, let us ask what our nation could do to give those who come legal status, either on a permanent basis or, at the very least, until they may safely return. Both questions will lead us into public-policy discussion and action, proper alternatives to meeting immediate needs of threatened persons through giving unlawful asylum.

b. Seek to distinguish between persons who are fleeing a homeland for political reasons ("a well-founded fear of persecution") and those who have left for economic reasons. Often, making such distinctions is not easy. But U.S. law and honesty in the discussion require that the distinction be maintained. Not all who would claim "refugee" status are able to qualify as politically endangered.

c. Give all possible *legal* support to undocumented persons who are among us. Learn from them about the causes of their flight from home and provide them with a caring community while their cases are in process. Help them with material support and social services. And advocate for them as they seek to legalize their status in the U.S. and to avoid deportation.

d. Before seeking a decision on sanctuary, give thoughtful attention to questions such as these:

1) Has careful study of sanctuary been done, giving opportunity for participation by the full membership in the study and decision?

2) Have all legal courses of action been exhausted for the protection of undocumented persons in our community before turning to an act of civil disobedience?

3) Is there readiness to accept the consequences of violating U.S. law (penalties may include such results as a fine of up to $2,000, a sentence of up to five years in prison, plus the confiscation of any vehicle used in transporting undocumented persons)?

4) Would sanctuary be declared primarily in order to safeguard human beings who are endangered, or to make a dramatic statement against U.S. immigration or foreign policy? (There may be more appropriate ways to make the policy statement.)

IV. POLICY AFFIRMATIONS

1. The American Lutheran Church asserts its commitment to government of human societies by law. Challenges to or changes in specific laws will normally be pursued through judicial or electoral channels. Disobedience of a law, for purposes of seeking greater social justice or keeping faith with one's conscience, is justifiable only within a framework of respect for our society's system of governance through law, which means the conditions under which civil law may be broken (Section II-B-7 above) are always to be honored.

2. The American Lutheran Church further asserts its commitment to the claims of discipleship in the Gospel, which in particular circumstances may call believers to disobedience of a civil law they consider to be in clear violation of established Christian commitments to the sacredness of life, to peace, to justice, to freedom, or to the independence of religious organizations from improper government regulation.

3. The American Lutheran Church promises to remain in ministry with[3] those who, having seriously reviewed all the points above, make decisions of Christian conscience to undertake actions of civil disobedience—without implying corporate agreement with particular stands taken. This affirmation includes actions of individual Christians, groups, pastors, and congregations.

4. The American Lutheran Church promises to remain in ministry with persons who, with regard to military service, conscientiously choose to do combatant service, to refuse combatant service at any time (general conscientious objection) or to refuse combatant service in particular circumstances on the basis of just/unjust war criteria (selective conscientious objection). To remain in ministry with persons choosing any of these options does not imply corporate agreement with particular stands taken. The ALC also reaffirms its pledge to stand by persons in the military who refuse to use weapons of mass destruction in combat, on grounds that they are proscribed under the criteria of the just/unjust war ethic (see *Mandate for Peacemaking,* 1982 ALC General Convention statement, Sections A-10, B-1-a, B-2-a).

5. The American Lutheran Church promises to remain in ministry wih persons who struggle with other decisions of conscience in the war-peace arena, based on their understanding of biblical ethics, without implying corporate agreement with particular stands taken. Examples would be behavior with regard to payment of taxes for weapons of mass destruction or nonviolent protests against production and deployment of such weapons.

6. The American Lutheran Church recognizes that giving public sanctuary is by definition, a *local* decision, since it can be done only by a particular congregation or sanctuary group in a particular community. The ALC therefore leaves the decision on the giving of public sanctuary to each congregation. The ALC reminds all congregations of the biblical call to care for the sojourner and stranger in our midst and commends those congregations which seriously pursue justice and compassion for any persons who seek safe haven among us. Such commenda-

tion is equally proper whether a congregation chooses to offer public sanctuary or finds other ways to be faithful to the call of the gospel in ministering among undocumented persons. The ALC encourages all of its members to petition the federal administration and their members of Congress to grant (1) a stay of deportation on humanitarian grounds or (2) extended voluntary departure status to persons who have emigrated to this country and remain under threat of deportation to life-threatening situations in their countries of origin.

Notes

Introduction

1. M. Perry, The Constitution, the Courts, and Human Rights: An Inquiry into the Legitimacy of Constitutional Policymaking by the Judiciary (1982).

2. See S. Toulmin, R. Rieke, & A. Janik, An Introduction to Reasoning 165 (2d ed. 1984):

> The society in which we live (unlike, for instance, Homeric Greece) is just as faction-ridden as it is coherent. We are apt to be misled by the fact that we use a single term, *society*, to designate a complicated system of cultures and subcultures, each with its own values . . . There are every bit as many contested beliefs as there are shared assumptions in our "society." This very fact ought to put us on guard against simply assuming that everyone shares the generalization that they find crystal clear and compellingly reasonable with other members of their society.

By "moral community" (including religious community) I mean a group of persons, not necessarily occupying a common space, who share a conception of human good—a belief or set of beliefs about what way of life is good for them and perhaps for some others, perhaps even for human beings generally.

Some philosophers argue that "the Right" is prior to "the Good". However, "the Good" is prior to "the Right". For a discussion, see chapters 3 & 4.

3. See A. MacIntyre, After Virtue 6 et seq. (1981).

4. By "moral discourse" I mean conversation or dialogue in pursuit of consensus among the interlocutors as to how the issue that engages them—and perhaps has divided them—ought, as a moral matter, to be resolved. See F. Dallmayr, Polis and Praxis: Exercises in Contemporary Political Theory 203–5 (1984). Put another way, moral discourse is aimed at moral knowledge in the sense of moral beliefs discursively justified among the interlocutors. Moral discourse is "productive" even if it does not remove all disagreement but merely diminishes it.

5. Throughout this book I tend to refer, implicitly as well as explicitly, to "the United States" or "American" society. I do so, first, because the United States is the country in which I've always lived and with which, therefore, I'm most familiar and, second, because the United States seems to me not merely an

example but a paradigm of a morally pluralistic society. However, most of what I say here is meant to apply, more or less, to any morally pluralistic society.

6. For my earlier effort to defend a position on constitutional interpretation, see M. Perry, note 1.

Part I

1. For a discussion of the matter, see chapter 1, section V, in particular notes 56 & 67. On the "moral/nonmoral distinction", including the Kantian version, and the absence of any such distinction in classical Greek thought, see M. Nussbaum, The Fragility of Goodness 5 n. * & 25–50 (1986).

Chapter 1

1. N. Chomsky, For Reasons of State 404 (1973). See Steinfels, "The Search for an Alternative," Commonweal, Nov. 30, 1981, at 660, 661 (commenting on the importance of the distinction "between the human and the 'truly human' ").

2. For a discussion of "truth" as "idealized rational acceptability", see chapter 2, section V.

3. J. Finnis, Natural Law and Natural Rights 59 (1980). See M. Adler, Six Great Ideas 49 (1981): "There cannot be false knowledge, as there can be false opinions and beliefs. The phrase 'true knowledge' is redundant; the phrase 'false knowledge' is self-contradictory."

4. The philosophical literature discloses a bewildering variety of names for the position that there can be no moral knowledge. One such name is moral "nihilism" (see G. Harman, The Nature of Morality 11 [1977]), which seems to me to have a pejorative connotation (though Harman is not pejorative). Another is moral "noncognitivism"; still another, "metaethical relativism" (see Brandt, "Ethical Relativism," in 3 The Encyclopedia of Philosophy 75 [P. Edwards ed. 1967]); both of which sound a bit technical. For better or worse, I've opted for the name "moral skepticism".

The position that moral claims function merely as expressions of attitude has sometimes been called "emotivism". See A. MacIntyre, After Virtue 11–21 (1981). If one is a moral skeptic, then one might also be an emotivist, but not necessarily. Moral skepticism holds that moral claims cannot be true-or-false statements about the world, and thus gives rise to the question: What, then, *are* moral claims? One answer—the emotivist answer—is: They are merely (they function merely as) expressions of attitude. No one denies that moral claims can and usually do function as expressions of attitude. But that they function "merely" as expressions of attitude is simply wrong, as MacIntyre (among others) has demonstrated. See id. at 12–13.

5. Walzer, "Teaching Morality," New Republic, June 12, 1978, at 12–13.

This and the next three quotes are of passages reporting the morally skeptical position, not defending it.

6. A. MacIntyre, note 4, at 11–12.

7. Moore, "Moral Reality," 1982 Wisconsin L. Rev. 1061, 1081. See id. at 1063:

> A moral skeptic is one who says things like, "there are no moral facts." These statements are usually joined, however, to others to the effect that values are inherently subjective, not objective; that there are no "absolutes", only values relative to a person or a culture; that value choices are irrational or arbitrary; that these choices are matters of emotion, attitude, or feeling and not of cognition or knowledge; that statements of the conclusions of these choices cannot by their nature be true or false; that arguments in support of these conclusions cannot be valid or invalid, correct or incorrect; that values, when all is said and done, are simply a matter of taste and "there's no disputing taste."

8. J. Fishkin, Beyond Subjective Morality 1 (1984). See Brandt, note 3, at 75; T. Regan & D. VanDeVeer, eds., And Justice for All 4 (1982).

9. S. Hampshire, Two Theories of Morality 3 (1977). See id. at 3:

> As for the word "ought", the study of modal words shows that the word "ought" has no particular connection with morality, but rather that practical reason of any kind involves the use of a whole panoply of modal words, of which "must" and "ought" are probably the most interesting. As for the word "good", exhaustive inquiries into semantics and into practical reasoning have ensured that the word "good" will no longer be segregated as belonging to some peculiar kind of discourse, or as indicating some peculiar speech-act. The thought that something is good, or the belief that it is, or the doubt whether it is, will be accepted as being normal thoughts, normal beliefs and normal doubts, whether in moral contexts or elsewhere.

See also id. at 33.

10. For examples of the morally skeptical views of an earlier generation of legal philosophers, see H. Kelsen, General Theory of Law and State 6 (1945) ("These questions [of justice] cannot be answered by means of rational cognition. The decision of these questions is a judgment of value, determined by emotional factors, and is, therefore, subjective in character, valid only for the judging subject and therefore relative only."); A. Ross, On Law and Justice 274 (1959):

> A person who maintains that a certain rule or order—for example, a system of taxation—is unjust, does not indicate any discernible quality in the order; he does not provide any reason for his attitude, but merely gives to it an emotional expression. *A* says: I am against this rule, because it is unjust. What he should say is: This rule is unjust because I oppose it.
>
> To invoke justice is the same thing as banging on the table: an emotional expression which turns one's demand into an absolute postulate.

See also Kelsen, "The Pure Theory of Law," 50 L. Q. Rev. 474, 482 (1934). Compare R. Unger, Knowledge and Politics 103 (1975): "[A]s long as the principle of subjective value is maintained, the making and application of laws will depend on choices that cannot be justified and therefore have to be perceived as pure domination exercised by some men over others."

For examples of the morally skeptical views of the contemporary generation of American lawyer-academics, see Bork, "Neutral Principles and Some First Amendment Problems," 47 Indiana L. J. 1, 8, 9, 10 (1971); Leff, "Unspeakable Ethics, Unnatural Law," 1979 Duke L. J. 1229. See id. at 1249:

> Napalming babies is bad.
> Starving the poor is wicked.
> Buying and selling each other is depraved.
>   Those who stood up to and died resisting Hitler,
>   Stalin, Amin, and Pol Pot—and General Custer
>   too—have earned salvation.
> Those who acquiesced deserve to be damned.
> There is in the world such a thing as evil.
> (All together now:) Sez who?
> God help us.

Apparently lawyer-academics are not the only contemporary moral skeptics. See Tannenbaum & Rowan, "Rethinking the Morality of Animal Research," Hastings Center Rep., Oct. 1985, at 32, 33: "Ethical skepticism is the view that moral claims cannot be true or false, as can statements of fact. It has some currency among scientists. To Sam Shuster, a vocal defender of animal research, moral claims are simply expressions of the desires of those who proclaim them."

11. To say that a claim has truth value is not to say that its truth value is known. Under the "internalist" account of "truth" discussed in chapter 4, however—which is the account implicit in my discussion throughout this essay—it is to say that its truth value *can be* known. Under the "externalist" or "correspondence" or "copy" account of "truth" discussed in chapter 2, to say that a claim has truth value is not to say that its truth value can be known.

12. See J. Segundo, Faith and Ideologies 21 (1982; Eng. tr. 1984):

> I am starting off from the *basic, undeniable fact* that every human being is moved by a quest for *satisfaction.* The reader might ask: Satisfaction of what? But that very question is not pertinent at this initial stage. Here I am simply referring to the fact that in our lives all of us are always comparing possible "satisfactions" and "pleasurable sensations or experiences" of every type. This work of comparison takes place long before we think about cataloguing these satisfactions as (e.g.) instinctual or deliberate, direct or subliminated, material or spiritual. From early childhood on, we are in the habit of mixing all kinds of satisfaction, delight, or pleasure in a common bowl. We want to compare them in their unique, general character as "satisfactions," so that we can then decide which one is more satisfying. So we compare things as unlike each other as martyrdom and sexual intercourse, the miser's hoarding of money and the suffering of the masochist, and eating oysters versus sacrificing oneself for a more just

society. An interesting problem is explaining how we can "compare" things that are so different and perhaps even contradictory. But that we do make such comparisons is a basic fact. It is to the credit of great thinkers that they have discovered or pointed up this fact.

Cf. R. Scruton, Sexual Desire: A Moral Philosophy of the Erotic 326 (1986): ". . . Aristotle's invocation of happiness, as the final end of human conduct, is essentially correct. Happiness is the single final answer to the question 'why do that?', the answer that survives the conflict with every rival interest or desire. In referring to happiness we refer, not to the satisfaction of impulses, but to the fulfillment of the person. . . . But what is happiness? Kant dismissed the idea as empty: happiness, he argued, simply stands for the generality of human desires: it means different things for different people, and provides no coherent motive of its own. Following Aristotle, however, I shall propose an idea of happiness as a kind of 'flourishing'."

13. It is not my purpose here to develop a naturalist moral theory. However, I do want to portray the naturalist conception of moral knowledge in a way that accounts for any of the various species of naturalist moral theory that have been taken seriously from time to time, including a "theological" naturalism in which human beings are understood to be, *inter alia*, "spiritual" entities. My statement that human beings are entities both biological and social in character accounts for the possibility that they are also spiritual in character. If human beings are spiritual entities, then their spirituality is an aspect of their sociality: Their society includes God.

14. J. Segundo, note 12, at 308.

15. See C. Taylor, Philosophy and the Human Sciences 190–91 (1985):

What has been argued in the different theories of the social nature of man is not just that men cannot physically survive alone, but much more that they could only develop their characteristically human capacities in society. The claim is that living in a society is a necessary condition of the development of rationality, in some sense of this property, or of becoming a moral agent in the full sense of the term, or of becoming a fully responsible, autonomous being. These variations and other similar ones represent the different forms in which a thesis about man as a social animal have been or could be couched. What they have in common is the view that outside society . . . our distinctively human capacities could not develop. From the standpoint of the thesis, . . . it is irrelevant whether an organism born from a human womb would go on living in the wilderness; what is important is that this organism could not realize its specifically human potential.

See also J. Maritain, The Rights of Man and Natural Law 7 (1958):

The person is a whole, but it is not a closed whole, it is an *open* whole. . . . It tends by its very nature to social life and to communion.

This is true not only because of the needs and the indigence of human nature, by reason of which each one of us has need of others for his material, intellectual and moral life, but also because of the radical generosity inscribed within the very being of the person, because of that openness to the communications of the intelligence and love which is the nature of the spirit, and which demands an entrance into relationship with other persons. To state it rigorously, the person cannot be alone. It wants to tell what it knows, and it wants to tell what it is—to whom, if not to other people. We can say with Jean-Jacques Rousseau that the breath of man is deadly to man; we can say with Seneca: "Every time that I have been among men I have returned a diminished man." All that is true—and yet by a fundamental paradox we cannot be men and become men without going among men; we cannot make life and activity burgeon within us without breathing in common with our fellow-men.

16. Cf. R. Scruton, note 12, at 327: "We may divide the answer to that question ['what constitutes a person's flourishing?'] into two parts: health and happiness. Health is the state in which I flourish as an animal; happiness the state in which I flourish as a person. And it is an important feature of the ontological dependence of personhood—of its need to find *embodiment* in an animal life—that health is such an important precondition of happiness. But health is not everything; happiness requires that we flourish as rational beings. . . . [W]e must be fulfilled as persons, through the decisions which guide our lives."

To say that one must live a certain way so as to flourish is not to say that the way of life in question bears an instrumental relation to flourishing—that it is a "means" to the "end" of flourishing. Rather, the way of life is constitutive of flourishing. The question "how to live so as to flourish" is the question "how to flourish" or "how to live a flourishing life, a life of well-being".

See H. Putnam, Meaning and the Moral Sciences 83 (1978): "[I] take the question [for moral philosophy] to be the simple three-worded question 'how to live'. . . . [T]his starting point[] not only seems fresh and unhackneyed in comparison with the usual academic ways of beginning the investigation of ethical topics, but . . . it has the effect of making ethics at once a branch of practical knowledge, and I think that this is a very important idea." See also J. Finnis, Fundamentals of Ethics 1, 3 (1983):

> [I]n calling ethics practical, Aristotle . . . meant that one does ethics properly, ade-
> quately, reasonably, if and only if one is questioning and reflecting *in order to be able
> to act*—i.e., in order to conduct one's life rightly, reasonably, in the fullest sense
> "well". . . . [E]thics is practical because my choosing and acting and living in a certain
> sort of way (and thus my becoming a certain sort of person . . .) is not a secondary
> (albeit inseparable and welcome) objective and side-effect of success in the intellectual
> enterprise; rather it is *the very objective primarily envisaged* as well as the subject-
> matter about which I hope to be able to affirm true propositions.

Bernard Williams' comment on what he calls "Socrates' question"—"How should one live?"—is relevant to our question—"How should particular human beings live (if they are to live the most deeply satisfying lives of which they are capable)?" See B. Williams, Ethics and the Limits of Philosophy 4 (1985):

Socrates' question is the best place for moral philosophy to start. It is better than "what is our duty?" or "how may we be good?" or even "how can we be happy?" Each of these questions takes too much for granted, although not everyone will agree about what that is. In the case of the last question, some people, such as those who want to start with the first question, will think that it starts in the wrong place, by ignoring the distinctive issues of morality; others may simply find it rather optimistic. Socrates' question is neutral on those issues, and on many others.

On the difference between our question and Socrates' question, see note 11.
  17. See S. Hampshire, note 9, at 53–54, 57–58:

[A] strength of Aristotle's moral theory . . . is the thoroughgoing naturalism of his approach to moral problems in the Nicomachean Ethics. He starts in Book I from biological concepts, and he continues his argument with the use of them. The word . . . soul marks the domain of biology, being the principle of life in living things. The vegetative part of the soul is no less a part of the soul than is the complex of human desires, and no less than the third and distinctive part, which is the complex capacity to think and to form designs for a whole life and for a complete way of life. The purposes proper to the species can only be attained in a complete life, and through the natural unfolding of the potentialities of the species, in the fitting social environment, and after the proper intellectual and emotional diet and training. Moral injunctions are to be thought of as a protection against a warped character, monstrous ambitions, corrupt appetites, and stunted and inhuman sentiments. They are to be thought of as a protection of innately preferred activities and sentiments, which bring pleasure with them, and against inhuman and conflict-laden activities and sentiments, which bring unhappiness with them. There is no independent, and no transcendental, sanction of moral restraints, and no authority external to men's experience of the workings of their own nature. The experience of ease and enjoyment of a way of life, as opposed to frustration and suffering, makes the crucial test, and men will in fact be guided by this test, if they are not governed by perverse passions. As felt pain warns us of some wound or infection in the body, so suffering warns us of some wound or corruption in thought or feeling.

By naturalism I here mean the habit of representing judgments about the moral strengths and defects of persons as resembling in most respects judgments about the physical strengths and defects of persons, and of representing virtue as an excellent state of the soul or mind, and vice as a diseased state of the soul or mind, manifested in action, just as health is an excellent state of the body. . . .

. . . Spinoza considered the individual organism, which has to be both a receptacle of knowledge and an agent in pursuit of it, in an entirely naturalistic way, without ascribing to a person any unexplained or supernatural powers, or any powers that are not to be understood as a complication of the powers of living creatures generally. Therefore moral enlightenment, and the improvement of men and of society, have to be the effects of understood and controlled causes in the natural order of things. In so far as radical improvement is attainable, it is attainable in much the same way that an improvement in men's physical condition may be attainable, by the application of a more systematic knowledge of causes: both of causes operating in society, as indicated in Spinoza's two political works, and also causes operating in the individual.

See also B. Williams, note 16, at 121–22; S. Lovibond, Realism and Imagination in Ethics 15 (1983): "[A] naturalistic realism . . . represents moral discourse—like other human institutions—as embedded in the world of (physical) nature."

James Griffin's important book, *Well-Being: Its Meaning, Measurement and Moral Importance* (1986), was published after I'd virtually completed this essay. Griffin's work should be consulted by anyone who wants to think about human "well-being" and its place in moral theory.

18. R. Beiner, Political Judgment 144 & 186 n. 18 (1983) (quoting McDowell, "Virtue and Reason," 62 Monist 331, 347–48 [1979]). See B. Williams, note 16, at 4–5:

> [Socrates' question "how should one live?"] is not immediate; it is not about what I should do now, or next. It is about a manner of life. The Greeks themselves were much impressed by the idea that such a question must, consequently, be about a whole life and that a good way of living had to issue in what, at its end, would be seen to have been a good life. . . . The idea that one must think, at this very general level, about *a whole life* may seem less compelling to some of us than it did to Socrates. But his question still does press a demand for reflection on one's life *as a whole*, from every aspect and all the way down, even if we do not place as much weight as the Greeks did on how it may end.

19. G. Allport, Becoming 73 (1955). See R. Beiner, note 18, at 73: "[W]e approach the experience of virtue not 'from the outside in' (on the basis of codified principles of right conduct), but 'from the inside out' (on the basis of a tacit understanding of what it is to live virtuously)." See also Toulmin, "How Medicine Saved the Life of Ethics," 25 Perspectives in Biology and Medicine 736, 748 (1982): "We are who we are: we stand in the human relationships we do, and our specific moral duties and obligations can be discussed in practice *only* at the point at which these questions of personal standing and relationship have been recognized and taken into account."

The naturalist conception of moral knowledge, as I'm portraying it, presupposes the conception of the person presented in chapter 3—the conception according to which a particular human being's commitments, projects, and character, and also the convictions that underlie her decision to make certain commitments, pursue certain projects, and cultivate certain traits of character, are all partly constitutive of the person she is. See chapter 3.

20. See note 51; chapter 2, section V.

Although our question—"How should particular human beings live (if they are to live the most deeply satisfying lives of which they are capable)?"—does not presuppose even that all human beings are alike in any significant respect, what Williams calls "Socrates' question"—"How should one live?"—is a different matter. See B. Williams, note 16, at 4:

"How should one live?"—the generality of *one* already stakes a claim. The Greek language does not even give us *one*: the formula is impersonal. The implication is that something relevant or useful can be said to anyone, in general, and this implies that something general can be said, something that embraces or shapes the individual ambitions each person may bring to the question "how should I live?" . . . This is one way in which Socrates' question goes beyond the everyday "what shall I do?"

See also id. at 20. Cf. note 53.

21. As this and the next chapter illustrate, the naturalist conception of moral knowledge (as I portray it) avoids "two mistakes often made in modern philosophy: to think of the individual as primary, the social as secondary (made by individuals interacting with each other); and, within the individual, to think of cognition and logic as primary, the emotive, associative, and imaginative as secondary (to be replaced if possible by the superior primary modes)." White, "The Judicial Opinion and the Poem: Ways of Reading, Ways of Life," 82 Michigan L. Rev. 1669, 1690 (1984). See R. Isaac, The Transformation of Virginia 1740–90 311 (1982): "Our twentieth-century outlook induces us to see unquestioningly the individual as the primary social reality whose self-fulfillment supplies the ultimate meaning and purpose in life. Yet 'the individual' is no less a great metaphor applied to the interpretation of social realities than hierarchies of ruling fathers have been."

22. For an illuminating discussion addressed to lingering doubts, see MacKenzie, "Moral Scepticism and Moral Conduct," 59 Phil. 473, 473–74 (1984).

23. M. Adler, note 3, at 79.

24. Id. at 80.

25. Id. at 79.

26. Id. at 80.

27. See note 33 and accompanying text.

28. Cf. J. Rawls, A Theory of Justice 578 (1971): "[T]here are great obstacles to maintaining that [first principles] are necessarily true, *or even to explaining what is meant by this*." (Emphasis added.)

29. J. Finnis, note 3, at 59.

30. Id. at 69–70.

31. L. Wittgenstein, On Certainty 28e (1969). See id. at 46e-47e:

357. One might say: "'I know' expresses *comfortable* certainty, not the certainty that is still struggling."

358. Now I would like to regard this certainty, not as something akin to hastiness or superficiality, but as a form of life. (That is very badly expressed and probably badly thought as well.)

359. But that means I want to conceive it as something that lies beyond being justified or unjustified; as it were, as something animal.

32. See J. Finnis, note 3, at 69.

33. P. Singer, Practical Ethics 203 (1979).

34. The commitment to rationality—to answers that work for us, that enable us, in Richard Rorty's word, to "cope" (see chapter 2, section V)—is best understood as an aspect of the commitment to flourishing. Cf. H. Putnam, Reason, Truth and History 134 (1981): "[W]hat we are trying to do in science is to construct a representation of the world which has the characteristics of being instrumentally efficacious, coherent, comprehensive, and functionally simple. But why? . . . [T]he reason . . . is that having this sort of representation system is *part of our idea of human cognitive flourishing*, and hence part of our idea of total human flourishing, of Eudaemonia."

35. See R. Bambrough, Moral Scepticism and Moral Knowledge 146 (1979):

> The sense in which, in Hume's phrase, morality rests upon 'the particular fabric and constitution of the human species' is paralleled by a sense in which logic also rests upon the particular fabric and constitution of the human species. Logic is not rendered subjective by this dependence, and morality is not rendered subjective by the corresponding dependence. For the dependence is not a dependence of the truths of logic or of morality upon facts about human beings. It is rather that the intelligibility to us of both agreement and conflict, both in logic and in morality, depends on our sharing a set of responses, upon our reacting in closely similar ways.

See also Flanagan, "Quinean Ethics," Ethics, Oct. 1982, at 56, 69 *et seq.* Cf. P. Strawson, Skepticism and Naturalism: Some Varieties 39 (1984):

> [Hume's] point . . . is that arguments, reasonings, either for or against the skeptical position, are, in practice, equally inefficacious and idle; since our natural disposition to belief, on the points challenged by the skeptic, is absolutely compelling and inescapable; neither shaken by skeptical argument nor reinforced by rational counter-argument. Where Nature thus determines us, we have an original nonrational commitment which sets the bounds within which, or the stage upon which, reason can effectively operate, and within which the question of the rationality or irrationality, justification or lack of justification, of this or that particular judgment or belief can come up. . . . [A parallel point obtains with respect to] the moral life. We are naturally social beings; and given with our natural commitment to social existence is a natural commitment to that whole web or structure of human personal and moral attitudes, feelings, and judgments of which I spoke. Our natural disposition to such attitudes and judgments is naturally secured against arguments suggesting that they are in principle unwarranted or unjustified just as our natural disposition to belief in the existence of body is naturally secured against arguments suggesting that it is in principle uncertain.

36. Hinman, "Can a Form of Life Be Wrong?," 58 Phil. 339, 341–42 (1983).

37. Werner, "Ethical Realism," Ethics, July 1983, at 653, 664–65. Cf. R. Scruton, note 12, at 325: "The weakness of the Kantian position lies in its attribution of a 'motivating force' to reason—in its denial of Hume's principle

that reason alone cannot be a motive to action. The Aristotelian position involves no commitment to the idea of a 'pure practical reason'. It recognises that practical reasoning concludes in action only because it begins in desire. The 'practical syllogism' has a practical premise, and to the agent with evil desires no reason can be given that will, by its sheer force as a reason, suffice to make him good."

38. R. Unger, note 10, at 196.

One might want to argue that every human being is necessarily committed to flourishing in the sense that every human being necessarily deems that at which she aims as good for her to achieve. However, that sense of "good" seems empty—tautalogical—to me. At any rate, I'm not making that argument. I'm open to the possibility that a human being might perversely aim at something she deems antithetical to her well-being. Or, at least, she might imagine that she is a nonhuman creature—a snow leopard, for example—and, so, act so as to serve not her well-being *qua* human being, but her well-being *qua* snow leopard. See B. Williams, note 16, at 58–59.

39. J. Mackie, Ethics: Inventing Right and Wrong 33, 35 (1977).

40. See Zimmerman, "Meta-Ethics Naturalized," 10 Can. J. Phil. 637, 644–45 (1980):

> Some expressions occur both in ordinary discourse and in scientific theorizing. But there is no particular reason to think that an investigation of the meaning-rules governing the use of such terms in natural language(s) will be of much use to the scientist in his investigations. Even if the sentence "atoms are indivisible" were analytically true circa 1850 this would still not settle any question of interest about the ultimate constituents of physical reality. One point to be emphasized is that moral theories are theories about value and obligation. The *linguistic* intuitions of speakers of natural languages have no greater controlling role in moral investigations than they do in scientific.

Cf. A. MacIntyre, note 4, at 57:

> [M]oral judgments are linguistic survivals from the practices of classical theism which have lost the context provided by these practices. In that context moral judgments were at once hypothetical and categorical in form. They were hypothetical in so far as they expressed a judgment as to what conduct would be teleologically appropriate for a human being: "You ought to do such-and-such, if and since your *telos* is such-and-such" or perhaps "You ought to do so-and-so, if you do not want your essential desires to be frustrated." They were categorical in so far as they reported the contexts of the universal law commanded by God: "You ought to do so-and-so: that is what God's law enjoins." But take away from them that in virtue of which they were hypothetical *and* that in virtue of which they were categorical and what are they? Moral judgments lose any clear status and the sentences which express them in a parallel way lose any undebatable meaning. Such sentences become available as a form of expression for an emotivist self which lacking the guidance of the context in which they were originally at home has lost its linguistiç as well as its practical way in the world.

41. See Foot, "Morality as a System of Hypothetical Imperatives," in P. Foot, Virtues and Vices 157–73 (1978); id. at 174–88; Scheffler, "Moral Scepticism and Ideals of the Person," 62 Monist 288 (1979). Cf. MacKenzie, note 22.

42. Cf. B. Williams, note 16, at 192:

> When we say that someone ought to have acted in some required or desirable way in which he has not acted, we sometimes say *there was a reason* for him to act in that way—he had promised, for instance, or what he actually did violated someone's rights. Although we can say this, it does not seem to be connected in any secure way with the idea that he had a reason to act in that way. Perhaps he had no reason at all. In breaking the obligation, he was not necessarily behaving irrationally or unreasonably, but badly. We cannot take for granted that *he had a reason* to behave well, as opposed to our having various reasons for wishing that he would behave well.

43. See R. Unger, Passion: An Essay on Personality 48 (1984): "The *should* of the existential project or the social vision means: execute this project and enact this vision, or find a better vision and a better project, or else fail at self-affirmation. In Kantian language this *ought* is hypothetical rather than categorical. But the rejection of its hypothesis—the effort at self-assertion— involves something far more drastic than the repudiation of a discrete goal of striving. It is more like the repudiation of striving itself."

44. See P. Foot, note 41, at 178–79; Scheffler, note 41, at 291. The categorical character of such judgments is the source of the "inescapability" of morality. See P. Foot, note 41, at 171–72.

45. To say that moral imperatives are not categorial is not necessarily to reject the nonhypothetical use of "ought". For a discussion of the point, and of the consequences of changing (or not changing) "our linguistic usage by dropping the nonhypothetical use of 'ought' ", see id. at 177–79. See also Scheffler, note 41, at 298:

> The sceptic may retreat to the position that it is at least inappropriate to offer moral evaluations of the actions of people who reject the underlying individual ideal. But it should be clear by now why this claim need not be accepted. The truth value of the judgment that a certain action does or does not conform to a moral rule in no way depends on the acceptance by the agent of the ideal underlying the relevant system of rules. (There remains the independent question . . . of whether it is appropriate to use the moral "ought" in evaluating the conduct of someone who rejects morality.)

46. J. Mackie, note 39, at 30.

47. See P. Singer, note 33, at 7: "In their denial of a realm of ethical facts which is part of the real world, existing quite independently of us, they are no doubt correct" (referring *inter alia* to Mackie).

Mackie said that "[o]ne way of stating the thesis that there are no objective values is to say that value statements cannot be either true or false." J. Mackie, note 39, at 25. By "value statements" he meant "statements that presuppose the objectivity of values". Naturalist moral statements, however, don't make that presupposition. Sometimes Mackie seemed to say that value statements are false. He meant, however, not that they are false, but, as he explicitly said, that they are neither true nor false. What is false, on Mackie's view, is not the value statement itself (which is neither true nor false) but the further, implicit claim that values are objective. See, for example, id. at 40: "The assertion that there are objective values or intrinsicially prescriptive entities or features of some kind, which ordinary moral judgements presuppose, is, I hold, not meaningless but false." (In this passage Mackie was in part taking issue with the logical positivists' "verifiability theory of descriptive meaning". He wrote: "I . . . not only reject the verifiability principle but also deny the conclusion commonly drawn from it, that moral judgements lack descriptive meaning." Id. at 39–40.)

Charles Taylor has described Mackie's argument as "a *naturalist* attack on the objectivity of value". Taylor, "The Diversity of Goods," in A. Sen & B. Williams, eds., Utilitarianism and Beyond 129, 141 n. 2 (1982) (emphasis added). And the description is apt: In the constructive portion of his book, Mackie developed a moral theory of the naturalist sort, contending that certain constraints on conduct are "needed for *the flourishing of human life*" and that "*general human well-being* [is] in some way the foundation of morality." J. Mackie, note 39, at 125 (emphasis added).

48. See Williams, "Ethics and the Fabric of the World," in Morality and Objectivity 203, 213 (T. Honderich ed. 1985):

> Mackie's theory, and any like it, leaves a real problem of what should happen when we know it to be true. . . . [T]he first victim of this knowledge is likely to be the Kantian sense of presented duty. . . . [I]t is the starkest example of objectification, and since there is virtually nothing to it except the sense of being given, it stands to suffer most if that sense is questioned. There are other ethical desires and perceptions which are better adapted to being seen for what they are. It is an important task for moral philosophy to consider what they may be, and into what coherent pictures of ethical life, philosophical, psychological and social, they will fit.

49. Price, "Varieties of Objectivity and Values," 83 Procs. Arist. Soc'y 103, 106 (1983). See id. at 118: "[V]alues are relative, at best anthropocentric, but often far more narrowly relative than that . . ." See also Lovin, "Empiricism and Christian Social Thought," Annual of Society of Christian Ethics 25, 41 (1982) ("Ethics will never be like physics, chemistry, or certain types of sociology, because it understands the moral reality to be about an interaction between persons and the world which can only be known from the reports of those who experience that interaction"); D. Hume, A Treatise of Human Nature 469 (L. Selby-Bigge ed. 1973): "Vice and virtue, therefore, may be compar'd to sounds, colours, heat and cold, which, according to modern philosophy, are not qualities in objects, but perceptions in the mind: And this discovery in morals, like that other in physics, is to be regarded as a considerable advance-

ment of the speculative sciences; tho', like that, too, it has little or no influence on practice."

Even in a theocentric ethics the category of values must be anthropocentric. If one believes that human beings ought to try to discover and value what God values, presumably it is because one believes that it is in their interest, in some way, to do so. Perhaps one believes that valuing what God values is the way to "salvation" (however that term is understood).

50. See J. Finnis, note 16, at 62–63:

> No doubt we cannot detach the meaning of "good" and "well-being" from the notion of "taking an interest in"; for we cannot detach the notion of good from the notion of what it is intelligent to take an interest in (favour, promote . . .). But what is *in my interests* is certainly not sufficiently to be determined by asking what I *happen* to *take an interest in* (desire, aim for . . .). The decisive question is always what it is *intelligent* to take an interest in. There are no "interests" (desires) that are immune from that question. Accordingly, there is no reason to assume that the answer to that question is provided by desires (even "standard desires") or feelings, or by reference to "the fact that some people do care about such things". So there is no reason to deny the . . . intelligibility and reasonableness . . . of statements about what constitutes someone's well-being (and is *therefore* in his interests).

See also Veatch, "The Rational Justification of Moral Principles: Can There Be Such a Thing?," 29 Rev. Metaphysics 217, 234–38 (1975).

51. See S. Hampshire, note 9, at 48–49:

> The correct answer to the old question—"why should it be assumed, or be argued, that there is just one good for man, just one way of life that is best?"—is . . . an indirect one and it is not simple. One can coherently list all the ideally attainable human virtues and achievements, and all the desirable features of a perfect human existence; and one might count this as prescribing the good for man, the perfect realization of all that is desirable. But the best selection from this whole that could with luck be achieved in a particular person will be the supreme end for him, the ideal at which he should aim. It is obvious that supreme ends of this kind are immensely various and always will be various. There can be no single supreme end in this particularized sense, as both social orders and human capabilities change. . . .
>
> That there should be an abstract ethical ideal, the good for men in general, is not inconsistent with there being great diversity in preferred ways of life, even among men living at the same place at the same time. The good for man, as the common starting-point, marks an area within which arguments leading to divergent conclusions about moral priorities can be conducted. The conclusions are widely divergent, because they are determined by different subsidiary premises. Practical and theoretical reason, cleverness, intelligence and wisdom, justice, friendship, temperance in relation to passions, courage, a repugnance in the face of squalid or mean sentiments and actions; these are Aristotle's general and abstract terms, which do not by themselves distinguish a particular way of life, realizable in a particular historical situation. The forms that intelligence and friendship and love between persons, and that nobility of sentiment and motive, can take are at least as various as human cultures; and they are more

various still, because within any one culture there will be varieties of individual temperament, providing distinct motives and priorities of interest, and also varieties of social groupings, restricting the choice of ways of life open to individuals.

See also J. Finnis, note 3, at 93–94; R. Unger, note 10, at 239–40; chapter 2, section V.

52. See note 50.

53. Cf. S. Hampshire, note 9, at 12:

Moral theory, like any practical theory and theory of action, does not purport to be accurate in the sense in which a scientific theory must be accurate if it is to be acceptable at all. A moral theory is not necessarily, or even usually, falsified by a clear and indisputable negative instance. It is sufficient, as Aristotle remarked, that the moral theory, and the set of more or less general propositions that compose it, should turn out to be acceptable for the most part and on the whole, in actual experience, political and private.

54. I don't mean to imply "an intellectualist thesis about the good life. People might well be able to live a life in which they realized their essence [i.e., satisfied their real interests] without knowing that that is what they were doing. Neither must one assume that knowledge of the appropriate life will suffice to ensure that the person who knows will actually lead such a life. I may know what the right life is, but be unable to lead it for any of a variety of reasons—I may be weak-willed or have developed unalterably wicked habits." Geuss, "Freedom and Preference," unpublished ms. at 3 (1985).

55. Consider, in connection with the ideal of self-critical rationality, Alasdair MacIntyre's suggestion that "the good life for man is the life spent in seeking for the good life for man, and the virtues necessary for the seeking are those which will enable us to understand what more and what else the good life for man is." A. MacIntyre, note 4, at 219.

56. Indeed, it is sometimes claimed that an egoistic theory is not a *moral* theory at all. See Schueler, "Moral Scepticism," 15 South. J. Phil. 117, 118 (1977). That claim relies on a problematic distinction—a most un-Aristotelian distinction—between acting "prudentially" or in a "self-regarding" way and acting "morally" or in an "other-regarding" way. See Wilkes, "The Good Man and the Good for Man in Aristotle's Ethics," in A. Rorty, ed., Essays on Aristotle's Ethics 341, 354–56 (1980). See also notes 57–58 and accompanying text. As Charles Taylor has argued, "the boundaries of the moral are an open question . . ." C. Taylor, note 15, at 233. See id. at 233, 236:

We could easily decide—a view which I would defend—that the universal attribution of moral personality is valid, and lays obligations on us which we cannot ignore; but that there are also other moral ideals and goals—e.g. of less than universal solidarity, or of personal excellence—which cannot easily be coordinated with universalism, and can even enter into conflict with it. To decide *a priori* what the bounds of the moral are is just to obfuscate the question whether and to what degree this is so, and to make it incapable of being coherently stated. . . .

The really important question may turn out to be how we combine in our lives two or three or four different goals, or virtues, or standards, which we feel we cannot repudiate but which seem to demand incompatible things of us. Which of these we dignify with the term "moral", or whether we so designate all of them, may end up appearing as a mere question of labelling—unless, that is, it confuses us into thinking that there is in principle only one set of goals or standards which can be accorded ultimate significance. In certain contexts, it might help clarify to drop the word, at least provisionally, until we get over the baleful effects of reductive thinking on our meta-ethical views.

Cf. Flanagan, "Admirable Immorality and Admirable Imperfection," 83 J. Phil. 41, 49–60 (1986):

> [W]e have (at least recently) been addressing issues concerning the good life without any moral theory or principle (certainly any single one) doing much work. This suggests that we have been addressing such problems without the concept of "morality" itself being of much service, despite the ubiquity of the word "moral". What we have been doing, sometimes well and sometimes badly, is talking about the order of goods and obligations from a wide variety of perspectives—talking, that is, about actual and possible worlds and visions of human flourishing therein. This seems to me to be a good way, indeed the only way, to do things. Acknowledging this much may, if we are lucky, help break the grip of the view that, when things go well, it is because the actors involved understand the true nature of morality and its supreme importance; and that, conversely, when things go badly, it is because those involved lack such understanding. That view, I think, is based on the deeply mistaken view that morality has a nature that can be revealed by moral philosophy.

For the naturalist-altruist, an egoistic theory is defective not because it is not a moral theory, but because it is a flawed moral theory—a moral theory whose conception of flourishing is flawed.

57. For an example of the position, see P. Singer, note 33, at 10–12:

> From ancient times, philosophers and moralists have expressed the idea that ethical conduct is acceptable from a point of view that is somehow *universal*. The "Golden Rule" attributed to Moses tells us to go beyond our own personal interests and "do unto others as we would have them do unto us." The same idea of putting oneself in the position of another is involved in the Christian commandment that we love our neighbor as ourself. . . . Kant developed this idea into his famous formula: "Act only on that maxim through which you can at the same time will that it should become a universal law." Kant's theory has been modified and developed by R. M. Hare, who sees "universalizability" as a logical feature of moral judgments. . . . Ethics takes a universal point of view. . . . [I]n making ethical judgments we go beyond our own likes and dislikes. From an ethical point of view the fact that it is I who benefits from . . . [something] and you, say, who lose by it, is irrelevant. Ethics requires us to go beyond "I" and "you" to the universal law, the universalizable judgments, the standpoint of the impartial spectator or ideal observer, or whatever we choose to call it. . . . In

accepting that ethical judgments must be made from a universal point of view, I am accepting that my own interests cannot, simply because they are my interests, count more than the interests of anyone else. Thus my very natural concern that my own interests be looked after must, when I think ethically, be extended to the interests of others.

58. See MacLean, "What Morality Is," 59 Phil. 21, 22 (1984): "Consistency, rationality—these notions clearly apply whenever we have a judgment for which reasons are or can be given. The judgment need not be moral, or even evaluative in character."

59. For an effective rejoinder to the claim that "not acting on the needs, interests and desires of others involves not treating them as people at all", see Schueler, note 56, at 127:

> The sceptic who denies that the needs, interests and desires of others give him reason to act while allowing that his own do is not shifting the meaning of "need," "interest" or "desire" when he uses them in first and in third person cases. For in allowing that his acceptance of "I need a bath" commits him to accepting "I have a reason to seek one" the sceptic need not allow that his acceptance of "Smith needs a bath" commits him to accepting "I have reason to seek a bath for Smith." It is enough that if he agrees that "Smith needs a bath" he also agrees that "Smith has reason to seek one." In the refusal to allow that the needs, interests and desires of others provide one with a reason to act there is no shift of meaning between the third and first person uses of these terms. In each case the principle being followed is something like "'X needs (or has an interest in or wants) Y' entails 'X has a reason to seek Y'," . . . It is completely consistent with this principle to hold that someone else needs something but that I have no reason to help him get it.

60. See J. Mackie, note 39, at 83–90.

61. See Schueler, note 56, at 128 n. 4: "[T]he problem with Hare's 'universalizability' [condition] . . . is obviously that even if one is committed to universal principles, they need not be altruistic."

62. Cf. J. Rawls, note 28, at 251: "It is a mistake . . . to emphasize the place of generality and universality in Kant's ethics. . . . It is impossible to construct a moral theory on so slender a basis, and therefore to limit the discussion of Kant's doctrine to these notions is to reduce it to triviality."

63. See Whiteley, "The Justification of Morality," 57 Phil. 435, 438–39 (1983):

> It is pretty obvious that a human life can only be lived in a community, and that life in a human community is possible only if there is among its members a certain amount of friendliness—I mean that the members abstain from doing each other serious damage, that they give some help to each other when in distress, that they combine in activities in which effort, risk and reward are shared, that they do not habitually deceive one another but give each other promises and keep them, that they follow such rules as the community adopts for the direction of mutual aid and mutual rivalry. Without a minimum of such friendly behavior (which is of course consistent with plenty of

competition of various kinds) a community cannot exist at all and its members cannot survive; without a fairly high level of friendliness they cannot prosper, that is, they cannot effectively pursue their most important aims and enjoy the fulfillment of them. So mutual goodwill is a necessary means for a group of people to fulfill an adequate proportion of their desires and aims to give them satisfaction in life. It follows that any rational man will prefer to belong to a community in which friendliness flourishes, since he cannot do without the cooperation of his fellows to realize whatever aims he has. Even the criminal relies on the fact that most people are law-abiding most of the time. I am not denying that there are and have been men who prefer, or imagine that they would prefer, a nasty, brutish and short life of constant mayhem and treachery: I deny that this preference can be rational, the outcome of a judicious estimate of gains and losses, just as I would deny rationality to the preferences of one addicted to alcohol or heroin, or completely in the grip of a passion of infatuation or revenge.

64. See Schueler, note 56, at 125:

[It] is usually very difficult indeed to see how acting on some moral code in a particular case, or even for a whole lifetime, will automatically be in one's interest. The usual argument is that it is clearly in one's interest for society in general to operate according to an altruistic moral code and that only by following this code oneself one can remain in such a society and do what one can to assure that the society itself continues to exist. But clearly this is only enough to show that it is in one's interest to be in such a society and to continue to seem to be acting on its moral code. Only if the actual existence of this society depended on one's acting . . . [in accordance with its moral code] would such an argument show that it is in one's interest to do so and surely such a situation is so unlikely as not to merit attention.

65. See J. Mackie, note 39, at 243: "D. D. Raphael, in 'The Standard of Morals', in Proceedings of the Aristotelian Society 75 (1974–75) follows Edward Ullendorff in pointing out that whereas 'Thou shalt love thy neighbor as thyself' represents the Greek of the Septuagint (Leviticus 19:18) and of the New Testament, the Hebrew from which the former is derived means rather 'You shall treat your neighbor lovingly, for he is like yourself.' " For a recent discussion of the Gospel ideal of agape, see G. Meilaender, Friendship (1981).

66. See Goldworthy, "God or Mackie?: The Dilemma of Secular Moral Philosophy," 1985 American J. Jurisprudence 43, 77; Maguire, "Ethics and Immortality," Annual of Society of Christian Ethics 42 (1978); D. Maguire, The Moral Revolution: A Christian Humanist Vision 268 (1986). See also note 68 and accompanying text.

67. See Wilkes, note 56, at 356:

[Aristotle's and Plato's] shared conviction is that nothing can be an arete unless it benefits its possessor—that there is no *genuine* "doing well" that does not leave the doer better off, in some way, than before . . . The clearest, if slightly misleading, way of putting this into modern terminology is to say that an enlightened prudentiality presupposes or requires morality. . . . The attempt to derive "the good life" from the requirements of rationality is a worthy and an interesting aim; many contemporary moralists would like to answer the amoralist's challenge, "Why should I be moral?" by saying, "Because no other course of action is in your interests, placed in the circumstances in which you are." But if this is so, then the foundation of morality is identical with that of enlightened prudentiality. Certainly such an enterprise is more exciting and intellectually satisfying than the attempt to base morality in the emotions, in intuitions, in conscience, or in a social contract.

(I wonder why Wilkes includes "the emotions". See note 49 and accompanying text.) See also M. Nussbaum, The Fragility of Goodness 5 n. * & 25–50 (1986); B. Williams, note 16, at 11–12, 31–32, 49–53; P. Singer, note 33, at 211–12.

68. See Goldworthy, note 66, at 54. See also R. Nozick, Philosophical Explanations 403 (1981):

> Recall Glaucon's challenge to Socrates in Plato's *Republic*: show that being moral is better for the agent, apart from its external consequences. To isolate these consequences, Glaucon imagines a ring that makes someone invisible. With this ring he is able to act immorally with no external penalty: he can rob, murder, and rape without being caught or punished. Is there any reason why he should not do this? Glaucon sharpens the issue by imagining that the immoral man has the reputation of being moral, he is honored and praised as moral, while another man is thought to be immoral and so is condemned and shunned. Glaucon asks Socrates to show, despite this, that the second moral person is better off than the first immoral one, that we would be better off being that second than the first.

"[T]he answer that [Plato] puts into the mouth of Socrates is that the just man is happy because his soul is harmoniously ordered, because, as we would say, he has an integrated personality, whereas the unjust man's personality is disintegrated, and the man who represents the extreme of injustice is psychotic, his soul is a chaos of internal strife." J. Mackie, note 39, at 190–91. Cf. B. Williams, note 16, at 46:

> There is also the figure, rarer perhaps than Callicles supposed, but real, who is horrible enough and not miserable at all but, by any ethological standard of the bright eye and the gleaming coat, dangerously flourishing. For those who want to ground the ethical life in psychological health, it is something of a problem that there can be such people at all. But it is a significant question, how far their existence, indeed the thought of their existence, is a cultural phenomenon. They seem sleeker and finer at a distance. Some Renaissance grandee fills such a role with more style than the tawdry fascist bosses, gangsters, or tycoons who seem, even as objects of fantasy, to be their chief contemporary instances. Perhaps we deceive ourselves about the past.

James Griffin addresses the problem of the relation of "prudence" and "morality" in chapter 8 ("From Prudence to Morality") of his recent book *Well-Being*, note 17.

69. See Overvold, "Morality, Self-Interest, and Reasons for Being Moral," 44 Philosophy & Phenomenological Research 493, 506 (1984).

70. A. MacIntyre, note 4, at 152.

John Finnis seems to argue, in his *Natural Law and Natural Rights* (1980), that the conception of human flourishing he develops there is self-evidently true. I don't know what it means to say that a conception of human flourishing is self-evidently true. I do know, however, that to adjudicate among competing conceptions of human flourishing is to give reasons, and that the claim that a conception is self-evidently true is, at best, an opaque reason. At worst, "[a]n appeal to self-evidence is no argument at all but rather states a conclusion in a rather dubious form." Richards, Review of J. Finnis, note 3, Ethics, Oct. 1982, at 169, 170.

Chapter 2

1. Unger, "The Critical Legal Studies Movement," 96 Harvard L. Rev. 561, 615 (1983).

2. Scanlon, "Contractualism and Utilitarianism," in A. Sen & B. Williams, eds., Utilitarianism and Beyond 103, 103 (1982). I discuss and criticize Scanlon's essay in chapter 4.

3. A. MacIntyre, After Virtue 152 (1981).

4. The naturalist conception of moral knowledge sketched in the preceding chapter is not foundationalist. Although a person's commitment to her own flourishing is foundational for naturalism, the commitment to or value of flourishing—which, like the value of rationality, cannot be justified but needs no justification (see chapter 1, section III)—is not a principle of morality. That is, the fact that I am committed to my own flourishing or that my flourishing is, for me, a value does not begin to tell me how to live or what to do (except in the formal or empty sense that it tells me to live and to act so as to flourish). The value of flourishing, as distinct from a particular conception of flourishing, offers no moral guidance. I don't mean to deny that a naturalist can be a foundationalist. John Finnis seems to be a naturalist who is a foundationalist, because Finnis seems to believe that the conception of flourishing he elaborates in his book *Natural Law and Natural Rights* (1980) is "self-evidently true" and, in that sense, unquestionable. See chapter 1, section III. However, a naturalist moral theory is not necessarily foundationalist, and the naturalist conception of moral knowledge portrayed in chapter 1 is not foundationalist. No conception of flourishing is beyond question, in my view; no conception of flourishing can serve as the *unquestionable* ground of moral justification.

5. The account of moral reasoning I offer here is also an account of reasoning generally, as will be apparent. Thus my account is opposed, at one extreme, to epistemological foundationalism and, at the other, to epistemological skepticism. Epistemological foundationalism is the position, roughly, that there are first principles of rationality—criteria of what beliefs to accept and what beliefs to reject—that are beyond question and serve as the unquestionable ground of justification. While an epistemological skeptic is necessarily a moral skeptic—epistemological skepticism holds that there can be no knowledge of any kind, including, therefore, moral knowledge—an epistemological founda-

tionalist is not necessarily a moral foundationalist: An epistemological foundationalist might believe that there are no first principles of morality; indeed, she
might believe that while there can be, and is, knowledge of some kinds—
scientific knowledge, for example—there can be no *moral* knowledge. (Recall
that twentieth-century "logical positivists" were epistemological foundationalists who tended to be moral skeptics.)

6. R. Bambrough, Moral Scepticism and Moral Knowledge 130 (1979).
See id. at 130–31.

7. My portrayal of reasoning and my terminology rely heavily on S.
Toulmin, R. Rieke, & A. Janik, An Introduction to Reasoning (2d ed. 1984).
Cf. id. at 10: "[R]easoning is less a way of hitting on new ideas—for that, we
have to use our imaginations—than it is a way of testing and sifting ideas
critically." (Emphasis deleted.)

8. See J. Rawls, A Theory of Justice 580 (1971): "[J]ustification is argument addressed to those who disagree with us, or to ourselves when we are of
two minds. It presumes a clash of views between persons or within one person,
and seeks to convince others, or ourselves, of the reasonableness of the principles upon which our claims and judgments are founded. Being designed to
reconcile by reason, justification proceeds from what all parties to the discussion hold in common." See also C. Perelman, Justice, Law, and Argument 132
(1980) ("Every effort to convince presupposes the existence of an agreement on
certain notions and principles. What is well-known and is the object of a general
consensus does not have to be proved"); C. Perelman, The Realm of Rhetoric
2–3, 31 (1982).

9. See C. Perelman, Justice, Law, and Argument 150 (1980); R. Geuss,
The Idea of a Critical Theory 31 (1981).

10. Toulmin et al., note 7, at 61–72, include a fourth element—*backing*—
in addition to claims, warrants, and grounds. It seems to me, however, that a
backing is simply an argument in support of a belief one wants to use as the
warrant in a subsequent argument—a belief at issue and thus in need of support.
Backing does not seem to be a functionally distinctive element of reasoning in
the way claims, warrants, and grounds are all functionally distinctive elements.

11. Haack, "Theories of Knowledge: An Analytic Framework," 83 Procs.
Arist. Soc'y 143, 156 (1983). See id.: "Like Quine (and before him, Dewey and
Peirce), I conceive of the theory of knowledge naturalistically, as centrally
concerned with the ways in which human beings learn about the world by means
of their interactions with it. And, like them, I think of experience as playing an
important role in the justification of a person's beliefs." Some of our beliefs
may be a part of our genetic program. Our beliefs about space, time, and
causality, for example, can be seen not as rooted in our experience of the world
but rather as preconditions for our experiencing the world as we do.

12. See notes 23 & 24 and accompanying text. Cf. Hardwig, "Epistemic
Dependence," 82 J. Phil. 335 (1985).

13. See N. MacCormick, Legal Theory and Legal Reasoning 273 (1978); C. Perelman, The Realm of Rhetoric 123, 160 (1982).

14. See Nussbaum, " 'Finely Aware and Richly Responsible': Moral Attention and the Moral Task of Literature," 82 J. Phil. 516 (1985). See also H. Putnam, Meaning and the Moral Sciences 85–86 (1978); Flanagan, "Quinean Ethics," Ethics, Oct. 1982, at 56, 71, 73.

15. Another important question, which I need not address here, is why some persons cling tenaciously to beliefs that seem obvious candidates for revision. See Rubin, "Why We Stick Our Heads in the Sand," N.Y. Times Book Rev., June 16, 1985, at 9 (reviewing D. Goleman, Vital Lies, Simple Truths: The Psychology of Self-Deception [1985]).

16. See generally W. Quine & J. Ullian, The Web of Belief (2d ed. 1978).

17. See Hinman, "Can a Form of Life be Wrong?," 58 Phil. 339, 342 (1983):

> No doubt can be completely presuppositionless; every doubt must take something for granted as true, as the firm foundation from which it can then exert some leverage. Doubting the reliability of pen and ink will only make sense if we assume the reliability of something else against which the trustworthiness of pen and ink can be measured; yet it is by no means evident what this other reliable point of comparison could be and how its reliability could be established in the first place.

See also C. S. Peirce, Philosophical Writings of Peirce 229 (J. Buchler ed. 1975). Cf. H. Putnam, Reason, Truth and History 662–63 (1981) on "Sextus Empiricus, who eventually concluded that his own scepticism could not be expressed by a statement (because even the statement, 'I do not know' could not be one he *knew*)".

18. L. Wittgenstein, Philosophical Investigations, sec. 217 (1953). (Quoted in H. Putnam, The Many Faces of Realism 85 [1987].)

19. See H. Putnam, note 18, at 85–86.

20. For a much fuller discussion of belief revision, see N. MacCormick, note 13, at 102, 124, 273–74; C. Perelman, note 9, at 169–70; Haack, note 9; Hinman, note 15; Lilla, "On Goodman, Putnam, and Rorty: The Return to the 'Given'," 51 Partisan Review 220 (1984); S. Burton, An Introduction to Law and Legal Reasoning 132–43 (1985); G. Harman, Change in View: Principles of Reasoning (1986). See also Stout, "Holism and Comparative Ethics," 11 J. Rel. Ethics 301, 312 (1983): "For the holist . . . the justification of moral knowledge neither depends upon independently known foundations nor is called into question by the impossibility of placing any given moral judgment beyond doubt. Practical justification is a dialectical affair, intelligible only in relation to the simultaneously social and intellectual setting of a particular time and place." The "holistic" conception of reasoning is ascendant. See B. Williams, Ethics and the Limits of Philosophy 113 (1985):

> [T]he [linear] model . . . is wrong. No process of reason-giving fits this picture, in the sciences or elsewhere. In theoretical connections, the foundationalist enterprise, of

resting the structure of knowledge on some favored class of statements, has now generally been displaced in favor of a holistic type of model, in which some beliefs can be questioned, justified, or adjusted while others are kept constant, but there is no process by which they can all be questioned at once, or all justified in terms of (almost) nothing. In von Neurath's famous image, we repair the ship while we are on the sea.

For an excellent discussion of legal reasoning from a holistic perspective, see Stick, "Can Nihilism Be Pragmatic?," 100 Harvard L. Rev. 332 (1986).

21. See Blackburn, "Rule-Following and Moral Realism," in Wittgenstein: To Follow a Rule 163, 178–79 (S. Holtzman & C. Leich eds. 1981).

22. L. Wittgenstein, On Certainty 46e (1969).

23. See MacIntyre, "Epistemological Crises, Dramatic Narrative and the Philosophy of Science," 60 Monist 453 (1977).

24. Bambrough, "The Roots of Moral Reason," in Gewirth's Ethical Rationalism 39, 48 (E. Regis ed. 1984).

25. See J. Segundo, Faith and Ideologies 6, 7, 22–23, 24–25 (1984).

26. See id. at 317:

Adhesion to a tradition is the basis for saving energy so that the latter may be invested in more important tasks. No tradition could perform that function if its content were thoroughly foreign, so that people would have to stop and ask questions and make personal decisions with every step they took.

To be left without a tradition would be akin to being left without genetic instructions. In like manner, too complete or rapid change in traditions would overload our homeostatic mechanisms for dealing with the external world. Even if that world remained unchanged, we would be brought to a standstill as was our poor elephant.

We need complementary doses of both elements: What we receive ready-made or half-made from tradition and what we must pose to ourselves as problems. However, we cannot prescribe any precise dosage that would be universal and valid once and for all. The fact that we need a dose of tradition does not exempt us from the task of wisely criticizing the shoulders on which we are mounted. Evolution requires that we introduce alterations, perhaps even radical alterations, into the foundation prepared by earlier generations and other social models. But we must do this prudently, following a delicate energy calculus comparable to the types mentioned so far . . .

The human being is not a cultural being simply because it is given a ready-made culture as the launching pad for its own individual creation. It is a cultural being because its individual creation, in turn, leaves an imprint on that culture.

27. A. MacIntyre, note 3, at 207.

28. On tradition, see J. Pelikan, The Vindication of Tradition (1984). On the notion of a "form of life", see Hinman, note 17.

29. S. Hauerwas, A Community of Character 60 (1981).

30. B. Williams, note 20, at 191.

31. Id.

32. See Hardwig, note 12. Hardwig concludes that "we could retain the idea that the knower must understand and have evidence for the truth of what he knows, but in doing so we deny that the knower is always an individual or even

a class of individuals. This alternative may well point to part of what [Charles Sanders] Peirce may have had in mind when he claimed that the *community* of inquirers is the primary knower and that individual knowledge is derivative." Id. at 349.

33. See note 20.

34. On self-critical rationality, see chapter 1, section IV. Cf. Schneewind, "Moral Knowledge and Moral Principles," in Revisions 113, 124–25 (S. Hauerwas & A. MacIntyre eds. 1983):

> The claim that morality is "cognitive" and that we now have some moral knowledge is not the claim that all our moral convictions as they now stand are true or justifiable. We do not think any such implication to be involved in the claim that we have knowledge of geology or physics or mathematics. We are aware that many of the particular opinions and theories we now hold in these disciplines will eventually be discarded as mistaken, but we have no hesitation in claiming knowledge within these fields nonetheless. The situation is the same as regards morality. . . . Our morality has been derived from many sources and shaped by many influences. It is moreover deeply involved with our factual and metaphysical or religious beliefs. There is no guarantee that it is free from inconsistency, error, or superstition, either on the purely moral plane or in its nonmoral involvements. Though it is bound to be our main starting point in thinking about practical matters, we must assume that progress and improvement in moral knowledge are possible. This is no more, and no less, than we must assume in every area of thought where truth is an aim.

35. See M. Walzer, Interpretation and Social Criticism 64 (1987): "Perhaps there are some societies so closed in upon themselves, so rigidly confined even in their ideological justifications, that they require asocial criticism; no other kind is possible. Perhaps—but it is my own belief that such societies are more likely to be found in social science fiction than in the real world." See also id. at 64 n. 19.

36. R. Unger, Passion: An Essay on Personality 10, 264 (1984).

37. See chapter 3, section I.

38. See White, "The Judicial Opinion and the Poem: Ways of Reading, Ways of Life," 82 Michigan L. Rev. 1669, 1698 (1984):

> [We cannot] start completely fresh, in a place we alone have made, to realize our own ideal . . . for there is no such place, and our ideals are never purely our own. But even if [we] could, who are we to claim to know so much better than our predecessors and contemporaries? The truth is a simple but hard one, that neither our acceptance nor our rejection of our inheritance should be unquestioned; it is in the life of our questioning of it and of ourselves, in our remaking the language that defines us, that our true work goes on, and our true community is defined.

39. See Unger, note 1, at 579–80:

> You start from the conflicts between the available ideals of social life in your own social world or legal tradition and their flawed actualizations in present society. You imagine the actualizations transformed, or you transform them in fact, perhaps only by

extending an ideal to some area of social life from which it had previously been excluded. Then you revise the ideal conceptions in the light of their new practical embodiments. You might call this process internal development. To engage in it self-reflectively you need make only two crucial assumptions: that no one scheme of association has conclusive authority and that the mutual correction of abstract ideals and their institutional realizations represents the last best hope of the standard forms of normative controversy.

40. H.-G. Gadamer, Philosophical Hermeneutics 34–35 (D. Linge ed. 1976). See R. Unger, note 36, at 42: "Inevitably, we must accept a conservative presumption. To question the legitimacy of our fundamental practices is somewhat like asking us why we should continue to be ourselves. The reasonable answer often falls somewhere between—Why shouldn't we?—and—We can't help it." Readers familiar with the Gadamer-Habermas debate should consult Rorty, "Habermas and Lyotard on Postmodernity," in R. Bernstein, ed., Habermas and Modernity 161 (1985) (criticizing Habermas and defending, *inter alia*, Gadamer).

41. Cf. R. Beiner, Political Judgment 150 (1983): "Here we have the intimation of a perspective capable of reconciling the truths contained in Aristotle and Kant respectively; confronting an established structure of actualities and possibilities, but bringing to bear a concept of right that critically judges, and therefore distances itself from, the established reality. The concrete achievement of political judgment is a living synthesis of detachment and involvement, of passionate commitment and critical distance."

42. J. Pelikan, note 28, at 54. Cf. id. at 57–58:

Whatever each of them may mean for his special disciples, Moses, Socrates, and Jesus have been linked so often throughout most of the history of the tradition that we must see in them the primary source and chief inspiration for the very critique of a tradition that presumes to speak for them. Moses smashed the tablets of the divine law itself in protest against idolatry; Socrates was executed as an enemy of the tradition because he believed that "an unexamined life is not worth living" and an unexamined tradition not worth following; and Jesus went to the cross because he would not have any earthly form of the divine (not even, let it be remembered, his own) become a substitute for the ultimate reality of the living God. Therefore no criticism of the tradition that was voiced by the evangelicalism of the Reformation or the rationalism of the Enlightenment or the historicism of the nineteenth century can ever match, for severity and power, the criticism that came from these, its noblest products and its most profound interpreters. Tradition has the right to vindicate itself by appropriating much of what its critics say, for it was said, not only against the tradition but within the tradition, long before.

43. Murray and Bernardin are quoted in Unsworth, "Seamless Garment Shredded," National Catholic Rptr., Dec. 20, 1985, at 8. Cf. D. Tracy, The Analogical Imagination 100 (1981):

[F]undamentalist and authoritarian theologies, properly considered, are not theologies at all.

Nor is this the case merely because such theologies will not take account of contemporary experience. More basically, these theologies are finally not interpretations of the tradition itself. They are but simple repetitions. The heart of any hermeneutical position is the recognition that all interpretation is a mediation of past and present, a translation carried on within the effective history of a tradition to retrieve its sometimes strange, sometimes familiar meanings. But the traditionalist's use of tradition betrays the enriching, even liberating notion of tradition. It is naive to assume that a thinker is so autonomous as to be no longer affected by the effects and influences of that tradition in our very language, a presence carrying us along by providing our initial prejudgments and often unconscious presuppositions as to the nature of reality. It is equally naive, and equally destructive of systematic theology's hermeneutical task, to assume with the traditionalist and fundamentalist that so autonomous in one's heteronomous obedience is the theologian that one can be faithful to the tradition to which one belongs by repeating its *tradita* rather than critically translating its *traditio*.

The systematic theologian, on the contrary, must operate in a manner more faithful to the actual finitude and historicity of every thinker in any cultural tradition. Indeed, the surest mark of contemporary systematic theology is precisely a profound acceptance of finitude and historicity.

44. R. Panikkar, Myth, Faith and Hermeneutics 208 (1979). See Cornell, "Toward a Modern/Postmodern Reconstruction of Ethics," 133 U. Pennsylvania L. Rev. 291, 346 (1985): "To recreate ourselves, in accordance with the most expansive vision of human possibility open to us on the basis of what we have learned, is the humanist project as I define it."

45. See M. Walzer, note 35. See also H.-G. Gadamer, Truth and Method 250 (Eng. tr. 1975). Cf. N. MacCormick, note 13, at 273–74: "Revolution is no doubt possible, as in cases of religious or ideological conversion. But even then one does not invent a whole new moral position . . . Even the great moral reformers like Jesus and Socrates appear to have argued their position by testing out the consistency and coherence and the acceptability all in all of elements of the currently received morality, and by extrapolating from it. They came not to destroy the law but to fulfill it."

46. Hauerwas, "On Keeping Theological Ethics Theological," in Revisions 16, 33 (S. Hauerwas & A. MacIntyre eds. 1983). See R. Unger, note 36, at 47–48:

The most important repositories of enacted social visions are the actual normative orders—especially the legal systems and the traditions of legal doctrine—that make a social world into something more than an arena of violent and unlimited struggle. The most significant articulation of existential projects can be found in the major religions and religiously inspired ethics of world history. Far more than the abstract doctrines of moral and political philosophers, these legal and religious traditions embody visions and projects that have withstood the test of experience, enabling large numbers of people over long periods of time to make sense of their experience.

The point extends beyond moral beliefs to other sorts of beliefs, including scientific ones. See note 32. See also J. Pelikan, note 28, at 20: "[T]he continuity of tradition [is] what Edmund Burke called 'a partnership in all science, all art, every virtue.' But, Burke added, 'As the ends of such a partnership cannot be obtained in many generations, it becomes a partnership not only between those who are living, but between those who are living, those who are dead, and those who are to be born.' And that, come to think of it, is not a bad definition of a living tradition." (Quoting E. Burke, Reflections on the Revolution in France 194–95 [C. O'Brien ed. 1982].)

47. On the role of experience in moral theorizing, see V. Held, Rights and Goods, chs. 4 & 15 (1984); Flanagan, note 11. See also note 59 and accompanying text.

48. Burtchaell, "The Sources of Conscience," 13 Notre Dame Mag. 20, 20–21 (Winter 1984–85). See id. at 21: "And when debate and dialogue and testimony do fructify into conviction, and conviction into consensus, nothing could be more absurd than to expect that consensus to be confined within a person's privacy or a church's walls. Convictions are what we live by. Do we have anything better to share with one another?" See generally J. Fuchs, Christian Ethics in a Secular Arena (1984).

49. Schneewind, note 34, at 113.

50. Id. at 118–19. For similar statements, see C. Perelman, The New Rhetoric and the Humanities 33 (1979); Moore, "Moral Reality," 1982 Wisconsin L. Rev. 1061, 1150.

51. See N. Goodman, Fact, Fiction, and Forecast 64 (4th ed. 1983) (emphasis deleted): "A rule is amended if it yields an inference we are unwilling to accept; an inference is rejected if it violates a rule we are unwilling to amend."

52. R. Bambrough, note 6, at 130, 137–38. For similar statements, see Lehman, "Rules in Law," 72 Georgetown L. J. 1571, 1601 (1984); note 53; note 58 and accompanying text. Cf. Toulmin, "How Medicine Saved the Life of Ethics," 25 Perspectives in Biology and Medicine 736, 747 (1982): "[W]e can grasp the moral force of principles only by studying the ways in which they are applied to, and within, particular situations."

53. American lawyers should find this a familiar and congenial emphasis. See T. Grey, The Legal Enforcement of Morality 34 (1983):

> The characteristic mind-set of the Anglo-American lawyer is intuitionistic and biased toward the concrete and particular. Offer a lawyer trained in our tradition a theory or principle, and he will respond in terms of cases—first asking for a typical case to illustrate what the theory means in application, then challenging the theory with a "hard case," where application seems to produce a counterintuitive result. If you respond by holding to the principle while agreeing that the result it compels seems wrong, you are not speaking the lawyer's language. He will expect you to recast or reconstrue the theory, however much it seems to you rooted in the nature of things.

See also id. at 34–35; V. Held, note 47, at 285 n. 24.

54. See H.-G. Gadamer, note 45, at 287–88:

> [I]t is a knowledge of the particular situation that completes moral knowledge, a knowledge that is nevertheless not a perceiving by the senses. For although it is necessary to see from a situation what it is asking of us, this seeing does not mean that we perceive in the situation what is visible as such, but that we learn to see it as the situation of action and hence in the light of what is right. Just as we "see" from the geometrical analysis of plane surfaces that the triangle is the simplest two-dimensional plane figure, so that we can go no further with our subdivisions, but must stop here, so in moral consideration the "seeing" of what is immediately to be done is not a mere seeing, but nous. This is also confirmed by what constitutes the antithesis to this kind of seeing. The antithesis to the seeing of what is right is not error or deception, but blindness. A person who is overwhelmed by his passions suddenly no longer sees in the given situation what is right. He has lost his self-mastery and hence lost his own rightness, ie the right orientation within himself, so that, driven by the dialectic of passion, whatever his passion tells him is right seems so. Moral knowledge is really a knowledge of a special kind. It embraces in a curious way both means and end and hence differs from technical knowledge. That is why it is pointless to distinguish here between knowledge and experience, as can be done in the case of a techne. For moral knowledge must be a kind of experience, and in fact we shall see that this is perhaps the fundamental form of experience, compared with which all other experience represents a denaturing.

See also Kekes, "Moral Intuitions," 23 Am. Phil. Q. 83 (1986). Cf. J. Segundo, note 25, at 18 (emphasis deleted):

> The third abstraction lies in the fact that we leave aside the role of imagination in these various forms by which our energy is stabilized. We do not concretely choose between values, but between imagined representations of possible satisfactions. We do not opt for the "virtue" or the "value" of peace; we opt for our imagined picture of the satisfaction we would get from knowing that those we loved dearly were living in a situation of peace or greater peace. And then we put an abstract name on this prospective piece of imagining. It is the role of imagination which logically explains why a human being often operates in a very complicated way with what we might call a scale of values. Human beings will not implement the same "values" in dealing with different types of people, for example. Yet they will be consistent with the concrete image and ideal that their imagination fashioned, while still regarding different people in different ways.

55. This is not to deny, of course, that "to a certain extent particulars already come to us subsumed in virtue of our speaking the language that we do. There is no such thing as a 'pure' particular: particulars are always given to us as instantiations of some universal or other; or expressed differently, the very recognition of particulars is necessarily mediated by linguistic concepts." R. Beiner, note 41, at 144.

56. Cf. Dewey, "Logical Method and Law," 10 Cornell L. Q. 17, 26–27 (1924):

Failure to recognize that general legal rules and principles are working hypotheses, needing to be constantly tested by the way in which they work out in application to concrete situations, explains the otherwise paradoxical fact that the slogans of the liberalism of one period often become the bulwarks of reaction in a subsequent era. There was a time in the eighteenth century when the great social need was emancipation of industry and trade from a multitude of restrictions which held over from the feudal estate of Europe. Adapted well enough to the localized and fixed conditions of that earlier age, they became hindrances and annoyances as the effects of methods, use of coal and steam, showed themselves. The movement of emancipation expressed itself in principles of liberty in use of property, and freedom of contract, which were embodied in a mass of legal decisions. But the absolutistic logic of rigid syllogistic forms infected these ideas. It was soon forgotten that they were relative to analysis of existing situations in order to secure orderly methods in behalf of economic social welfare. Thus these principles became in turn so rigid as to be almost as socially obstructive as "immutable" feudal laws had been in their day.

57. For Bruce Ackerman the master norm is the neutrality principle; for Ronald Dworkin, the principle of equal concern and respect. See chapter 3, sections II & III.

58. B. Williams, note 20, at 116–17. See Toulmin, note 52, at 749: "At this moment, . . . the style of . . . discussion appears to be shifting away from attempts to relate problematic cases to general theories—whether those of Kant, Rawls, or the utilitarians—to a more direct analysis of the practical cases themselves, using methods more like those of traditional 'case morality.' " Cf. Singer, "The Player and the Cards: Nihilism and Legal Theory," 94 Yale L. J. 1, 62 (1984).

59. Cf. Schneewind, note 34, at 124:

[T]he quest for moral knowledge did not begin yesterday. The moral principles most of us accept have had to survive a fair amount of testing and sifting in the course of time. There is therefore a fair amount of evidence to show that they can give acceptable guidance and can form the nucleus of a moral community. To say that we *know* some of them to be correct is to express our reasoned confidence that they, or something very close to them, will, of those available for our consideration, come out best in relation to all the evidence, future as well as past.

60. For a similar point, emphasizing the importance of narrative, see M. Walzer, note 35, at 65–66.

In American society, the relevant "shared particular beliefs" may even be religious—especially biblical—in character. See J. Coleman, An American Strategic Theology 197–98 (1982):

If I understand [Bryan] Hehir's proposal correctly, he would not allow or, at the least, discourage a public appeal to the Judaeo-Christian or larger religious heritage in societal debates about normative questions of social policy. I would agree if the appeal violated respect for the specifically pluralistic faith-context of American public life or involved a cultural imposition through some form of force or coercion rather than persuasion in common debate and discussion. Moreover, it may be the case that the most important place for theological symbols in public debate is more as an ethical horizon and set of value preferences than in specific and concrete policy discussion.

But I think Hehir is mistaken inasmuch as he seems to neglect a patrimony which is already very much a *public* strand of our cultural heritage. I also suspect that he is more sanguine than I am about the possibility of escaping the "permanent hermeneutical predicament" of particular languages and community traditions in a conflict of interpretive schemes through the emergence of a common, universal language. I fear that his proposal could court the risk of a continuation of the pernicious intertwining of an ethic of deep concern with an ethic of looking out for number one. But finally, and most persuasive for me, I simply do not know anywhere else to look in American culture besides to our religious ethical resources to find the social wisdom and ethical orientation we would seem to need if we are to face as Americans our new context of increasing interdependence at the national and international level.

61. See note 49 and accompanying text.

62. B. Barber, Strong Democracy: Participatory Politics for a New Age 164 (1984) (quoting M. Oakeshott, On Human Conduct 66 [1975]).

63. J. Pelikan, note 28, at 17, 61 (quoting G. Chesterton, Orthodoxy 47–48, 79 [1959]). See B. Barber, note 62, at 194: "Democrats have trouble with the past: government is for the living, they cry, echoing Thomas Paine. Yet if they are honest they must admit with Burke that the true majority in every community lies dead in the grave. The dead are heard through custom and tradition, but they can speak only with the aid of the living, who have an obligation to find appropriate formulations to encapsulate the beliefs and experiences of their forebears."

64. J. Pelikan, note 28, at 81–82.

65. See note 26.

66. Schneewind's description of an aspect of the process of bringing past to bear on present is illuminating:

> Principles of morality function in some ways like the formulations of laws which scientists propose. There are, at any given time, a number of specific judgements, rules and ideals, the correctness of which we have no hesitation in affirming. Formulations of moral principles serve to systematise and generalise these beliefs, and in doing so they articulate what may be called the spirit of our morality. They pick out the aspects of our less general beliefs which are not tied to specific circumstances and which would remain constant in a variety of situations. This enables them to express the point or rationale of specific moral convictions. And this in turn enables us to carry out a critical and explicit projection of our moral beliefs to new kinds of problems and new combinations of circumstances. The formulation of a principle to cover classes of cases where we know the rights and wrongs, and the application of the principle thus formed to the solutions of difficulties which arise where we have no firm convictions, are analogous, in a rough but fairly clear way, to the formulation of a law to cover a set of well-established data and its use to predict results of new combinations of causal factors.

Schneewind, note 34, at 120–21.

For an interesting account of the slow but eventual emergence in Roman law of rule-governed adjudication, see Toulmin, "The Tyranny of Principles," Hastings Center Rep., Dec. 1981, at 31, 33.

67. H. Hart, The Concept of Law 125 (1961).

68. Id.

69. Id. at 126.

70. But not always. "To escape this oscillation between extremes we need to remind ourselves that human inability to anticipate the future, which is at the root of this indeterminacy, varies in degree in different fields of conduct." Id. at 127. See id. at 127–32.

71. Id. at 126.

72. J. Meiland & M. Krausz, eds., Relativism: Cognitive and Moral 4 (1982).

73. See H. Putnam, note 14, at 84–89:

Practical knowledge is not scientific knowledge. . . . The reason that knowledge of, say, *wines* or *cooking* is not scientific knowledge is that the criterion of successful cooking or of a successful wine is a satisfied human palate—and not just any palate, at that. The question whether good cooking or good winemaking could be reduced to a science "in principle" is an uninteresting one, because "in principle" has nothing to do with actual human life in the foreseeable future. To be sure, it is not "logically impossible" that someday we might have so complete a theory of our own nature that we could program a computer to determine what would and would not satisfy us. But, if that ever comes to be the case, then it cannot but alter our nature itself. If we ever become so transparent to ourselves that the distinction between practical knowledge and theoretical knowledge disappears, then no doubt such institutions as science, philosophy, and literature may well disappear in their present forms too. And if one cannot reduce cooking well or making wine well to a "science", then how much less can one hope to reduce living well to a "science"!

Yet the fact that one cannot reduce living well to a science does not mean that reflecting on how to live well is not a rational enterprise, or that there cannot be any . . . knowledge about it.

74. See J. Meiland & M. Krausz, note 72, at 167:

The type of relativism which is capable of definitive refutation is that which maintains each of these two propositions: (1) the term "right" means "right for a given society" and (2) it is wrong for people in one society to condemn or interfere with the values and moral behavior of another society. This version . . . contradicts itself by asserting in the first proposition that all uses of "right" and "wrong" are relative to a society and then in the second proposition employing the term "wrong" in a nonrelative way.

No wonder Bernard Williams has said that moral relativism thus conceived is "possibly the most absurd view to have been advanced even in moral philosophy." Williams, "An Inconsistent Form of Relativism," in id. at 171, 171.

75. The position put forward by Gilbert Harman, for example, is not mor-

ally relativist in the relevant sense. In his essay "Moral Relativism Defended," in id. at 189, Harman explicitly says that he "is not denying (nor am I asserting) that some moralities are 'objectively' better than others or that there are objective standards for assessing moralities. My thesis is a soberly logical thesis about logical form." Id. at 190. Harman's thesis is about, at least in part, the nonhypothetical use of "ought". See chapter 1, note 47.

With respect to Bernard Williams' well-known essay, "The Truth in Relativism," in id. at 175, see B. Williams, note 20, at 220 n. 3: "I no longer want to say without qualification as I do there [in "The Truth in Relativism"], that for ethical outlooks a relativistic standpoint, defined in these terms, is correct."

76. For a discussion of "truth" as "idealized rational acceptability", see note 92 and accompanying text.

77. See chapter 1, section III.

78. One or more of one's own beliefs can be false relative to one's more basic beliefs. See J. Meiland & M. Krausz, note 72, at 4:

> [J]ust as our ordinary conception of truth allows a person to hold beliefs which are false, so too the notion of relative truth must allow an individual to hold beliefs which are false *for him* or *her*. If it were not possible for an individual to hold beliefs which were false for him or her, then the notion of relative truth would be superfluous; for then to say that a belief is true for Jones would only be a roundabout way of saying that it was one of Jones' beliefs. And we do not need a new way of saying *that*.

See also Devine, "Relativism," 67 Monist 405, 406 (1984):

> [R]elativism is not individualistic subjectivism, for which anything goes intellectually; nor is it collective subjectivism, which would settle intellectual questions by voting. The analogy with law makes this point clear: while law is relative to a particular society, law and public opinion are not the same thing. Not anything goes by way of legal argument—the precedents and statutes have to be taken into account. But one can say, so long as one does not do so too often, that the decision of the courts, even those of the last resort, are legally and not just morally or politically wrong. Likewise a moral relativist who finds his basic standards in the ethos of a given society can disagree with the majority of that society (though perhaps not the overwhelming majority) on some moral issue, so long as he is prepared to defend his disagreement on grounds whose relevance the majority is prepared to accept. In brief, while the standards we employ are (according to the relativist) grounded in the fact of their acceptance by a group to which we belong, the application of these standards is objective and not a matter of what people think.

Unlike Meiland and Krausz in the passage above, I prefer to speak in terms of relativity to a community rather than to an individual: The basic beliefs a person accepts—especially the basic moral beliefs—she accepts less *qua* individual than *qua* member of a particular community. "[F]orms of life are communal property; there is no private practice." Baker, "On the Very Idea of a Form of Life," 27 Inquiry 277, 278 (1984). Of course, one can conceive of relative truth in individual rather than communal terms. See Foot, "Moral Relativism," in J. Meiland & M. Krausz, note 72, at 152, 157:

[I]ndividualistic subjectivism may itself be a form of moral relativism. (Perhaps we would call it a limiting case.) For even if the truth of moral judgments is not relative to local community standards it . . . could still be relative to the standards of the individual. This is how it is, in effect, in emotivist and prescriptivist theories, since these theories deny the presence of objective criteria, or any objective method by which differences between individuals with radically different basic moral principles could in principle be resolved. If these theories are correct, anyone who queries the truth of a moral judgment, and still possesses the resource of testing it by his more basic moral principles, uses "true" substantially; but beyond this point he does not. It follows that the emotivist or prescriptivist is committed to a form of relativism, however little he may like the label. [C. L.] Stevenson, who claimed to have refuted moral relativism, turns out to be himself a kind of moral relativist.

79. R. Rorty, Consequences of Pragmatism xx (1982). I discuss aspects of Rorty's views later in this chapter.

80. Several short statements of the epistemologically relativist, or "holist", position, are collected in Van Cleve, "Epistemic Supervenience and the Circle of Belief," 68 Monist 90 (1985).

81. M. Adler, Six Great Ideas 43, 44 (1981).

82. R. Rorty, note 79, at vi, xix (emphasis added).

83. H. Putnam, note 17, at ix, 49, 128, 130, 134 (emphasis added).

84. See 0. Flanagan, The Science of the Mind (1984).

85. See J. Stout, The Flight from Authority 151, 152, 153–54 (1981):

[Steven] Lukes argues that there are universal criteria of rationality as well as context-dependent ones, and that the former include . . . the notion of truth as correspondence to reality. . . . At times he seems to be insisting only that all language users "share a reality which is independent of how it is conceived," but he will have trouble finding live opponents for that thesis. . . . The issue [Thomas] Kuhn seems to be raising has to do with how "correspondence to reality" could ever function nontrivially as a criterion of rationality. Yet it is this question that Lukes begs. To say that something is a *criterion* of rationality or of truth is to imply that it is the kind of thing one could appeal to in a dispute over what should be counted as rational or as true, but to say that a theory corresponds to reality seems to add nothing to the notion that it is true and therefore ought to be accepted. What we want to be told is how to tell the true from the false, the justified from the unjustified. That is what we expect from criteria of truth and rational acceptance. For "correspondence" to become a criterion in this sense, we would have to characterize the "reality" to which correspondence is sought. But the characterization we choose will place us within the logical space of one or another theory of the way things are. What Lukes seems to want, however, is a theory-independent criterion for judging which theory gets it right. The problem is that "reality" cannot be theory-independent without ceasing to be a criterion. We are perfectly free to use "reality" to signify "the purely vacuous notion of the ineffable cause of sense and goal of the intellect," but we would be foolish to suppose that any notion this vacuous could help us award the title of truth. A less vacuous notion of "reality," on the other hand, would be theory-dependent and therefore relative in a way that might encourage just the worries Lukes is trying to undercut.

(Citing S. Lukes, Essays in Social Theory [1977]). See also J. Meiland & M. Krausz, note 72, at 13–17 (discussing Nelson Goodman, Ways of Worldmaking [1978]).

86. This is not to deny that we *can* use "truth" in a sense such that there are no accessible criteria for determining if a statement is true. (Cf. K. Popper, Conjectures and Refutations 225: "The objective theory of truth . . . allows us to make assertions such as the following: A theory may be true even though nobody believes it, and even though we have no reason for accepting it, or for believing that it is true; and another theory may be false, although we have comparatively good reasons for accepting it." Quoted in Wonnell, "Truth and the Marketplace of Ideas," 19 U. California/Davis L. Rev. 669, 678 n. 50 [1986].) See note 85.

To reject the correspondence or copy theory of truth (sometimes called "metaphysical realism") is *not* to reject scientific (or "empirical") realism. See Smith, "Plausible, If Not True," Times Lit. Supp., Sept. 4, 1987, at 963. "One can be *both* a realist *and* a conceptual relativist." H. Putnam, note 18, at 17. For an elegant statement of an attractive scientific-realist position, see McMullin, "A Case for Scientific Realism," in Scientific Realism 8 (J. Leplin ed. 1984).

87. Quoted by R. Bellah, "American Civil Religion in the 1970s," Anglican Theological Rev., Supp. Ser. No. 1, July 1973, at 9.

88. R. Rorty, note 79, at vi. See J. Meiland & M. Krausz, note 72, at 16.

89. Recently David Tracy has cautioned that:

[T]he present debate on pluralism within the disciplines and within the culture is not, with very few exceptions, explicitly a debate on the nature of ultimate reality. (Derrida, for example, may be an exception; Foucault probably is not.) The present debate on pluralism is initially a debate on culture and often on rules for public civility, not on ultimate reality. Pluralism is today first a debate, within the disciplines on the nature of a discipline, not on the nature of "nature." For that reason, it seems wise to me to bracket for the moment the traditional metaphysical terms "pluralism vs. monism" and reserve those terms for the substantive discussion on pluralism and monism in metaphysics and theology.

Tracy, "Christianity in the Wider Context: Demands and Transformations" (1987). This essay is due to appear in W. Schweiker & P. Anderson, Worldviews and Warrants: Plurality and Authority in Theology (1987).

90. R. Rorty, note 79, at iii.

91. Id. at v, ix, xvii.

Max Horkheimer wrote that "one might be tempted to deny any philosophical pedigree to a doctrine that holds not that our expectations are fulfilled and our actions successful because our ideas are true, but rather that our ideas are true because our expectations are fulfilled and our actions successful." M. Horkheimer, Eclipse of Reason 42 (1974). Horkheimer apparently wanted to say that "our expectations are fulfilled and our actions successful because our ideas are true". But what is the criterion of truth? Rorty's (and Dewey's) answer, which Horkheimer's criticism fails to dent, is that our ideas are "rationally acceptable" (Putnam's term; see note 92 and accompanying text) to the extent "they [better than competitor ideas] seem to be paying their way and fit in with other sentences which are doing so." Of course, one can say: "But *why* does system of ideas (or theory) *A* seem to be paying its way better than any competitor system? The best answer, all things considered, is that *A* converges asymptotically on the Real." That may indeed be the best answer, all things considered. See note 86. The point, however, is that the Real cannot be our criterion of truth, because we lack access to the Real. See note 85.

92. H. Putnam, note 17, at 49–50, 52. See id. at 55, 56:

> To reject the idea that there is a coherent "external" perspective, a theory which is simply true "in itself", apart from all possible observers, is not to *identify* truth with rational acceptability. Truth cannot simply be rational acceptability for one fundamental reason; truth is supposed to be a property of a statement that cannot be lost, whereas justification can be lost. The statement "The earth is flat" was, very likely, rationally acceptable 3,000 years ago; but it is not rationally acceptable today. Yet it would be wrong to say that "the earth is flat" was *true* 3,000 years ago; for that would mean that the earth has changed its shape. In fact, rational acceptability is both tensed and relative to a person. In addition, rational acceptability is a matter of degree. . . . [T]ruth is an idealization of rational acceptability. We speak as if there were such things as epistemically ideal conditions, and we call a statement "true" if it would be justified under such conditions. "Epistemically ideal conditions", of course, are like "frictionless planes": we cannot really attain epistemically ideal conditions, or even be absolutely certain that we have come sufficiently close to them. But frictionless planes cannot really be attained either, and yet talk of frictionless planes has "cash value" because we can approximate them to a very high degree of approximation. . . . [T]he two key ideas of the idealization theory of truth are (1) that truth is independent of justification here and now, but not independent of *all* justification. To claim a statement is true is to claim it could be justified. (2) truth is expected to be stable or "convergent"; if both a statement and its negation could be "justified", even if conditions were as ideal as one could hope to make them, there is no sense in thinking of the statement as *having* a truth-value.

93. Rorty has indicated that he finds Putnam's conception of truth—which Putnam calls "naturalist" or "pragmatist"—congenial. See Rorty, "Solidarity or Objectivity?," in Post-Analytic Philosophy 3, 7 (J. Rajchman & C. West eds. 1985).

94. D. Wong, Moral Relativity 158 (1984). See B. Williams, note 20, at 153–55. See also Kekes, "Human Nature and Moral Theories," 28 Inquiry 231, 244 (1985).

95. See Williams, "Auto-da-Fé," N.Y. Rev., Apr. 28, 1983, at 33: "Rorty is so insistent that we cannot, in philosophy, simply be talking about human beings, as opposed to human beings at a given time. . . . Rorty . . . contrasts the approach of taking some philosophical problem and asking . . . 'What does it show us about *being human*?' and asking, on the other hand, 'What does the persistence of such problems show us about *being twentieth-century Europeans*?' " Id. (emphasis in original). See R. Rorty, note 79, at 173–74:

> [The pragmatist] can only say . . . that truth and justice lie in the direction marked by the successive stages of European thought. This is not because he knows some "necessary truths" and cites these examples as a result of his knowledge. It is simply that the pragmatist knows no better way to explain his convictions than to remind his interlocutors of the position they both are in, the contingent starting points they both share, the floating, ungrounded conversations of which they are both members. This means that the pragmatist cannot answer the question "What is so special about Europe?" save by saying "Do you have anything non-European to suggest which meets *our* European purposes better?" He cannot answer the question "What is so good about the Socratic virtues, about Miltonic free encounters, about undistorted communication?" save by saying "What else would better fulfill the purposes we share with Socrates, Milton, and Habermas?"

See also Rorty, note 93.

96. Joseph de Maistre, quoted in E. Leach, Social Anthropology 56 (1982).

97. H. Putnam, note 17, at 171–72. In the following passage, Putnam compares human beings *as a species* to other possible species:

> When I claim that the murder and suffering of innocent people is wrong, I do not, I think, really care about the question whether this judgment would be valid for a being of a totally alien constitution and psychology. If there are beings on, say, Alpha Centauri, who cannot feel pain and who do not mind individual death, then very likely our fuss about "murder and suffering" will seem to them to be much ado about nothing. But the very alienness of such a life form means that they cannot understand the moral issues involved. If our "objectivity" is objectivity humanly speaking, it is still objectivity enough.

Id. at 167–68.

98. R. Rorty, note 79, at xlii.

99. Id.

100. See Taylor, "Rationality," in Rationality & Relativism 103, 104, 105 (M. Hollis & S. Lukes eds. 1982).

101. Even "primitive" or "magical" belief-systems are aimed, in some measure, at understanding, predicting, and controlling the environment. Consider these two passages:

> It may sound convincing that the Azande are among other things "expressing an attitude to contingencies" in their magical rites. But can we say that they are doing this *as against* trying to control certain of these contingencies? It would seem not. And

Winch himself makes this point: the rites have a relation to consumption; they are undertaken to make the crops grow free of the hazards that threaten them. Winch's thesis is that they also have this other dimension which he stresses.

That is why the position Winch criticizes will always have a certain plausibility. We can all too easily find analogies between primitive magical practices and some of our own, because they do overlap. Thus a lot of what Robin Horton says . . . concerning the analogies between African religious thinking and Western scientific theory is very convincing: both bring unity out of diversity, place things in a wider causal context, and so on.

Id. at 87, 93. See also id. at 100 (on the common project shared by "the science of the High Renaissance" and its successor, Galilean science).

[T]he traditional astrocosmology performed many and varied functions at the same time. (One of its charms, indeed, was the fact that a single system of ideas appeared capable of serving so many varied human purposes.) Some of these functions were practical ones: keeping track of the changes of the seasons, forecasting solar eclipses, and the like. Others were purely theoretical: providing an intellectual basis for explaining the makeup and workings of the natural world. Others were symbolic and expressive: that is, iconographic. Others, again, were more strictly religious: testifying to the relationships between things divine and things human. The balance of emphasis as between all these varied functions differed from one culture and context to another. In Babylonia, practical functions on the whole weighed more than theoretical; in Athens, it was the other way about. Yet in none of the cultures of classical antiquity do we find people single-mindedly preoccupied with any one function, to the absolute exlusion of the others. Thus, in their own ways and on their own terms, Kidinnu and his colleagues in Babylon were capable astronomical theorists; while the Greek philosophers never ignored the practical significance of astronomical and cosmological issues, any more than the poet Hesiod had done. The great strength of the traditional world picture thus was the fact that it could be understood at once as an astronomical, a technological, and a theological picture.

S. Toulmin, The Return to Cosmology: Postmodern Science and the Theology of Nature 225 (1982).

102. Rorty, note 93, at 11 (emphasis added).

103. Foot, note 78, at 164. See Kekes, note 92.

104. S. Hampshire, Morality and Conflict 155 (1983). See note 94 and accompanying text.

105. H. Putnam, note 17, at 148. See B. Williams, note 20, at 153:

[T]here are many and various forms of human excellence which will not all fit together into a one harmonious whole, so any determinate ethical outlook is going to represent some kind of specialization of human possibilities. That idea is deeply entrenched in any naturalistic or . . . historical conception of human nature—that is, in any adequate conception of it—and I find it hard to believe that it will be overcome by an objective inquiry, or that human beings could turn out to have a much more determinate nature than is suggested by what we already know, one that timelessly demanded a life of a particular kind.

See also chapter 1, note 53.

106. H. Putnam, note 17, at 148. See id. at 140 (referring to "sick standards of rationality" and "sick conception[s] of human flourishing"), 147: "We have just as much right to regard some 'evaluational' casts of mind as sick (and we all do) as we do to regard some 'cognitional' casts of mind as sick."

107. Compare R. Rorty, note 79, at xvii, with Baker, note 78, at 286:

> On the one hand, there is little doubt that Wittgenstein supports the ubiquity thesis: a major thrust of the later work is to oppose any assumption of prelinguistic knowledge against which the adequacy of language can be tested. (". . . [A] language-game does not have its origin in *consideration*. Consideration is part of a language-game.") On the other hand, our language is not arbitrary or freely chosen: it develops out of our "primitive reactions". For example, regarding our "primitive reaction to tend, to treat, the part that hurts when someone else is in pain", Wittgenstein comments: "But what is the word 'primitive' meant to say here? Presumably that this sort of behaviour is pre-linguistic: that a language-game is based on it, that it is the prototype of a way of thinking and not the result of thought".
>
> Rorty writes as if the only two alternatives are to hold that there is extra-linguistic intuition to which each of us has privileged access and to which we can compare our linguistic formulations or to deny that there are any privileged vocabularies. That is, Rorty takes an endorsement of immediate awareness in the spirit of Descartes to be the only possible basis for a privileged vocabulary.
>
> If the interpretation here of forms of life is correct, then one of Wittgenstein's important results is that there is another, nonprivate basis for a privileged vocabulary— viz., forms of life. It is important that forms of life are not just temporary arrangements, convenient for the moment, which may be adjusted or replaced at will. Our practices, and hence the vocabularies possible for us, are "materially" constrained by our "mindedness" (Lear's term), by the actual set of responses that we agree upon without reflection, e.g. ". . . 998, 1000, 1002 . . .". On Wittgenstein's view, not just any invented vocabulary is a live option for us; our being minded as we are shapes the possibilities for us; our being minded as we are shapes the possibilities for usable vocabularies. (This last point, along with others that I want to make, is, for Wittgenstein, more showable than statable.)
>
> The interpretation of the idea of forms of life given here thus supports the ubiquity thesis and undercuts the thesis of linguistic convenience. It appears, then, that Rorty is wrong to conflate the two theses: not only would Wittgenstein deny Rorty's view that vocabularies are freely chosen for convenience, but also he would offer considerations that actually cast doubt on that view.

108. J. Elster, Sour Grapes 2 (1983). Cf. D. Parfit, Reasons and Persons 452–53 (1983): "We should not assume that the objectivity of Ethics must be all-or-nothing. There may be a part of morality that is objective. In describing this part, our claims may be true. . . . There may be other questions about which we shall never agree. There may be no true answers to these questions. *These* questions may be subjective."

109. Cf. Hinman, note 17, at 348:

There is something right-hearted—but wrong-headed—about the claim that forms of life are the autonomous arbiters of meaning and justification within their own domains and thus insulated from criticism from the standpoint of some other form of life. Only in recent years have we come to realize the degree to which we unwittingly impose our own socio-cultural framework of meaning and value on other cultures which we seek to understand. All too often we have presupposed that our own form of life was the unquestionable standard in terms of which all others were to be measured. In attempting to overcome what some have seen as cultural chauvinism, many have gone in the other direction by claiming that each culture or form of life is right in its own domain and none has a right beyond that. No form of life could be judged from the standpoint of another form of life. We have moved from passing judgment on everyone to passing judgment on no one.

There is a common assumption shared by both of these positions, namely, that our own form of life cannot be criticized from outside, that it cannot be held up to another form of life and found wanting. Both of these extremes serve to insulate our own form of life from criticism, and it is precisely this which makes them philosophically suspect.

110. Drucilla Cornell has written that "[t]he problem with the attempt to establish a definitive view of human nature . . . is that any such vision appears to undermine plurality and the possibility of an ever-expanding vision of what we might become. This is so, at least, if one purports to argue from an accurate representation of what we truly and necessarily are—an approach that denies the historical element." Cornell, note 44, at 359. I hope that by now it is clear that my pluralistic naturalism—a naturalism in which the ideals of self-critical rationality and self-transcendence play an important role and which includes a (moderate) anthropological relativism—avoids the two difficulties identified by Cornell.

111. See note 103 and accompanying text.

112. Devine, note 78, at 412.

113. Rorty, "Science as Solidarity," unpublished ms. at 5 (1984). (This essay has recently appeared in J. Nelson *et al.*, eds., Rhetoric of the Human Sciences [1987].)

114. See Baker, note 78, at 279:

[W]hen we think of forms of life as conventional, . . . "we are thinking of convention not as the arrangements a particular culture has found convenient, in terms of its history and geography, for effecting the necessities of human existence, but as those forms of life which are normal to any group of creatures we call human, any group about which we will say, for example, that they have a past to which they respond, or a geographical environment which they manipulate or exploit in certain ways for certain humanly comprehensible motives. Here the array of 'conventions' are not patterns of life which differentiate human beings from one another, but those exigencies of conduct and feeling which all humans share." This passage makes it clear that—the amorphousness of life notwithstanding—most fundamentally, the human species is the locus of forms of life. For specific purposes, "form of life" is sometimes applied to practices that are not universal, as when writers take religion (or a particular religion) to be a form of life, or when writers speak of different societies as exhibiting different forms of life. Although I think that these narrower uses of "form of life" illustrate the elasticity of the idea, and suggest that forms of life, though not clearly demarcated, are thoroughly interwoven and even "nested", they do not tell against the point that Wittgenstein's first concern is with human practices, not with local options.

(Quoting S. Cavell, The Claim of Reason: Wittgenstein, Skepticism, Morality and Tragedy 111 [1979].) Cf. Sharrock & Anderson, "Criticizing Forms of Life," 60 Phil. 394, 395, 398 (1985):

Whether there are insuperable obstacles to mutual understanding (and, therefore, to external criticism) is not, then, something to be determined *a priori*, for the simple reason that the answer will depend on the nature of the differences and disagreements involved. . . .

There is no basis in Wittgenstein's numerous comments on the nature of human beings and their lives for supposing that understanding between them must be either impossible or inevitable. He seems to try to maintain a perspicuous view of the balance of homogeneity and heterogeneity among human beings. He tries not to lose sight of the fact that human beings are, after all, human beings, members of the same species with their animal constitution (which has ramifying consequences for the lives they do lead) in common. At the same time he emphasizes how much the practices which they create may diverge from one another. Human lives develop in very different directions from the common "starting points" provided by their species inheritance. It is the fact that human beings are the kinds of creatures that they are which lets them take to training, to learn language and other practices. The fact that a human being might, with equal ease, have been inducted into either of two ways of life does not, however, mean that having been drawn into the one he can now adopt the other with the same facility as if he had been brought up to it—learning a second language is not the same as learning a first and, of course, a language like ours makes Chinese harder to learn than French. Two ways of life might, then, be organized in such ways that the grasp of one is inimical to the understanding of the other.

115. If such a position supports epistemological foundationalism (see note 5), it is a very weak foundationalism indeed. Such transcendental constraints radically underdetermine resolution of the real-world intellectual/ideological conflicts that have engaged members of our species.

116. B. Williams, note 20, at 158. See Rorty, note 93, at 8–9: "It is a consequence of this holistic view of knowledge . . . that alternative cultures are not to be thought of on the model of alternative geometries. Alternative geometries are irreconcilable because they have axiomatic structures, and contradictory axioms. They are *designed* to be irreconcilable. Cultures are not so designed, and do not have axiomatic structures."

117. F. Dallmayr, Polis and Praxis: Exercises in Contemporary Political Theory 196 (1984) (quoting H.-G. Gadamer, note 45, at 321, 323–25). See Hinman, note 17, at 349–51:

[Gadamer's model] suggests that understanding is possible between forms of life, and looks upon differences between their presuppositions as opportunities for fuller understanding(self-understanding as well as understanding of the other) rather than as impediments to it. . . . Gadamer describes this process as a "fusion of horizons". Although he discusses this in relation to historical understanding, we can easily reformulate his point in relation to forms of life. . . . This is not to deny that to some extent forms of life differ from one another, presuppose somewhat different standards of meaning and value, and are constituted in part by rules which vary from one form of life to another. It is to suggest, however, that understanding is a task which involves the creation as well as the discovery of shared structures of meaning and value. Perhaps the most disturbing aspect of the contemporary belief in the absence of any such shared standard between different forms of life is that it invites resignation and passivity rather than dialogue, disagreement, and the eventual creation of mutual understanding.

Ecumenical moral discourse is a principal constituent of a deliberative, transformative politics as distinct from a politics that is merely manipulative and self-serving. (I discuss the former sort of politics in chapter 6.) Benjamin Barber has put the point well:

[T]alk as communication obviously involves receiving as well as expressing, hearing as well as speaking, and empathizing as well as uttering. The liberal reduction of talk to speech has unfortunately inspired political institutions that foster the articulation of interests but that slight the difficult art of listening. . . .

"I will listen" means to the strong democrat not that I will scan my adversary's position for weaknesses and potential trade-offs . . . It means, rather, "I will put myself in his place, I will try to understand, I will strain to hear what makes us alike, I will listen for a common rhetoric evocative of a common purpose or a common good." . . .

The empathetic listener becomes more like his interlocutor as the two bridge the differences between them by conversation and mutual understanding. Indeed, one measure of healthy political talk is the amount of *silence* it permits and encourages, for silence is the precious medium in which reflection is nurtured and empathy can grow. Without it, there is only the babble of raucous interests and interests vying for the deaf ears of impatient adversaries. . . . The Quaker meeting carries a message for . . . [liberals], but they are often too busy articulating their interests to hear it.

B. Barber, note 62, at 174, 175–76. See Brest, Review of id., 13 Pol. Theory 465 (1985).

118. The problems (and the possibilities) of conducting productive moral discourse *among* modern societies are not different from the problems of conducting such discourse *within* a pluralistic society. See Rorty, note 93, at 9: "[T]he distinction between different cultures does not differ in kind from the distinction between theories held by members of a single culture. The Tasmanian aborigines and the British colonists had trouble communicating, but this trouble was different only in extent from the difficulties in communication experienced by Gladstone and Disraeli."

119. Foot, note 78, at 164. For Foot's perceptive explanation why "rela-

tivists, and subjectivists generally," are not able to take the whole journey, see id. at 165–66.

120. R. Beiner, note 41, at 186 n. 17.

121. See J. Dewey, The Quest for Certainty 262 (1929):

> The word "taste" has perhaps got too completely associated with arbitrary liking to express the nature of judgments of value. But if the word be used in the sense of an appreciation at once cultivated and active, one may say that the formation of taste is the chief matter wherever values enter in, whether intellectual, esthetic or moral. Relatively immediate judgments, which we call tact or to which we give the name of intuition, do not preclude reflective inquiry, but are the funded products of much thoughtful experience. Expertness of taste is at once the result and the reward of constant exercise of thinking. Instead of there being no disputing about tastes, they are the one thing worth disputing about, if by "dispute" is signified discussion involving reflective inquiry. Taste, if we use the word in its best sense, is the outcome of experience brought cumulatively to bear on the intelligent appreciation of the real worth of likings and enjoyments. There is nothing in which a person so completely reveals himself as in the things which he judges enjoyable and desirable. Such judgments are the sole alternative to the domination of belief by impulse, chance, blind habit and self-interest. The formation of a cultivated and effectively operative good judgment or taste with respect to what is esthetically admirable, intellectually acceptable and morally approvable is the supreme task set to human beings by the incidents of experience.

Chapter 3

1. Rawls is also our most prominent Kantian political philosopher. See Rawls, "Kantian Constructivism in Moral Theory," 77 J. Phil. 505, 517 (1980). However, I'm not sure precisely what it means to say that Rawls is Kantian. For a recent clarifying comment by Rawls, see "Justice as Fairness: Political Not Metaphysical," 14 Phil. & Pub. Aff. 223, 224 n. 2 (1985).

Although contemporary contractualist thought is sometimes said to be Kantian, it "differs from Kant among other things in making no demands on a theory of noumenal freedom, and also, importantly, in admitting considerations of a general empirical kind in determining fundamental moral demands, which Kant at least supposed himself not to be doing." Williams, "Persons, Character, and Morality," in B. Williams, Moral Luck 1, 1 (1981). See M. Sandel, Liberalism and the Limits of Justice 39 (1982). Perhaps the Kantian character of contemporary contractualist thought resides in its abstraction from—its annihilation of?—the identities of persons. Kant's view (according to Roger Scruton, a sympathetic interpreter) was that

> [i]f we are to find an imperative that recommends itself on the basis of reason alone, then we must abstract from all the distinctions between rational agents, discounting their interests, desires and ambitions, and all the "empirical conditions" which circumscribe their actions. Only then will we base our law in practical reason alone, since we will have abstracted from any other ground. By this process of abstraction I arrive at

the "point of view of a member of the intelligible world." This is a point of view outside my own experience, which could therefore be adopted by any rational being, whatever his circumstances. The law that I formulate will then be an imperative that applies universally, to all rational beings.

R. Scruton, Kant 69 (1982). The affinity between Kant's view and the view of contractualist thinkers like Rawls is apparent. For them,

> the moral point of view is basically different from a non-moral, and in particular self-interested, point of view, and by a difference of kind; . . . the moral point of view is specially characterized by its impartiality and its indifference to any particular relations to particular persons, and . . . moral thought requires abstraction from particular characteristics of the parties, including the agent, except in so far as these can be treated as universal features of any morally similar situation; and . . . the motivations of a moral agent, correspondingly, involve a rational application of impartial principle and are thus different in kind from the sorts of motivations that he might have for treating some particular persons (for instance, though not exclusively, himself) differently because he happened to have some particular interest towards them.

Williams, this note, at 2.

The Kantian perspective is problematic, as Ronald Beiner, among others, has noted:

> Because the rational subject, for Kant, may be viewed from two perspectives, empirical and transcendental, it is always problematical how the transcendental perspective that guides Kant in the three Critiques can be related back to the actual human concerns of knowing, acting, and judging subjects in the phenomenal world. Here we are presented with problems that apply generally within transcendental idealism. If the transcendental subject is a universal subject and if the only way for it to win a rationally compelling basis for its principles of judgment is by ascending to a universal standpoint detached from all contingent empirical conditions, what is it that gives the deliberations of this subject enough determinacy to have any content at all? In the ascent to universality, at what point is one sufficiently distanced from the particular and the contingent to satisfy the transcendental requirement, and what particularities of human experience can be tolerated without this requirement being violated? And if it is through shedding all particularity and contingency that the Kantian subject secures transcendental validity for its judgments, doesn't the standpoint of the transcendental subject turn into no standpoint at all, and isn't the universal self in danger of becoming self-less? How far can the "enlarged mentality" expand without ceasing to be the possession of an individuated subject retaining its own identity?

R. Beiner, Political Judgment 33–34 (1983). See R. Scruton, Sexual Desire: A Moral Philosophy of the Erotic 324–25 (1986).

2. J. Rawls, A Theory of Justice 11 (1971). See generally id., chapter 1, §3. Cf. id. at 12, 18 ("[T]he original position . . . is understood as a purely hypothetical situation characterized so as to lead to a certain conception of justice. . . . The idea . . . is simply to make vivid to ourselves the restrictions that it seems reasonable to impose on arguments for principles of justice, and therefore on these principles themselves."); Rawls, "Justice as Fairness: Political Not Metaphysical," 14 Phil. & Pub. Aff. 223, 237–38 (1985):

> [T]he original position is simply a device of representation: it describes the parties, each of whom are responsible for the essential interests of a free and equal person, as fairly situated and as reaching an agreement subject to appropriate restrictions on what are to count as good reasons. . . . [T]his position models what we regard as fair conditions under which the representatives of free and equal persons are to specify the terms of social cooperation in the case of the basic structure of society . . .

Compare Scanlon, "Contractualism and Utilitarianism," in Utilitarianism and Beyond 103, 111–12 (A. Sen & B. Williams eds. 1982):

> [My] contractualist account of moral wrongness refers to principles "which no one could reasonably reject" rather than to principles "which everyone could reasonably accept" for the following reason. Consider a principle under which some people will suffer severe hardships, and suppose that these hardships are avoidable. That is, there are alternative principles under which no one would have to bear comparable burdens. It might happen, however, that the people on whom these hardships fall are particularly self-sacrificing, and are willing to accept these burdens for the sake of what they see as the greater good of all. We would not say, I think, that it would be unreasonable of them to do this. On the other hand, it might not be unreasonable for them to refuse these burdens, and, hence, not unreasonable for someone to reject a principle requiring him to bear them. If this rejection would be reasonable, then the principle imposing these burdens is put in doubt, despite the fact that some particularly self-sacrificing people could (reasonably) accept it. Thus it is the reasonableness of rejecting a principle, rather than the reasonableness of accepting it, on which moral argument turns.

3. Rawls, "Kantian Constructivism in Moral Theory," 77 J. Phil. 505, 542–43 (1980).

No one should doubt that Rawls' theory of justice is a moral theory, his principles of justice, moral principles. As Rawls has recently emphasized, "a political conception of justice is, of course, a moral conception . . ." Rawls, note 2, at 224. See id. at 245. He continues: "[I]t is a moral conception worked out for a specific kind of subject, namely, for political, social, and economic institutions. In particular, justice as fairness is framed to apply to what I have called the 'basic structure' of a modern constitutional democracy. . . . By this structure I mean such a society's main political, social, and economic institutions, and how they fit together into one unified system of social cooperation." Id. at 224–25.

4. See Lovin, "Empiricism and Christian Social Thought," Annual of Society of Christian Ethics 25 (1982). See also A. MacIntyre, After Virtue 112 (1981).

5. MacIntyre, "Does Applied Ethics Rest on a Mistake?," 67 Monist 498, 498–99 (1984).

6. Rawls, note 3, at 518. See id. at 524.

7. Id. at 518. See Rawls, note 2, at 225: "Whether justice as fairness can be extended to a general political conception for different kinds of societies existing under different historical and social conditions, or whether it can be

extended to a general moral conception, or a significant part thereof, are altogether separate questions. I avoid prejudging these questions one way or another."

8. Rawls, note 3, at 536.
9. Id. at 539, 542.
10. Id. at 543.
11. See Rawls, note 2, at 225:

> [A]s a practical matter no general moral conception can provide a publicly recognized basis for a conception of justice in a modern democratic state. The social and historical conditions of such a state have their origins in the Wars of Religion following the Reformation and the subsequent development of the principle of toleration, and in the growth of constitutional government and the institutions of large industrial market economies. The conditions profoundly affect the requirements of a workable conception of political justice: such a conception must allow for a diversity of doctrines and the plurality of conflicting, and indeed incommensurable, conceptions of the good affirmed by members of existing democratic societies.

See also id. at 223, 226, 230.

According to Rawls, the transcendent justification (if there is one) cannot take into account "the whole truth, if the whole truth is to include the truths of religion and of philosophy and of moral and political doctrine." Rawls, note 3, at 542. Because there are deep and persistent differences as to which religious, etc., claims are true, "there is no alternative . . . to founding a conception of justice suitable for a well-ordered democratic society on but a part of the truth, and not the whole . . ." Id. Rawls emphasizes that point time and again: "Justice as fairness tries to construct a conception of justice that takes deep and unresolvable differences on matters of fundamental significance as a permanent condition of human life." Id.

As I explained in chapter 1, the naturalist conceives of moral knowledge as knowledge of how to live so as to flourish, and so seeks to ground her moral theory, including her theory of justice, in the whole of the relevant truth. For the naturalist, justification is an epistemological problem; to seek to justify a naturalist moral claim is to argue for its truth. By contrast, Rawls seeks to ground his theory of justice not in truth, but in a hypothetical agreement. For Rawls, justification "is not primarily an epistemological problem." Id. at 519. The following passages suggest the difference, with respect to the matter of truth and justification, between Rawls' liberal project and the naturalist one:

> The search for reasonable grounds for reaching agreement . . . replaces the search for moral truth . . . [R]ather than think of the principles of justice as true, it is better to say that they are the principles most reasonable for us . . . [T]he idea of approximating to moral truth has no place in a [contractualist] doctrine: the parties in the original position do not recognize any principles of justice as true or correct and so as antecedently given; their aim is simply to select the conception most rational for them, given their circumstances . . . [N]o assumptions have been made about a theory of truth. A

[contractualist] view does not require an ideal or a verificationist, as opposed to a realist, account of truth . . . These principles are not . . ., as in some naturalist doctrines, to be derived from the truths of science and adjusted in accordance with advances in human psychology and social theory . . . [I]t seems better to say that in [contractualism] first principles are reasonable (or unreasonable) than that they are true (or false) . . .

Id. at 519, 554, 564, 565, 567, 569. See also Rawls, note 2, at 230: "[T]he aim of justice as fairness as a political conception is practical and not metaphysical or epistemological. That is, it presents itself not as a conception of justice that is true, but one that can serve as a basis of informed and willing political agreement between citizens viewed as free and equal persons." See Rawls, note 3, at 569:

This usage, however, does not imply that there are no natural uses for the notion of truth in moral reasoning. To the contrary. For example, particular judgments and secondary norms may be considered true when they follow from, or are sound applications of, reasonable first principles. These first principles may be said to be true in the sense that they would be agreed to if the parties in the original position were provided with all the relevant true general beliefs.

12. For a discussion of a different justification Rawls advances in support of his principles of justice—in effect, a "Good prior to Right" justification as distinct from the "Right prior to Good" justification criticized in this chapter—see chapter 4, section II.

13. For a recent elaboration by Rawls of what he means by "citizens as free and equal persons", see Rawls, note 2, at 233–34.

14. Rawls, note 3, at 517, 519, 554, 569.

15. See M. Sandel, note 1, at 10–11, 12, 55, 58–59, 172–73; Sandel, "The Procedural Republic and the Unencumbered Self," 12 Pol. Theory 81 (1984). See also Scheffler, "Moral Scepticism and Ideals of the Person," 62 Monist 288, 295 (1979) ("[i]t is the ideal of a person who . . . regards the conception of himself or herself as rational chooser of his or her own ends as more dear than any particular end"); Galston, "Moral Personality and Liberal Theory: John Rawls' Dewey Lectures," 10 Pol. Theory 492 (1980).

16. See Rawls, note 3, at 569: "Recall that a Kantian view, in addressing the public culture of a democratic society, hopes to bring to awareness a conception of the person and of social cooperation conjectured to be implicit in that culture, or at least congenial to its deepest tendencies when properly expressed and presented."

17. Rorty, "Postmodernist Bourgeois Liberalism," 80 J. Phil. 583, 585–86 (1983). See M. Sandel, note 1; Galston, note 15. Cf. Scheffler, note 15, at 294:

Many of Rawls' critics and commentators have argued that at least some of the conditions characterizing the original position are nevertheless neither weak nor widely shared. Rather, it is urged, they are controversial conditions, and they are controversial precisely because they arise directly out of an ideal of the person that is itself an object of controversy, and place the stamp of that ideal indelibly on the original position. Thus it is said that even though the parties in the original position do not explicitly accept the ideal, the characterization of the original position and of the parties themselves constitutes a kind of model of the full-blown ideal. Now in itself, the idea that the original position models the ideal is far from uncongenial to Rawls; indeed, he explicitly intends for the original position to be regarded as a model, among other things. But unless the model is constructed out of elements that are weak and widely shared, as Rawls had hoped it was but as his critics suggest that it is not, serious questions are raised about the justificatory relevance of any hypothetical choice in the original position.

For examples of the sort of criticism to which Scheffler refers, see B. Ackerman, Social Justice in the Liberal State 338–40 (1980); Raz, "Liberalism, Autonomy, and the Politics of Neutral Concern," 7 Midwest Stud. Phil. 89, 96–98 (1982); Unger, "The Critical Legal Studies Movement," 96 Harvard L. Rev. 561, 658 (1983).

18. Rawls, note 2, at 238.

19. Id. at 223 (passages rearranged).

20. See note 2.

21. Rawls, note 2, at 238–39.

22. See, for example, R. Beiner, note 1, at 126. See also R. Scruton, note 1, at 324.

23. See note 1 (passage from R. Beiner noting the problematic character of the Kantian "transcendental" perspective).

24. Rorty, "The Priority of Democracy Over Philosophy," unpublished ms. at 21 (1986) (due to appear in M. Peterson & R. Vaughan, eds., The Virginia Statute of Religious Freedom [1987]).

25. See note 17 and accompanying text. See also Lomasky, "Personal Projects as the Basis for Basic Rights," 1 Soc. Phil. & Pol'y 35, 42, 43 (1984):

At bottom, the two conceptions of morality that have been opposed rest on different analyses of relations persons bear to their own ends. There is a metaphysical gulf that separates one from the other. Emphasis on the moral significance of project pursuit is based on a conception of personal identity over time which incorporates not only criteria of memory retention and bodily continuity but also persistent attachment to one's ends. As an active being, one's identity is not simply a given but is created and recreated continuously through identifying oneself with one's projects. One understands a life as a life, and not merely a jumble of discrete episodes, by focusing on motivational patterns that persist over long periods of time and order a large number of particular variations. "This is someone who, three years ago, decided to plant tomatoes in his backyard garden," provides insubstantial information about the person's purposive dimension. But saying, "She is an ardent Zionist"; "He is a Cicero scholar," is to begin to explain a life.

A coherent life, coherent from both the outside and the inside, is not open to motivation from just any direction. Rather, it will systematically embrace some potential source of value and stand aloof from others. Consider a variation on a theme from Kafka in which a person awakens one morning to find that he has the body of a loathsome insect. Suppose that instead of a bodily metamorphosis he had undergone an equally radical volitional transformation. That to which he was formerly drawn he is now indifferent; outcomes he had previously worked to avert now command his allegiance. And suppose further that such shifts occurred regularly and could assume an unlimited variety of forms. In such a scenario, the unity of the person as an acting, purposive being would have completely broken down. Indiscriminate evaluators of this sort are different in kind from project pursuers, and even if it makes sense to suppose them bound by some moral framework, it would be a morality different from that applied by and to project pursuers. . . .

[A] correct analysis of what we fundamentally take persons to be must incorporate project pursuit.

In thinking of the conception of the person presupposed by Rawls' theory, interpreted as a Right-prior-to-Good theory, I'm reminded of a song—"Freezing," lyrics by Suzanne Vega, music by Philip Glass—on Glass' 1986 album *Songs from Liquid Days*:

If you had no name
If you had no history
If you had no books
If you had no family

If it were only you
Naked on the grass
Who would you be then?
This is what he asked
And I said I wasn't really sure
But I would probably be
Cold

And now I'm freezing
Freezing

26. See M. Sandel, note 1.
27. MacIntyre, note 5, at 509–10.
28. Scheffler, note 15, at 295. A different revisionist strategy is pursued by Charles Larmore, who suggests that Rawls' principles of justice are best understood as

a *modus vivendi* among people having different ultimate commitments (often at home in different subcommunities), a system of mutual advantage, to which we primarily adhere, not because it expresses our deepest self-understandings, but rather for the more prudential reason that it serves our other values. . . . [Rawls' principles are] primarily a *modus vivendi* among persons having constitutive views of the good life which are shared with some but differ from those of many others.

Larmore, Review of M. Sandel, Liberalism and the Limits of Justice (1982), 81 J. Phil. 336, 338, 340 (1984). For Larmore, then, Rawls' principles of justice are not prior to the good; a person ought to accept Rawls' principles (or something like them), in Larmore's view, because doing so is a means to the end of achieving her good (as she conceives it). For a discussion of "liberal" principles thus understood and of Rawl's theory thus construed, see chapter 4, section II.

29. Galston, note 15, at 506. See id.: "And he must answer more fully the contentions of those who . . . see in Rawls' Kantian universalism a systematic violation of the individualistic particularity that characterizes the human good."

30. B. Ackerman, note 17, at 11.

Rawls' project was to locate principles of justice whose justification is impartial among the differences that constitute the subjective circumstances. The project failed, because Rawls' justification of his principles of justice did not transcend the subjective circumstances. Indeed, if as it seems there is no transcendent justification of principles of justice, Rawls' project was doomed to failure. Ackerman's project fails too, but not because Ackerman supposes there to be a transcendent justification for his master principle—a neutral justification of the neutrality principle. Ackerman understands that there is no such justification:

> [W]hile Neutrality excludes a broad range of normative argument from the practice of liberal politics, it does not follow that these arguments should also be excluded when the subject is the justification of the entire practice of liberal argument, considered as a whole. Indeed, it would be a category mistake to imagine that there could be a Neutral justification for the practice of Neutral justification—for Neutrality makes no sense except as a part of the practice it constitutes.

Ackerman, "What is Neutral About Neutrality?," Ethics, Jan. 1983, at 372, 387.

31. Imagine two human beings, A and B. To say that A is superior to B seems to be to say that A compares favorably to B in terms of some factor X, like strength, intelligence, or race. But what does it mean to say that A is *intrinsically* superior to B? That A compares favorably to B not in terms of some X, but *period*? If that is what it means, then the statement is incoherent, because A and B cannot be compared at all except in terms of some X. Perhaps "A is intrinsically superior to B" means that A compares favorably to B in terms of some X, which is not merely intrinsically good, but better than any other factor, including any factor in terms of which B compares favorably to A. In that case, X would have to be the ultimate standard of comparison. How might one defend the claim that X is the ultimate standard of comparison? By asserting that one simply knows—"intuits"—it? Perhaps that (in addition to claims about the worth of conceptions of human good) is what the neutrality principle bans:

assertions of an intuition that a particular standard of comparison (strength, intelligence, being-white, not-being-a-Jew, etc.) is the ultimate standard.

32. See note 38 and accompanying text.

33. Ackerman adopts the simplifying strategy of addressing the problem of distributive justice in an idealized world before turning to the real world with all its complications. The principle of equal distribution holds that in establishing the State in the idealized world and making an initial distribution of resources, every citizen is entitled to an equal share.

34. See Harman, "Liberalism Without Foundations?," 91 Yale L. J. 397, 401 (1981); Fletcher, "The Watchdog of Neutrality," 83 Columbia L. Rev. 2099, 2109–10 (1983).

35. See Harman, note 34, at 397–98: "[Ackerman] argues that an equal distribution of power can be justified on the ground that because each person is at least as good as any other, each person is entitled to at least as much (power, wealth, etc.) as any other person. This principle, he asserts, does not violate neutrality. It does not say that anyone is *better* than anyone else, only that each person is *at least as good as* anyone else."

36. See id. at 401.

37. Id.

38. Fletcher, note 34, at 2108. See Harman, note 34, at 400–1.

39. Dworkin, "Liberalism," in Public and Private Morality 113, 115 (S. Hampshire ed. 1978).

40. Id. at 127.

41. Id. at 125.

42. Dworkin, "Why Liberals Should Believe in Equality," New York Rev., Feb. 3, 1983, at 32.

43. Dworkin, note 39, at 127.

44. Dworkin, "What Liberalism Isn't," New York Rev., Jan. 20, 1983, at 47. See R. Dworkin, Taking Rights Seriously 272–73 (rev. ed. 1978):

> Government must treat those whom it governs with concern, that is, as human beings who are capable of suffering and frustration, and with respect, that is, as human beings who are capable of forming and acting on intelligent conceptions of how their lives should be lived. Government must not only treat people with concern and respect, but with equal concern and respect. It must not distribute goods or opportunities unequally on the ground that some citizens are entitled to more because they are worthy of more concern. It must not constrain liberty on the ground that one citizen's conception of the good life of one group is nobler or superior to another's. These postulates, taken together, state what might be called the liberal conception of equality . . .

See also Dworkin, note 42, at 32 (arguing that the equality principle "insists on an economic system in which no citizen has less than an equal share of the community's resources just in order that others may have more of what he lacks").

45. In "What Liberalism Isn't," note 44, Dworkin seems to argue that the neutrality principle is somehow derived from the equality principle, which is foundational.

46. Id. at 33.

47. Cf. Holborow, "Dworkin on Treating Citizens as Equals," 3 Oxford J. Leg. Stud. 371, 375 (1983): "Dworkin owes us some other account of why his conception of equality is to be preferred. In the absence of such an account he has shown merely that the conception of equality that he has outlined is a possible one, not that it is compelling."

48. Dworkin has criticized Ackerman for arguing that liberalism's commitment to "neutrality" is more basic than its commitment to "equality". See Dworkin, note 44. According to Dworkin, the commitment to equality is basic and the commitment to neutrality (Dworkin seems to say) somehow derives from it. See id. Dworkin's criticism rests on a misunderstanding of Ackerman's position. Ackerman argues that there are several paths to his neutrality principle, and that the path one person finds most attractive is not necessarily the path another finds most attractive. Ackerman's principal concern, however, is not with the relative merits of the various paths, but with the neutrality principle. Nothing Ackerman says is inconsistent with Dworkin's argument that the equality principle is fundamental and somehow leads to the neutrality principle, although nothing he says requires that conclusion either. See B. Ackerman, note 17, at 11–12, 359–69. (I don't mean to suggest that Dworkin's neutrality principle is the same as Ackerman's, although it's not clear that it isn't.)

49. See A. MacIntyre, note 4, at 112:

> Ronald Dworkin has recently argued that the central doctrine of modern liberalism is the thesis that questions about the *good life for man* or the ends of human life are to be regarded from the public standpoint as systematically unsettlable. On these individuals are free to agree or disagree. The rules of . . . law hence are not to be derived from or justified in terms of some more fundamental conception of the good for man. In arguing thus Dworkin has, I believe, identified a stance characteristic not just of liberalism, but of modernity.

50. In his recent book *Well-Being: Its Meaning, Measurement and Moral Importance* (1986), James Griffin reaches the same conclusion. See id. at 50 & 121–24. See also Frug, "Why Neutrality?," 92 Yale L. J. 1591 (1983); "Should We Legislate Morality?," in Phil. & Pub. Pol'y, Summer 1982, at 1, 3–4 (reporting comments of Mark Sagoff). Cf. Boyle, "A Catholic Perspective on Morality and the Law," 1 J. L. & Rel. 227, 233–34 (1983): "There is no neutral ground on which legislators, judges or citizens can stand and rationally arbitrate the conflicts between moral perspectives. Any such ground will in fact be *some* moral perspective and the illusion that it is neutral will have the effect of disregarding the moral views of some citizens."

51. Geuss, "Freedom and Preference," unpublished ms. at 5 (1985).

52. I. Berlin, Against the Current 289 (1980). The passage continues: "To understand such thinkers, it is more important to grasp this central notion or image, which may be implicit, but determines their picture of the world, than even the most forceful arguments with which they defend their views and refute actual and possible objections." Id. Cf. J. Coleman, An American Strategic Theology 196 (1982): "As every philosophy contains an implicit anthropology and sociology, it contends, at crucial points, with theological visions of the human and the social and vice versa."

53. Dworkin, note 39, at 142–43.

54. See Rawls, note 2; chapter 4, section II.

55. See Dworkin, note 44, at 47: "When Ackerman tries to rebut certain familiar justifications of economic inequality, . . . he tacitly relies on the idea that neutrality forbids any appeal to any principle of justice whatsoever."

56. See chapter 2, section III.

57. J. Finnis, Natural Law and Natural Rights 221–22 (1980).

58. See id. at 222–23.

59. Cf. note 48.

60. See A. Gewirth, Reason and Morality (1978); A. Gewirth, Human Rights (1982).

61. For an effective critique of Gewirth's theory, drawing on several earlier critiques of the theory, see Bishop, "Gewirth on the Justification of Moral Rights," unpublished ms. (1985). See also E. Regis, ed., Gewirth's Ethical Rationalism (1984).

62. Ackerman, note 30, at 389–90.

63. See notes 17 & 25 and accompanying text.

64. See Barry, "Introduction to the Symposium [on B. Ackerman, Social Justice in the Liberal State (1980)]," Ethics, Jan. 1983, at 328, 329: "[I]f . . . [Ackerman's] critics are correct and the project of constructing a coherent political theory on the basis of neutrality fails, and fails not in ways that simply require more ingenuity to fix up the weaknesses but because of its intrinsic impossibility, where does that leave us?"

Political philosophers like Rawls, Ackerman, and Dworkin tend simply to *assume*—to take for granted—that basic moral and religious differences are

> insusceptible to the kind of assessment that could lead to rational agreement . . . The real contest between Rawlsian liberalism and its most interesting critics relates to whether conceptions of the good incompatible with liberalism can in fact be rationally justified. But on this issue Rawls himself has nothing much to say. What can be granted without hesitation is that liberal principles were the right ones to adopt when competing religious beliefs and divergent conception of the good embroiled Europe in the religious wars. Religious beliefs and conceptions of the good were, in that highly particular context, part of a dialectical impasse that made the attainment of rational agreement on a whole range of issues impossible. Whether they remain so is another question—and one well worth asking.

J. Stout, The Flight from Authority 240–41 (1981). See Galston, note 15, at 516: "Few contemporary theorists (and Rawls is surely no exception) are more willing than were their overtly skeptical predecessors to entertain perfectionist, intuitionist, or naturalist theses."

Chapter 4

1. In chapter 6 I address the questions in what sense and to what extent American society, given its morally pluralistic character, can be said to be a political *community*. See R. Beiner, Political Judgment 142–43 (1983). See also J. Murray, We Hold These Truths 9–10 (Image books ed. 1964).

2. Cuomo, "Religious Belief and Public Morality: A Catholic Governor's Perspective," 1 Notre Dame J. L., Ethics & Pub. Pol. 13, 13 (1984). See Bernardin, "Religion and Politics: The Future Agenda," 14 Origins 321 (1984).

3. Bedau, "The Limits of Utilitarianism and Beyond," Ethics, Jan. 1985, at 333, 333.

4. See A. Sen & B. Williams, eds., Utilitarianism & Beyond 1 (1982).

5. See note 29.

6. Id. at 334.

7. Frey, "Introduction: Utilitarianism and Persons," in Utility and Rights 3, 4 (R. Frey ed. 1984).

8. According to act-utilitarianism, an action is to be evaluated by reference to the consequences of the action "in comparison with [the consequences] of . . . alternatives [to the action]." Brock, "Utilitarianism," in And Justice for All 217, 226 (T. Regan & D. VanDeVeer eds. 1982). See also Brandt, "The Real & Alleged Problems of Utilitarianism," Hastings Center Report, Apr. 1983, at 37, 37: "[Act-utilitarianism is] the thesis that a particular act is right if, and only if, no other act the agent could perform at the time would have, or probably would have (on the agent's evidence), better consequences."

9. According to rule-utilitarianism, "particular actions are to be evaluated by their conformance to moral, social, or legal rules, and . . . only the rules are evaluated by the utilitarian standard." Brock, note 8, at 226. See also Brandt, note 8, at 37: "[Rule-utilitarianism is the thesis] that an act is morally right if, and only if, it would be as beneficial to have a moral code permitting the act as to have any moral code that is similar but prohibits the act."

10. According to utilitarian generalization, "a particular action is to be evaluated not by *its* consequences, but by the consequences of *everyone* performing acts of a similar kind." Brock, note 8, at 226. See id.: "A bewildering variety of versions of rule utilitarianism and utilitarian generalization have been developed."

11. See D. Regan, Utilitarianism and Co-operation (1980). One reviewer has described Regan's cooperative utilitarianism (CU) this way:

What CU requires is that each agent " . . . cooperate with whomever else is cooperating, in the production of the best consequences possible given the behavior of non-cooperators" . . . To do this, one must ascertain who is willing to cooperate, identify the optimal pattern of behavior for such potential cooperators, and then do one's part in this pattern—*provided* that the other cooperators have identified the same pattern and remain willing to cooperate. What CU requires is not merely that one do some act but rather that each follows a certain procedure for identifying fellow cooperators and then coordinating one's behavior with theirs.

Nelson, Book Review, Ethics, July 1982, at 751, 752–53.

12. Frey, note 7, at 4.

With respect to "the range component", see J. Finnis, Natural Law and Natural Rights 157–58 (1980):

[Utilitarianism] provides no reason for preferring altruism to egoism or to exclusive concern for one's family or party or class or country or church. Jeremy Bentham oscillated and equivocated for sixty years about whether his utilitarianism was to maximize his own happiness or the happiness of "everybody". A given [utilitarian] may happen to find (or think he finds) his own good in maximizing the good of others or of "all"; but this [utilitarian] analysis and method of practical reasoning affords him no principle by reference to which he could criticize as unreasonable or immoral those who set out to maximize their own happiness regardless of the welfare of others.

13. See J. Finnis, Fundamentals of Ethics 80–108 (1983).

14. See Perry, "Some Notes on Absolutism, Consequentialism, and Incommensurability," 80 Northwestern U. L. Rev. 967 (1985).

15. Any effort to justify a standard of value on the basis of a theory, including a utilitarian theory, employing the standard is of course circular. Thus, there is no such thing as a utilitarian justification of the utilitarian standard of value (the standard employed in the justification).

16. And for sentient creatures generally. See Brock, note 8, at 221.

17. Id. at 222.

18. It is important to keep distinct the entirely separate question of who's in the best position to know if she might be living a life as deeply satisfying as any of which she is capable (the woman herself? her best friend? her therapist?), and also the entirely separate question of to what extent government ought to be in the paternalistic business of second-guessing a person's judgment that she's living a damned fine life, thank you. See note 26.

19. For a different comment on the happiness conception, see Sen, "Well-being, Agency and Freedom," 82 J. Phil. 169, 188–89 (1985).

20. See id. at 190–91:

The evidential role of desires is . . . deeply problematic in the context of *interpersonal* comparisons. Comparative intensities of desire may be a very dubious guide indeed to well-being intensities in comparing one person with another, since these intensities are influenced by many contingent circumstances that are arbitrary for well-being comparisons. Our reading of what is feasible in our situation and station may be crucial to the intensities of our desires and may even affect what we dare to desire. Desires reflect compromises with reality, and reality is harsher to some than to others. The hopeless destitute desiring merely to survive, the landless laborer concentrating his efforts on securing the next meal, the round-the-clock domestic servant seeking a few hours of respite, the subjugated housewife struggling for a little individuality, may all have learned to keep their desires in line with their respective predicaments. Their deprivations are gagged and muffled in the interpersonal metric of desire fulfillment. In some lives small mercies have to count big.

21. See H. Putnam, Reason, Truth and History 169 (1981):

The "Benthamite" conception does allow one case in which an individual can be persuaded to abandon a goal (or, at any rate, to abandon pursuit of the goal) by rational criticism: this is the case in which he had misestimated consequences in the direction of badly underestimating the costs of attaining the goal (relative to other goals he has). This opens the door to a question which has to do as much with imagination as with propositional intelligence: the question of what it would actually be like, experientially, to attain the goal. Many human beings pursue goals they would not actually enjoy attaining or would not enjoy nearly as long or nearly as much as they think. Even within a Benthamite framework, it would be possible to improve the account of rational decision making by taking into account the possibility of misestimating the actual existential feel of various goals. And this begins to introduce a sense in which goals themselves can be criticized as irrational, and not just means.

22. See J. Elster, Sour Grapes 109 (1983):

[W]hy should individual want satisfaction be the criterion of justice and social choice when individual wants themselves may be shaped by a process that preempts the choice. And in particular, why should the choice between feasible options only take account of individual preferences if people tend to adjust their aspirations to [what they believe are] their possibilities? For the utilitarian, there would be no welfare loss if the fox were excluded from consumption of the grapes, since he thought them sour anyway. But of course the cause of his holding them to be sour was his conviction that he would be excluded from consuming them, and then it is difficult to justify the allocation by invoking his preferences.

23. See J. Finnis, note 12, at 113–14:

If . . . someone asserts that each and every human desire has the same prima-facie entitlement to satisfaction, . . . we must repeat that this has no plausibility at all. . . . What reason can you find to deny that truth (and knowledge) is a good? What reason, then, can be found for treating the desire of someone who wants to keep people ignorant as a desire that even prima facie is just as much entitled to satisfaction as the desire of someone who loves knowledge? Why should anyone who desires (as consequentialists obviously do) to regulate his conduct by practical reasonableness treat as of equal value the desire (which he may find in himself or in others) to live according to sheer whim, or according to a programme adopted and loved for its sheer arbitrariness? And we can ask the same question in relation to all those desires that focus on death, pain, joylessness, trash, hatred and destruction of others, incoherence, and any other form of human ruin. These evils can be embraced as if they were intrinsic goods, by persons who once accepted them only as means to ends and whose personalities were skewed by their wrongdoing. To say that one who gives vent to these desires is "mentally sick" (and hence not to be counted in the grand calculus of satisfaction) is, often enough, a mere form of words disguising a moral evaluation made tacitly on non-consequentialist lines.

24. Brock, note 8, at 223. See Unger, "The Critical Legal Studies Movement," 96 Harvard L. Rev. 561, 656–60 (1983). Cf. A. Sen & B. Williams, note 4, at 6: "[S]omething can be valuable even if it is not desired by anyone. A person may not have the courage to desire freedom under a severely repressive regime, or may not have the wits to do so because of lack of experience, or social conditioning."

25. Elster, "Sour Grapes—Utilitarianism and the Genesis of Wants," in A. Sen & B. Williams, note 4, at 219, 237. See J. Elster, note 22, at 35.

26. As I indicated above (text accompanying note 5), adherence to a utilitarian theory—for example, preference-utilitarianism—as a decision procedure for public policymaking might be based on acceptance of the theory as a general moral theory, but not necessarily. One might accept preference-utilitarianism, for example, not as a general moral theory, but merely as a decision procedure for public policymaking. Why? On the ground that "liberty" or "autonomy" require government to stay out of the business of evaluating preferences. See note 29.

27. Of course, such a position is incoherent: If preferences are simply a matter of taste and there's no disputing taste, then there's no disputing one's distaste for preference-utilitarianism. Adherence to preference-utilitarianism as a decision procedure for public policymaking is more sensibly rooted in acceptance of preference-utilitarianism as a general moral theory—a *cognitivist* theory, and thus one that rejects the there's-no-disputing-taste shibboleth—or, more narrowly, in the belief that it is illegitimate for government to be in the business of evaluating preferences. See note 26. It is not inconsistent to accept that there *is* reasoning about taste/preferences, and even that politics is in part a proper occasion for such reasoning, while at the same time insisting that, when the time for talk is over and the time for action is at hand, preference-utilitarianism is the proper decision procedure.

28. F. Dallmayr, Polis and Praxis: Exercises in Contemporary Political Theory 219 (1984).

29. Sensitive to the fact that many preferences are defective in one way or another, some preference-utilitarians have proposed that only *some* preferences be allowed to count. "Hare demands 'perfectly prudent' preferences—'fully informed and unconfused.' Harsanyi wants that, and *more*; to wit, to 'exclude all antisocial preferences, such as sadism, envy, resentment, and malice.'" Sen, note 19, at 191. See A. Sen & B. Williams, note 4, at 9–10. That strategy is unavailing. See Sen, note 19, at 191–92; A. Sen & B. Williams, note 4, at 10–

11, 14–15. Pursuing that strategy involves abandoning the very heart of preference-utilitarianism—the preference-satisfaction conception of human good—for a very different conception, one according to which what matters is the satisfaction not of actual preferences but of interests. (Of course, most of us have an interest in the satisfaction of at least some of our preferences.) The sort of utilitarianism based on that conception of good is distinct from preference-utilitarianism and ought not to be confused or conflated with it. See Brock, note 8, at 222–23.

See text accompanying note 5. For a compelling critique of preference-utilitarianism taken as a decision procedure for public policymaking, see Sagoff, "Values and Preferences," Ethics, Jan. 1986, at 301. See also Sunstein, "Legal Interference With Private Preferences," 53 U. Chicago L. Rev. 721 (1986).

A comment on "economic analysis of law", understood as a normative theory of adjudication, is in order at this juncture. As Jules Coleman has indicated, "[W]hat is [economically] efficient depends on what people are willing to pay . . ." Coleman, "Law and Economics," in J. Murphy & J. Coleman, The Philosophy of Law: An Introduction to Jurisprudence 211, 256 (1984). What people are willing to pay depends, in turn, not merely on the factor identified by Coleman, namely, "what they are capable of paying". Id. A person's willingness to pay depends more fundamentally on the character and strength of her preferences. A basic problem with normative economic analysis of law—the basic problem, in my view—is that it presupposes the authority of existing preferences, thereby ignoring the fundamental question of "what our preferences should be, or what sorts of people we should become." Chapman, "Raising Johnny to be Good: A Problematic Case for Economic Analysis of Law," 34 U. Toronto L. J. 358 (1984). See Peller, "The Politics of Reconstruction," 98 Harvard L. Rev. 863, 873 (1985). As James B. White has observed:

> [T]he current habit of regarding law as the instrument by which "we" effectuate "our policies" and get what "we want" is wholly inadequate. It is the true nature of law to constitute a "we" and to establish a conversation by which that "we" can determine what our "wants" are and should be. Our motives and values are not, in this view, to be taken as exogenous to the system (as they are taken to be exogenous to an economic system) but are in fact its subject. The law should take as its most central question what kind of community we should be, with what values, motives and aims.

White, "Law as Rhetoric, Rhetoric as Law: The Arts of Cultural and Communal Life," 52 U. Chicago L. Rev. 684, 698 (1985). See White, "Economics and Law: Two Cultures in Tension," 54 Tennessee L. Rev. 161, 174 (1987). The argument that courts have no legitimate role to play in dealing with that question (see, for example, Easterbrook, "Method, Result, and Authority," 98 Harvard L. Rev. 622, 627–29 [1985]) is one I address, and reject, in chapter 6.

30. See note 3 and accompanying text.

31. Scanlon, "Contractualism and Utilitarianism," in A. Sen & B. Williams, note 4, at 103, 103. (Scanlon's essay is reprinted at J. Rajchman & C. West, Post-Analytic Philosophy 215 (1985).)

32. Id.

33. Id. at 104.

34. Id. See B. Williams, Ethics and the Limits of Philosophy 73 (1985): "[I]t is now obvious (once again obvious) that what one thinks about the subject matter of ethical thought, what one supposes it to be about, must itself affect what tests for acceptability or coherence are appropriate to it; and the use of those tests must affect any substantive ethical results."

35. Scanlon, note 31, at 105, 106.

36. Scanlon doesn't use the term "naturalism". He uses, instead, "philosophical utilitarianism". But, as Amartya Sen has remarked, "the term 'philosophical utilitarianism' is a little misleading [since] even nonutilitarian approaches can be consistent with 'the thesis that the only fundamental moral facts are facts about individual well-being' . . ." Sen, note 19, at 185. The term "naturalism" seems to fit much better. In any event, I'm interested in comparing contractualism, as Scanlon portrays it, with naturalism, not with utilitarianism, which I've criticized in this chapter.

37. Scanlon, note 31, at 108.

38. Id. at 110.

39. Id. See B. Williams, note 34, at 75: "This account of wrongness goes with a particular theory of what moral thought is about, or of what ultimate moral facts there are. On this theory, moral thought is concerned with what agreements people could make in these favored circumstances, in which no one was ignorant or coerced. . . . It is a question of what rules would be acceptable to people who are assumed to be already interested in reaching agreement." A contractualist morality, then, is an example of what John Mackie described as a "morality in the narrow sense". See J. Mackie, Ethics: Inventing Right and Wrong 106–07 (1977).

40. Scanlon, note 31, at 111. See id. at 111–12:

> The contractualist account of moral wrongness refers to principles "which no one could reasonably reject" rather than to principles "which everyone could reasonably accept" for the following reason. Consider a principle under which some people will suffer severe hardships, and suppose that these hardship are avoidable. That is, there are alternative principles under which no one would have to bear comparable burdens. It might happen, however, that the people on whom these hardships fall are particularly self-sacrificing, and are willing to accept these burdens for the sake of what they see as the greater good of all. We would not say, I think, that it would be unreasonable of them to do this. On the other hand, it might not be unreasonable for them to refuse these burdens, and, hence, not unreasonable for someone to reject a principle requiring him to bear them. If this rejection would be reasonable, then the principle imposing these burdens is put in doubt, despite the fact that some particularly self-sacrificing

people could (reasonably) accept it. Thus it is the reasonableness of rejecting a principle, rather than the reasonableness of accepting it, on which moral argument turns.

41. See R. Beiner, note 1, at 126:

Rawls forgoes substantive judgments about the good life and the good for man—the classical questions of western political philosophy—leaving rational individuals to decide for themselves their own "rational plan of life." Rather than theorizing about the proper ends of life, Rawls thinks that the way forward is by means of a theory of political *right* formulated in conjunction with "a thin theory of good." (More precisely: right is to *take priority* over the good. A fuller theory of the good can be elaborated, subsequent to, and on the basis of, a fully developed conception of right.) The implicit assumption is that there is no reliable way of arbitrating between "thick" theories of the good. We can devise rules that tell us what is *right*, namely the rules of a just society, without being able to specify what the substantive good for man consists in.

42. See B. Williams, note 34, at 103–4:

If the model is that of coexistence with creatures very different from us, why should that lead us to imagine a universal republic rather than a confederation or—less than that and most appropriately of all—a mere nonaggression treaty? The most schematic code against interference and mutual destruction may be enough for parties who merely have a shared requirement to live, not a requirement to share a life. If that schematic code were taken to provide all the ethical substance of a shared life, it would yield too little: the shared life needs more than a bare defensive individualism.

43. Larmore, Review of M. Sandel, Liberalism and the Limits of Justice (1982), 81 J. Phil. 336, 338, 340 (1984). (In his review, Larmore accuses Sandel of overlooking a liberalism in which the Good is prior to the Right. However, Sandel did not overlook such a liberalism; he was concerned with a very different sort of liberalism. Sandel's critique was directed against "deontological liberalism", in which the Right is prior to the Good.)

44. Raz, "Liberalism, Autonomy, and the Politics of Neutral Concern," 7 Midwest Stud. Phil. 89, 105 (1982). See id.: "[T]he common feature of most routes will be the reliance on a rational reconstruction of a process of bargaining by which the common overriding goal to reach an agreement leads the parties to compromise by accepting a less than perfect doctrine as the optimally realizable second best."

45. Rawls, "Justice as Fairness: Political Not Metaphysical," 14 Phil. & Pub. Aff. 223, 225–26 (1985).

46. Id. at 247. See, more recently, Rawls, "The Idea of an Overlapping Consensus," 7 Oxford J. Legal Studies 1 (1987).

47. Rawls, note 45, at 250.

48. Id. at 247.

49. See chapter 1, notes 56 & 67.

50. See note 43 and accompanying text. Nothing Rawls says in his most recent essay, "The Idea of an Overlapping Consensus," note 46, at 9–12, overcomes this conclusion.

51. See Rorty, "The Priority of Democracy Over Philosophy," unpublished ms. (1986) (due to appear in M. Peterson & R. Vaughan, eds., The Virginia Statute of Religious Freedom [1987]). For an interesting construal of Rawls' theory of justice, according to which it is of the Good-prior-to-Right sort, see Beckley, "A Christian Affirmation of Rawls' Idea of Justice as Fairness: Part I," 13 J. Rel. Ethics 210 (1985).

52. See Rorty, note 51, at 14–15.

53. See id. at 30.

54. Scanlon, note 31, at 113.

55. Id. at 104.

56. Flanagan, "Quinean Ethics," Ethics, Oct. 1982, at 56.

57. V. Held, Rights and Goods, chs. 4 & 15 (1984).

58. See, for example, A. MacIntyre, After Virtue (1981); S. Hampshire, Morality and Conflict (1983).

59. Lovin, "Empiricism and Christian Social Thought," Annual of Society of Christian Ethics 25, 41 (1982).

60. V. Held, note 57, at 60.

61. Scanlon, note 31, at 116.

62. See Machan, "Metaphysics, Epistemology, and Natural Law Theory," 31 American J. Jurisprudence 65, 68–69 (1986).

63. Seanlon, note 31, at 128.

64. Id. at 103.

65. H. Putnam, note 21, at 148–49. See id. at 161–62.

66. See, generally, Harrison, "Relativism and Tolerance," in J. Meiland & M. Krausz, eds., Relativism: Cognitive and Moral 229 (1982). See also J. Raz, The Authority of Law 271 (1979); Scheffler, "Moral Scepticism and Ideals of the Person," 62 Monist 288, 300–1 (1979); Blackburn, "Rule-Following and Moral Realism," in Wittgenstein: To Follow a Rule 163, 176 (S. Holtzman & C. Leich eds. 1981). Cf. Harman, "Human Flourishing, Ethics, and Liberty," 12 Phil. & Pub. Aff. 307, 321 (1983): "[We can] condemn other people as evil, bad, or dangerous by our lights, or take them to be our enemies. Nothing prevents us from using our values to judge other people and other moralities. But we only fool ourselves if we think our values give *reasons* to others who do not accept those values."

67. Rorty, "Postmodernist Bourgeois Liberalism," 80 J. Phil. 583, 589 (1983). See H. Putnam, note 21, at 161–62.

68. J. S. Mill, On Liberty 9 (E. Rapaport ed. 1978).

69. J. F. Stephen, Liberty, Equality, Fraternity 66 (R. White ed. 1967).

70. J. S. Mill, note 68, at 11.

71. Id. at 80.

72. C. L. Ten, Mill on Liberty 40 (1980). See Raz, note 44, at 90.

73. J. F. Stephen, note 69, at 61.

74. J. S. Mill, note 68, at 10–11.

75. P. Devlin, The Enforcement of Morals 7–8 (1965).

76. Id. at 16, 21.

77. Id. at 16–17.

78. R. Dworkin, Taking Rights Seriously 254–55 (2d ed. 1978).

79. Of course, there may be—and in the United States there are—constitutional norms that govern the decision whether to pursue a coercive strategy.

80. See Matthew 25:34–40. See also note 92.

81. Boyle, "Positivism, Natural Law, and Disestablishment: Some Questions Raised by MacCormick's Moralistic Amoralism," 20 Valparaiso U. L. Rev. 55, 59 (1985) (quoting T. Aquinas, Summa Theologiae at First Part of the Second Part, Question 96, Article 2).

82. See B. Mitchell, Law, Morality and Religion 134 (1967): "The function of the law is not only to protect individuals from harm, but to protect the essential institutions of a society. These functions overlap, since the sorts of harm an individual may suffer are to some extent determined by the institutions he lives under."

83. J. S. Mill, note 68, at 74. See Harrison, note 66, at 242.

84. See B. Williams, note 34, at 159–60:

If we become conscious of ethical variation and of the kinds of explanation it may receive, it is incredible that this consciousness should just leave everything where it was and not affect our ethical thought itself. We can go on, no doubt, simply saying that we are right and everyone else is wrong (that is to say, on the nonobjectivist view, affirming our values and rejecting theirs), but if we have arrived at this stage of reflection, it seems a remarkably inadequate response. What else is possible? In trying to answer this, we once again turn the question of relativism around. The question has traditionally been whether we *have* to think in a relativistic way, for conceptual or logical reasons, or whether that is impossible. We should rather ask how much room we can coherently find for thinking like this, and how far it provides a more adequate response to reflection.

85. H. Putnam, note 21, at 148.

86. See chapter 1, section IV.

87. R. Geuss, The Idea of a Critical Theory 53–54 (1981).

88. Cuomo, note 2, at 16. See Harrison, note 66, at 242.

89. Although to coerce someone to make a choice she does not want to make is to cause her to suffer, it might be to prevent her from suffering, too. To prevent someone from crossing a bridge she believes to be safe but that is in fact unsafe is to prevent her from suffering, even though, at least initially, she suffers the frustration of being stopped from crossing the bridge. Bear in mind that the considerations I'm now sketching are *not* being offered as conclusive

reasons against coercing someone to make a choice she does not want to make, but merely as reasons. In a given situation, there may well be better reasons for pursuing a coercive strategy, as the unsafe-bridge example suggests.

90. See id. at 242.

91. Sibley, "Religion and the Law: Some Thoughts on Their Intersections," 2 J. L. & Rel. 41, 53 (1984).

92. Quoted in Woodward, "Noonan's Life of the Law," Newsweek, Apr. 1, 1985, at 82. Cf. McBrien, "The Church and Politics," 1 J. L., Ethics & Pub. Pol. 57, 61 (1984):

> The letter entitled Political Responsibility, issued by the Administrative Board of the United States Catholic Conference in March 1984 [13 Origins 732 (1984)], grounded political involvement in love of neighbor, which goes beyond individual relationships to embrace the entire human community, and in Christ's specific call to reach out and help those in need, which also goes beyond individual relationships to embrace the institutions and structures of society, the economy, and politics. The purpose of such involvement is to promote human rights and to denounce violations of such rights; to call attention to the moral and religious dimensions of secular issues; to keep alive the values of the Gospel as a norm of social and political life; and to point out the demands of Christian faith for a just transformation of society.

93. Boyle, "A Catholic Perspective on Morality and the Law," 1 J. L. & Rel. 227, 235, 236 (1983). See id. at 235:

> Given this conception of morality the question arises as to what the purpose might be for seeking to legally proscribe actions which one judges to be immoral. For, surely it is doubtful that such legal proscription can in any efficient way contribute to the moral goal of a person's choosing to do what is right because he or she sees it to be right. Legal enforcement of a prohibition can guarantee only behavioral compliance; it cannot guarantee—and can in many cases do little to promote—the person's making the right choices or making them for the morally appropriate reasons. Fear of punishment might cause a person to comply with a norm—it might even be a motive for choosing to comply with the norm; but it does not contribute and, in fact, may hinder a person's making the choice to conform to the norm precisely because this is judged to be the right thing to do. In fact, even if one judges that obeying the law is the right thing to do—because it is obeying the law—this morally relevant ground for choosing in accord with the law is not the initial moral reason for judging that the action in question should not be done. So, even if there is morally significant compliance with the law the reason could be quite different from the reason the act was morally proscribed in the first place.

As Michael Walzer has recently reminded us, John Locke, too, based his brief for religious tolerance on his (Protestant) theology. See M. Walzer, Interpretation and Social Criticism 52–56 (1987).

94. J. Murray, note 1, at 164.

95. Of course, some of these values can support a coercive legislative strategy as well as oppose it. For example, the values of compassion and

community support a law criminalizing behavior that causes suffering and destroys community. Consider, in that regard, a law banning racial discrimination. Implicit, I think, in the principal consideration supporting a coercive legislative strategy are the values of compassion and community.

96. B. Mitchell, note 82, at 135.

97. Do the six considerations call for a legal system like Italy's? See "On the Record," Time, Mar. 18, 1985: "Newton Minow, 59, attorney and former FCC chairman, on his study of the legal systems of four European countries: 'In Germany, under the law everything is prohibited except that which is permitted. In France, under the law everything is permitted except that which is prohibited. In the Soviet Union, everything is prohibited, including that which [under the law] is permitted. And in Italy, . . . everything is permitted, especially that which [under the law] is prohibited.' "

98. See MacCormick, "A Moralistic Case for A-Moralistic Law?," 20 Valparaiso U. L. Rev. 1, 14 (1985): "Toleration, unlike indifference, does not shirk criticism of rival views; merely, it insists on the difference between a critique, however trenchant, of a rival view and a suppression of that view."

99. See note 2 and accompanying text.

100. J. Murray, note 1, at 9.

101. Id.

102. See chapter 3, section I.

103. See Rorty, note 51.

104. Recall that John Locke based his argument for religious tolerance on his (Protestant) theology. See M. Walzer, note 93, at 52–56.

105. See Rabkin, "Disestablished Religion in America," 86 Public Interest 124, 124–25 (Winter 1987):

> Religion may help people to develop the self-restraint required by a constitutional democracy. "Our Constitution was designed for a religious and moral people and for no other" was how John Adams put it. But such formulations, gratifying as they may be to the American self-image, tend to obscure an important fact about "religion": Not every kind of religion is compatible with a liberal constitutional order. The stability of our constitutional order owes much to the fact that the dominant religious tendencies through most of American history have, in fact, been quite compatible with liberal democracy and religious tolerance and have not, by and large, forced people to make wrenching choices between religious and civil obligations.

Chapter 5

1. Oscar Arnulfo Romero, Archbishop of San Salvador, in words spoken one day before his assassination. Quoted in Buckley, "Letter from El Salvador," New Yorker, June 22, 1981, at 41, 64.

2. Anyone interested in the problem of conscientious disobedience should

consult K. Greenawalt, Conflicts of Law and Morality (1987). (This chapter was completed before publication of Greenawalt's exhaustive and definitive analysis.)

3. See chapter 4, notes 99–105 and accompanying text.

4. See, for example, Boyle, "A Catholic Perspective on Morality and the Law," 1 J. L. & Rel. 227, 228–30 (1983); "Human Law and the Conscience of Believers: A Statement of the American Lutheran Church," 2 J. L. & Rel. 177 (1984) (reprinted as Appendix B to this book).

5. That is, one ought always to obey all laws to the extent one can. ("'Ought' implies 'can'.") If two laws contradict each other, then one can't obey them both.

6. See Perry, "Some Notes On Absolutism, Consequentialism, and Incommensurability," 80 Northwestern U. L. Rev. 967 (1985).

7. I'm assuming that "no law" means "no determinate law". An indeterminate law—one to the effect, for example, "Never intentionally kill a human being unless morally justified in doing so"—is a law of a different color.

8. In rejecting Claim 3, as I do below, I'm assuming that there is at least one imaginable situation in which one knows that some disobedient act will not be detected or punished.

9. Greenawalt, "Promise, Benefit, and Need: Ties that Bind Us to the Law," 18 Georgia L. Rev. 727, 763 (1984).

10. For a fuller discussion, see Smith, "Is There a Prima Facie Obligation to Obey the Law?," 82 Yale L. J. 950, 954–60 (1973); Mackie, "Obligations to Obey the Law," 67 Virginia L. Rev. 143, 146–47 (1981); D. Lyons, Ethics and the Rule of Law 212 (1984); Greenawalt, note 9, at 754–64. In his essay Greenawalt claims that the hypothetical "tennis court scheme" he sets forth "shows that the duty of fair play can be violated though no one is actually harmed." Id. at 763. Not so: Although, as Greenawalt says, the Monroes' use of the tennis court "would not add to the cost of upkeep", id. at 755, their failure to pay fifty cents for each hour of use has the effect of not diminishing the per capita cost of upkeep.

11. Mackie, note 10, at 145. See Soper, "The Obligation to Obey the Law," unpublished ms. at 19 (1983): "Some people, judges perhaps, may expressly promise to obey the law. But most do not." (Soper's unpublished paper is adapted from a chapter in his book *A Theory of Law* [1984]. A revised version of Professor Soper's paper has recently appeared in R. Gavison, ed., Issues in Contemporary Legal Philosophy [1987].)

12. D. Lyons, note 10, at 211.

13. Smith, note 10, at 960. See Simmons, "Consent, Free Choice, and Democratic Government," 18 Georgia L. Rev. 791, 804 (1984):

> Continued residence cannot be taken to ground political obligation unless residence is understood as one possible choice in a mandatory decision process. Residence must

be seen as the result of a morally significant choice. It is not enough that the choice is available; it must be understood by each man to be a required choice, with mere residence not constituting, for instance, a way of declining to choose. And in Hume's view, of course, these conditions are not satisfied in our actual political lives. Residence requires no "act of the mind" as consent does.

See also id. at 809–18; R. Dworkin, Law's Empire 192–93 (1986).

14. Id. at 800. See Mackie, note 10, at 145: "[P]olitical participation as such carries no general implication of . . . [agreement to obey the law], since it is well known that people often make use of a political system that they do not endorse."

15. Mackie, note 10, at 145. See J. Raz, The Authority of Law 237–38 (1979).

16. Mackie, note 10, at 145.

17. See J. Raz, note 15, at 241:

[T]he duty to support and uphold good institutions, the existence of which need not be denied, is insufficient to establish an obligation to obey. It extends directly to those laws setting up and maintaining the just institutions (e.g. those guaranteeing the functioning of a democratic government in the society). It provides reasons to obey other laws only to the extent that by doing so one sets a good example or that by failing to so act one sets a bad example: That is, only to the extent that obedience to these other laws strenghthens or prevents weakening the laws on which the democratic character of the government is founded.

See id. at 241–42 (criticizing Peter Singer's argument in *Democracy and Disobedience* [1973]); Mackie, note 10, at 147–49.

18. G. J. A. Warnock, The Object of Morality 41 (1971).

19. Soper, note 11, at 3 (emphasis deleted and added).

20. This is how Kent Greenawalt has fairly characterized Soper's argument. Greenawalt, "Comment [on Soper, note 11]," in R. Gavison, ed., Issues in Contemporary Legal Philosophy 156, 157 (1987). See Soper, note 11, at 40–47.

21. Id. at 61. See P. Soper, A Theory of Law 80 (1984): "[The] features [that should be sufficient to establish political obligation] are (1) the fact that the enterprise of law in general—including the particular system, defective though it may be, that confronts an individual—is better than no law at all; and (2) a good faith effort by those in charge to govern in the interests of the entire community, including the dissenting individual." For an effective critique of Soper's argument, see Book Note, 98 Harvard L. Rev. 1346 (1985).

22. See id. at 1346 & n. 3:

Soper's . . . legal theory restricts the definition of "law" to only those state directives that citizens are obligated to obey. . . . Soper uses the word "law" in two ways. In presenting his political theory, he uses "law" to refer to all orders issued by the state. This pre-analytic sense of law is the relevant sense of the word in the question "is there an obligation to obey the law?" The second sense, the post-analytic, refers only to those orders of the state that citizens are morally obligated to obey, as distinct from those orders to which no obligation attaches. The merit of the second sense is the subject of Soper's legal theory.

23. See note 22.

24. Greenawalt, note 20, at 10, 14. Cf. Book Note, note 21, at 1350:

. . . Soper never convincingly establishes why respect engenders political obligation. He suggests that the connection between respect and political obligation is the product of a general moral theory but never articulates that theory. Without the theory, the reader is forced to intuit a connection between respect and obligation that is not intuitively obvious. Respect for a person does not necessarily confer authority on that person: because we respect someone who is concerned about us, we are likely to listen carefully to what she has to say; but that does not mean that we should feel even the weakest obligation to obey. Perhaps Soper could devise a convincing moral theory in which respect for the ruler would imply political obligation, but he has not done so.

25. A final argument perhaps worth mentioning proceeds in terms of the normative commitment to showing gratitude to persons, including lawmakers, who act in our interests and thereby confer benefits on us. This argument seems close to Soper's. Like all the other arguments we've examined, it doesn't work. See Smith, note 10, at 4–5; J. Harris, Legal Philosophies 211–12 (1980).

26. D. Lyons, note 10, at 211.

27. Cf. Greenawalt, note 20, at 30: "[M]uch more promising than the search for an elusive general obligation [to obey the law] is close attention to the scope and power of those sources of obligation that have been identified."

28. See notes 39 & 40 and accompanying text.

29. Cf. Greenawalt, "The Natural Duty to Obey the Law," 84 Michigan L. Rev. 1, 37 (1985): "[O]ne might understand the duty as an obligation to comply with laws of the state directed toward what are the state's proper ends—including security, liberty, justice, and welfare—when one's compliance and that of one's fellows may reasonably be thought necessary to success. Such a duty . . . would not reach evidently foolish laws or applications of laws when general noncompliance plainly will not interfere with the state's legitimate ends."

30. I follow Kent Greenawalt in that my "analysis proceeds on the assumption that the law to be obeyed or disobeyed is plainly valid within the system of positive law, that is, is legally valid in the sense that any law passed by the Parliament in Great Britain is valid. . . . [T]he core issues of disobedience are most clearly seen when an apparently illegal act cannot be defended as consistent with underlying positive law." Greenawalt, "A Contextual Approach to Disobedience," 70 Columbia L. Rev. 48, 50 (1970). See J. Rawls, A Theory of Justice 365 (1971).

31. I refer, of course, to the Socrates of the *Apology*, who in his speech before the assembly insists that he will continue to perform his sacred work of teaching philosophy no matter what the state says or threatens. Cf. D'Amato,

"Obligation to Obey the Law: A Study of the Death of Socrates," 49 Southern California L. Rev. 1079 (1976).

32. These words appear in par. 1 of the Introduction.

33. See chapter 4, note 100 and accompanying text.

34. R. Dworkin, Taking Rights Seriously 186 (rev. ed. 1978).

35. Hook, "Social Protest and Civil Disobedience," in Civil Disobedience and Violence 53, 56 (J. Murphy ed. 1971).

36. See R. Dworkin, A Matter of Principle 105 (1985):

> . . . Americans accept that civil disobedience has a legitimate if informal place in the po-litical culture of their community. Few Americans now either deplore or regret the civil rights and antiwar movements of the 1960s. People in the center as well as on the left of politics give the most famous occasions of civil disobedience a good press, at least in retrospect. They concede that these acts did engage the collective moral sense of the community. Civil disobedience is no longer a frightening idea in the United States.

37. Cf. Greenawalt, note 30, at 57–58:

> . . . I do not, as do most writers, start with a definition of civil disobedience. The breadth of the definition often seems to depend on the writer's approval or disapproval of particular kinds of violations of law, the unspoken implication being that illegal acts that cannot be defined as "civil" disobedience are impossible, or at least more diffi-cult, to justify. To qualify as "civil disobedience" under a relatively narrow and fairly common definition, an illegal act must be committed to change a law or policy, and better society; the act must be nonviolent and public; and the actor must intend to accept punishment. . . . No one, I think, would dispute that acts meeting . . . [these] criteria are acts of civil disobedience. What are generally thought of as typical acts of civil disobedience, those of the civil rights movement in this country and those led by Gandhi in India, do conform to them. One could, of course, try to decide which of the elements of those acts are essential for acts to qualify as "civil" disobedience and which are not. My concern, however, is with whether disobedient acts are morally justified, and I do not think the line between morally justified and morally unjustified illegal acts is coincident with the line between acts that are considered to be civil disobedience, however defined, and those that are not. Thus, I do not attempt a definition of my own.

For an elaborate definition of "civil disobedience", see Bay, "Civil Disobe-dience: Prerequisite for Democracy in Mass Society," in Civil Disobedience and Violence 73, 76–79 (J. Murphy ed. 1971).

38. See Appendix B, §§II.B.3 & II.B.8.

39. Hook, note 35, at 57.

40. See id. at 59:

> [W]here civil disobedience is undertaken, there must be some rhyme and reason in the time, place, and targets selected. If one is convinced, as I am not, that the Board of Education of New York City is remiss in its policy of desegregation, what is the point of dumping garbage on bridges to produce traffic jams that seriously discomfort com-muters who have not the remotest connection with educational policies in New York?

Such action can only obstruct the progress of desegregation in the communities of Long Island. Gandhi, who inspired the civil disobedience movement in the twentieth century, was a better tactician than many who invoke his name but ignore his teachings. When he organized his campaign of civil disobedience against the Salt Tax, he marched with his followers to the sea to make salt. He did not hold up food trains or tie up traffic.

Finally, there is such a thing as historical timing. Democrats who resort to civil disobedience must ask themselves whether the cumulative consequences of their action may in the existing climate of opinion undermine the peace and order on which the effective exercise of other human rights depends. This is a cost which one may be willing to pay but which must be taken into the reckoning.

41. J. Raz, note 15, at 267.

42. Greenawalt, note 30, at 66, 69. See Bay, note 37, at 89.

43. Greenawalt, note 30, at 66. For historical counterexamples to the argument that violence is invariably counterproductive, see H. Zinn, Disobedience and Democracy 50–52 (1968).

44. Appendix B, §II.B.7.b.

45. See, for example, Hook, note 35, at 58; R. Dworkin, note 34, at 108–9. See also the Statement of the American Lutheran Church, Appendix B, §II.B.7.a. Compare J. Rawls, note 30, at 373.

46. J. Raz, note 15, at 269, 275 (sentences rearranged).

47. A. Fortas, Concerning Dissent and Civil Disobedience 63 (1968).

48. See H. Zinn, note 43, at 32–33. See id. at 35:

[Fortas'] position leads to another oddity. What if some terrible grievance is represented not by an evil law, but by a failure on the part of the government to enforce a good law? Civil disobedience is okay in the first instance, wrong in the second, although the same grievance is involved. For instance, if the government were to pass a law ordering Negroes to register for eventual execution, they could violate that law in protest. But what if Negroes were being systematically killed by state officials, and the President refused to invoke Section 333, Title 10 of the U.S. Code, which gives him the power to use armed force against state officials to protect citizens? There is no law Negroes can violate that represents this inaction; they may therefore be forced to violate the law against "sitting in" at the White House, in order to pressure the President to stop the murder of black people.

49. Greenawalt, note 30, at 68. See id. at 68–69:

The breadth of the example provided to others who believe laws are unjust or would like to change policies is, one could argue, also relevant to the Fortas distinction. Thus, if action is directed only at the unjust law itself, the example has a self-limiting scope: the principle extends only to acts of disobedience directed at other laws believed by the actors to be unjust. (For reasons suggested earlier, however, the limiting principles in the mind of the actor are unlikely to be fully perceived by others, and disobedience directed to an unjust law may give others some encouragement to engage in broader forms of disobedience not directed at the law to which the actors object.) Since the only limiting principles for disobedience of laws not the focus of complaint are highly flexible weighings of probable social harm against probable social good, the misapplication of these principles by others is quite likely. Therefore, it may be that an act of disobedience will create a more dangerous precedent if not directed at an unjust law. But that hardly leads to the absolute principle laid down by Fortas. It would only lead one to conclude that some stronger grounds are necessary to justify such an act than one directed at an unjust law itself. If, contrary to the assumption of the immediately preceding analysis, one accepts Professor Zinn's view that people are too prone to obey the law, then the fact that a particular kind of disobedience would serve as a broad example might even be counted in its favor.

50. Appendix B, §II.B.6 (emphasis added). See J. Rawls, note 30, at 364–65. Cf. Statement of the American Lutheran Church, §II.B.3:

> *Protest of Military Preparations.* This area is not as well defined as the issues of conscripting people or their money into military service. It is not a matter of opposing a law which demands an action in violation of one's conscience (direct civil disobedience). It is rather a matter of acting to protest a process or system one believes will have evil results, such as military preparations or production of weapons of mass destruction. This indirect civil disobedience seeks to awaken public awareness and to have impact on public policy, through nonviolent, public, symbolic, illegal actions, taken only after regretfully concluding that less drastic actions have proved insufficient.

Cf. Warnock, note 18, at 42:

> [There is] the obvious possibility that, though some rule may be perfectly appropriate in general, and I may clearly be one of those to whom the rule applies, I may think that in this case I need not, or even should not, comply with it—that is, that a breach of the rule is on this occasion "justified", or even required. I have in mind here not the case already mentioned, where one may think that noncompliance with some rule sometimes does not matter, but the case—or rather, the enormous range of cases—where compliance with a rule may be thought to be outweighed by quite other considerations. There is perhaps nothing to be said quite in general about this, except that, as of course is very obvious, the applicability in a certain situation of some rule, however "good" the rule may be, is not in general a conclusive reason for acting, in that situation, as the rule requires; thus, it is always possible that one might ask, without questioning either the rule or its applicability: should I—or, why should I—comply with it here and now? The question here is, not whether there is any reason to act as the rule requires, but whether there may not be—as there might be—better reason, here and now, for acting otherwise.

51. See J. Rawls, note 30, at 366–67.

52. Greenawalt, note 30, at 69.

53. See, for example, Statement of the American Lutheran Church, Appendix B, §II.B.7(e); Hook, note 35, at 59:

> [T]hose who resort to civil disobedience are duty bound to accept the legal sanctions and punishments imposed by the laws. Attempts to evade and escape them not only involve a *betrayal of the community*, but erode the moral foundations of civil disobedience itself. Socrates' argument in the *Crito* is valid only on democratic premises. The

rationale of the protesters is the hope that the pain and hurt and indignity they volun-
tarily accept will stir their fellow citizens to compassion, open their minds to second
thoughts, and move them to undertake the necessary healing action. When, however,
we observe the heroics of defiance being followed by the dialectics of legal evasion, we
question the sincerity of the action.

See also J. Rawls, note 30, at 366.

54. See Greenawalt, note 30, at 69–70:

At first glance the distinction between avoiding and accepting punishment may
appear to coincide with that between surreptitious and open violation of law. But the
perpetrator of a carefully planned surreptitious murder may, as soon as he is successful,
give himself up and willingly subject himself to legal penalties. Conversely, open
violations are not always accompanied by even the first element of this willingness. A
rioter may count on not being apprehended; those engaging in unlawful strikes may
rely on the pressure they can bring to bear to avoid penalties; students who take over
buildings may similarly attempt to gain amnesty as a condition of settlement.

55. Id. at 70.

56. See Olsen, "Socrates on Legal Obligation: Legitimation Theory and
Civil Disobedience," 18 Georgia L. Rev. 929, 960 (1984).

To reject the position that the disobedient person must always accept the legal
consequences is not to deny that in a particular situation a willingness to accept
the consequences might be essential to justifying disobedient activity. For a
thoughtful discussion, see Greenawalt, note 30, at 70–71.

57. Sidney Hook's arguments—for example, see note 53—presuppose the
context of a democratic society like the United States, as do Fortas' arguments
(see note 47 and accompanying text) and the Statement of the American
Lutheran Church (see note 53). See also J. Rawls, note 30, at 363.

58. See Greenawalt, note 29, at 72–73.

59. Id. at 72. See id. at 73–75 (raising questions about how close to, or
how far from, the democratic model is the United States).

60. Id. at 72.

61. See Shane, "Equal Protection, Free Speech, and Selective Prosecution
of Draft Nonregistrants," 72 Iowa L. Rev. 359, 387 (1987) (quoting Martin
Luther King, Jr.,'s "Letter from Birmingham City Jail" 4 [1963], reprinted in
Aspen Institute Executive Seminar Readings [D. Barron ed.]):

Nonviolent direct action seeks to . . . establish such creative tension that a community
that has constantly refused to negotiate is forced to confront the issue. It seeks so to
dramatize the issue that it can no longer be ignored. . . . Just as Socrates felt that it was
necessary to create a tension in the mind so that individuals could rise from the bondage
of myths and half-truths to the unfettered realm of creative analysis and objective
appraisal, we must see the need of nonviolent gadflies to create the kind of tension in
society that will help men to rise from the dark depths of prejudice and racism to the
majestic heights of understanding and brotherhood.

Cf. J. Rawls, note 30, at 387:

A community's sense of justice is more likely to be revealed in the fact that the majority cannot bring itself to take the steps necessary to suppress the minority and to punish acts of civil disobedience as the law allows. Ruthless tactics that might be contemplated in other societies are not entertained as real alternatives. Thus the sense of justice affects, in ways we are often unaware of, our interpretation of political life, our perception of the possible courses of action, our will to resist the justified protests of others, and so on. In spite of its superior power, the majority may abandon its position and acquiesce in the proposals of the dissenters; its desire to give justice weakens its capacity to defend its unjust advantages. The sentiment of justice will be seen as a more vital political force once the subtle forms in which it exerts its influence are recognized, and in particular its role in rendering certain social positions indefensible.

Chapter 6

1. Several years ago I wrote a book in constitutional theory: M. Perry, The Constitution, the Courts, and Human Rights (1982). In this chapter, in the course of revising and refining the vision of constitutional adjudication I presented there, I do two things I was not yet ready to do in that earlier work. First, I offer an account of the role of the constitutional text in constitutional adjudication. (No one can deny that the text plays a fundamental role, though it is a matter of controversy precisely what that role is or should be.) Second, I specify the sense in which constitutional adjudication is a species of political-moral reasoning.

2. I'm concerned here with adjudication of constitutional issues, not adjudication of common-law or of statutory issues. The questions of to what extent and in what ways my discussion of constitutional adjudication is relevant to common-law or to statutory adjudication I leave to those more familiar than I with the latter sorts of adjudication.

3. Brennan, "The Constitution of the United States: Contemporary Ratification," 27 South Texas L. Rev. 433, 434 (1986).

4. See Linde, "*E Pluribus*—Constitutional Theory and State Courts," 18 Georgia L. Rev. 165 (1984); Symposium, "The Emergence of State Constitutional Law," 63 Texas L. Rev. 959 (1985). See also Pear, "State Courts Move Beyond U.S. Bench in Rights Rulings," New York Times, May 4, 1986, at p. 1; Marcotte, "Federalism and the Rise of State Courts, American Bar Ass'n J., Apr. 1987, at 60.

5. See J. Choper, Judicial Review and the National Political Process, chs. 4–6 (1980); M. Perry, note 1, chapter 2. See also note 84 and accompanying text.

6. See M. Perry, note 1, at 4 & 186 n. 17.

7. Paul Brest introduced the terminology. See Brest, "The Misconceived Quest for the Original Understanding," 60 Boston University L. Rev. 204 (1980). I don't claim to be using the terminology precisely the way Brest does.

Although it is serviceable for present purposes, I'm not comfortable with the "originalist/nonoriginalist" terminology. There is a sense in which we are all originalists: We all believe that constitutional adjudication should be grounded in the origin—the text that is *at* our origin and, indeed, *is* our origin. But there is a sense, too, in which none of us is an originalist: As Gadamer, for one, has taught us, we cannot travel back to the origin, no matter how hard we try, and we deceive ourselves if we think we can. "It is enough to say that we understand in a different way, if we understand at all." H.-G. Gadamer, Truth and Method 264 (Eng. tr. 1975). I'll happily abandon the originalist/nonoriginalist terminology as soon as someone suggests a terminology that better captures the fundamental difference animating contemporary constitutional-theoretical debate.

8. For examples of originalist theory, see R. Berger, Government By Judiciary: The Transformation of the Fourteenth Amendment (1977); R. Berger, Death Penalties: The Supreme Court's Obstacle Course (1982); Bork, "Neutral Principles and Some First Amendment Problems," 47 Indiana L. J. 1 (1971); Bork, "The Impossibility of Finding Welfare Rights in the Constitution," 1979 Washington U. L. Q. 695; R. Bork, Tradition and Morality in Constitutional Law (1984); Bork, "Styles in Constitutional Theory," 26 South Texas L. J. 383 (1985); Bork, "The Constitution, Original Intent, and Economic Rights," 23 San Diego L. Rev. 823 (1986); Meese, "The Battle for the Constitution," 35 Pol'y Rev. 32 (1985); Meese, "Toward a Jurisprudence of Original Intention," 2 Benchmark 1 (1986); Meese, "The Supreme Court of the United States: Bulwark of a Limited Constitution," 27 South Texas L. Rev. 455 (1986); Monaghan, "Our Perfect Constitution," 56 New York University L. Rev. 353 (1981); Rehnquist, "The Notion of a Living Constitution," 54 Texas L. Rev. 693 (1976).

9. Cf. Twining, "Talk About Realism," 60 New York University L. Rev. 329, 337 (1985): "It should be a working precept of all jurisprudential criticism and polemics that before launching an attack one should first identify worthy opponents and attribute to them what one considers to be the least vulnerable interpretation of their views that the relevant texts will sustain. Intellectual debate is impoverished when one attacks caricatures; soft targets generally only suit weapons with correspondingly low firepower."

10. For an example of a different nonoriginalist theory—a "process-based" one—see J. Ely, Democracy and Distrust (1980). For a critique of Ely's theory, see M. Perry, note 1, at 76–90. See also Brest, "The Substance of Process," 42 Ohio State L. J. 131 (1981); R. Dworkin, A Matter of Principle 57–69 (1985); L. Tribe, Constitutional Choices 9–20 (1985); Tushnet, "Darkness on the Edge of Town: The Contributions of John Hart Ely to Constitutional Theory," 89 Yale L. J. 1037 (1980).

11. The "only if", as distinct from "if and only if", indicates that the condition is necessary, but not sufficient. A theory of proper judicial role—

whether originalist or nonoriginalist—can contain a theory of judicial self-limitation according to which a judge should sometimes decline to invalidate governmental action *even if* the beliefs on which the judge is to rely, according to the theory of judicial role, entail the conclusion that government has done something it may not do or failed to do something it must do. For my effort to sketch a theory of judicial self-limitation, in the context of a nonoriginalist theory of judicial role, see section VIII.

A theory of judicial role can also include a theory of precedent. Although a theory of precedent complicates any theory of judicial role, including an originalist theory, I'm presenting originalism without much attention to the matter of precedent. For one originalist theorist's view of the role of precedent in constitutional adjudication, see Monaghan, "Taking Supreme Court Opinions Seriously," 39 Maryland L. Rev. 1 (1979). Cf. M. Perry, note 1, at 67–68 (commenting on Raoul Berger's seemingly inconsistent views with respect to the role of precedent). For one nonoriginalist Justice's view, see Brennan, note 3, at 444:

> [T]he unique interpretive role of the Supreme Court with respect to the Constitution demands some flexibility with respect to the call of *stare decisis.* Because we are the last word on the meaning of the Constitution, our views must be subject to revision over time, or the Constitution falls captive, again, to the anachronistic views of long-gone generations. . . . [W]hen a Justice perceives an interpretation of the text to have departed so far from its essential meaning, that Justice is bound, by a larger constitutional duty to the community, to expose the departure and point toward a different path.

12. See section IV.

13. Rakove, "Original Meanings of the Constitution: The Historian's Contribution," unpublished ms. at 11–12 (1985). Rakove's footnote reads as follows: "Madison to Nicholas P. Trist, December 1831; speech of April 6, 1796; and Madison to J.G. Jackson, December 27, 1821; and see Madison to Thomas Ritchie, September 15, 1821; in Farrand, *Records,* III, 516–518, 374, 447–450." Id. at 12 n. 9. See Powell, "The Original Understanding of Original Intent," 98 Harvard L. Rev. 885, 887–88 (1985).

14. See U.S. Const., Art. V:

> The Congress, whenever two thirds of both Houses shall deem it necessary, shall propose Amendments to this Constitution, or, on the Application of the Legislatures of two thirds of the several States, shall call a Convention for proposing Amendments, which, in either Case, shall be valid to all Intents and Purposes, as Part of this Constitution, when ratified by the Legislatures of three fourths of the several States, or by Conventions in three fourths thereof, as the one or the other Mode of Ratification may be proposed by the Congress.

15. Monaghan, note 8, at 375 n. 130.

16. See R. Dworkin, note 10, at 41.

17. See id.

18. See note 23.

19. See Bennett, "The Mission of Moral Reasoning in Constitutional Law," 58 Southern California L. Rev. 647 (1985).

20. But cf. note 11.

21. See R. Dworkin, Law's Empire 323 (1986).

22. See R. Epstein, Takings: Private Property and the Power of Eminent Domain 28 (1985). See also R. Dworkin, note 21, at 323–24.

23. Thus, Dworkin misconceives the originalist (or, as Dworkin says, "historicist") position when he writes:

> A historicist . . . has settled on a style of constitutional adjudication that limits eligible interpretations of the Constitution to principles that express the historical intentions of the Framers. He will not accept that the equal protection clause outlaws state-imposed segregation unless he is satisfied that those he counts as framers thought it did. Or, somewhat weaker, unless he is satisfied that the framers did not think the clause did not outlaw segregation.

Id. at 360. For a more accurate statement by Dworkin of the (sophisticated) originalist position, see Dworkin, "The Bork Nomination," New York Rev., Aug. 13, 1987, at 3.

24. For one example, see Bennett, note 19. For a citation to others, see Schauer, "An Essay on Constitutional Language," 29 UCLA L. Rev. 797, 805 n. 27 (1982).

25. Bork, "Original Intent and the Constitution," Humanities, Feb. 1986, at 22, 26. See Bork, "The Constitution, Original Intent, and Economic Rights," 23 San Diego L. Rev. 823, 826–27 (1986) (arguing that his originalist theory does not require "judges . . . invariably [to] decide cases the way the Framers would if they were here today", but does require them to "confine themselves to the principles the Framers put into the Constitution"). Cf. Powell, "Rules for Originalists," 73 Virginia L. Rev. 659 (1987). For a critique of the misconception of originalism Judge Bork properly distances himself from, see Perry, Appendix to "The Authority of Text, Tradition, and Reason: A Theory of Constitutional 'Interpretation,'" 58 Southern California L. Rev. 597 (1985).

26. Dworkin, note 23, at 6.

Recall the discussion, in chapter 2, section III, of "the priority of the particular". Notice how, in the passage accompanying this note, Dworkin implicitly gives the place of privilege in the justificatory hierarchy not to the particular, but to the general, that is, to "principles or values more general still". For a critical comment on this tendency of "liberal" political philosophy to privilege the general, see chapter 2, notes 56–60 and accompanying text.

27. Bork, Foreword to G. McDowell, The Constitution and Contemporary Constitutional Theory at xi (1985).

28. Id. Dworkin's suggestion that the framers of the equal protection clause

of the fourteenth amendment should be understood to have constitutionalized "the principle that government should not act out of prejudice against any group of citizens"—a principle, Dworkin emphasizes, that applies to everyone, women and homosexuals included, and not just to racial minorities (Dworkin, note 23, at 8)—seems to me less sensitive to available historical materials and more likely an instance of wishful thinking than Bork's suggestion that the framers of the equal protection clause should be understood to have constitutionalized a principle against discrimination or prejudice on the basis of race. The *reductio ad absurdum* of Dworkin's way of (man)handling history is the suggestion that the framers of the equal protection clause—and of the first amendment and indeed of all constitutional provisions pertaining to human rights—should be understood to have constitutionalized the principle that "government should not act unjustly". For a concise but powerful criticism of this aspect of Dworkin's theory of interpretation, see Alexander, "Striking Back at the Empire: A Brief Survey of Problems in Dworkin's Theory of Law" (1987) (due to be appear in a forthcoming issue of *Law and Philosophy*). For an elegant statement of what motivates judges and commentators to engage in what Henry Monaghan has called "excessive generalization" of the ratifiers' beliefs (see note 38 and accompanying text), see Sandalow, "Constitutional Interpretation," 79 Michigan L. Rev. 1033, 1038–39, 1046, 1060 (1981).

29. H.-G. Gadamer, note 7, at 264.

30. Cf. Monaghan, note 8, at 377:

Although the difficulties of establishing original intent are formidable, they are by no means intractable. Significant difficulty in historical reconstruction is not present with respect to some constitutional provisions, and with respect to others it is at least partially ameliorated by the extensive body of precedent accumulated over the years by courts nearer in time to the origins of the relevant provision. Most importantly, the language of the Constitution itself remains. Whatever the difficulties, the language itself constitutes the best evidence of original intention. In any event, the core question remains: do the basic postulates of the constitutional order require that the court undertake the task of ascertaining original intent, *as best it can?*

31. Epstein, "Bork-bashing: Easy, Unedifying and Irresponsible," Chicago Tribune, Aug. 31, 1987, § 1, p. 9.

32. For a more elaborate catalogue of various possible bases for originalism, see Simon, "The Authority of the Framers of the Constitution: Can Originalist Interpretation Be Justified?," 73 California L. Rev. 1482 (1985).

33. See Powell, note 13. But see Kay, "Adherence to the Original Intentions in Constitutional Adjudication: Three Objections and Responses," unpublished ms. (1986).

34. Federal judges are electorally unaccountable in that they enjoy lifetime tenure in office. See M. Perry, note 1, at 9 & 170 n. 5.

35. See Easterbrook, "Legal Interpretation and the Power of the Judiciary," 7 Harvard J. L. & Pub. Pol'y 87, 97 (1984).

36. J. Ely, note 10, at 41.

37. Raoul Berger, for one, seems to be a constitutional originalist, though he doesn't distinguish constitutional originalism from democratic originalism and sometimes makes democratic-originalist claims. See R. Berger, Government By Judiciary: The Transformation of the Fourteenth Amendment (1977).

38. Monaghan, "The Constitution Goes to Harvard," 13 Harvard Civ. Rts.-Civ. Lib. L. Rev. 117, 127–28 (1978). See M. Perry, note 1, at 70–75; Kay, note 33; note 28.

39. See Bennett, "Objectivity in Constitutional Law," 132 U. Pennsylvania L. Rev. 445, 456 (1984).

40. See id.

41. Rakove, note 13, at 4. See Kay, note 33. Jeff Powell's "Rules for Originalists," note 25, seems to affirm Rakove's point, at least implicitly, in the course of insisting that there are better and worse ways for originalists to do their job.

42. Tushnet, "Following the Rules Laid Down: A Critique of Interpretivism and Neutral Principles," 96 Harvard L. Rev. 781, 804 (1983).

43. See note 28; Schauer, "Easy Cases," 58 Southern California L. Rev. 399, 437 n. 99 (1985). See also Kay, note 33.

44. Cf. Taylor, "Meese v. Brennan: Who's Right About the Constitution?," New Republic, Jan. 6 & 13, 1986, at 17, 18:

> When the Constitution's language and history provide little or no guidance on a subject, why can't . . . [the Court] leave the law-making to legislatures? Those who work so hard to prove that the Constitution cannot supply the values for governance of modern society seem to think it follows that judges must do it, with a little help from their friends in academia. But their argument rebounds against the legitimacy of judicial review itself. [Judge Robert] Bork poses a question to which they have no good answer: "If the Constitution is not law—law that, with the usual areas of ambiguity around the edges, nevertheless tolerably tells judges what to do and what not to do—. . . what authorizes judges to set at naught the majority judgment of the American people?"

45. Sanford Levinson tried to make a challenge of the first sort. See Levinson, "Law as Literature," 60 Texas L. Rev. 373 (1982). But he failed. See Graff, " 'Keep Off the Grass,' 'Drop Dead,' and Other Indeterminacies: A Response to Sanford Levison," 60 Texas L. Rev. 405 (1982). For another example of such a challenge, see Tushnet, note 42. Tushnet's basic claim is that an originalist approach to constitutional adjudication is available only on the basis of assumptions that contradict originalism's "liberal" (in the sense of "individualist") political-philosophical premises. Originalism, however, is much more plausibly understood to rest on Burkean conservative premises. Tushnet's suggestion that a conservative (or other communitarian) political philosophy has no need for a constitutional theory, and that, therefore, originalist constitutional theory cannot plausibly be understood to rest on Burkean

conservative premises, is simply wrong. In a political community with a constitution and a judiciary charged with enforcing it, even a conservative (or other communitarian) political phisolophy must offer a constitutional theory in the sense of a theory of what role the judicary should play in enforcing the Constitution.

Robert Bennett has argued that originalism faces "the conceptual difficulty of defining what in an individual's mental framework counts as a relevant part of intention." Bennett, note 39, at 456. For a critical comment on Bennett's point, see Perry, note 25, at 601.

After I'd finished drafting this chapter, I had the opportunity to read Richard Kay's unpublished essay, "Adherence to the Original Intentions in Constitutional Adjudication: Three Objections and Responses," note 33. In my view, Kay's essay elaborates cogent responses to several of the prevalent academic criticisms of originalism. For another recent essay defending originalism, see Maltz, "The Failure of Attacks on Constitutional Originalism," 4 Constitutional Commentary 43 (1987).

46. See Tribe, "Contrasting Constitutional Visions: Of Real and Unreal Differences," 22 Harvard Civ. Rts.-Civ. Lib. L. Rev. 95, 95 (1987): "[F]or all the ballyhoo, overall approaches differ far less than might appear. Both Judge Robert Bork and I, for example, . . . start with the recognition that any 'legitimate theory of constitutional adjudication begins from the premise that the Constitution is law,' and that it must therefore provide genuine constraints on choice." (Quoting Bork, note 27, at 22.) Cf. Dworkin, note 23, at 10: "[Judge Bork's] writings show no developed political philosophy . . . beyond frequent appeals to the truism that elected legislators, not judges, ought to make law when the Constitution is silent. No one disputes that, of course; people disagree only about when the Constitution *is* silent."

47. Tom Grey has written that "[c]onvention specifies that judges are bound always and only to interpret existing law in the decision of cases." Grey, "Advice for 'Judge and Company,'" New York Rev., Mar. 12, 1987, at 32, 33. However, that convention or axiom coexists with deep disagreement as to what it means to "interpret" existing law—that is, as to what interpretive moves judges should make. Grey's article (a review of Ronald Dworkin's *Law's Empire* [1986]) comments on, and this chapter participates in, that disagreement. Indeed, one might reasonably conclude that the convention is indeterminate to the point of vacuity, since such different interpretive moves or strategies are consistent with it.

48. Cf. Verhey, "The Use of Scripture in Ethics," in The Use of Scripture in Moral Theology 213, 213 (C. Curran & R. McCormick eds. 1984):

> To say scripture is an authority is not yet to say what moves are authorized in an argument "from the Bible to the modern world." . . . The question of *whether* (and, within believing communities, the agreement that) scripture is a source and canon for

moral discernment and judgment must be distinguished from the question *what* this source provides or *how* this canon functions as a norm. In spite of agreement that scripture is an authority, there are wide disagreements about the authorization for moving from scripture to moral claims.

49. The inquiries *why* the constitutional text *is* authoritative and *whether* it *should be* are interesting but not pressing. To say that in American political-legal culture the constitutional text is axiomatically authoritative in constitutional adjudication is to say that, in American political-legal culture, the proposition "the constitutional text is authoritative in constitutional adjudication" is not in question. It bears mention that there is no reason to think that the "why" and "whether" questions have single answers. As the discussion in the text makes clear, the constitutional text—"the Constitution"—does not mean the same thing to everyone; in that sense, the constitutional text is not the same thing for everyone. To explain why the Constitution, understood one way, is authoritative for some people is not to explain why the Constitution, understood another way, is authoritative for other people. To argue that the Constitution, understood one way, should be authoritative is not to argue that the Constitution, understood another way, should be authoritative.

The extent to which "interpretation" of legal materials—particularly cases, statutes, and constitutional provisions—is or is not a constrained activity has been a concern of several recent articles. See R. Dworkin, note 10, at 146–77; Fish, "Working on the Chain Gang: Interpretation in Law and Literature," 60 Texas L. Rev. 551 (1982); Fish, "Wrong Again," 62 Texas L. Rev. 299 (1983); Fish, "Fish v. Fiss," 36 Stanford L. Rev. 1325 (1984); Fiss, "Objectivity and Interpretation," 34 Stanford L. Rev. 739 (1982); Fiss, "Conventionalism," 58 Southern California L. Rev. 177 (1985). I want, therefore, to make a few brief comments about the matter of interpretation and constraint.

Imagine that you see in front of you something you conclude to be a small rubber ball. To see something as a small rubber ball is to interpret that something. To interpret something as one thing rather than another is to make a constrained choice. No choice is unconstrained. Every choice, indeed every act, is determined—or so, with John Mackie, I believe (see J. Mackie, Ethics: Inventing Right and Wrong 203–26 [1977])—even if the crucial determinants are sometimes "internal" (e.g., one's values) rather than "external" (e.g., a gun held to one's head) and even if it is difficult or impossible to specify all the determinants. See Taylor, "Determinism," in 2 Encyclopedia of Philosophy 359 (P. Edwards ed. 1967). (To interpret something as one thing rather than another might be to make a mistaken choice, too. To interpret something as a parachute rather than as a small rubber ball might be to make a fatal mistake.) Imagine that you see in front of you something you conclude to be the text of the Constitution. (For present purposes, the distinction between the original text, on display at the National Archives, and copies of the original is not important.) To see something as the constitutional text is to interpret that something, and that interpretive choice is not unconstrained (or necessarily correct).

Assume that the small rubber ball is one with which we can play any of several games. To say "let's play ball" (without otherwise indicating which game) is to suggest not that a particular game be played, but that some game be played—presumably one that can be played with the ball. As contemporary debates in constitutional theory illustrate, the constitutional text is one with which we—in particular, the Court—can play more than one game. See Nickel, "Uneasiness About Easy Cases," 58 Southern California L. Rev. 477 (1985). To say "let's interpret the Constitution" (without otherwise indicating which interpretive game) is to suggest not that a particular game be played, but that some game be played—presumably one that can be played with the constitutional text. See D. Kelsey, The Uses of Scripture in Recent Theology 151 (1975):

> [A] theologian's remark "Scripture is authority for theology," said in reference to biblical texts taken as scripture, is like a boy's exclamation "Come on, let's play ball," said in reference to a ball not evidently designed for use in any one ball-game in particular. It no more makes a claim about the texts than the boy's exclamation does about his ball; rather, it self-involvingly invokes an activity. In saying "Scripture is authority for theology," the theologian commits himself to participate in one or another of a family of activities called "doing Christian theology." Moreover, he thereby acknowledges and commits himself to observing a rule governing the practice of theology (on certain understanding of "theology"): In defending theological proposals, scripture shall be used in such a way that helps authorize the proposals.

The ball does not itself constrain us to play a particular game. Of course, our decision to play with the ball does rule out some games—those that require a different sort of ball and those that aren't played with a ball. One can't do just anything with a ball—use it as a parachute, for example. Similarly, the constitutional text does not itself constrain us to play a particular game, although, of course, our decision to interpret *the Constitution* does rule out some interpretive games—those that require a different sort of text. It is difficult to see how the Steppenwolf Theatre Company could interpret the Constitution in the sense it has interpreted Sam Shepard's *True West*.

Our decision to play a particular game with the ball, and our decision to play a particular interpretive game with the Constitution, are constrained and constraining: constrained just as every choice is constrained, and constraining us to engage in the practices constitutive of the game in question.

What is the originalist game—the interpretive game that, according to originalism, the Court should play with the constitutional text? And what is the nonoriginalist game I would have the Court play? (I hope it's clear I'm not using "game" in a demeaning or pejorative sense.)

50. To interpret any text—or "text analogue", such as a human practice—

is more fully to disclose its meaning, to make the text less strange or alien, to make it more familiar. This is true even of the interpretation of a dramatic or a musical work by an artist—actor or musician—performing the work. Is it true, too, of the interpretation of observational data by a natural scientist trying to "make sense of" the data? That is, is *all* understanding, even natural-scientific understanding, "interpretive" or "hermeneutic"? Is there something to be gained in maintaining a distinction between "scientific" understanding, on the one hand, and "interpretive" or "hermeneutic" understanding, on the other? "Every time we act, deliberate, judge, understand, or even experience, we are interpreting. To understand at all is to interpret." D. Tracy, Plurality and Ambiguity 9 (1987). In particular, Tracy argues—correctly, in my view—that even scientific understanding, despite now discredited positivist pretensions to the contrary, is interpretive or hermeneutic. See id. at 31–33 & 47–48.

51. To ask about a constitutional provision—or about any text—"What does it say?" is not the same as asking "What does it mean?" Yet, if what the provision says is sufficiently familiar in the relevant community—if what it says is not alien or strange—then we shouldn't be surprised if the question "What does it mean?" elicits the impatient reply "It means what it says!" Imagine a law setting a speed limit of 55 miles per hour. What seems strange is not the law but the question "What does it mean?" It means what it says. We might say that its preliminary meaning is simply what it says. Of course, this is not to deny that to say of the speed-limit law "It means what it says!" is to interpret the law/text, just to emphasize that the question "What does it mean?" becomes real, explicit, when what the text says is at least a little alien or strange in the relevant community. Imagine a law forbidding a state to deny the equal protection of the laws to any person within its jurisdiction. To say that the law means what it says is not very helpful, if in the relevant community what it says is more than a little alien or strange; thus, the need to interpret the law, to render it more familiar and hence usable, is obvious (in a way that the need to interpret the speed-limit law is not obvious).

52. The point can be made in terms of "understanding" as well as "meaning": "A text can be understood in multiple ways. (Indeed, one understanding of a text can contradict another understanding of the text.) Understanding is always understanding by someone, and the way in which a text is understood by one person is not necessarily the way in which it is understood by another. But is it the case that a text can be understood in more than one way by a person?" And so on.

53. For an instructive study of "constitutional aspiration", see G. Jacobsohn, The Supreme Court and the Decline of Constitutional Aspiration (1986).

54. See note 115 and accompanying text.

55. Whether a particular constitutional provision is aspirational can be controversial, of course. To say—whether from the perspective of a participant

observer in the political-legal culture, which is the judge's perspective, or from the perspective of the outsider, like de Tocqueville—that a particular provision does not signify a fundamental aspiration of the American political tradition is to say either, or both, of two things: (1) that the provision does not signify an aspiration; (2) that the aspiration the provision signifies is not now, if it ever was, a fundamental aspiration of the tradition.

56. Article VI of the Constitution provides in relevant part that "all . . . judicial Officers, both of the United States and of the several States, shall be bound by Oath or Affirmation, to support this Constitution."

57. I'm not claiming that a judge ought never to violate her oath, anymore than I would claim that a person ought never to break a promise. See Perry, "Some Notes on Absolutism, Consequentialism, and Incommensurability," 80 Northwestern U. L. Rev. 967 (1985). I do suppose, however, that a judge has a strong presumptive obligation not to violate her oath. Cf. R. Dworkin, note 21, at 218–19 .

58. Cf. id. at 358:

> Justices who are called liberal and those who are called conservative agree about which words make up the Constitution as a matter of preinterpretive text. The disagree about what the Constitution is as a matter of postinterpretive law, about what standards it deploys for testing official acts. Each kind of justice tries to enfore the Constitution as law, according to his interpretive judgment of what is is, and each kind thinks the other is subverting the true Constitution. So it is useless as well as unfair to classify justices according to the degree of their fidelity to their oath.

59. It can be difficult, even impossible, to distinguish an originalist position with respect to some issue from a nonoriginalist one. An opinion written by an originalist judge who thinks that the relevant original belief is so general as to constitute, in effect, an aspiration or "principle"—call it aspiration X—is likely to look much the same, perhaps even identical to, an opinion written by a nonoriginalist judge who thinks that the constitutional provision at issue signifies, means, X. Indeed, it would not be surprising for the latter judge to join the opinion of the former judge, or vice versa. Query, however, whether *disinterested* historical inquiry will disclose many, or any, original beliefs so general as to constitute aspirations or principles. (Moreover, a *democratic* originalist must face the possibility that reliance on an original belief so general—indeterminate—as to constitute an aspiration or principle is inconsistent with originalism's democratic premises. See note 36 and accompanying text.) If not, then originalism allied to good history will yield opinions that look significantly different from the opinions yielded by nonoriginalism. Of course, a judge who professes to be an originalist but who has an instinct to do justice in a particular case or sort of case may succumb to the temptation to ally her originalism to bad history—that is, she may succumb to the temptation to credit bad history—so as to have the latitude to do justice. See notes 27 & 28 and accompanying text.

60. See Hoy, "The Interpretation of Sacred Texts: Methodological Issues," 9 Proceedings of the General Education Seminar (Columbia University) 26, 28 (1980–81): "At this point . . . I borrow from Professor John Gager the distinction between texts that are religious and those that are sacred. To identify a text as religious is simply to say something about its subject matter—God, revelation, apocalypse, etc. A text is sacred only if it is also adoped by a tradition as the object of, or for purposes of, the institution of worship. Being institutionalized as an integral part of tradition is crucial. The sacredness of a text is thus determined not only by its genesis and original context but, perhaps more markedly, by its *Wirkungsgeschichte* (the history of its effects and interpretations)." One might be tempted to say that a text is sacred for a community *because* it is authoritative in a special way for the community. Building on Hoy, however, it seems to be the case that to say that a text is sacred for a community is just to say, in part at least, that the text is authoritative in a special way for the community. See also Proudfoot, "Comment [on Hoy, this note]," 9 Proceedings of the General Education Seminar (Columbia University) 33, 33 (1980–81): "[T]o understand a text as a sacred text is not particularly a textual issue, or at least it need not be restricted to that. One really needs to look at the functions a text has served in a community, its liturgical context, for instance. To study the Bible as scripture might be less a study of the history of ancient Israel and of the early Christian community than a history of the interpretation of the Bible, its liturgical uses and its use within the Jewish or Christian community."

61. A. MacIntyre, After Virtue 207 (1981). Cf. S. Hauerwas, A Community of Character 63 (1981): "Scripture is not meant to be a problem solver. It rather describes the process whereby the community we call the church is initiated by certain texts into . . . the 'vivid and lively pattern of argument and controversy' characteristic of biblical traditions."

62. Cf. D. Tracy, The Analogical Imagination 105 (1981): "The text can become a classic for the reader only if the reader is willing to allow that present horizon to be vexed, provoked, challenged by the claim to attention of the text itself."

63. See id. at 154.

64. See id.

65. See id. at 112, 122–24. See also P. Ricouer, Hermeneutics and the Human Sciences 143–44 (J. Thompson ed. 1981):

> Ultimately, what I appropriate is a proposed world ["the world of the work"], which is not *behind* the text, as a hidden intention would be, but *in front of* it, as that which the work unfolds, discovers, reveals. Henceforth, to understand is *to understand oneself in front of the text*. It is not a question of imposing upon the text our finite capacity of understanding, but of exposing ourselves to the text and receiving from it an enlarged self, which would be the proposed existence corresponding in the most suitable way to the world proposed. So understanding is quite different from a constitution of which the subject would possess the key. In this respect, it would be far more correct to say that the self is constituted by the "matter" of the text.

66. See D. Tracy, note 62, at 99.
67. See note 115 and accompanying text.
68. See D. Tracy, note 62, at 100.
69. Id. at 105. See D. Tracy, note 50, at 68–69.
70. See R. Ruether, Sexism and God Talk (1983); Ruether, "Of One Humanity," Sojourners, Jan. 1984, at 17. See also S. Heschel, ed., On Being A Jewish Feminist: A Reader (1983).
71. See D. Tracy, note 62, at 99–100.
72. See A. Bickel, The Least Dangerous Branch 103 (1982): "No answer is what the wrong question begets, for the excellent reason that the Constitution was not framed to be a catalogue of answers to such questions. And, indeed, how could it have been, consistently with the intention to write a charter for the governance of generations to come—for a period, it was hoped, stretching far into the future?"
73. Cf. H.-G. Gadamer, note 7, at 264, 270:

> Because what we are now concerned with is not individuality and what it thinks, but the objective truth of what is said, a text is not understood as a mere expression of life, but taken seriously in its claim to truth. . . .

> The text that is understood historically is forced to abandon its claim that it is uttering something true. We think we understand when we see the past from a historical standpoint, ie place ourselves in the historical situation and seek to reconstruct the historical horizon. In fact, however, we have given up the claim to find, in the past, any truth valid and intelligible for ourselves. Thus this acknowledgement of the otherness of the other, which makes him the object of objective knowledge, involves the fundamental suspension of his claim to truth.

See note 91; note 97 and accompanying text.
74. A. Bickel, note 72, at 31. See Saphire, "Making Noninterpretivism Respectable: Michael J. Perry's Contributions to Constitutional Theory," 81 Michigan L. Rev. 782, 794–95 (1983).
75. Brennan, note 3, at 1.
76. Poe v. Ullman, 367 U.S. 497, 540 (1961) (Harlan, J., dissenting).
77. Id.
78. Brennan, note 3, at 3–4.
79. P. Ricouer, note 65, at 37. See id. at 139–40.
80. See Fiss, "Objectivity and Interpretation," 34 Stanford L. Rev. 739, 743 (1982): "It should also be understood that generality and comprehensiveness do not discourage interpretation but are the very qualities that usually provoke it. Interpretation is a process of generating meaning, and one important (and very common) way of both understanding and expressing the meaning of a text is to render it specific and concrete." See also K. Burke, A Grammar of Motives 366–67 (1969).
81. Brennan, note 3, at 1.
82. For example, section 5 of article I of the Constitution provides, in part,

that "a majority of each [House] shall constitute a Quorum to do business; but a smaller Number may adjourn from day to day."

83. See note 5 and accompanying text.

84. See Wechsler, "The Political Safeguards of Federalism: The Role of the States in the Composition and Selection of the National Government," 54 Columbia L. Rev. 543 (1954); J. Choper, note 5, chs. 4–6; M. Perry, note 1, chapter 2. But cf. Van Alstyne, "The Second Death of Federalism," 83 Michigan L. Rev. 1709 (1985).

85. Cf. Curtis, "A Better Theory of Legal Interpretation," 3 Vanderbilt L. Rev. 407, 425 (1950): "Words in legal documents . . . are simply delegations to others of authority to give them meaning by applying them to particular things or occasions. The only meaning of the word meaning . . . is an application to the particular. And the more imprecise the words are, the greater is the delegation, simply because then they can be applied or not to more particulars. This is the only important feature of words in legal draftmanship or interpretation."

86. Cf. Schauer, note 24, at 829.

87. For an important argument that the case for an originalist approach to the interpretation of recently ratified amendments is often, though not necessarily, compelling, but that the strength of the case "decreases with the passage of time" and, moreover, that that case does not support an originalist approach to constitutional interpretation generally, see Simon, note 32, at 1535–38. Simon's argument, which I find attractive, is not inconsistent with anything I'm arguing in this chapter.

88. Brennan, note 3, at 7.

89. See, for example, R. Dworkin, note 10, at 146–77.

90. See S. Fish, Is There a Text in this Class?: The Authority of Interpretive Communities (1980). For an instructive comment on Fish's views, see T. Eagleton, Literary Theory 86–88 (1983).

91. See H.-G. Gadamer, note 7, at 275:

> In both legal and theological hermeneutics there is the essential tension between the text set down—of the law or of the proclamation—on the one hand and, on the other, the sense arrived at by its application in the particular moment of interpretation, either in judgment or in preaching. A law is not there to be understood historically, but to be made concretely valid through being interpreted. Similarly, a religious proclamation is not there to be understood as a merely historical document, but to be taken in a way which exercises its saving effect. This includes the fact that the text, whether law or gospel, if it is to be understood properly, ie according to the claim it makes, must be understood at every moment, in every particular situation, in a new and different way. Understanding here is always application.

See also note 73; note 97 and accompanying text.

92. See Grey, "The Constitution as Scripture," 37 Stanford L. Rev. 1 (1985).

93. See note 102.

94. Steven Knapp and Walter Benn Michaels have argued that "to interpret a text" means "to search for what the author(s) of the text intended it to mean". See Knapp & Michaels, "Against Theory," 8 Critical Inquiry 723 (1982); Knapp & Michaels, "A Reply to Our Critics," 9 Critical Inquiry 790 (1983). See also Michaels, "Is There a Politics of Interpretation?," 9 Critical Inquiry 248 (1982); Michaels, "Response to Perry and Simon," 58 Southern California L. Rev. 673 (1985). As a matter of ordinary language, however, "interpretation" has no single, canonical meaning. Like many other words, "interpretation" is used in more than one way, it has more than one sense. The "search for what the author intended" meaning is one sense, but not the only one, as, for example, theological-hermeneutical discussion of sacred texts makes clear. As Ronald Dworkin has observed, a literary "intentionalist cannot suppose that all his critics and those he criticizes mean, when they say 'interpretation,' the discovery of the author's intention. Nor can he think that his claims accurately describe what every member of the critical fraternity actually does under the title 'interpretation.' If that were so, then his strictures and polemics would be unnecessary." R. Dworkin, note 10, at 155. Cf. Hoy, "Interpreting the Law: Hermeneutical and Poststructuralist Perspectives," 58 Southern California L. Rev. 135, 137 (1985): "[H]ermeneutics cannot decide in advance what interpretation is and then tell interpreters what they are doing, whatever the interpreters may think they are doing."

95. Pelikan is the author of the five-volume *The Christian Tradition: A History of the Development of Doctrine*, published by the University of Chicago Press.

96. J. Pelikan, The Vindication of Tradition 58 (1984). Pelikan adds: "The analogy first came to my attention when I heard my late colleague from the Yale Law School, Alexander Bickel, speaking about 'development of doctrine'—a technical term that was, I am quite sure, invented in its modern sense by John Henry Newman in his *Essay on Development*." Id. See id. at 58–60. In addition to Pelikan, see Bruns, "Law as Hermeneutics: A Response to Ronald Dworkin," in The Politics of Interpretation 315, 319–20 (W. Mitchell ed. 1982); Barry, "Courts and Constitution," Times Lit. Supp., Oct. 25, 1985, at 1195, 1196.

97. Bruns, note 96, at 317. See id. at 317–20. See also notes 73 & 91. I don't mean to deny that an originalist understanding of constitutional adjudication can be hermeneutical. See notes 29–31 and accompanying text.

98. For a discussion of how Congress has given meaning to the equal protection clause, and the President to the treaty clause, see Munzer & Nickel, "Does the Constitution Mean What It Always Meant?," 77 Columbia L. Rev. 1029, 1047–50 (1977).

99. See M. Perry, note 1, at 100–1.

100. Why would anyone want each and every legislator to exert moral leadership with respect to each and every issue? J. William Fulbright was a U.S. senator from Arkansas during the 1950s and 1960s. Senator Fulbright surely wanted to see the various pieces of civil rights legislation proposed during that period enacted into law. Had he supported such legislation, however, much less sponsored it, in all likelihood he would have lost his senate seat and therefore not been around to play the invaluable role he did with respect to foreign policy. Assuming that his vote was not crucial to the passage of the civil rights legislation, and given the sort of person who would probably have defeated him, did Senator Fulbright act improperly in failing to exert moral leadership with respect to—or even support—the civil rights legislation? (I don't recall Fulbright playing a significant role in opposition to such legislation. I suspect he studiously avoided playing any such role.)

101. See J. Choper, note 5, at 67–68. For a confirmatory case study, see Barnum, "Decision Making in a Constitutional Democracy: Policy Formation in the Skokie Free Speech Controversy," 44 J. Politics 480 (1982).

102. See note 112 and accompanying text; Grey, note 92, at 24 (making fun of the notion of judges-as-prophets). *Of course* judges are not priests or prophets. They are merely human beings, and lawyers at that. To say that they are not prophets, however, is *not* to deny that at their best judges can play a prophetic role. See Fiss, "Foreword: The Forms of Justice," 93 Harvard L. Rev. 1, 12 (1979): "Judges are most assuredly people. They are lawyers, but in terms of personal characteristics they are no different from successful businessmen or politicians. Their capacity to make a special contribution to our social life derives not from any personal traits or knowledge, but from the definition of the office in which they find themselves and through which they exercise power."

On the relation between prophecy, in the biblical sense, and internal social critique, see M. Walzer, Interpretation and Social Criticism, ch. 3 (1987).

103. A. Bickel, note 72, at 26.

104. See chapter 2, section III.

105. P. Bator, P. Mishkin, D. Shapiro & H. Wechsler, Hart & Wechsler's The Federal Courts and the Federal System 82 (2d ed. 1973).

106. Later in this chapter I explain why the nonoriginalist judicial role should be a *restrained* one—restrained both as to what issues the Court chooses to deal with, at least in more than a cursory, formal way, and also as to how it chooses to resolve them.

107. Brennan, note 3, at 7.

108. See Thornburgh v. American College of Obstetricians and Gynecologists, 54 LW 4618, 4629 (White, J., joined by Rehnquist, J., dissenting) (1986): "The Constitution is not a deed setting forth the precise metes and bounds of its subject matter; rather, it is a document announcing fundamental principles in

value-laden terms that leave ample scope for the exercise of normative judgment by those charged with interpreting and applying it."

For a comment on the "integrating" function of indeterminacy, see notes 132 & 136 and accompanying text.

109. Cf. J. Fuchs, Christian Ethics in a Secular Arena 43 (1984):

[I]t is . . . [the judge's] duty to establish the concrete law . . . on the basis both of his knowledge of the current law . . ., on the one side, and of the legal . . . particularity of the concrete human situation, on the other. Must the subject in search of the correct solution simply classify the concrete situation (as if no subjectivity were involved) as a case covered by the existing . . . law? . . . Hermeneutics says that a subject seeking understanding, without giving up subjectivity, must understand both the general declaration [law] in itself, and the concrete human situation in itself, and both in their true mutual relationship; only so is it possible to establish a meaningful relationship between the already existing declaration and the given human situation.

110. Cf. Dahl, "Decision-Making in a Democracy: The Supreme Court as a National Policy-Maker," 6 J. Pub. L. 279, 293 (1957): "[T]he Supreme Court is inevitably a part of the dominant national alliance."

111. See M. Perry, note 1, chapter 4; note 102 and accompanying text.

112. See note 102. Cf. M. Weber, Law in Economy and Society 320 (1954):

Prophets are the only ones who have taken a really consciously "creative" attitude toward existing law; only through them has new law been consciously created. For the rest, as must be stressed again and again, even those jurists who, from the objective point of view, have been the most creative ones, have always, and not only in modern times, regarded themselves to be but the mouthpiece of norms already existing, though, perhaps, only latently, and to be their interpreters or appliers rather than their creators.

My thanks to Tom Grey for this quote.

113. See Greenawalt, "Discretion and Judicial Decision: The Elusive Quest for the Fetters that Bind Judges," 75 Columbia L. Rev. 359, 397–98 (1975): "[L]ower court decisions are subject to review, and the higher the court the more judges must approve the decision. . . . [O]n many issues a judge might assume that if his values are far wide of community standards, he will be outvoted by his brethren or reversed by a higher court."

114. See Saphire, "Judicial Review in the Name of the Constitution," 8 U. Dayton L. Rev. 745, 790–91 (1983). Cf. J. Pelikan, note 96, at 54: "We do well to recognize as infantile an attitude toward our parents that regards them as all-wise or all-powerful and that is blind to their human foibles. But we must recognize no less that it is adolescent, once we have discovered those foibles, to deny our parents the respect and reverence that is their due for having been, under God, the means through which has come the only life we have."

115. Hoy, note 94, at 147. See also Hoy, note 60, at 28: "[Hermeneutics insists that] the reception of a text in a tradition is also constitutive of its

meaning and, therefore, of its interpretation. The claim is that this history of the text's effects (*Wirkungsgeschichte*) itself conditions, or qualifies, the interpretation and so must be taken into account in the interpretation."

116. A. Bickel, note 72, at 236.

117. See note 138 and accompanying text.

118. A. Bickel, note 72, at 39. See Saphire, note 74, at 792.

119. Brest, "Interpretation and Interest," 34 Stanford L. Rev. 765, 773 (1982).

120. I take the modern period of American constitutional law to be the period since *Brown* v. *Board of Education*, 347 U.S. 483 (1954). See C. Black, Decision According to Law 33 (1981) (describing *Brown* as "the decision that opened our era of judicial activity").

121. See chapter 3, section I.

122. F. Dallmayr, Polis and Praxis: Exercises in Contemporary Political Theory 211 (1984) (quoting Oakeshott, "The Voice of Poetry in the Conversation of Mankind," in M. Oakeshott, Rationalism and Politics 206–10 [1962]).

123. B. Barber, Strong Democracy: Participatory Politics for a New Age 173–74 (1984).

124. Elster, "Sour Grapes—Utilitarianism and the Genesis of Wants," in A. Sen & B. Williams, eds., Utilitarianism and Beyond 219, 237 (1981).

125. F. Dallmayr, note 122, at 211 (quoting Oakeshott, "The Voice of Poetry in the Conversation of Mankind," in M. Oakeshott, Rationalism and Politics 206–10 [1962]).

The distinction between deliberative politics and manipulative politics is largely the same as Cass Sunstein's distinction between the "republican" and the "pluralist" conceptions of politics. Sunstein's elaboration of the distinction is illuminating. See Sunstein, "Interest Groups in American Public Law," 38 Stanford L. Rev. 29, 31–35 (1985).

126. F. Dallmayr, note 122, at 196 (quoting H.-G. Gadamer, note 7, at 321, 323–25). See chapter 2, note 117 (quoting Benjamin Barber).

127. R. Beiner, Political Judgment 152 (1983). See Singer, "The Player and the Cards: Nihilism and Legal Theory," 94 Yale L. J. 1, 64–65 (1984).

128. At the beginning of this section of the chapter, I noted the tenuousness of any separation of politics from law, in particular from adjudication. It is not surprising, therefore, that a distinction between two visions of law tracks the distinction between the two visions of politics. In manipulative politics law is regarded principally "as the instrument by which 'we' effectuate 'our policies' and get what 'we' want." White, "Law as Rhetoric, Rhetoric as Law: The Arts of Cultural and Communal Life," 52 U. Chicago L. Rev. 684, 689 (1985). In deliberative politics, by contrast, law is more richly understood: "It is the true nature of law to constitute a 'we' and to establish a conversation by which that 'we' can determine what our 'wants' are and should be. Our motives and values

are not, in this view, to be taken as exogenous to the system (as they are taken to be exogenous to an economic system) but are in fact its subject. The law should take as its most central question what kind of community we should be, with what values, motives, and aims. It is a process by which we make ourselves." Id.

129. See chapter 3, section I.

130. R. Beiner, note 127, at 142–43. See id. at 129–52; MacIntyre, "Moral Arguments and Social Contexts," 80 J. Phil. 590 (1983).

131. See Solum, "On the Indeterminacy Crisis: Critiquing Critical Dogma," 54 U. Chicago L. Rev. 462, 473 (1987).

132. MacIntyre, "Does Applied Ethics Rest on a Mistake?," 67 Monist 498, 510 (1984). See H. McCloskey & A. Brill, Dimensions of Tolerance: What Americans Believe About Civil Liberties 48–58 (1983); Prothro & Grigg, "Fundamental Principles of Democracy: Bases of Agreement and Disagreement," 22 J. Pol. 276 (1960). My thanks to Erwin Chemerinsky for the McCloskey/Brill and Prothro/Grigg citations.

133. See S. Hauerwas, note 61, at 60: "A community is a group of persons who share a history and whose common set of interpretations about that history provides the basis for common actions. These interpretations may be quite diverse and controversial even within the community, but are sufficient to provide individual members with the sense that they are more alike than unalike."

134. R. Beiner, note 127, at 141. Cf. id. at 138–44.

135. See R. Dworkin, note 21, at 72–73.

136. D. Levine, The Flight From Ambiguity 42–43 (1985). See id. at 41–43.

137. R. Beiner, note 127, at 138–39.

138. Id. at 138.

139. Id.

140. D. Tracy, note 50, at 19 (quoting B. Lonergan, Method in Theology 231 [1972]). See id. at 26. Cf. id at 26–27: "[A]rguments on ideal-speech conditions are transcendental in the sense that they claim to provide the necessary conditions for a contingent situation, namely, the implicit claim to validity in all communication. This is a claim to contingent, not absolute, necessity. By contrast, transcendental arguments on the existence or nonexistence of the universe or God are strictly transcendental arguments. Communication could be other than it is, but in fact is not. We reason discursively. We inquire. We converse. We argue. We are human beings, not angels."

141. Id. at 142–43, 146 (passages rearranged).

142. White, note 128, at 684.

143. Cf. id. at 697: "[T]he United States Constitution can be regarded as a rhetorical text; one that established a set of speakers, roles, topics, and occasions for speech. So understood, many of its ambiguities and uncertainties

become more comprehensible, for we can see the text as attempting to establish a conversation of a certain kind and its ambiguities as ways of at once defining and leaving open the topics for conversation."

144. Brennan, note 3, at 3.

145. The courts can play that role well or poorly. Remember that I'm elaborating an idealized vision of constitutional adjudication—of what constitutional adjudication, at its best, can be. For an important argument that the rhetorical and analytic devices often deployed by the Court in the modern period of American constitutional law serve—and indeed might be intended to serve— to distance the Court from, rather than engage it in a truly collaborative, discursive enterprise with, the polity, see Nagel, "The Formulaic Constitution," 84 Michigan L. Rev. 165 (1985). See also Nagel, "Rationalism in Constitutional Law," 4 Constitutional Commentary 9 (1987). Even if one is persuaded by Nagel's argument, which is certainly impressive, it doesn't follow that the problem is irremediable.

In conversation my colleague Carol Rose has pressed the question whether judicial language isn't inevitably of a kind—whether it isn't inevitably talk about "rights" or "entitlements"—that shuts down, rather than opens up, discourse with the other branches and agencies of government (as, according to Carol, rights- or entitlement-talk tends to do). Her question is important and must be addressed. I'm inclined to think that courts can learn to talk in ways that open up rather than shut down such discourse, but that's a topic, and a challenge, for another day.

146. See chapter 1, section IV.

147. See note 33 and accompanying text. See also Perry, note 25, at 583–87 & 587–88 n. 107.

148. See Easterbrook, note 35. See also Easterbrook, "Method, Result, and Authority: A Reply," 98 Harvard L. Rev. 622, 629 (1985).

149. What if the decision is justified on both originalist and nonoriginalist grounds? Or if it is justified on nonoriginalist grounds but is justifiable on originalist ones?

150. At the Third Midwest Constitutional Law Teachers Conference, held at the Northwestern University School of Law, Oct. 18–19, 1985.

151. 410 U.S. 113 (1973).

152. See Easterbrook, note 35, at 97–98:

[T]he transmutation of the nature of judicial review from a power to guide one's *own* conduct by one's best lights into a power to dictate how others shall behave has some implications for the quality of the justifications that a judge must supply. A judge cannot expect obedience just because he announces what he thinks a wise and just result would be. He must always be prepared to give an answer to the question: Why should other people pay attention? Why is the opinion any more binding than a law review article?

The reason the judge gives about why obedience must be forthcoming usually will take the form of asserting that someone other than the judge really decided the issue. The question was settled by the Framers of the Constitution or the drafters of statute. There is a rule, binding on judges and others alike, to which all must conform. The judge's authority to compel obedience comes from that external decision, not from the judge's own desires.

This is not to say that judges must "find" rather than "make" law. Finding versus making is a false dichotomy. All interpretation involves meaning added by the reader. The point of this discussion is that the more meaning added by the judge, the less powerful the judge's claim to obedience.

When a judge issues a ruling under the authorization of a statute or proviso entitling a judge to invent a common law on the subject (antitrust law and the "reasonableness" clause of the fourth amendment are again good examples), the court's claim to obedience is as strong as if the judge were enforcing a "plain" statute. The judge can point to an external rule calling for obedience—in one case to the "plain" rule, in the other to whatever rule the judge makes up using the grant of law-making authority. The judge's claim is at least as good as Congress's claim to be obeyed in executing power under the Commerce Clause.

When a court's claim to obedience is based on its belief that it is doing what legislators would have wanted had they thought about the subject, it is on much weaker ground. If the legislators did not settle some issue and did not authorize courts to fill in the blanks, why should anyone listen to what the judge says? The judge's claim to obedience is little better than that of a professor of law. Similarly, a judge who claims power to make decisions based on a . . . [nonoriginalist] approach to the Constitution is bold indeed. Why should people obey if all the judge can say in support of the decision is that (a) the decision lays down a good rule, and (b) the decision . . . is not starkly contrary to an actual decision of the Framers?

153. A variation on this argument allows that if government is morally obligated to obey nonoriginalist decisions—or at least some nonoriginalist decisions—the reason or reasons have nothing to do with any supposed moral authority of the decisions themselves. Nonoriginalist decisions lack the moral authority of originalist ones (according to the argument). The reasons have to do, rather, with the need for political stability, etc. Government is obligated to obey originalist decisions for those reasons, too. However, the *principal* reason government is obligated to obey originalist decisions—the fact that the decisions possess the moral authority of original beliefs—has no force with respect to nonoriginalist ones.

154. See Simon, note 32, at 1499–1500:

The Constitution was adopted by propertied, white males who had no strong incentives to attend to the concerns and interests of the impoverished, the nonwhites, or nonmales who were alive then, much less those of us alive today who hold conceptions of our interests and selves very different from the ones held by those in the original clique. These are hardly small or overly theoretical problems for a theory that proposes to bind us to the clique's intent for reasons that, if coherent, must ultimately be rooted in our own autonomy and welfare. They are thus fatal criticisms for any contract-based claim for originalism as the exclusive method of constitutional interpretation.

See also Wald, "The Role of Morality in Judging: A Woman Judge's Perspective," 4 L. & Inequality 3 (1986).

155. For a fuller discussion, see M. Perry, note 1, at 9.

156. R. McCloskey, The American Supreme Court 12–13 (1960). Cf. A Bickel, note 72, at 27–28: "Democratic government under law—the slogan pulls in two opposed directions, but that does not keep it from being applicable to an operative polity. If it carries the elements of explosion, it doesn't contain a critical mass of them. Yet, if the critical mass is not to be reached, there must be an accommodation, a degree of concord between the diverging elements."

157. See M. Perry, note 1, at 9, 137–38.

158. Brennan, note 3, at 6.

159. Rakove, note 13, at 22, 23. See B. Barber, note 123, at 17: "[I]n reality the American political system places many curbs on majoritarianism, and it is probably correct to say with Louis Hartz that 'what must be accounted one of the tamest, mildest, and most unimaginative majorities in modern political history has been bound down by a set of restrictions that betray fanatical terror.' "

160. Alexander, "Painting Without Numbers: Noninterpretive Judicial Review," 8 U. Dayton L. Rev. 447, 458 (1983).

161. Brennan, note 3, at 16.

162. Of course, many persons who for one reason or another are unhappy with some or many aspects of modern constitutional doctrine will contest this judgment, which I can't defend here. An adequate defense would require a detailed analysis and evaluation of the modern Court's constitutional workproduct in a variety of doctrinal areas. That's work enough for several scholars. For present purposes I must be content to acknowledge my "on balance" judgment about that workproduct as a contestable element in my defense of nonoriginalist judicial review.

163. See Rehnquist, note 8, at 701–4.

164. See Commager, "Judicial Review and Democracy," 19 Va. Q. 417 (1943).

165. See Commager, "Keynote Statement," in The Future of Our Liberties: Perspectives on the Bill of Rights 3 (S. Halpern ed. 1982).

166. Cover, Book Review, New Republic, Jan. 14, 1978, at 26, 28.

167. A. Bickel, note 72, at 16. See Cover, note 166, at 27.

168. The *locus classicus* of this argument is Dahl, note 110. See Barnum, "The Supreme Court and Public Opinion: Judicial Decision Making in the Post-New Deal Period," 47 J. Pol. 652 (1985) (arguing "that the Court's decisions overturning legislation and/or protecting minority rights were often supported

by the distribution or at least the trend of nationwide public opinion and that when such support was lacking, the Court seemed reluctant to act", and that, therefore, "the policymaking activism of the post-New Deal Supreme Court was perhaps more consistent with majoritarian principles than is sometimes supposed").

169. Recall, too, the point I made in section V of this chapter: It is unrealistic to expect federal judges to be radicals, either of the left or of the right, but even if some were (or are) radicals, their beliefs cannot, in the nature of things, be determinative in constitutional adjudication, since no belief can be determinative in constitutional adjudication unless it is widely shared among the several judges who must agree before a constitutional ruling can be established.

170. See M. Perry, note 1, 111–14. For an interesting study of the dialectical interplay between judiciary and legislature in the state of New York between 1870 and 1920, see Lindgren, "Beyond Cases: Reconsidering Judicial Review," 1983 Wisconsin L. Rev. 583.

171. See Hammer v. Dagenhart, 247 U.S. 251 (1918), *overruled*, United States v. Darby, 312 U.S. 100 (1941).

172. See Kay, "Preconstitutional Rules," 42 Ohio St. L. J. 187, 201–2.

173. See Alexander, note 160, at 459–60, 462.

174. Id. at 462–63. By now I hope it's clear that my justification for a nonoriginalist/hermeneutical judicial role of the sort presented in this chapter is no less "secular" than Tom Grey's. See Grey, note 92, at 20.

175. See Komesar, "Taking Institutions Seriously: Introduction to a Strategy for Constitutional Analysis," 51 U. Chicago L. Rev. 366 (1984).

176. 410 U.S. 113 (1973).

177. See San Antonio Independent School District v. Rodriguez, 411 U.S. 1, 56–59 (1973).

178. 349 U.S. 294 (1955) (Brown II).

179. Moeller, "Alexander M. Bickel: Toward a Theory of Politics," 47 J. Pol. 113, 135 (1985). Cf. Taylor, "Key 1954 Bias Case: A Drama Backstage," New York Times, Mar. 22, 1987, p. 1; Editorial, "With All Deliberate Impropriety," New York Times, Mar. 24, 1987, p. 26. See Moeller, this note, at 133–35; Kronman, "Alexander Bickel's Philsophy of Prudence," 94 Yale L. J. 1567, 1584–90. See also M. Perry, note 1, at 124. Ronald Dworkin has recently remarked that "[a]n actual [Supreme Court] justice must sometimes adjust what he believes to be right as a matter of principle, and therefore as a matter of law, in order to gain the votes of other justices and to make their joint decision sufficiently acceptable to the community so that it can continue to act in the spirit of a community of principle at the constitutional level." R. Dworkin, note 21, at 380–81.

180. Cf. Gunther, "Some Reflections on the Judicial Role: Distinctions, Roots, and Prospects," 1979 Washington U. L. Q. 817, 824:

I am naive enough to think that a court should not shrink from announcing legitimate constitutional rights simply because of remedial concerns. . . . *Worcester v. Georgia*, [31 U.S. (6. Pet.) 536,] the 1832 case that rejected Georgia's claim of authority over Indian lands and held the imprisonment of two missionaries illegal[,] . . . engendered the most threatening consequences for the Marshall Court, and yet I think it represents the Marshall Court's noblest hour. When *Worcester* was decided in the spring of 1832, John Marshall and his colleagues knew that Andrew Jackson's White House and a large part of Congress were ready to defy the Court. When John Marshall and his fellow Justices voted in that case, they genuinely believed that the decision might well mean the end of effective Court authority. But they also thought that it was legally right, and so it was. And, unflinchingly, they did their duty: they decided the case on the merits, even though the immediate prospects were anxiety-producing, even though the survival of the Court was truly at stake. I think theirs was the proper judicial stance. If a decision is right on the merits, it *should be* handed down, despite fears about the consequences.

See also In re Grand Jury Subpoena Duces Tecum Issued to Richard M. Nixon, 360 F. Supp. 1, 9 (D.C.C.), *aff'd sub nom.* Nixon v. Sirica, 487 F.2d 700 (D.C. Cir. 1973): "That the Court has not the physical power to enforce its order to the President is immaterial to a resolution of the issues. The court has a duty to issue appropriate orders. It would tarnish the court's reputation to fail to do what it could in pursuit of justice."

181. Kurland, "Public Policy, the Constitution, and the Supreme Court," 12 Northern Kentucky L. Rev. 181, 200 (1985).

182. Cf. Karst, "The Freedom of Intimate Association," 80 Yale L. J. 624, 673, 691–92 (1980).

183. Constitutional adjudication is a species of politics, but politics of an electorally unaccountable sort. Thus, the dialectical interplay is between electorally unaccountable politics and electorally accountable politics.

184. 410 U.S. 113 (1973).

185. A fetus is viable when it is "potentially able to survive outside the womb, albeit with artificial aid." Rhoden, "Trimesters and Technology: Revamping *Roe v. Wade*," 95 Yale L. J. 639, 640 (1986). "This is simply the standard definition of the term. The Court relied for this definition [410 U.S. at 163] on the then-current edition of a well-known medical text, L. Hellman & J. Pritchard, Williams Obstetrics 493 (14th ed. 1971)." Id. at 640 n. 6.

186. 347 U.S. 483 (1954).

187. To say that the Court had no business making abortion its business is in effect to say that the Court should have sustained the Texas statute challenged in *Roe* on the ground that the statute did not give rise to any serious constitutional question. Such a ground is distinct from the ground that although a serious constitutional question is raised, requiring careful analysis, in the end, after such analysis, the statute is constitutional.

188. Ely, "The Wages of Crying Wolf: A Comment on *Roe* v. *Wade*," 82 Yale L. J. 920 (1973).

189. Id. at 935–36 & 947–49.

190. In 1927, in *Meyer* v. *Nebraska*, 262 U.S. 390 (1923), the Court remarked that "liberty"

> denotes not merely freedom from bodily restraint but also the right of the individual to contract, to engage in any of the common occupations of life, to acquire useful knowledge, to marry, establish a home and bring up children, to worship God according to the dictates of his own conscience, and generally to enjoy those privileges long recognized at common law as essential to the orderly pursuit of happiness by free men.

191. See notes 187 & 190.

192. See *Roe* v. *Wade*, 410 U.S. at 153. See also Ely, note 188, at 923: "Let us not underestimate what is at stake: Having an unwanted child can go a long way toward ruining a woman's life."

193. 410 U.S. at 169–70. See Heymann & Barzelay, "The Forest and the Trees: *Roe* v. *Wade* and Its Critics," 53 Boston U. L. Rev. 765, 775 (1973):

> At the core of this sphere [of constitutionally protected "liberty" or "privacy" interests] is the right of the individual to make for himself [the] fundamental decisions that shape family life: whom to marry; whether and when to have children; and with what values to rear those children. [Plainly] the right [to an abortion] falls within [this] class of [interests]. The question of constitutionality [in *Roe*] is a more difficult one than that involved in *Griswold* and *Eisenstadt* only because the asserted state interest is more important, not because of any difference in the individual interests involved.

194. 410 U.S. at 117–18 (citing Texas Penal Code 1191, 1196 [Vernon 1961]).

195. See Rhoden, note 185, at 457–62.

196. For an argument that the Texas statute was unconstitutional, but that the Court's decision in *Roe* went too far, see Ginsburg, "Some Thoughts on Equality and Autonomy in Relation to *Roe* v. *Wade*," 63 N. Carolina L. Rev. 375 (1985); Freund, "Storms Over the Supreme Court," 69 A.B.A. J. 1474, 1480 (1983).

197. Cf. G. Calabresi, Ideals, Beliefs, Attitudes, and the Law 105–6 (1985).

198. See 410 U.S. at 175–78.

199. See id. at 206–7.

200. See Perry, "Modern Equal Protection: A Conceptualization and Appraisal," 79 Columbia L. Rev. 1023, 1028–67 (1979). See also Brest, "Foreword: In Defense of the Antidiscrimination Principle," 90 Harvard L. Rev. 1, 7–8 (1976); Note, "Discriminatory Purpose and Disproportionate Impact: An Assessment After *Feeney*," 79 Columbia L. Rev. 1376, 1397–99 (1979).

201. All the poll data I've seen indicates widespread support among the American people for exceptions like the three I've enumerated. Moreover, see notes 198 & 199 and accompanying text. See also *Roe* v. *Wade*, 410 U.S. 113,

298 (Burger, C.J., concurring): "In oral argument, counsel for the State of Texas informed the Court that early abortion procedures were routinely permitted in certain exceptional cases, such as nonconsensual pregnancies resulting from rape and incest."

202. The burden of legislative inertia—of capturing the attention of a sufficient number of legislators, of surviving various institutional hurdles (such as committee votes), of winning the support of a majority of legislators, etc.—is borne by those who want either to put a law on the books or to take a law off the books. There tends to be a presumption in favor of the status quo: The parties who want to change it, in this instance the parties who want to put a criminal law against abortion on the books, have to overcome that presumption, which, in the form of the burden of legislative inertia, has a certain institutional force. In carrying that burden they likely have to attend to competing considerations in a way they probably would not were they merely protecting the status quo.

203. M. Perry, note 1, at 113. Cf. A. Bickel, The Supreme Court and the Idea of Progress 91 (1970):

> Virtually all important decisions of the Supreme Court are the beginnings of conversations between the Court and the people and their representatives. They are never, at the start, conversations between equals. The Court has an edge, because it initiates things with some immediate action, even if limited. But conversations they are, and to say that the Supreme Court lays down the law of the land is to state the ultimate result, following upon a complex series of events, in some cases, and in others it is a form of speech only. The effectiveness of the judgment universalized depends on consent and administration.

One important way to enhance the dialogical character of constitutional decisionmaking and the moderate character of constitutional judgment is to maintain the Supreme Court as an ideologically balanced institution. See Dellinger, "Free to Choose," New Republic, Dec. 16, 1985, at 38, 41: "[W]hen a president . . . attempt[s] to direct the Court's future course by submitting a nominee known to be committed to a particular philosophy, it should be a completely sufficient basis for a senator's negative vote that the nominee's philosophy in one the senator believes would be bad for the country. In making this judgment, the senator should consider the present composition of the Court, and how this appointment would affect the Court's overall balance and diversity. As the contributions of justices with backgrounds as diverse as Hugo Black, John Harlan, and Thurgood Marshall make clear, a thoughtful Court should draw upon a rich diversity of backgrounds and experiences." See also L. Tribe, God Save This Honorable Court: How the Choice of Supreme Court Justices Shapes Our History (1985).

204. See Hutchinson, "Alien Thoughts: A Comment on Constitutional Scholarship," 58 Southern California L. Rev. 701 (1985).

205. See Brest, "Who Decides?," 58 Southern California L. Rev. 661 (1985).

206. See Brennan, note 3, at 10:

As government acts ever more deeply upon those areas of our lives once marked "private," there is an even greater need to see that individual rights are not curtailed or cheapened in the interest of what may temporarily appear to be the "public good." And as government continues in its role as provider for so many of our disadvantaged citizens, there is an even greater need to ensure that government act with integrity and consistency in its dealings with these citizens. . . . [T]he possibilities for collision between government activities and individual rights will increase as the power and authority of government itself expands, and this growth, in turn, heightens the need for constant vigilance at the collision points. . . . All the talk in the last half-decade about shrinking the government does not alter this reality or the challenge it imposes. The modern activist state is a concomitant of the complexity of modern society; it is inevitably with us. We must meet the challenge rather than wish it were not before us.

See also M. Perry, note 1, at 163–65.

207. This is, of course, a contestable judgment. The issue, the importance of which cannot be doubted, is on the intellectual agenda of American constitutional theory. For an argument that there *is* a serious tension between a large judicial role and the empowerment/participation goals, see Brest, "Constitutional Citizenship," 34 Cleveland State L. Rev. 1 (1986). See also Monahan, "Judicial Review and Democracy: A Theory of Judicial Review," 21 U. British Columbia L. Rev. 87 (1987); B. Barber, note 123, at 142–43, 145–48.

Conclusion

1. To make that claim is not to deny that sometimes such convictions can be unconscious and only be inferred from behavior. Nor is it to deny that such convictions, unconscious or not, can be repulsive. The category of the moral does not exclude what some or even most of us might believe to be deeply immoral. Cf. chapter 1, section V.

2. See chapter 6, sections VII & IX.

3. See Solum, "On the Indeterminacy Crisis: Critiquing Critical Dogma," 54 U. Chicago L. Rev. 462 (1987); Stick, "Can Nihilism Be Pragmatic?," 100 Harvard L. Rev. 332 (1986); Williams, "Critical Legal Studies and the Rise of the New Langdells," unpublished ms. (1987) (to appear in a forthcoming issue of the *New York University Law Review*).

4. See Cover, "The Bonds of Constitutional Interpretation: Of the Word, the Deed, and the Role," 20 Georgia Law Review 815 (1986).

5. See R. Beiner, Political Judgment (1983); chapter 6, section VI.

6. See chapter 1, note 1 and accompanying text.

7. See R. Unger, Passion: An Essay on Personality 47–48 (1984). (This passage is quoted in chapter 2, note 46.)

8. See L. Boff & C. Boff, Introducing Liberation Theology (1987).

9. Women who take seriously religious thought about the human have been playing an important role in the development of feminist theory. For but one recent example, see C. Keller, From a Broken Web (1986).

10. See chapter 1, section IV; chapter 2, section V. Cf. H. Putnam, The Many Faces of Realism 77 (1987).

11. See chapter 2, note 18 and accompanying text (quoting Wittgenstein).

12. H. Putnam, note 10, at 60.

13. Id. at 60–61. Putnam goes on to say:

> . . . I myself find Kant's moral philosophy defective in two respects. Kant does not want to supplement earlier moral images, but to replace them completely, and to replace them with a monistic moral standpoint. We need a more pluralistic vision than the eighteenth century could foresee. I can also sympathize with those who think that the replacement of a notion of fraternity which stresses the idea of having fraternal *feelings* towards one another by a notion of fraternity that stresses doing one's *duty* towards one another involves a real loss. Thus I disagree with Kant's rigorism *and* I think we need a more multi-faceted moral image of the world.

Id. at 61.

14. See chapter 4, note 92 and accompanying text; see also chapter 2, note 48 and accompanying text.

15. John 14:34. See John 15: 12, 17. A footnote in the *New Jerusalem Bible* says: "Though enunciated in the Mosaic Law, this precept is 'new' because Jesus sets the standard so high by telling his followers to love one another as he himself loved them, and because love is to be the distinguishing mark of the 'new' era which the death of Jesus inaugurates and proclaims to the world."

Other principal moral texts include the Prophets of the Hebrew Bible (about which Rabbi Heschel wrote so compellingly; see A. Heschel, The Prophets [1962]), the Sermon on the Mount (Matthew 5–7; Luke 6:20–49), and the Last Judgment scene in Matthew's Gospel (25:31–46).

Appendix A

1. Sophocles, Antigone lines 744–45. This translation is problematic: The ancients did not have the notion of a right. See note 9.

2. See, for example, R. Dworkin, Taking Rights Seriously (1978); C. Fried, Right and Wrong (1978); A. Gewirth, Human Rights (1982); Human Rights (J. Pennock & J. Chapman eds. 1981); R. Nozick, Anarchy, State, and Utopia (1974); Richards, "Rights and Autonomy," Ethics, Oct. 1981, at 3.

3. See Galston, "On the Alleged Right to Do Wrong," Ethics, Jan. 1983, at 320, 322–23:

> To say that A and B are morally permissible is to assert that:
> a) neither A nor B contravenes any duty and
> b) the moral considerations that bear on our evaluation of A and B are insufficient to render an unequivocal judgment between them.

Thus, morality may well have a great deal to say about morally permissible alternatives, and they may well occupy spheres of considerable human importance. Moral permissibility rules out only a clear choice of a *single* morally most preferred alternative.

This is, I submit, more than a formal possibility. It is rather the usual outcome of real-life moral reflection. Among a vast array of alternatives, many can be readily eliminated, in two ways. Some can be shown to rest on indefensible moral premises. And some are *dominated* alternatives—that is, the values they serve are more effectively promoted by other valuable alternatives. Typically, the end product of this process of elimination is a relatively small range of alternatives, each buttressed by powerful considerations, no one of which clearly dominates the others. This is not to say that, with the identification of the undominated set, argument necessarily comes to a halt. It is only to say that even after all available arguments and considerations have been exhausted, reasonable people of good will may continue to disagree . . . and that they cannot be *morally* blamed for doing so.

4. See id.

5. That *A* may choose *X*—that choice *X* is morally discretionary for *A*— does not entail that *B* ought not to interfere with *A*'s choice of *X*, although it might happen to be the case that *B* ought not to interfere with *A*'s choice, and it might happen to be the case, too, that one reason why *B* ought not to interfere is that *A*'s choice of *X* is discretionary.

6. See Mackie, "Can There be a Right-Based Moral Theory?," 3 Midwest Stud. Phil. 350, 351 (1978): "[I]f someone, A, has the moral right to do X, not only is he entitled to do X if he chooses—he is not morally required not to do X—but he is also protected in his doing of X—others are morally required not to interfere or prevent him. . . . [W]hat is primary is A's having this right in a sense indicated by the prescription 'Let A be able to do X if he chooses,' and the duty of others not to interfere follows from this . . ." (Mackie seems not to have understood that to say that *A* may do *X* is not necessarily to say that *B* may not interfere with *A*'s doing *X*.) See also Montague, "Two Concepts of Rights," 9 Phil. & Pub. Aff. 372, 381 (1980): "[T]he distinction between rights which are the grounds of obligations and those which are not corresponds to the distinction between exercisable and nonexercisable rights."

To say that "a rights-claim that is primarily a way of talking about a discretionary choice can be a ground of duty" is not to say that it can be an *ultimate* ground or reason. The rights-claim can always be put in question. Nor is it to deny that in some cases the reason *B* ought not to interfere with *A*'s choice of X is the same reason *A*'s choice is thought to be discretionary in the first place, rather than the fact that *A*'s choice is thought to be discretionary.

7. J. Finnis, Natural Law and Natural Rights 205 (1980).

8. Brandt, "The Concept of a Moral Right and Its Function," 80 J. Phil. 29, 29 (1983). See Montague, note 6, at 375.

As I've indicated, a rights-claim that is primarily a way of talking about a discretionary choice can be a ground of duty. However, rights-claims of the other sort—those that are primarily a way of talking about obligations (from the viewpoint of the beneficiary)—cannot ground duties. Without distinguishing between the two sorts of rights-claims, Joseph Raz has written that "[r]ights are grounds of duties in the sense that one way of justifying holding a person to be subject to a duty is that this serves the interest on which another's right is based." Raz, "On the Nature of Rights," 93 Mind 194, 211 (1984). If we may interpret Raz as arguing, at least in part, that rights-claims that are primarily a way of talking about obligations are grounds of duties, then we must conclude that Raz is wrong. Assuming that "one way of justifying holding a person to be subject to a duty is that this serves the interest on which another's right is based", it does not follow that "rights are grounds of duties". It follows merely that *interests* are grounds both of rights and of the duties in terms of which those rights are explained (in Brandt's terms, the duties those rights "logically entail"). Raz has also written: "To say that a person has a right is to say that an interest of his is sufficient ground for holding another to be subject to a duty, i.e. a duty to take some action which will serve that interest, or a duty the very existence of which serves such interest. One justifies a statement that a person has a right by pointing to an interest of his and to reasons why it is to be taken seriously." Raz, "Legal Rights," 4 Oxford J. Leg. Stud. 1, 5 (1984). However, to say that "a person, *A*, has a right" *in the sense that* "an interest of *A*'s, along with reasons why it is to be taken seriously, are sufficient ground for holding another person, *B*, to be subject to a duty" is *not* to say that rights are grounds of duties. Rather, it is to say that *A*'s interest and the reasons for taking it seriously constitute sufficient ground for holding (a) *B* "to be subject to a duty to take some action which will serve *A*'s interest or a duty the very existence of which serves such interest", and, *equivalently*, (b) *A* to have a right that *B* be subject to such duty. Raz seems to think that whereas one justifies a statement that *A* has a right that *B* be subject to a particular duty by "pointing to *A*'s interest and the reasons why it is to be taken seriously", one justifies a statement that *B* is subject to the duty by pointing to the fact that *A* has a right that *B* be subject to it. However, given Raz's premises, what follows is that one justifies both the statement that *B* is subject to the duty *and* the *equivalent* statement that *A* has a right that *B* be subject to it by "pointing to *A*'s interest and the reasons why it is to be taken seriously". In short, Raz has said nothing to undermine the position that rights-claims that are primarily a way of talking about obligations cannot ground duties.

    9. See T. Benditt, Rights 3 (1982):

> If we wish to determine whether we can come up with a useful notion of rights, we are immediately faced with the question "Why bother?" After all, the ancients and the medievals did not have the notion of a right—was their moral life stunted in some way as a result? Did they lack the tools for dealing with certain aspects of the moral enterprise? Among them moral questions were dealt with in terms of what is right and

wrong, what is in accordance with or required by the natural law, what people ought to do or are obliged to do, but not in terms of what someone has a right to, or has a right to do.

See also J. Finnis, note 7, at 209–10:

[I]t is salutary to bear in mind that the modern emphasis on the powers of the right-holder, and the consequent systematic bifurcation between "right" (including "liberty") and "duty", is something that sophisticated lawyers were able to do without for the whole life of classical Roman law. . . .

And in this, the vocabulary of Roman law resembles more than one pre-modern legal vocubulary. Anthropologists studying certain African tribal regimes of law have found that in the indigenous language the English terms "a right" and "duty" are usually covered by a single word, derived from the verbal form normally translated as "ought". This single word (e.g. *swanelo* in Barotse, *tshwanelo* in Tswana) is thus found to be best translated as "due", for "due" looks both ways along a juridical relationship, both to what one is due to do, and to what is due to one. This is linked, in turn, with a "nuance in tribal societies, in that they stress duty and obligation, rather than the nuance of modern Western society, with a stress on right[s]".

(Quoting M. Gluckman, The Ideas in Barotse Jurisprudence xxv [2d ed. 1972]). For an essay "confess[ing] to a moderate skepticism about the necessity of the language of rights", see Golding, "The Primacy of Welfare Rights," 1 Soc. Phil. & Pol'y 121, 121 (1984).

   10. See T. Benditt, note 9, at 7–8:

One might say: Well, at least rights-talk is as important as duty-talk in that we can regard duties as redundant and think entirely in terms of rights. This does not, however, seem intuitively plausible. Duties seem to be the indispensable items, perhaps because the language of duty has been around a lot longer, but more likely because in the end it is people's behavior that we are concerned with, and duties are more directly tied to what people are to do. There is, though, yet another argument for the indispensability of duties. The strongest correlativity thesis says that not only is there a corresponding duty wherever there is a right, but a corresponding right wherever there is a duty. The latter half of the thesis, however, turns out to be demonstrably false. . . .

Among one's duties is the duty of charity. A person's duty to give for charitable purposes can be fulfilled by giving to charities of his own choice, and (within limits) in amounts of his choosing. But there is no particular object of charity to which one owes anything; no potential object of charity can demand anything from a giver as its due. Thus, though there is a duty, there is no corresponding right. Another example is the supererogatory duty, or "ultra obligation." . . . Though we think of Albert Schweitzer's becoming a missionary doctor as an exemplary undertaking that was not morally required of him, he himself seems to have thought it his duty, and it seems true that there is a sense in which (given his ideals) even we can say that he had a duty. But of course we would not say that any of the beneficiaries of his mission had a right to it.

What we see, then, is that there are situations in which there are duties without corresponding rights. The language of duties is essential in characterizing these situations. So if it is a question whether it is duties or rights that are indispensable, duties so far get the nod—unless other cases can be found which argue the indispensability of rights. This then remains a standing challenge for partisans of rights. For any theory of rights we may ask: is there a unique contribution being made by the notion of a right in this theory? Or are the rights in this theory merely echoes of other moral concepts which are really the significant ones. Are the references to rights merely summaries of other, more essential, moral information, or do they have independent moral standing, such that they constitute the basis for ascribing duties (or whatever) to others?

See also Golding, note 9, at 129, 132 (noting that the existence of a duty does not entail the existence of a corresponding right).

11. J. Finnis, note 7, at 210. See Brandt, note 8, at 43–45; note 18.

12. J. Finnis, note 7, at 210. See Churchill & Siman, "Why the Abortion Debate is Sterile: Abortion and the Rhetoric of Individual Rights," Hastings Center Rep., Feb. 1982, at 9; Montague, note 6, at 374–75.

13. Becker, "Individual Rights," in And Justice For All 197, 197 (T. Regan & D. Van De Veer eds. 1982).

14. Cf. Montague, note 6, at 384:

[I]ndividuals who are incapable of intentional activity are incapable of exercising [exercisable] rights, and may not even possess those rights that are exercisable. (I am inclined to say that individuals who have never been capable of performing intentional actions have no exercisable rights, while those who once were capable of such activity, and hence who had exercisable rights, have not lost these rights even though they may have lost the power to exercise them.) I take it that such individuals would include (most) non-human animals, human fetuses, human infants, and those human adults who, for whatever reason, are incapable of the kind of mental activity required for the performance of intentional actions. Since it may appear to be implicit in what I have said that exercisable rights, as the only rights that are distinct from obligations, are the only *genuine* rights; and since I have claimed that only individuals capable of acting intentionally are capable of exercising rights; it may seem that I am committed to denying that, for example, infants, fetuses, animals, and mentally incompetent persons have rights. And many people would find such a position morally objectionable.I suppose there is a sense in which I would deny that those incapable of acting intentionally have rights, but I do not see that doing so has any morally objectionable consequences. It isn't as if, for example, that by denying that infants have a right to self-defense I am sanctioning infanticide; what I have said here implies only that the immorality of infanticide cannot be *grounded* on the rights of infants. Infanticide—as well as such things as cruelty to animals and non-therapeutic experimentation on the severely retarded—is immoral even if infants, animals, and the severely retarded have no (exercisable) rights. What we cannot do is argue that such actions are immoral *because* infants, animals, and so on, have the right not to be dealt with in certain ways, since, if I am right, such arguments are question-begging.

15. See Golding, note 9, at 122, 124, 127–28. Cf. note 14.

16. See Becker, note 13, at 197–200.

17. I've argued elsewhere that no determinate rule of conduct is absolute. See Perry, "Some Notes on Absolutism, Consequentialism, and Incommensurability," 80 Northwestern U. L. Rev. 967 (1985).

18. See Westen, "On 'Confusing Ideas,' " 91 Yale L. J. 1153, 1158 n. 15 (1982): "This is not to deny that the term 'rights' can also be used . . . narrowly as a term of art for prescriptive claims of a certain sort, such as claims of particular importance or force" (referring to "Ronald Dworkin's usage of 'rights' to refer to prescriptive claims that have sufficient force to 'trump' other prescriptive claims"). For an example of such usage, see Brandt, note 8, at 36–37, 44. As Brandt acknowledges, however, "It is true that it is only convenient, not necessary, that there be a special term with [these] connotations, as distinct from 'moral obligation'; we could simply speak of certain obligations as being very strong." Id. at 44. In his essay "On the Nature of Rights," note 8, Joseph Raz uses "rights" in a special, term-of-art sense. See id. at 195.

Appendix B

1. The World Peace Tax Fund Act would amend the Internal Revenue Code to provide that a taxpayer conscientiously opposed to participation in war could have that portion of her/his taxes equal to the military share of the federal budget designated for a special trust fund, which would finance specific non-military, peace-related activities (such as national peace academy of retraining of workers displaced by conversion of industry from weapons production). In 1984 the chief Senate sponsor is Mark Hatfield (R-OR) and the bill has some 50 House co-sponsors.

2. Traditional criteria say a war, to be justifiable, may be entered only (1) for a just cause (e.g., defense); (2) as a last resort; (3) upon declaration by lawful authority; (4) if there is reasonable prospect of achieving the just goals. Further, war to be justifiable may be prosecuted only (5) by means proportionate to the ends sought; (6) in ways that insure the immunity of non-combatants; (7) with promise of mercy to a vanquished enemy.

3. To "remain in ministry with" implies (1) no breaking of the fellowship of the faith community because of disagreement over particular acts of civil disobedience; (2) support through prayer, counsel, pastoral care, and acts of love on behalf of those who may be in violation of law; (3) no commitment on the part of the American Lutheran Church to provide financial or legal support for persons who engage in acts of civil disobedience.

Index

ABA. *See* American Bar Association
Abortion legislation. See also *Roe* v.
    Wade
    as constitutional question, 173–74,
        302*n*187
    judicial self-restraint and, 170–71
    moral discourse and, 55
    women's rights and, 174–76,
        303*n*192
Accountability. *See* Electoral
    accountability
Ackerman, Bruce, 63–66, 67, 69, 72,
    237*n*57, 257*n*30, 259*n*48
Act-utilitarianism, 78, 261*n*8. *See also*
    Utilitarianism
Adjudication. *See* Constitutional
    adjudication
Adler, Mortimer, 13–14, 40, 41–42
Alexander, Larry, 165
Alienation, coercive legislation and,
    100
Allport, Gordon, 12
Altruism, 21–23
AMA. *See* American Medical
    Association
American Bar Association (ABA), 176,
    177
American Law Institute Model Penal
    Code, 176
American Lutheran Church, statement
    on "Human Law and the
    Conscience of Believers," 114,
    115, 118, 189–207
American Medical Association (AMA),
    176, 177

American society
    conditions for civil disobedience and,
        118–19
    as constitutional community, 158–59
    fundamental aspirations in, 133–35,
        139, 145–48, 150
    as judging community, 154–55
    as morally pluralistic, 3, 51–52,
        154–56
Anthropological relativism, 44–50, 51,
    180
Antigone, 114
Aquinas, Thomas, 98, 100
Aristotle, 11, 23, 99
Aspirations. *See* Fundamental
    aspirations
Authenticity, human, 182–83
Authority
    of fundamental aspirations, 162
    respect for, and obedience, 113
Autonomy. *See* Freedom

Backing, 229*n*10
Barber, Benjamin, 249*n*117
Beiner, R., 153, 236*n*55
Beliefs. *See also* Moral/religious
    convictions; Web of beliefs
    reasoning and, 26
    revision of, 27–28, 29, 30–33
    shared, and moral discourse, 49, 51
    sources of, 27, 29–30. *See also*
        Experience transcendental
    constraints on, 51
    truth of, as relative, 39–40

313